15.00
TH 0210-H

Catholics, Anglicans and Puritans

Catholics, Anglicans and Puritans
Seventeenth Century Essays

by

Hugh Trevor-Roper

The University of Chicago Press

The University of Chicago Press, Chicago 60637
Martin Secker & Warburg Limited, London
Copyright © by Hugh Trevor-Roper 1987
All rights reserved. Published 1987
University of Chicago Press edition 1988

96 95 94 93 92 91 90 89 88 87   5 4 3 2 1

Library of Congress Cataloging-in-Publication Data
Trevor-Roper, H. R. (Hugh Redwald), 1914–
Catholics, Anglicans, and puritans.

Includes bibliographical references and index.
1. England—Church history—17th century.
2. England—Intellectual life—17th century.
I. Title.
BR756.T73   1988   941.06   87-12304

ISBN 0-226-81228-6

PRINTED IN GREAT BRITAIN BY
MACKAYS OF CHATHAM LIMITED,
CHATHAM, KENT

Contents

Introduction

The five essays in this volume are all concerned, in one way or another, with English intellectual history before and during the Puritan Revolution. But how can we speak of 'English intellectual history'? Intellectual history can never be pursued in isolation. It is conditioned by its social and political context, quickened and distorted by events. Nor can it be localized. Though local conditions may give them a particular direction, ideas cannot be confined in space. They overflow national boundaries. They also overflow the boundaries of time. Ancient philosophies, rediscovered, are found to possess a disturbing vitality even in modern times. In these essays I shall refer to some such ancient philosophies and I shall hope to show that even the domestic controversies of the English Church were influenced by European events.

The most important of the ancient philosophies which disturbed the Aristotelean orthodoxy of Renaissance Europe was Neoplatonism, which, as interpreted by Ficino in Italy and Paracelsus in Germany, animated all branches of thought. Orthodox Christianity sought to come to terms with it but found it increasingly difficult and, in the end, repudiated it. The Italian 'philosophers of Nature' at the close of the sixteenth century found themselves persecuted by Rome. Tommaso Campanella, having sought in his youth to set up a Platonic utopia in Calabria, spent most of his life in Neapolitan or Roman prisons. Giordano Bruno, who formulated and expressed his bold ideas in England, ended on a bonfire in Rome. In Germany Paracelsianism was swept up into a general revolution. In the 1620s the tide ebbed, driven back by more disciplined ideas which, though at first no less disturbing, would ultimately be absorbed as a stabilizing force into European

vii

thought: the empiricism of Bacon, the mathematically based science of Galileo, the deductive rationalism of Descartes.

Another ancient philosophy, more persistent and more dangerous, because more open-ended, was the 'Pyrrhonism' of the Academic Sceptics which, by calling all received opinions into doubt, undermined the faith of all Churches. This 'Pyrrhonist crisis' was most acute in the early seventeenth century. It forced men to seek a new canon of certainty, an irrefutable basis from which reason could operate. The Roman Church found that basis in its own infallibility, dogmatically asserted. Protestants transferred that infallibility to the texts and prophecies of Scripture, as interpreted by themselves. Mathematics too could supply an answer; and mathematics and prophecy could join forces to establish a scientific chronology and an interpretation of history which could sustain the theological system on which it was based.

Such were some of the ideas which troubled men in the years 1600–1660: the years covered by this volume. The first essay, which is somewhat peripheral to the main theme of the book, introduces a mysterious Englishman who, at Elizabethan Oxford, had been converted to Catholicism and then captivated by the ideas of Giordano Bruno. An English 'philosopher of Nature', he seems to have imitated Campanella and involved himself in a strange, utopian conspiracy in the remote toe of England, as Campanella had done in the remote toe of Italy. Like Campanella, he failed, and a new generation forgot him; but he has his place in the history of ideas, as an abortive precursor of the atomists of the next generation. My essay on him first ventured forth as a lecture at the Warburg Institute, under the aegis of that remarkable scholar, the late Charles Schmitt. I have often been urged to publish it, but have hesitated because of the difficulty of establishing my hero's genealogy and identity. In a lecture one can slide over such difficulties, but in print one prefers to have solved them. However, all my efforts to solve this problem have failed, and in the end I have decided to take the risk: to publish and perhaps be damned by the discovery of some new document which may destroy a speculative link in the thin chain of argument. If so, I shall console myself by reflecting that the remaining links are still interesting and the curious story of Nicholas Hill still deserves to be explored.

Nicholas Hill the atomist, rogue Catholic, conspirator and exile, made no greater impact on the 'high Calvinist' doctors of the English Church than his master Bruno had done during his famous visit to Oxford. He is a very marginal figure, interesting indeed, as the only known English disciple of the great Italian heretic, but elusive and obscure. But he was accidentally associated with a very different man who made a far more notable, and in the end disastrous, attack on the Calvinist establishment: a man who dominates English Church history in the next forty years and the next essay in this book. This was the future Archbishop of Canterbury, William Laud, who for two years, from 1589 to 1591, was a colleague of Hill at that seminary of unconventional thinkers, afterwards the citadel of Laudian orthodoxy: St John's College, Oxford.

What was Laudianism? What was its function in the crisis which began in England in 1640 and led to civil war in 1642? Was Laud an innovator or a conservative? Why was he – or was he? – so generally detested? Was the civil war fought about religion or about politics? What was the new-fangled 'Arminianism' of which he and his followers were accused? Was he in fact an Arminian? What were his real relations with the Church of Rome? What lay behind the secret offer to him of a cardinal's hat? How was it that his allegedly detested form of religion triumphed at the Restoration? These are questions that are still debated by historians. In the two long complementary essays, the first on 'Laudianism and Political Power', the second on 'the Great Tew circle', I have offered my answer. The first of these two essays grew out of a lecture delivered at Peterhouse, the citadel of Laudianism in Cambridge. The second began, no less appropriately, as a seminar paper in Oxford.

I have suggested that there was indeed an 'Arminian' tradition in early seventeenth-century England; that it was not an innovation in the long term (though it could be represented as such in that short term); that it was an intellectual movement which had a well-established pedigree in England, which appealed to humane and liberal men, and which offered, at one time, a solution to the still recent, and therefore still reparable, schism of Western Christendom. For although Anglicanism may seem to us a purely English form of Christianity – a national religion established in one country only – it was not always so. In the reign of James I, the Church of England had pretensions to be an ecumenical Church, a third force, competing with the international Church of Rome and international Calvinism. It attracted French Huguenots like Casaubon, Dutch Arminians like Grotius, dissident Italian Catholics like Paolo Sarpi and Marcantonio de Dominis, Greek patriarchs like Cyril Lucaris. However, that phase did not last. After the international crisis of the 1620s, which coincided with the change of reign in England, this originally unpolitical movement was diverted by

a series of historical accidents into the support of a particular political
system and thus became an inseparable, organic part of a new
synthesis. With that synthesis, eleven years later, it foundered.
Through a national revolution, the Church which had recently aspired
to be universal was destroyed at home, and its destruction, since it had
no base abroad, seemed final and total.

The man who, insensibly, under the pressure of events, was
responsible for that diversion, was Archbishop Laud, and so he bears
the greatest responsibility for the disasters to which it led. However,
those disasters were not, I believe, inevitable: but for certain historical
accidents the synthesis might have been firmly established. Nor were
they in fact final, for the Church was afterwards restored, in the form
which Laud had imposed upon it; which shows that that form was not,
in itself, rejected. How did this happen? I have suggested that the
restoration of the Anglican Church after 1660 owed something to the
survival, throughout the revolutionary period, of the original intellectual movement which had inspired it, before it had been diverted into
the political synthesis, and that that survival was ensured by the group
of men who, during the personal rule of Charles I, met together at the
country house of Lord Falkland at Great Tew, and who were not, as is
often supposed, dispersed and finally broken up by the death of their
patron and the events of the civil war.

Politically, the men of Great Tew were all critics of Laudianism; but
intellectually, I have argued, they continued, in its pure form, the
movement which the Laudians had captured and distorted. They too
were 'Arminians' – genuine Arminians. They were also distinguished,
and denounced, as 'Socinians', that is, rationalists – as were several of
the Laudians. 'Socinianism', the application to religion of constructive
reason, was their answer to the 'Pyrrhonist crisis' of the time. In the
mouths of the orthodox of all parties the word was a term of abuse, for
such rationalization dissolved some of their distinguishing doctrines:
those doctrines which had been confirmed for the Catholics at Trent
and for the Calvinists at Dordt. The English Arminians, committed to
neither of these Councils, were happy to reject their decrees. But their
'reason' went further than this: it also repudiated certain distinctive
historic claims of the Protestant Church in England as in Europe.

In particular, it repudiated, implicitly if not explicitly, the claim that
the Protestant Church, and it alone, was justified by biblical prophecy.
This claim was essential to the Protestant Church of England in 1600.
It was the intellectual cement which united 'moderate Anglican', 'high
Calvinist' and 'Puritan' behind the formally precarious 'Elizabethan

compromise' and constituted their chief bulwark against the Pyrrhonist threat. It entailed the doctrine that the Papacy was Antichrist; that the visible Church had been represented in the Dark and Middle Ages not by Rome but by an underground society of the faithful which had periodically surfaced as Waldensian, Albigensian or Lollard heresy; and that the Reformation was its decisive breakthrough. The human agent of that breakthrough, as of the original breakthrough in the Roman Empire, had been the Christian Prince, who was thus recognized as an important instrument of the divine will. After the breakthrough, the rest of history, it was argued, would run at a faster pace: there would be terrible convulsions, 'shakings' of Heaven and Earth and all political systems, followed by the fall of Antichrist, the universal triumph of the Gospel, the second coming of Christ, perhaps (for here there were different schools of thought) the millennium.

In England, these doctrines had a special character, largely supplied by the work of John Foxe, who had himself been inspired, during the Marian exile, by German Protestants, and whose *Acts and Monuments* – vulgarly known as 'the Book of Martyrs' – was the staple diet of Elizabethan readers. According to this view, the English monarchs, following the example of Henry VIII, Edward VI and Elizabeth, were the Christian Princes under whose guidance England, an 'Elect Nation' like ancient Israel, would assume the leadership of Christendom and prepare the way for the second coming of Christ. The discoveries and achievements of Elizabethan England were evidence of its fitness for this glorious role. Had not the Prophet Daniel said that, in the run-up to the Last Days, there would be great voyages and universal enlightenment? James I would see himself (at least for a time) as the type of Christian Prince and Francis Bacon would make use – perhaps only rhetorical use – of these ideas in order to give depth and resonance to his projects for the advancement of learning.

Ideas which had come to England from Germany, naturally continued to flourish in their native country. In an earlier essay,[1] I have shown how, in Germany, the ideas of Paracelsus were combined with such metaphysical speculations: how there too a new era of enlightenment was expected to follow the return of a chemical prophet, 'Elias Artista', who would make all things new; and how the beginnings of the Thirty Years War were seen as the 'shakings' which would precede the fall of Antichrist and, as it were, light the fuse for the great eschatological explosion. That did not work out according to plan; but in 1640, when a new series of 'shakings' began in England, hope was rekindled. The English Puritan Revolution, which we see as a purely

national struggle, appeared to many European Protestants as an event
of international significance, the second stage of the Bohemian
revolution of 1618. So messianic expectations were renewed and central
European enthusiasts looked, and sometimes came, to an England
which, they hoped, having reclaimed its historic role, would realize the
Baconian promise of enlightenment as the prelude to the millennium.[2]

These ideas, woven into the very texture of Protestant thought, form the
intellectual climate of the early seventeenth century in England. Inherited, as part of conventional wisdom, by the post-Elizabethan opponents
of Charles I, and expressed for them by their oracle, the belated
Elizabethan polymath Archbishop Ussher, they were repudiated by the
'Arminians' both of Lambeth and of Great Tew, and given a new,
revolutionary content by radical 'Puritans' like Milton, who was not
content with the Elizabethan compromise but sought 'the reformation of
reformation itself'. All of these men were responding, in different ways, to
the same intellectual challenge. None of them produced a final answer.
But in the convulsions of their time the old compromise was destroyed, or
at least emptied of its real content, and all of them, out of its relics,
incidentally contributed something to the succeeding age: an acceptable system of chronology; a more rational form of religion; a great
poem.

Some historians, looking at this challenge and these responses, have
seen them in clear, even simple terms, as episodes in a struggle between
'progress' and 'reaction'. They have presented the Laudians as 'reactionary', the 'Puritans' as progressive, and the 'radical Puritans' as the most
progressive of all. For them, Milton looks forward, the prophet of modern
liberty; Laud looks back, a belated medieval prelate; Ussher stands in the
middle, the great 'moderate' whose views and policies, if adopted, might
have prevented the revolution; and the men of Great Tew are out on the
fringe, a mere house-party of ineffectual dilettanti, irrelevant to the harsh
realities of their time. I am afraid that I cannot accept these sharp
dichotomies, this linear view of history. 'Arminian', 'Calvinist', 'Puritan',
are imprecise terms, often terms of abuse. Laud resented the charge of
Arminianism; Abbot, Ussher, Prideaux declared their detestation of
'Puritanism'. It is only if we dissolve the imaginary spectrum stretching
from Right to Left that the ideas which have been artificially fitted into it
recover their individuality and can be studied in their true context. This is
particularly true of those who are so conveniently shoved into the middle,
between the antithetical poles, and so defined as 'moderate'. Sometimes,
when detached from their false position, these 'moderate' men acquire a
more definite character: they become real and their ideas distinct.

The supposed dilettanti of Great Tew, for instance, are found to be, intellectually, not very different from the Laudians on the far Right – and the Laudians to be far more 'rational' and 'liberal' than the 'Puritans' on the Left. The 'moderate' Archbishop Ussher, whose vast and genuine learning was devoted to the support of an obsolescent system, appears more 'reactionary' than Laud. As for Milton – who can ever approach Milton objectively, undazzled by his incomparable power over words, undisgusted by his savage use of it, unawed by the depth and darkness visible, the mysterious recesses and iridescent, icy stalactites of that great twilit treasure-cave, his mind? But who, having examined his expressed views, can say that, in politics or in ideas, he looked forward rather than back? Is he not rather, like so many great men of his age – like Bodin or Pascal or Sir Thomas Browne – Janus-faced, looking both ways, a law to himself?

Of course it can be replied that the politics of Laud led to the immediate ruin of his Church, and that the rationalism of Great Tew, which helped that Church to survive its immediate crisis, led in the long run to the deism which drained it of its vitalizing illusions. And it can be said that the ideas of Laud and the Laudians, however 'modern', when compared with those of their rivals, would have led, if successfully applied, to an authoritarian monarchy which it was therefore 'progressive' to resist by whatever means were necessary, even if that meant mobilizing violent and irrational passions by the pretence of 'popish plots'. However, that would be to introduce unhistorical criteria and perhaps to misuse words. Indeed, I believe that the whole concept of linear progress as the distinguishing property of certain political parties, whether 'puritan' or whig or marxist, is unhistorical. The function of the historian is not to judge but to understand.

None of these essays has been published before. Most of them began as lectures or seminar papers and have since grown as I have thought further about the problems raised. I have already stated the origins of some of them. Of the others, the essay on Ussher began as a lecture in Trinity College, Dublin, on the fourth centenary of the Archbishop's birth. That on Milton was written specially for this volume. I am grateful to my friends and former pupils in discussion with whom I have clarified and (I hope) corrected my own views: Richard Ollard, Charles Webster, Edward Chancey, Nicholas von Maltzahn, and, most particularly and regularly, Blair Worden and Kevin Sharpe. And as always I am indebted to my wife for her devoted work on the index.

Nicholas Hill, the English Atomist

1   The mystery man

The years around 1600 were years in which revolutionary scientific ideas were combined, sometimes in combustible form, with Neoplatonic cosmology, religious heresy, and utopian politics. In 1599 Tommaso Campanella, a Dominican friar and natural philosopher, attempted to set up a utopian republic by political rebellion in a remote part of Italy: an attempt which was at once crushed and caused its author to spend much of the rest of his life in Spanish or papal prisons. Next year another former Dominican friar, Giordano Bruno, was burnt in Rome for his combination of heretical science with Hermetic Neoplatonism. These emphatic condemnations had their effect for a time, at least in Catholic countries; but in the years which followed – the years of the comet and the new star, of Rosicrucianism and the expected coming of the chemical messiah – such ideas lived on. In Germany, in particular, Paracelsian cosmology was united with revolutionary utopian claims; and after 1618, when the Bohemian crisis, coinciding with another comet, convulsed all Europe, there was a fresh outbreak of cosmological heresy, and a fresh political persecution of it. The burning of Giulio Cesare Vanini at Toulouse in 1619, and the hysterical condemnation of atomism by the University and Parlement of Paris in 1624, can be seen as the second act of the drama of Campanella and Bruno.

In this essay I wish to suggest that there may have been a similar episode in England: that a disciple of Bruno, in the year after his death, may have sought to imitate, in a remote part of England, the example of Campanella. The suggestion is very tentative, for I am aware that the links in the chain of reasoning are slender and fragile. I have had to rely on inconclusive hearsay evidence because hard evidence has proved unattainable and on hypotheses which may be exploded by the discovery of some fatal fact. But at the worst, my story will not be much more fanciful than some of the accounts which still circulate about its hero, the natural philosopher Nicholas Hill.

Who was Nicholas Hill? According to John Aubrey, he was 'one of the most learned men of his time, a great mathematician and philosopher and traveller, and a poet'.[1] A modern writer has described his *Philosophia Epicurea, Democritiana, Theophrastica* (1601), his only published work, as one of the most important of all early seventeenth-century books in the history of ideas, and has hailed him as a precursor of Hobbes and Locke.[2] These are bold claims and have been contested: another writer has dismissed him as unoriginal and confused, 'a thinker of minor ability'.* At least we can say that Hill was an interesting and controversial man. He was an early advocate of a Copernican solar system, the first Englishman to advance the theory of a plurality of worlds, the first of the moderns publicly to preach Epicurean atomism. In spite of this, his personal life remains mysterious: mysterious but also tantalizing.

The great difficulty is the lack of contemporary evidence. I have failed to discover anything about Nicholas Hill's parentage or family. Once removed from the university, he left no trace of his movements. His only published book was printed abroad. He evidently died abroad, and although his widow apparently returned to England, her identity is unknown. So common a name is itself a protection against discovery. And he seems deliberately to have chosen a life of secrecy

---

* Robert Hugh Kargon, *Atomism in England from Hariot to Newton* (Oxford 1966), pp. 14, 15, 147. Kargon writes slightingly of McColley's 'attempt to make Hill important'. McColley undoubtedly exaggerates Hill's significance, but Kargon seems to me to dismiss Hill without sufficient examination. Thus he writes that Hill's work is 'a confused and self-contradictory melange ... particularly a blend of the thought of the atomists, Aristotle, Nicolas of Cusa, the fabled Hermes Trismegistus, Bruno, Gilbert and Copernicus.' Hill was explicitly anti-Aristotelean, and the last five names are cited together by Hill, reasonably enough, as authorities for the movement of the earth. That does not discredit his work or make it a mere *mélange*. The best account of Hill's philosophy seems to me to be Jean Jacquot, 'Harriot, Hill, Warner and the New Philosophy', in John W. Shirley (ed.), *Thomas Harriot, Renaissance Scientist* (Oxford 1974), pp. 110–14. Jacquot writes, implicitly refuting Kargon, that Hill's book 'is not exempt from confusion and contradictions, yet it is not a mere jumble of opinions derived from many sources': it yields 'a relatively consistent picture'. It is unfortunate that Kurd Lasswitz, in his standard work *Geschichte des Atomistik* (Hamburg and Leipzig 1890), does not deal with Hill, of whose work, as he writes (I, p. 465), he had been unable to find a copy.

and solitude. His writings give nothing away. His style is deliberately obscure. If his readers did not understand it, he wrote, 'I answer, *damnatum esse Luciferi nomen*: that the name of Lucifer' – that is, of the Light-bringer – 'is damned'. As a philosopher, he was of the School of Night, not Enlightenment: of Hermes Trismegistus, not of Francis Bacon. Such obscurity, both of style and of life, was no doubt useful to a man who was a Catholic recusant in Protestant England and – if his ideas were examined – a heretic in the Catholic Church. By lying low, he kept out of trouble. Thereby he also escaped the publicity, and denied historians the documentation, of a trial or a martyrdom.

Nicholas Hill did indeed publish his opinions, and it is that publication which has given him his place in intellectual history. But his book, which was published in Paris in 1601, attracted remarkably little attention at the time and aroused no curiosity about its author. Indeed, according to John Aubrey, his very name would have been lost had it not been accidentally associated with a single episode of a kind not usually thought compatible with the dignity of history: the Great Fart in the Parliament House. This unfortunate explosion seems to have taken place in 1610, and it inspired the poets of the time to celebrate it in verse and, incidentally, to couple it with the name of Nicholas Hill.

The first of these poets was Ben Jonson. In a poem written about that time, after a passing mention

Of the grave Fart late let in Parliament,

Jonson went on to describe an imaginary scene in which

several ghosts did flit
About the shore, of Farts but late departed,
White, black, blue, green; and in more forms outstarted
Than all those *atomi* ridiculous
Whereof old Democrite and Hill Nicholas
One said, the other swore, the world consists.[3]

Ben Jonson evidently had more than a nodding acquaintance with Nicholas Hill's book. He owned a copy of it – in which he wrote a somewhat derogatory comment[4] – and several years later he referred to it in conversation with the Scotch poet William Drummond of Hawthornden. Drummond recorded Jonson's remarks, but did not cite Hill by name: evidently he was himself unfamiliar with the book.[5]

However, if Jonson knew the book, he clearly did not know the author personally, for he described him as being an old man in 1601. In fact, at that time, Hill had just turned thirty.

The second poet inspired by the same untimely parliamentary incontinence was Jonson's friend and boon companion, John Hoskyns. Hoskyns (a rogue Wykehamist) was a lawyer – a 'sergeant at law' (he is often referred to as 'Sergeant Hoskyns') – a man of letters, and a man about town. He was also something of a line-shooter: he claimed to have polished the manners of Ben Jonson and the prose of Sir Walter Ralegh: he had been a prisoner in the Tower with Ralegh. His poem on 'The Great Fart in the Parliament House' was much commended by his fellow wits and was printed in some of 'the drolleries' – i.e. the contemporary collections of light verse.[6] In him too the idea of spectacular flatulency somehow led to thoughts of Nicholas Hill, whom he claimed to have known well. However, his known observations on the subject did not go beyond making this connexion.[7]

Meanwhile, similar thoughts had engaged yet another poet. About the time of the Great Fart, John Donne was compiling his 'catalogue of the courtier's library', a Rabelaisian *jeu d'esprit* consisting of a list of imaginary works by real authors, such as today might decorate a *trompe l'oeil* in a literary home. The first book in the list is 'How to distinguish sex and hermaphroditism in atoms', by Nicholas Hill, Englishman, together with a companion work by the same author on the anatomy and midwifery of such atoms. Later in the same catalogue we find another item, 'Cardanus de nullibietate crepitûs' – Cardanus on the non-existence in space of the Fart. Cardanus – Girolamo Cardano – was a well-known Italian 'philosopher of Nature', a precursor of Bruno and Hill. Thus to Donne, too, Nicholas Hill was somehow associated with flatulence. John Donne, incidentally, also owned a copy of Hill's work. It was Ben Jonson's copy, which Jonson had passed on to him.[8]

Ben Jonson, Sergeant Hoskyns, John Donne – these three contemporary poets were all personal friends, and all members of that poetical company which met at the Mermaid Tavern. Lovers of poetry like to imagine the elevated literary conversation in those brilliant symposia. Here, surely, we can actually overhear it. It is not quite what we expected. But let us keep to Nicholas Hill. At the moment all that we need say is that, for over thirty years after its publication, the work of Nicholas Hill was apparently unnoticed in England except in the ribald conversation of poets in the Mermaid Tavern.

At first, it seems to have been equally unnoticed abroad. However, after eighteen years of silence, foreigners gradually rediscovered this neglected work of natural philosophy, and began to take it seriously. Its rediscovery was incidental: a by-product of the controversy caused by the new astronomical discoveries of Galileo; but it also coincides with – indeed initiates – what I have called the second act of the drama of Campanella and Bruno.

In 1615–16 Galileo had his first brush with the Roman Inquisition, and the heretical idea of a heliocentric universe, which his astronomical observations had confirmed, was thereby given new publicity. Three years after this episode, a new edition of Hill's work was published in Geneva. This edition was revised and corrected, in some respects, from that of 1601. Greek words were accompanied by Latin translations; a marginal reference to the previous theorists of a heliocentric system was, perhaps out of prudence, omitted; and so was a crude poem which Hill had appended to his work in 1601. This second, Genevan, edition seems to have achieved a somewhat larger circulation than the first, Parisian, edition, whose very existence was unknown to later admirers of Nicholas Hill.

The republication of Hill's work in 1619 was followed by a rash of works on natural philosophy directed against the Aristotelean system and seeking to revive, in various forms, the atomic theories of Democritus and Epicurus. In the same year, the chemist Daniel Sennert of Wittenberg published an important work[9] which has been described as marking the renewal of atomist physics.[10] In 1620 came Bacon's *Novum Organum* and David van Goorle's *Philosophical Exercises*. In 1621 Sébastien Basson proposed the idea of the molecule, in a work which has been described as an important step on the road to modern chemistry and a link between Bruno and Descartes.[11] Then, in 1622, Hill's work received further publicity – once again in connexion with Galileo. In that year, Campanella, still a prisoner in Rome, through his German Lutheran friend Tobias Adami, published at Frankfurt the *Apologia pro Galileo* which he had written at the height of the crisis six years earlier. In the preface to the published text, Adami cited the previous proponents of a heliocentric universe. Among them he included Nicholas Hill.

By this time there were other reasons for noticing Nicholas Hill. For we are now in the period of European crisis following the Bohemian revolt. That crisis was ideological as well as political. The revolt had polarized ideas as well as parties, and led to intensified ideological war. In Protestant Germany, Paracelsian enthusiasts hailed the beginning of a new age of the world. In Catholic France the orthodox turned upon the 'libertines'. After November 1620, when the battle of the White

Mountain ended the Protestant advance, the Catholic counter-attack began. In 1621–2 there was religious war and persecution of witches in the reconquered lands. But the new crusade against heresy was not merely reactionary. The same years saw the beginning of the new 'mechanical' philosophy which would ultimately eclipse the Hermeticism of the Renaissance.

The man who prepared the way for this new philosophy was the Minim friar, Marin Mersenne. In 1623–5 he launched his massive attack on the anti-Christian anti-Aristotelean 'philosophers of Nature' from Cardano onwards, and in particular on the modern 'deists', 'atheists', 'chemists' and sceptics, and thereby opened the way for the new Cartesian orthodoxy. Mersenne's great enemy was Bruno; but around Bruno he saw a whole cluster of heretics, including, especially, Campanella, Vanini, Francis Bacon, van Goorle, Basson and Nicholas Hill. Francis Bacon would have felt uncomfortable in this company, but all of them were teachers of a philosophy fundamentally incompatible both with scholastic Catholicism and with the new doctrines of Mersenne and Descartes. 'As for the *Epicurean Philosophy* of Hill,' wrote Mersenne, 'it would have to be transcribed in full if we wished to recount his fantasies. To sum up, all these men were heretics. No wonder they agree with one another like robbers at the fair.'[12]

Thus by the early 1620s Hill's work was known in both Catholic France and Protestant Germany; but another fifteen years had to pass before it was seriously noticed in his own country. Here again, the stimulus seems to have been the attack on Galileo. In 1632 Galileo was finally condemned by the Roman Inquisition and thereby became famous in the Protestant world. In 1638 John Wilkins, in his *Discovery of a World in the Moon*, quoted Hill's arguments for a heliocentric universe. It is likely that Wilkins had been led to Hill by Campanella – or rather, by Adami's preface to Campanella. In the same year Robert Burton included in the fifth edition of his *Anatomy of Melancholy* a new chapter entitled 'A Digression on Air', and in this he speculated on the possibility of a plurality of worlds and quoted, with implicit approval, Hill's expression of that doctrine: '*sperabundus exspecto innumerabilium mundorum in aeternitate perambulationem* . . . why should not an infinite cause (as God is) produce infinite effects, as Nic. Hill, *Democrit. philos.*, disputes?'[13]

Thus by 1638 Hill was at last recognized as a serious scientist in two fields: Copernicanism and the doctrine of the plurality of worlds. His third contribution to natural philosophy, his atomism, had to wait a little longer for recognition. However, in the 1640s atomism was being freely discussed in Paris in the circle of Gassendi, Hobbes and Sir Charles Cavendish, and in 1647 Pierre Gassendi's *Life of Epicurus* made Epicurean atomism intellectually respectable. After that Hill's *atomi* were no longer 'ridiculous', and their author could be owned as a serious scientist. So, when the restoration of the monarchy brought stability back to England, scholars and antiquaries could look with less mocking eyes on this long dead and almost forgotten 'philosopher of Nature'. They might even seek to reconstruct his biography.

Unfortunately, by this time, such reconstruction was very difficult. Nicholas Hill had left very few traces of his personal life. In his own lifetime, nobody, as far as we know, mentioned his name. Even today, the archives have revealed no more solid contemporary evidence of his existence than was available then. That evidence consists of two documents: Hill's own book, as published by him in 1601, and the official records of the university of which, for a brief time, he had been an unsatisfactory member. Apart from this there was only fading memory and hearsay. Let us now turn to this evidence and see what the scholars of the seventeenth century made of it.

2 The evidence

From his own book it is known that Nicholas Hill was a Londoner, for he so describes himself on its title-page. From the dedication we know that he had a young son called Lawrence, who was an 'infant' in 1601, and to whom he was clearly devoted. It is clear, too, that he was at that time a Roman Catholic: for he states explicitly that if anything in his book is contrary to the Catholic and Apostolic faith, '*igni illud et inferis mando*', I consign it to fire and Hell.* But apart from these clear facts Hill himself, in his surviving work, tells us nothing about himself.

The records of Oxford University and of St John's College tell us a

---

* Dr Christopher Hill, reluctant to let any scientist slip out of his 'radical Puritan' net, overlooks this emphatic protestation and suggests that Nicholas Hill was not a Catholic at all but a Puritan. As evidence he refers to the publication of his book in Calvinist Geneva (he does not mention that this was a posthumous publication and that the author himself had published it in Catholic Paris) and to various allegedly 'puritan' statements in his book. Thus Nicholas Hill, we are told, approved of government by popular assemblies, rejected 'on principle' aristocratic patronage, and repudiated ecclesiastical traditions: all surely signs of puritan virtue (see his *Intellectual Origins of the Puritan Revolution*, Oxford 1965, pp. 92, 112, 114–15). Unfortunately none of these opinions was in fact expressed by Nicholas Hill: they are all mistranslations of his words which Dr Hill has taken on trust from Grant McColley's article, 'Nicholas Hill and the *Philosophia Epicurea*' (*Annals of Science* IV, 1939).

little more. From them we know that Hill matriculated as a scholar of St John's College in June 1587, being then described as sixteen years old. They describe him as *plebei filius*, born in Fleet Street,* and educated previously at Merchant Taylors' School. *Plebei filius* merely means that his father was not a nobleman or esquire: he was probably a city merchant – merchants found it economically advantageous so to describe themselves. The same records show that on 30 June 1590, Nicholas Hill was elected a Fellow of his college, but that within a year he was 'removed' (*amotus*) and another scholar elected in his place. A comment in the Catalogue of Fellows records that, after leaving St John's College, 'he applied himself to the Lullian doctrine' and 'published certain questions in philosophy'. This comment is precious, because at least it proves that the references are to our Nicholas Hill: without it, we could not be sure even of that. A marginal note in the Catalogue, 'mortuus est', in the hand of Archbishop Laud indicated that he was dead by 1621 when Laud ceased to be President of the College.[14] Laud himself had been an undergraduate of the college with Hill and must have known him personally; but he does not refer to him in any of his writings.

These new facts are the only solid contemporary evidence for the life of Nicholas Hill. They are the only evidence available to us, and it seems that they were the only solid evidence available in the late 1680s, when Anthony Wood, of Merton College, Oxford, sought to construct a brief biography of Hill for his great dictionary of Oxford writers, *Athenae Oxonienses*. Since all later writers who have noticed Hill have started from Wood's account, which was compiled some seventy years after Hill's death, it is important to examine this account critically and see upon what evidence it is based. Fortunately, documents have survived which enable us to do so.

In order to write his notice of Hill, Wood applied to his friend – the friend whom he so regularly used and abused – John Aubrey; and Aubrey in turn applied to his friend, Thomas Henshaw of Kensington. Henshaw, like Aubrey, was a Fellow of the Royal Society and a virtuoso of science: Elias Ashmole described him as 'one extraordinarily learned and a great ornament to our nation'. He proved a useful informant, for

---

* Fleet Street was in the parishes of St Bride and St Dunstan in the West. The baptismal registers of the former, for the relevant period, have not survived. Those of the latter are decayed and largely illegible, but among the partly legible entries is one for 'Nicholas son (?) of, [illegible] Hill, baptised (?) on 3 (or 30 or 31) April (or May) 1570' (Guildhall Library MS 10,342 unfoliated). I am grateful to Mr C. R. H. Cooper, Keeper of MSS, Guildhall Library, for this information.

he actually possessed part of a manuscript by Hill. Aubrey passed on Henshaw's information to Wood, and Wood then applied to Henshaw direct. Henshaw sent him a copy of his manuscript, together with an account of its history, and confirmed what he had told Aubrey. In the course of the correspondence it became clear that both the manuscript and much of the biographical information supplied by Henshaw derived ultimately from Edmund Sheffield, first Earl of Mulgrave, who had died in 1646.[15]

Postponing, for a moment, the question of Henshaw's manuscripts, let us consider the biographical account of Nicholas Hill, which he supplied both to Aubrey and direct to Wood. According to Henshaw, 'the Earl of Mulgrave had heard that this Hill was secretary to the great Earl of Oxford' – that is, Edward de Vere, 17th Earl of Oxford – and had accompanied him on his travels in Italy and Germany. Henshaw also retailed a story (which also came from Mulgrave) about an incident said to have occurred during those travels. A poor man, it was said, had begged Hill to give him a penny. 'A penny!' exclaimed Hill, 'what dost thou say to ten pound?' 'Ah, ten pound!' said the beggar, 'that would make me a man!' Whereupon Hill gave him £10 and entered it in the Earl's account, 'Item, £10 for making a man'; which the Earl at first questioned but later, on hearing the story, cheerfully allowed. Henshaw also told Aubrey that Hill had died about 1610, 'an old man', and suggested that his son Lawrence, to whom he had dedicated his book, might have been the Lawrence Hill who had been hanged for complicity in the Popish Plot in 1679.[16]

Aubrey eagerly accepted Henshaw's story of Hill's travels with 'the great Earl of Oxford'. It enabled him to tell again one of his favourite stories: how that magnificent young Earl, while 'making his low obeisance to Queen Elizabeth, happened to let a Fart; at which he was so abashed that he went to travel seven years. At his return, the Queen welcomed him home and said, "My Lord, I had forgot the Fart".' This story served to remind Aubrey of the other Great Fart of 1610, and its poet Sergeant Hoskyns, who claimed to be 'well acquainted' with Nicholas Hill; whereupon he consulted Hoskyns' grandson, 'Sir John Hoskyns, baronet, my honoured friend', and was reminded by him of Ben Jonson's poem bringing Nicholas Hill together with all those ghostly Farts. So we are back again in the Mermaid Tavern. Wood, a dry old stick, expurgated the Farts from Aubrey's commentary, but otherwise accepted everything that he had been told, directly or indirectly, from Henshaw.

In fact, we must now sadly admit, everything that Henshaw told

Aubrey and Wood about the biography of Nicholas Hill is demonstrably wrong. Hill cannot have accompanied the Earl of Oxford on his travels (which in fact lasted only two, not seven years). One of the few certain facts about Hill is that he was sixteen years old when he matriculated at St John's College, Oxford, in June 1587. He was therefore born in 1570–71, and was only three years old when the Earl went on his travels in 1574, and five years old when he returned in 1576. Nor could he have died 'an old man' in or about 1610, for he was then only forty. Henshaw's recollection of what the Earl of Mulgrave was said to have heard was evidently, to say the least, mistaken.

Meanwhile Wood was hearing another tradition which was, potentially at least, more reliable. For it had its source in a man who, by his own account, was 'an intimate acquaintance of Mr Hill'. This was the distinguished Elizabethan scientist Robert Hues.

Robert Hues was an Oxford man who in 1586–8 had accompanied Thomas Cavendish in his circumnavigation of the world. He had been a friend of Sir Walter Ralegh, to whom he had dedicated his work on the use of terrestrial and celestial globes, published in 1594.[17] He had then become a client of Lord Grey of Wilton whom he had enlivened by his conversation during Grey's long imprisonment in the Tower. After Grey's death, he had been taken on the pay-roll of Henry Percy, 'the Wizard Earl' of Northumberland, who was also a prisoner in the Tower. He was one of 'the three Magi' – the others were Thomas Harriot and Walter Warner – whom the Earl maintained at Syon House.* In 1616 the Earl sent his heir, Algernon Percy, afterwards Lord Admiral of the Parliament against the King, to study at Christ Church, Oxford. Algernon Percy had been an undergraduate at Cambridge, but was evidently sent to Oxford for what would now be called graduate studies. Hues accompanied him thither, and himself stayed on at Christ Church till his death, at the age of eighty, in 1632, when he was buried in the cathedral. While at Oxford, Hues naturally discussed his earlier experiences with his friends and in particular with Joseph Maynard, afterwards Rector of Exeter College. Maynard

---

* It has been regularly said that the three Magi were the Earl's constant companions in the Tower and formed a kind of 'academy' there. This, as Mr John W. Shirley has shown, is not true (see his essay 'Sir Walter Ralegh and Thomas Harriot', in Shirley ed., op. cit., pp. 29–30; also his book *Thomas Harriot, A Biography*, Oxford 1983), ch. IX, 'The Northumberland Circle'). But they may all have visited him there. Hues' epitaph in Christ Church Cathedral, Oxford, states explicitly that, after accompanying Cavendish round the world, he was companion to Lord Grey 'cui solator accessit *in Arce Londinensi*. Quo defuncto ad studia Henrici comitis Northumbriensis *ibidem* vocatus est . . .' (my italics).

retailed his stories to others, and one of those who heard them from him was Obadiah Walker, Master of University College – a man who would become notorious for his timely conversion to popery on the accession of James II. Walker recorded them, along with other academic and scientific gossip, in a commonplace book, which survives in the Bodleian Library.* From Walker, Wood obtained the story of Nicholas Hill as told by Hues. It is very different from that which he had received, both direct and via Aubrey, from Henshaw.

According to Hues, as recorded by Walker, Hill was steward not of the Earl of Oxford but of his own patron the Earl of Northumberland, and it was that Earl whom he had charged £10 'for making a man'. Then Walker goes on:

Afterwards he joined himself with Mr Basset, who after Queen Elizabeth's death pretended some right for the crown. But King James being admitted, and possessed, he fled and lived in Rotterdam, taking his son Lawrence with him, who died there of a pestilential disease; which put the old man into great passion and melancholy; who coming into his apothecary's shop demanded such a quantity of ratsbane, chop'd it into his mouth, swallowed it, and there with great pain died, blaspheming and cursing.

This story I cannot affirm, but I had it from one that heard Mr Hues tell it. He was a great chymist and is mentioned in Ben Jonson's *Alchymist*.† He professed himself a disciple of Jordanus Brunus, and according to his principles writ two books, one printed at Geneva, another never printed that I know; both full of mighty words and no great matter.

Hues, we observe, said nothing of any connexion between Nicholas Hill and the Earl of Oxford. To him, Hill is a client of the Earl of Northumberland and, after him, of 'Mr Basset', both of whom are unnamed by Henshaw or Aubrey. Indeed, the two accounts – that which Henshaw had based upon Mulgrave and that which Walker had obtained from Hues – are entirely inconsistent with each other. The only point in common between them is the story of making a man for £10: a story which one places in Italy, at the expense of the spendthrift

---

* MS Rawlinson B.158. That this document is by Obadiah Walker emerges from Henshaw's letter to Wood of 6 March 1689 where he explicitly ascribes 'that tragical story' of Hill's death to 'Mr Walker' (MS Wood F.42). This detail, unobserved by previous scholars, was shown to me by Mr Mordechai Feingold.

† A slip: he means Jonson's *Epigrams*.

Earl of Oxford, the other in England, at the expense of the prudent and economical Earl of Northumberland.

We have subjected Henshaw's evidence to some severe criticism, and it is only fair to look equally critically at that of Walker – for both alike are reporters of hearsay. First, we must note that there is no evidence in the recorded expenses of the Earl of Northumberland, of any payment made to Hill;* he was certainly not on the same footing, in that household, as Harriot, Hues and Warner to whom regular payments are registered. Secondly, if Hill fled abroad on the accession of James I, he could not have been with Northumberland at the time when Hues was established there; for Hues, according to his funeral monument in Christ Church, Oxford, only entered the Earl's service after the death of his previous patron, Lord Grey of Wilton, who died in 1614. However, these objections are not fatal; for Hues was in London in the 1590s, closely associated with Sir Walter Ralegh, the friend and ally of Northumberland, and no doubt he was noticed by Northumberland even before entering his service. Hues may have been less 'intimate' with Hill than he afterwards claimed, or was claimed, to have been; his account may have been tainted by transmission through Maynard and Walker; but it cannot be rejected, like that of Henshaw, as inconsistent with itself or with known facts.

If Hues is worthy of credit on Hill's connexion with the Earl of Northumberland, he is even more credible when he speaks of his connexion with 'Mr Basset'; for whereas it would have been natural, in the seventeenth century, to associate a scientist of that time with Northumberland, who was known as a great patron of science – and particularly Neoplatonic, Hermetic science – it is hardly conceivable that anyone would invent an association with the unknown Basset. It is clear from his language that Walker, who recorded Hues' evidence, himself knew nothing about Basset, whose 'conspiracy' had been so effectively buried that even today it is difficult to document it; and so it is likely that the information which he gives on this matter comes authentically from Hues, who was in a position to know. This being so, it would be unreasonable in us to ignore it.

When Wood was in possession of these two inconsistent accounts, he evidently wrote direct to Henshaw pointing out some of the difficulties. In particular, how could Hill's son Lawrence be the same Lawrence

* Mr Colin Shrimpton, archivist at Alnwick Castle, has kindly checked the 'breving books' of the 9th Earl of Northumberland, but has found no reference to Nicholas Hill there, or in the accounts of the Steward of the Household or Foreign Paymaster. 'I could find but one Hill', he writes, 'and he was a scrivener'.

Hill who had been hanged for alleged complicity in the Popish Plot in 1679, if he had died of the plague in Holland before the death of his father in about 1610? In his reply, Henshaw came clean. He admitted that much of his own account had been mere speculation: he had set down 'all I knew, and more than I knew, for some of it was only conjecture'. Moreover, this conjecture was based on an admitted error: Henshaw had not known about the original Paris edition of Hill's book, in 1601, and had assumed that the Geneva edition of 1619 was the first edition – he had never believed, he explained, that 'so humorous and obscure a piece would ever have held out to a second edition'. On this assumption, he had supposed that Hill's son was an infant in 1619 and so might still qualify for hanging sixty years later. That explained one mistake, but only at the expense of emphasizing another, for Henshaw had himself told Aubrey that he believed Hill to have died 'an old man' in 1610: how then could he have supposed that he had dedicated a book to his infant son in 1619? But let that pass. Henshaw saved what he could from the wreck of his statement by expressing his personal disbelief in the story of Hill's suicide. It was, he thought, inherently unlikely that a man of Hill's 'great parts and experience in the world should come to die the death of a fool or madman'. In another letter, he went further, dismissing the story as 'fabulous'.

Faced with these two entirely inconsistent accounts, what was Anthony Wood to do? A critical scholar would have tested the authority of each and probably rejected Henshaw's account altogether. But Anthony Wood was not a critical scholar: he was an industrious collector of material and he had little time to test his individual entries. So he simply threw together the two accounts with all their inconsistencies unresolved. Without citing his authorities he declared confidently that he 'knew' that Hill was 'a great favourite of Edward, the poetical and prodigal Earl of Oxford'; that he 'spent some time with him while he consumed his estate beyond the sea and at home'; and that 'after that count's death, or rather before' – this strange phrase was the only way in which he could 'save the phenomena'* – 'he was taken into the retinue of that noble and generous person, Henry Earl of Northumberland, with whom he continued for some time in great esteem. At length, being suspected to comply with certain traitors against King James I', he 'fled beyond the seas and there died'. After this, Wood includes Hues' more detailed information among 'several traditions going from

---

* Wood must suddenly have realized that Hill could not have joined Northumberland after Oxford's death, since Hill (according to the evidence supplied to him) fled abroad in 1603 and Oxford did not die till 1604.

man to man'. He tells the story of Hill's 'making a man' for £10 (which he gives in Henshaw's version, as having happened when Hill was steward to the Earl of Oxford); he refers to Hill's involvement with 'one Basset, who pretended some right to the crown'; and having retailed the story of Hill's suicide as told by Walker, he rejects it in the words of Henshaw: Hill, he concluded, was a person of good parts, but humorous and fantastical, but 'I cannot be convinced that he should die the death of a fool or a madman'.

It has been necessary to analyse Wood's account of Nicholas Hill in such detail because that account is the basis of all later notices of him. Every modern scholar who hitherto has written on Nicholas Hill – C. J. Robinson in *The Dictionary of National Biography*, Mr McColley, Mr Kargon, Dr Christopher Hill, M. Pierre Lefranc, M. Jean Jacquot[18] – has confidently declared that he travelled abroad with the Earl of Oxford, though this is demonstrably impossible, and no such scholar has paid any attention to the story of his alleged complicity in the plot of 'Mr Basset' against James I, although this is recorded on better authority – and indeed on exactly the same authority as the patronage of Hill by the Earl of Northumberland, which all these writers accept without question.* The essential fact is that Wood's account is a composite work, consisting of undigested matter from differing sources of differing value. The evidence can only be judged if the account is disintegrated and its individual parts carefully tested.

Apart from the evidence which he sent to Wood, there is one detail supplied independently by Aubrey. This is that Hill was one of the 'intimate acquaintance and friends of Sir Walter Ralegh'. Aubrey gives no source for this statement, for which he is the only authority. Modern writers on Ralegh assume it to be true, and there is nothing inherently unlikely in it: if Hill was associated with Northumberland, he would naturally come into the orbit of Ralegh; but as we cannot test it, the assumption is unsafe: the question must remain in suspense.

Before seeking to re-arrange the evidence for Nicholas Hill's life, we may seek to clear up the one part of Thomas Henshaw's evidence which deserves to be taken seriously. It concerns not the biography of Nicholas Hill but his manuscripts. Here Henshaw is a credible authority for he speaks from experience and actually possessed at least one such manuscript.

* Thus C. J. Robinson, who states as a fact that Hill was secretary to the Earl of Oxford and 'lived under the patronage of Henry, Earl of Northumberland, and shared in his philosophical studies', dismisses his involvement in 'a plot against James I', etc., as 'a gossiping story'.

According to Henshaw, the manuscript which he possessed was a copy taken by John Everard, a Neoplatonist who had translated the Hermetic writers, from 'an imperfect copy in the hands of Edmund Earl of Mulgrave, great-grandfather [in fact, grandfather] to the present earl'. The Earl's manuscript was anonymous, but presumably it was he who ascribed it to Hill since he was the source of Henshaw's information (or misinformation) about Hill's life. Mulgrave was a Yorkshire peer who had led an active public life, first as a commander at sea under Queen Elizabeth and later, under James I, as President of the Council at York. He suffered from religious melancholy and wavered between inclination to popery and persecution of it. When Henshaw had acquired Everard's transcript of the manuscript, about 1637, he showed it to the greatest expert on such arcane matters, his own kinsman William Backhouse of Swallowfield.* This William Backhouse was a patron and himself a student of alchemy and other mysteries: he was the alchemical 'father' – i.e. initiator – of the alchemical virtuoso Elias Ashmole; and in 1662, on his deathbed, he told Ashmole 'in syllables the true matter of the philosopher's stone', which, says Ashmole, 'he bequeathed to me as a legacy'.† On reading Henshaw's manuscript, Backhouse, who knew Hill's printed work, recognized it as being by the same writer and determined to discover more about him. Accordingly, he 'never left enquiring after him till he found his widow dwelling behind Bow Church, of whom,' says Henshaw, 'he bought this manuscript, written in her own hand, which confirmed him that nothing is to be found of him or her in the church register, for that they were papists.' It is unfortunate that Backhouse – the one person, who, through Hill's widow, could have discovered, and perhaps did discover, the true history of his life – left no record of it or indeed of anything else. But Backhouse was a strange and secretive character who led a hidden life – *sache cacher* was his chosen motto – and committed nothing to paper.

Henshaw's account, in his letter to Wood, is supplemented by his

---

* William Backhouse's brother Sir John Backhouse married Flower Henshaw, who died in 1651. She was presumably a relation of Thomas Henshaw, perhaps an aunt (in her will she refers to 'Thomas Henshaw the elder', her nephew – and also to another Thomas Henshaw).

† On Backhouse, see C. H. Josten, 'William Backhouse of Swallowfield', *Ambix* VI, i (Dec. 1949), 1–33. If Backhouse had left any papers, they would presumably have passed either to his alchemical 'son', Ashmole, or to his daughter and sole heir, Flower, who at her death in 1700 was married to Henry Hyde, 2nd Earl of Clarendon. I have not found any Backhouse papers in the Ashmole or Clarendon MSS.

account given, at the same time, to Aubrey, of which we only have Aubrey's version. According to Aubrey,

> Thomas Henshawe of Kensington, esq, *R.Soc. Socius*, hath a treatise of his [i.e. Hill's] in MS, which he will not print, *viz.* of the Essence of God, etc. Light. It is mighty paradoxicall: – *that there is a God*; what he is, in 10 or 12 articles: *Of the Immortality of the Soule*, which he does demonstrate παντουσίᾳ and ὀντουσίᾳ.

A little later, Aubrey says that Henshaw – he presumably means Backhouse, as reported by Henshaw – 'bought of Nicholas Hill's widow, in Bow Lane, some of his bookes; among which is a manuscript *de infinitate et aeternitate mundi*. He finds by his writings that he was (or leaning) a Roman Catholique'. In summary, Aubrey states that Hill's writings 'had the usuall fate of those not printed in the author's life-time' – i.e., they were fragmented, dispersed, destroyed.

Putting these statements together, the most natural inference seems to be that Hill wrote a second work, which he may not have completed; that 'an imperfect copy' of this work, or of part of it, had somehow come to Mulgrave and been copied by Everard for Henshaw; and that another fragment of it, written out by his widow, was acquired from her by Backhouse. This second work was evidently entitled *De infinitate et aeternitate mundi*. This inference is supported by the evidence of Hues as retailed by Walker; for Walker writes of two books, the printed *Philosophia Epicurea* and 'another, never printed that I know', which Hues seems to have seen, for he characterizes it as being, like the *Philosophia Epicurea*, 'full of mighty words and no great matter'. Although the second book of Nicholas Hill is evidently lost, two fragments of his manuscript work survive. One of these is the text sent by Henshaw to Wood, and preserved among Wood's papers.[19] It consists of two folios only and expresses Neoplatonic mysticism. It is consistent with Aubrey's description of it as a demonstration of the immortality of the soul 'παντουσίᾳ and ὀντουσίᾳ' – whatever that opaque phrase, worthy of Coleridge at his best, may mean.* Since Hill's second book was presumably in Latin and this text is in English, it may be a translation written out by Hill's widow. The other fragment is a Latin poem of eighteen lines, in elegiac couplets, which can certainly be described as a demonstration 'that there is a God' and 'mighty paradoxical': it may have formed part of the 'treatise'

---

* 'pantheistically and ontologically' would appear to be the meaning; but I would defer to Peacock's Mr Flosky.

mentioned by Aubrey. Two versions of this poem came into the hands of Archbishop Sancroft, and are preserved in the Bodleian Library.[20] One of them is heavily emended in Sancroft's hand: the other is subscribed 'Nicholas Hill' and endorsed 'Mr Hilles verses divine to prove that there is God'. The style – and the mixture of Latin and Greek terms – is typical of Hill.

Recently, one other manuscript has come to light, which may be relevant to our enquiry. This manuscript, which is now in the Brotherton Library, Leeds,[21] is a volume of 335 folios at the end of which a seventeenth-century hand has noted 'this book was written by my cosin Mr Nicholas Hill'. The note is unsigned, and there is no other evidence of authorship. The history of the manuscript before 1880 is unknown. By that time it had been acquired by Falconer Madan, afterwards Bodley's Librarian at Oxford. Madan commented on it in a brief contribution to *Notes and Queries*,[22] describing it as 'written by one Nicholas Hill, c. 1600', and quoting an autobiographical passage in it. To this passage, which describes the daily routine of the author, we shall return. The rest of the book is intrinsically unrewarding. It is simply a series of extracts, principally from moral and devotional works. The books cited are mainly patristic and medieval, and the author is clearly Roman Catholic. The latest book to be cited appears to be the *Promptuarium Morale* of the English Catholic *émigré* theologian Thomas Stapleton, published at Lyon in 1592. The book was therefore compiled after that date.

Is this commonplace book by our Nicholas Hill? When I first studied it, I came hesitantly to the conclusion that it was not. The name of the author, his date and his religion all pointed towards him, but the content was so different from our Nicholas Hill's published work and manuscripts that I could not see him as the same person. There is nothing in this commonplace book even remotely suggesting the bold, paradoxical scientific speculations of our author's work. However, on second thoughts, I am not so sure; for in spite of this omission, the character of our Nicholas Hill, as it emerges from his undoubted work, has certain general affinities, and one particular affinity, with that of the compiler of the commonplace book. Those affinities are Catholic contemplative mysticism and, in particular, a concern for the hermit life.

In his printed work, Hill states that all religion consists in giving thanks and celebrating the name of God; that all virtue is participation in divinity; that contemplation of the deity so elevates and captivates the soul of man that he cannot thereafter descend to common matters; that God is unintelligible and indescribable except by those to whom

He has granted a new criterion of vision; that worldly wisdom is a form of arrogance and that the faculties of the mind can only be exercised silently, humbly, with self-denial; that study, if it is to bring man to the highest pitch of virtue, must be 'in solitude and shadow, which cool the blood and spirits and take away occasion of sin'.[23] Similarly, in the fragment preserved by Henshaw, Hill quotes those who preach contempt of the world, citing especially St Macarius, 'a follower of St Anthony's, and many Eremitic divines', extolling 'the severe lives of Eremites, true adversaries of sensuality', and advocating contemplative union with an all-pervasive God as the highest form of happiness, which being achieved, 'all other appetites vanish like dismissed servants of whom there is no farther use'. These sentiments are compatible with those of the author of the commonplace book, who cites, above all, the mystical writers – St Bernard, St Bonaventure, St John Climacus, etc. – and writings on contempt of riches and the world. His account of his own daily routine describes a life of regular study and devotion at home – there is no reference at all to ritual – with occasional walks abroad or, for preference, in the garden, where there is 'ample room to stroll', and conversation at meals, 'but only on sacred subjects'. There are also occasional marginal notes of a personal kind, recommending the hermit life. One such note remarks how a Duke of Savoy, after the death of his wife, 'forsook the world and withdrew himself into a pleasant hermitage . . . in a delightful place adjoining to the sea . . . and there led a solitary life, with certain other knights of the same mind'. Another, in Latin, recalls how some scholars prefer to study 'in an open place, high up, in clear air, surrounded on all sides by sky and air. Such men have lived in the deserts and mountains where, if we believe Jerome, they find a quality of serenity that is lacking in smoky cities'. There are also citations against solitude and the hermit life, as if the writer was debating the question with himself.

Nicholas Hill, the author of this commonplace book, may not have been the same as Nicholas Hill, the natural philosopher. It is perfectly possible that there were two men of that name writing in the same decade, both literate in English and Latin, both devout Roman Catholics, both mystical in their devotion, with a leaning towards the hermit life. It is equally possible that the private commonplace book and the unpublished philosophical treatise represent different sides, or different phases, of the same person. At present we must be content to leave the question in suspense, and from this, as from so much of the evidence about this enigmatic personality, draw only the most tentative conclusions.

We are now in a position to review the available evidence of the early life of Nicholas Hill the philosopher. Very little of it is solid. He was certainly born in 1570–71 and described himself as a Londoner. His father was probably a London merchant. He was educated at Merchant Taylors' School and at St John's College, Oxford. In 1590 he was a Fellow of the College but in 1592 he was removed. Since we know that he was afterwards a Roman Catholic we can be reasonably certain he was deprived of his fellowship on account of his conversion. Thereafter his career is very uncertainly documented. He evidently led a solitary, self-contained life, and it may well be he who, after his conversion, steeped himself in Catholic contemplative writers and recorded his reading in the commonplace book. In spite of the repeated statements of successive scholars, he did not travel abroad with the Earl of Oxford, whose travels, by that time, were long past and who was now living quietly in Hackney writing (as some believe) the plays of Shakespeare. There is some reason to believe that he was patronized by the Earl of Northumberland at Syon House in the 1590s, and he may have become associated with Sir Walter Ralegh. Then – whether before or after publishing his book in Paris in 1601 is not clear – he 'joined himself with Mr Basset, who after Queen Elizabeth's death pretended some right for the crown'.

Who was this mysterious 'Mr Basset' – 'one Basset' as Wood unceremoniously calls him? In order to discover him, we must abandon the fabulous world of the migratory Earl of Oxford 'sending his patrimony flying' in the courts of Europe, and the famous intellectual laboratory of the 'wizard earl' of Northumberland at Petworth and Syon, and move westwards, to a bizarre and obscure episode in provincial Devonshire.

3   Sir Robert Basset and his conspiracy

Robert Basset of Heanton Punchardon and Umberleigh was a member of an ancient family seated in Devon and Cornwall which had been drawn into high politics in the reign of Henry VIII when Honor, the widow of Sir John Basset, had married Arthur Plantagenet, Viscount Lisle, the natural son of Edward IV. In 1533 Lisle was appointed governor of Calais, but in 1540, being suspected of complicity in the alleged Catholic plot of his West Country kinsmen, Henry Courtenay, Marquis of Exeter, and the Pole family, and of himself aspiring to the Crown, he had been arrested and had died in the Tower. One of the consequences of this marriage was the marriage of Lisle's daughter, and co-heiress, Frances Plantagenet, to his stepson John Basset; thus their son, Sir Arthur Basset, could claim – though illegitimate and through the female line – royal descent. Not that Sir Arthur ever made so dangerous a claim: he lived a blameless life in the West Country, represented Barnstaple and then Devonshire in Parliament, and was high sheriff of Devonshire. He died in 1586, aged forty-five, and was succeeded in his estates by his eldest son Robert, with whom we are concerned.[24]

The Basset family, in general, followed the religion of State, but they were conservative in their outlook and inclined to Catholicism. This inclination was increased when James Basset, the youngest stepson of Lord Lisle, married Mary Roper, the grand-daughter of Sir Thomas More. The family of Sir Thomas More was the most self-consciously Catholic group in England, and it made a cult of More himself. All the biographies of More were written, or originated, within his family circle, which also published his works. Mary Basset herself translated the Latin part of More's *Treatise of the Passion* into English. Thanks to this connexion, the family of James Basset remained firmly Catholic. In the Catholic reign of Mary Tudor, James Basset himself became one of the Queen's Privy Council and his wife a gentlewoman of her Privy Chamber. Their two sons, Philip, named after his godfather King Philip, and Charles, were both devout Catholic recusants whose lives would be made difficult by their recusancy. They were cousins of Sir Arthur, the father of our Robert Basset.

Robert Basset was born in 1574. He was matriculated at Queen's College, Oxford, in 1589 and then read law at the Inner Temple. In 1593 he represented Plymouth in Parliament. He had property scattered through Devonshire and Cornwall, and indeed elsewhere, but his main seat was Heanton Court at Heanton Punchardon near Barnstaple: a place, as a contemporary described it, 'whether you respect pleasure or profit, daintily situated by an arm of the sea'.[25] Like many West Country gentlemen, he owned a ship and was deeply involved, with various associates, in privateering ventures, some of which were barely distinguishable from piracy. These, in due course, would bring him into financial difficulties; for although possessed of ample estates, his family was always straitened for ready money. He was also, since Barnstaple was a port for shipment to Ireland, involved in Irish affairs; and thus he came into the orbit of that fatal figure, Robert Devereux, Earl of Essex. In 1599 he accompanied Essex to Ireland and was one of those knighted by him. By this time, like so many followers of Essex, he had begun to speculate on the political opportunities which would be created by the death of Queen Elizabeth. He was also – again like many Essexians – unsettled in religion.

It has been remarked that whenever there was speculation on the succession to the Crown there was a revival of interest, among the English recusants who hoped to profit by such a change, in Sir Thomas More.[26] More had, by now, become their totem figure, and the writing of biographies or hagiographies of him had become a regular industry of his family circle. In 1599 a new biography of him was written, by an author who was evidently within the same family circle, for his only original contributions come from personal knowledge of it: he cited the private expense accounts of More's son-in-law William Roper and added new details of the More and Roper families. He also cited, as if it were well known to its readers, the biography of More by Nicholas Harpsfield, which was unpublished at the time, and was based on the equally unpublished work of William Roper. Evidently the new work was addressed to the restricted circle of those to whom these manuscript works were already familiar. Apart from Harpsfield, its main documentary source was the Latin life of More by the Catholic *émigré* Thomas Stapleton, whom we have already had occasion to mention: this book had been printed in Louvain in 1588. The author of the new work showed himself to be a young man who had not previously tried his hand in literature: he describes himself as 'a young beginner'. He signed his manuscript 'Ro. Ba.'. Although the identification is not certain, all the signs point towards Robert Basset who, at precisely that time, had been drawn into Catholicism.[27]

The evidence of Basset's conversion to Catholicism comes from a letter which William Pole, of Shute, a Devonshire gentleman, wrote to his uncle, Sir John Popham, on 18 January 1600. Pole was Basset's brother-in-law: their wives were sisters, the daughters of a local judge, Sir William Periam. Popham, also a West Country man, was Lord Chief Justice, and had become notorious as a detector and repressor of recusancy. In his letter, Pole reminds his uncle that he had already, some two years ago, written to warn him that Basset was being 'corrupted and seduced to popery'. This places Basset's conversion in or about 1598, and is compatible with his authorship of the life of More, which he might well have written at such a time. However, for us, the particular interest of Pole's letter lies in the identity of the man who corrupted and seduced Basset, whom he names as 'one Hill'.

According to Pole, Popham, on this previous occasion, had caused this man Hill to be haled before Archbishop Whitgift. Hill had then taken the oath of Supremacy and subscribed to the Thirty-Nine Articles, 'and so rid himself of trouble'. But now, two years later, 'this blasphement fellow' had reappeared, in company with one John Sweet, who had already been cited before Popham and was now 'run away and thought to be a priest'. Hill, Pole went on, had been to see a Jesuit imprisoned in Newgate, and 'I fear the sequel thereof will be evil, if it be not prevented, for though Sir Robert Basset standeth not curious in any religion (with sorrow I write), yet lately he hath practised his frauds with popery and hath confessed privately that Sir William Courtenay and himself have combined themselves that way, and it is known that these kind of people prepare themselves for innovation'. In fact, said Pole, Basset had confessed to him a particular design in hand. Immediately, he planned to travel abroad with Hill. Meanwhile, he had 'resolved to have the isle of Lundy, and there to place a malcontent fellow, one Ansley, a Somersetshire man'. Pole felt obliged to inform Popham of these plans, out of loyalty to the government and love of his brother-in-law, and he urged Popham to nip them in the bud by stopping the projected foreign travel and imprisoning 'that most pernicious lewd man Hill, who otherwise will be the overthrow of the gentle nature of Sir Robert'.[28]

Pole had reason to be alarmed: Basset, it seemed, was threatening the security of the whole family. Recusancy itself was dangerous enough; but here it was associated with 'innovation', political revolution. Sir William Courtenay, with whom he was 'combining that way', was already deeply suspect: Cecil's agents had reported that he was in touch with the Spaniards, who expected him to co-operate with them if they should land in the West Country.[29] Although nothing like this happened, Pole's general apprehensions were justified next year, when Catholic extremists supported Essex's attempt to seize power in the State and Lord Chief Justice Popham found himself pronouncing sentence on the ringleaders of that rising. Pole was right too about John Sweet. Sweet, who was a Devonshire man and a kinsman of Lady Basset, did in fact make his way to Rome. By October 1602 he was in the English College at Rome, a Jesuit house. After four years' residence there, he would enter the order and, under the alias John Douse, would twice return to Devonshire, as a missionary, and re-visit his kinswoman Lady Basset. Finally, Pole was right about Basset – although three years would elapse before Basset carried out his plan. He would carry it out after the death of Queen Elizabeth, in 1603.

By this time, Basset was in deep financial trouble in consequence of his privateering adventures. In November 1601 one of his associates, for whom he had stood surety, had seized a ship belonging to some French merchants of St Jean de Luz. This was sheer piracy, and when the matter was brought to court, Sir Robert was adjudged liable in £15,000. This sudden liability seems to have been the immediate cause of his desperate act. Just as financial insolvency had caused Essex to plunge into conspiracy in 1601, and would drive his surviving followers into the Gunpowder Plot in 1605, so this heavy financial blow caused Basset to risk all on a lunatic political adventure. Remembering his royal descent, he 'pretended some right for the crown', and carried out the plan which he had mentioned to Pole three years earlier. That is, he raised his standard on that regular resort of desperate men, Lundy Island.* Then, when no one paid any heed to him, he decided to flee abroad. In July 1603 he 'took shipping at Appledore in the port of Barnstaple' and sailed to La Rochelle. At first he planned to go and fight the Turk in Hungary; but afterwards he changed his mind. He made his way overland to Marseille, and wrote thence to his family. Then he moved on to Pisa. From Pisa he wrote to his son expressing a wish that he was back in Lundy Island, 'in as poor case as I came from thence, where I would gladly spend my days in an obscure hermitage'. He asked that letters should be addressed to him c/o John Sweet, esq, at the English College, Rome.[30]

Basset's 'conspiracy', if it may be so called, excited very little notice at the time, and is remarkably ill-documented. Though it proclaimed him a traitor and a fugitive, the government of James I seems to have been more concerned by his debts than by his treason: for it found itself importuned 'with continual clamour' by the French merchants who had been robbed at sea by his associates and who could not obtain the indemnity legally awarded to them. Basset established himself at Rome, at the expense of John Sweet, and for a time was cultivated by the English *émigré* Catholics: he was taken up by Cardinal Allen and feasted by that most political of English Jesuits, Fr. Persons. But he soon tired of his exile. Though he still spoke indiscreetly of his title to

* Lundy Island had frequently been held by rebels against the Crown in the Middle Ages (see J. R. Chanter, *Lundy Island*, 1887). In the reign of Edward VI it had been the resort of pirates protected by the Admiral, Lord Seymour. A Spanish occupation of the island was apprehended in 1598 (HMC Marquess of Salisbury, VIII, p. 59). Later, in the reign of James I, a notorious pirate, Salkeld, declared himself king of Lundy and prepared for his coronation there but was dethroned by a mutiny of his prisoners and forced to flee from the island (SP Dom.Jac.I, liii.100). In the civil war, Lundy was one of the successive island retreats of the eccentric hermit-entrepreneur Thomas Bushell, who defended it for Charles I. It was the last royalist stronghold to surrender to the Parliament.

the Crown, he wrote pitiful letters to the King and to Lord Salisbury, confessing his 'enormous errors' and begging for permission to return home and for protection against his creditors. He begged in vain. The Gunpowder Plot, in 1605, made any concession to a Catholic plotter inopportune. In 1606 Sweet left Rome, *ad componendas res suas*, to arrange his own affairs, and returned to Devonshire, where he was arrested at the house of Lady Basset.[31] In 1609 Basset himself left Rome for Paris and Brussels, and pestered the English ambassadors there. He protested 'that he had rather be a gentleman in England, well at his ease, than a wandering Prince in imagination'.[32] Finally, in 1611, the King granted his pardon, for the financial benefit of a hungry Scotchman. At the instance of Henry Howard, Earl of Northampton, the crypto-Catholic who had eclipsed Salisbury as the King's political adviser, Basset was excused his crimes on the ground that he had lately been distracted, and allowed to return to England on condition that he remained in his house in Devonshire. There he lived, obscure and impoverished, having sold thirty manors to satisfy his creditors, till his death twenty years later.[33]

Such was the 'conspiracy' of Sir Robert Basset. On the face of it, it was a mad venture, so eccentric and futile that no historian, it seems, has condescended to notice it. Even at the time, it seems to have been immediately forgotten – unlike the equally lunatic Gunpowder Plot, which was so emphatically commemorated. The records of government ignore it. Local chroniclers slide tactfully over it. The contemporary antiquary of Devon, being Basset's brother-in-law, Sir William Pole, is discreetly silent about it. When Obadiah Walker and Anthony Wood learned of Hill's 'compliance' with it, they showed no sign of knowing what it was about: they merely recorded the report, shrugged their shoulders, and passed on. This suggests that at least they recorded faithfully what they heard, and that Robert Hues, on whose ultimate authority they both rely, did in fact state that Hill was compromised in it – or at least had felt himself to be compromised and had fled abroad to avoid trouble. If Hues said so, we cannot ignore his evidence. The very absurdity and eccentricity of the venture makes it unlikely that he invented it.

Moreover, we cannot help noticing a striking fact and a possible connexion. The striking fact is the accurate prophecy of Basset's brother-in-law William Pole. Pole had seen it all coming. Three years before the dramatic *dénouement* of the plot, he had recorded the perversion of Basset to popery, his association with Sweet, and his plan to establish himself on Lundy Island. The possible connexion is the name of Hill. Two years before that, he had named Basset's chief seducer, 'one Hill'. The question naturally arises, who is this fellow Hill? Is he our Nicholas Hill?*

The question is not easy to answer. Hill is a very common surname, common in the West Country as elsewhere in England, and we do not know the Christian name of the Hill who, according to Pole, was perverting Basset. Moreover there are other Hills who enter into the story of Basset at a later date. How can we distinguish these various Hills? All attempts to identify Nicholas Hill of London having failed, let us turn to see whether we can identify, in any way, the even more elusive Hill who was so close to Sir Robert Basset in Devonshire.

The first potential clue is supplied by John Sweet; for clearly Hill and Sweet were closely associated with each other and with Basset in 1598–1600. Moreover, the two names, Hill and Sweet, are joined together, in a similar context, for a second time, in 1621. In November of that year, Sweet, who was now a Jesuit priest, returned as a missionary to his native Devonshire. His name was well known to the English government, and his movements were watched. He was arrested and found to be in possession of 'superstitious and massing trinkets'. He was alleged to have been entertained in Devonshire by 'one Hill, who is fled and reputed to be a seminary priest'.[34] It is tempting to suppose that this is the same Hill who had been associated with Sweet in 1598–1600, in which case we have to admit that the evil genius of Sir Robert Basset in 1598–1600 cannot have been our Nicholas Hill, for we know, on the evidence of Archbishop Laud's notes in the Register of St John's College, that our man was dead by 1621. However, there are objections which seem fatal to such a simple identification.

The objections centre on the identity of the Hill who entertained Sweet in 1621. This man can almost certainly be identified with one Southcote Hill who had aroused the zeal of the local authorities in Devonshire in September 1617. A local justice, Richard Reynell of Creedy Wiger, had then informed the mayor and aldermen of Exeter that he had sent his servants 'with warrants for Southcote Hill etc.', but that the birds had flown. 'I wish,' he added, 'you had described S. Hill by his stature, apparel, etc.' Evidently Southcote Hill was not well known to the local JPs.[35]

* A. W. Reed, in his Appendix I to Ro. Ba.'s *Lyfe of Syr Thomas More* (EETS 1950), pp. 304–6, assumes without question that he is; and this assumption is taken over, on his authority, by Muriel St Clair Byrne (*The Lisle Letters* (Chicago 1981) VI, p. 287); but the identity cannot be thus easily assumed: it remains – alas – a tantalizing speculation.

Who was Southcote Hill? The Catholic antiquaries of the nineteenth century who examined the episode – George Oliver, the Devonshire antiquary, and, following him, Henry Foley, the chronicler of the English Jesuits – state categorically, though without giving any evidence, that the name Southcote Hill was assumed by one John Wood, *alias* John de Sylva, who was born in 1586, became a lay brother of the Jesuits in 1612, and died at Liège in 1663. If this is correct, 'Southcote Hill' cannot have been the seducer of Sir Robert Basset in 1598, for he would then have been only twelve years old. But in fact I suspect that Oliver (whom Foley merely copies) was wrong,[36] and that the true facts may help to solve our mystery. For I can see no reason to suppose that 'Southcote Hill' was the pseudonym of John Wood or anyone else. It was the real name of a person who perfectly fits the evidence.

The Southcotes of Southcote and Bovey Tracy and the Hills of Shilston, in the parish of Modbury, were established gentry families in Devonshire. They were neighbours in South Devon, and are mentioned together in interesting circumstances. From an account of the famous Jesuit Robert Persons (himself a West Country man), written by his brother, we learn that Persons, as a Fellow of Balliol College, Oxford, was so highly regarded that many West Country men particularly sought him out as tutor for their sons – as 'Lord Seymour, Mr Southcote, Mr Hill and others'.[37] Thus temptations to recusancy already lay in the way of these two families. In 1575 the two families were allied when Robert Hill of Shilston married Ursula, the daughter of Thomas Southcote of Bovey Tracy. Their first son, Edward, was born in 1580. Of Edward we only know that he and his father between them wasted their estate and were finally sold up in 1614. The second son, Edward's younger brother, was called Southcote Hill. Of him we know only that in 1620, at the time of a herald's visitation, he was abroad 'in partibus transmarinis'.[38]

This is surely the Southcote Hill of 1621. The younger son of a decayed gentry family, touched with popery, born, like Sweet, in the parish of Modbury, he is the natural associate of his older neighbour. In 1617 warrants are out for him in Devonshire; he flees, and in 1620 he is abroad; in 1621 he has returned in time to receive Sweet; and when Sweet is arrested, attention is directed, once again, towards him. But once again he evades his pursuers, contemporary JPs and modern historians alike, and we hear no more of him. However, we can say of him, positively, that he was not the 'lewd fellow Hill' who seduced Sir Robert Basset in 1598. He too was too young for that *rôle*. We do not know the date of his birth, but we know that his elder brother was born in 1580 and his younger brother in 1589; so it must have been between those dates. That makes him between nine and seventeen years old in 1598 – not an age at which to convert an educated and mature man of twenty-four, a university man and a member of Parliament. The blasphemous fellow of 1598 was clearly another and an older man, who is still to be identified.

However, by thus localizing the problem, we may have come a little nearer to its solution. We have established something about the conspiracy of Sir Robert Basset. Basset did not merely 'pretend some right to the crown': his 'conspiracy' was hatched in an atmosphere of political discontent and Roman Catholic resentments within a closely connected and interrelated social group. This group centred on a particular locality. The world of Sir Robert Basset had two bases: Barnstaple in North Devon and, in South Devon, the area from Plymouth to Exeter. It was from these two bases that he and his associates sent out their ships. His operations in the Bristol Channel were conducted from Barnstaple. That was his own home town. It was thence that he looked towards Ireland, thence that he plotted to seize Lundy Island, thence that he fled to La Rochelle. But his privateering ventures against foreign ships were directed from Plymouth. His wife's family were of Crediton, near Exeter. His friend, with whom he 'practised his frauds with popery', Sir William Courtenay, was of Powderham, south of Exeter. Sir William Pole, his brother-in-law, who was so concerned about it, lived at Colcombe and Shute, in South Devon. Lady Basset's other kinsmen, the Sweet family, came from Modbury, near Plymouth. So did the Hills of Shilston, with whom John Sweet was so closely involved. It was in the Exeter–Modbury–Powderham area that the plot – whatever it was – was discussed; and if Nicholas Hill was involved in it, as Robert Hues stated, it is a reasonable inference that it was because he too was one of that intimate circle: that he was one of the local family, the Hills of Shilston.

Perhaps his father was a younger son who had gone to London and become a merchant or tradesman in Fleet Street. The fact that he is not recorded in wills or pedigrees means nothing.* This would account for his birth in Fleet Street, and his description of himself as 'Londiniensis'; but he would retain a family connexion with his kinsmen in Shilston

---

* Unimportant, absentee or unlanded members of a family were often omitted from the herald's records, and wills are no sure guide: the will of Oliver Hill of Shilston, who died in 1573, mentions his son Robert but says nothing of his other two sons and three daughters.

and, through them, would be drawn into the world of Devonshire men in London and at home: the Sweets of Modbury, their closest neighbours in Devonshire, John Sweet's kinswoman Lady Basset, and her husband Sir Robert Basset. John Sweet may have been known to him at Oxford, for they were there together. If Aubrey is right in recording that he was an 'intimate' friend of Sir Walter Ralegh, that connexion too may have had a Devonshire base; for Ralegh had been born in Hayes Barton near Exmouth and his mother was Katherine Champernowne whose family were lords of Modbury.

Once we admit this hypothesis, Nicholas Hill's association with Sir Robert Basset in his remote Devonshire home becomes more intelligible. But why did he also involve himself in such an extraordinary conspiracy? Basset's claim to the throne of England was absurd, a fantasy: his royal descent was genuine, but it was illegitimate, and his family had never previously suggested that they could claim a right. His plot was a wild venture which arose out of the discontent of the Catholic gentry of the West, a general atmosphere of conspiracy engendered by political uncertainty – and memories, perhaps, of that earlier 'plot' which had been so disastrous to the very same families who were now involved: the Courtenays, the Poles and Basset's own forebear, Lord Lisle. What had Nicholas Hill to do with this? Local ties, friendship, Catholicism – these might provide an occasion, but 'compliance' requires a more compelling reason. In search of such a reason, we must go back from the recusant gentry of Devonshire to the intellectual development of Nicholas Hill the atomic philosopher, and, in particular, to the one period of his life which is securely documented: his student days at Oxford.

4   Bruno and Hill

We have seen that the member of St John's College who completed the entry in the college records concerning Nicholas Hill wrote that, after leaving Oxford, 'he applied himself to the Lullian doctrine'. Robert Hues, who knew him in those days, afterwards remembered that 'he professed himself a disciple of Jordanus Brunus'; and indeed Hill himself, in a marginal note to his book, explicitly cites Giordano Bruno, under his habitual Latin name 'Nolanus'. Mersenne also attacked him as a disciple of Bruno. Since Bruno was the great reviver of 'Lullianism' in the later sixteenth century, there is no conflict in these statements, although Hill's debt to Bruno is rather in the field of cosmology than in

that of the Lullian art of memory and cabalistic magic. The question
therefore arises, how did Hill become a disciple of Giordano Bruno?

An answer presents itself at once. Giordano Bruno came to England
in 1583 and for the next two years lived in the house of the French
ambassador in London. From the moment of his arrival, he was
determined to conquer England intellectually, preaching a new
philosophy that would transcend the differences between Catholicism
and Protestantism and so lay the ideological basis for an Anglo-French
alliance. It seems that he had the support of the French ambassador
and, behind him, of certain circles in the France of Henri III, torn by
ideological civil war. In order to make this conquest, Bruno made his
first appeal to the University of Oxford, and went thither in person to
advocate his ideas. He was rebuffed by the Protestant doctors of the
University, and thereafter he attacked the University in his writings as
having lapsed from its former glory as a centre of philosophical
thought and denounced its Protestant doctors as donkeys and swine.
During the next two years, while he remained in London, he wrote
half-a-dozen books – the most famous and challenging of his books –
which were published in London at the expense, probably, of the
French ambassador. Unlike his previous books, which he had written
in Latin, these books were all written in Italian – a sign that Bruno had
abandoned hope of converting the Protestant university establishment
and now addressed himself instead to the Italianate intellectuals of
London; in particular to the circle of Philip Sidney and his close friend
Fulke Greville. It was in these works that he advanced his cosmological
ideas of a world constructed of atoms, mobilized by magical forces, and
of an infinite universe containing a plurality of heliocentric worlds. In
October 1585, when the French ambassador was recalled, Bruno left
London, and the rest of his life was spent in France, Germany and Italy,
ending disastrously in the *auto da fe* in Rome.

Bruno's visit to Oxford, and his violent clash with the Oxford
doctors, were long remembered, on both sides. The puritanical George
Abbot, afterwards Archbishop of Canterbury, who had been a Fellow
of Balliol at the time, was still angry about it twenty years later.[39] In
1587, only two years after Bruno's departure from England, the
memory of the event must have been fresh in Oxford: indeed, in that
year, or soon afterwards, it was parodied in Robert Greene's play *Friar
Bacon and Friar Bungay*. When Nicholas Hill came to Oxford in that year,
he would certainly have heard about the episode, and natural curiosity
about it might well have caused him to read the works which Bruno had
since poured out. Moreover, in St John's College he would have found

an atmosphere more congenial to open-minded study of fashionable ideas than in the Balliol of George Abbot.

For St John's College was not a conventional Protestant college. It had been founded in the reign of Mary Tudor by a Catholic merchant of London, and under Elizabeth it still retained a Catholic flavour. Outwardly Protestant, it was inwardly semi-Catholic, or, later, 'Arminian'. It produced the Roman Catholic martyr Edmund Campion and the high-Anglican martyr Archbishop Laud. It also produced the Benedictine 'Leander Jones' who, like Bruno, though in a different way, sought to reconcile Catholicism and English Protestantism. In such a college, it was easy to slide, as Nicholas Hill evidently slid, into open popery. It was also easy to look for other escapes from sectarian conformity, such as the Hermetic irenism that was preached by Bruno. In 1592, the year after Hill was deprived of his fellowship, Robert Fludd came to St John's College. He would remain there for six years, and then spent several years travelling abroad, often as a tutor in Catholic French families. It was while he was at St John's that he laid the basis of his Hermetic philosophy. An older man, a Fellow of the College who lived there in both Hill's and Fludd's time, and was a personal friend of Fludd, was William Paddy. He also combined semi-Catholic religious opinions with semi-Catholic Hermetic ideas in philosophy.[40] Both Fludd and Paddy were doctors of medicine; both were fond of music; both were impatient of sectarian religion. Paddy, like Hill, had come to St John's from Merchant Taylors' School. So had another Fellow of St John's, his contemporary, who was also both an accomplished musician (he lectured on music) and a physician (he became Regius Professor of Medicine), Matthew Gwinn. Gwinn was a lover of Italy, who spoke Italian fluently; through his lifelong friend, the Italian *émigré* John Florio, he became intimate with Bruno in England, accompanying him in London and Oxford. He was present at the famous disputation and is one of the English friends and sympathizers named by Bruno. He was at St John's College, as junior proctor, when Hill was at the college, and could have been a link between him and the ideas of Bruno.[41]

To have been expelled by a society as tolerant as St John's College, Hill must have been more uncompromising in his unorthodoxy than Paddy or Fludd. His commonplace book (if it is his) suggests a decisive conversion and a hankering for the philosopher's ivory tower. Perhaps, in the 1590s, he found opportunities for study in the circle of the Earl of Northumberland and Walter Ralegh. Northumberland, who was himself a reader of Bruno, and owned and annotated his Italian works,[42] was indifferent, perhaps sceptical, in religion and kept papists in his household; which was to prove disastrous to him after the Gunpowder Plot. But by 1598 (if our identification is correct) Hill was in Devonshire, in the circle of Sir Robert Basset. Basset, it seems, had hitherto been either indifferent or sceptical in religion but now he was unsettled and ripe for conversion. By 1599 he was converted. By 1600, under a convergence of forces, he was prepared to carry out a coup; and Hill was ready to encourage him.

It was at this time that William Pole intervened. In order to save his brother-in-law from an act of folly which would ruin himself and his family, he wrote to his uncle, the Lord Chief Justice, urging him to intervene and remove the tempter. How Sir John Popham responded, we do not know; but he can hardly have ignored the appeal: that might have been fatal not only to the family but also to himself, for it could have shown him compounding an act of treason. All that we know is that in February 1601, when the Earl of Essex staged his coup in London, Basset, in Devonshire, did not move, and Sir John Popham, who condemned Essex and his fellow conspirators, was spared the task of judging his own kinsman. Later in the same year, Nicholas Hill's work was published in Paris. Presumably he had been working on it at the time when Basset had been planning to seize Lundy Island. Let us therefore turn to it to see what we can make of it.

5   Hill's utopia

In form, Hill's work is a series of terse philosophical propositions, like the *theses* which challenging philosophers or theologians undertook to defend against all comers. There are over five hundred of these propositions, and they set out, in a disorderly and sometimes obscure apophthegmatic form, a comprehensive picture of the universe. Essentially it is the universe of Giordano Bruno: a universe in which the cold, mechanical atomic theory which Bruno had found in Lucretius is extended to infinity and animated with divine life. Like Bruno, Hill repudiates the old Aristotelean universe entirely. Men whose minds had been conditioned by Aristoteleanism, or by traditional methods of thought, he says, will never attain to true knowledge of Nature. A radical breach is needed, and knowledge must be attained systematically, sense-perception proceeding to imagination and imagination to understanding, until we embrace the whole universe and see, through direct revelation, which is a sudden irradiation at the end of long and

methodical study, the whole scheme of things, uniformly ruled by the
four 'tetrarchs': God, matter, space and time.

The universe which Hill has thus discovered is infinite, in space as in
time, co-eternal with God, and contains innumerable world-systems
like our own, heliocentric and inhabited. It is alive, and its infinite
diversity is animated, and given unity, by God, who is not anthropo-
morphic or rationally comprehensible, but is an indestructible source
of energy and life diffused uniformly throughout the cosmos, by his
'only daughter and helper', Nature. The earth, and all other heavenly
bodies, are themselves animate and intelligent, generating from their
own substance the animals which live on them, the latest-born of which
is man. In an unlimited universe there is no hierarchy of position –
there can be no higher or lower stations and the concept of weight is
meaningless. All movement is by magnetic force – for Hill has read
William Gilbert's great work *On the Magnet*, published a year before, in
1600, and he ascribes what we know as gravity to magnetic force. Man
is a microcosm of the larger world; his soul, which is subject to
magnetism too, is a particle of divinity: his diseases are therefore
curable by chemistry and astral magic which harness the forces of the
macrocosm. Prolongation of life is thus possible: the elixir of life, the
philosopher's stone, can be discovered, and men's stature could be
greatly increased – they could become giants – if only medical art were
perfected. But death is final: it is the extinction of the vital principle, all
animal spirits being worn out. The idea of resurrection of the flesh is
therefore a stupidity and the desire to retain individuality after death
contrary to reason: after death the soul is liberated and reunited with
God, and thus enjoys the aesthetic prospect of a boundless universe,
teeming with life: 'the exploration and comprehension through eternity
of innumerable worlds'.

*Innumerabilium mundorum in aeternitate perambulationem et aitiologicam
explicationem* – the vivid phrase seized upon by Robert Burton – is Hill's
cri de coeur. Like Bruno, he is excited, exhilarated, by the thought of the
crumbling of the old Aristotelean prison-walls, 'the bursting of the
spheres that separated us from the wide open spaces and inexhaustible
treasures of the ever-changing, eternal and infinite universe'.[43] Other
philosophers shrank from that prospect, equally disturbing to Christian theology and the humanist conception of the nobility of man. Bacon
feared it; Campanella would defend Galileo against the charge of
believing in it; Kepler had 'a secret hidden horror' of it.[44] But Hill will
have none of this. To the objection that the infinity of the universe
destroys the special dignity of man, reducing us to mere ants, he replies

that, on the contrary, while increasing the glory of God, it inspires us with new hopes and gives us, intellectually, new worlds to conquer.[45] In his enthusiasm, as in his cosmology, Hill is a true disciple of Bruno.

Such cosmology, which draws on the pagan Plato and the infidel Lucretius, which cites Hermes Trismegistus, Paracelsus, Copernicus and Bruno, as well as (slightly) more consistent philosophers like Cardano and Patrizi, is hardly compatible with any Christian orthodoxy; and indeed Hill explicitly repudiates some of the essential truths of the religion which, outwardly, he professes. In the uniformity and determinism of Nature, he denies the existence of Providence, both general and particular. Special providences, he says, are merely convenient moral fictions. Even God is not free from the necessity entailed by his own perfection and symmetry. Hill envisages no act of creation. He doubts miracles, has no use for martyrs or images, hates the regular clergy. He is a mystic who is at best uninterested in the apparatus of the Church and the details of theology. Such things he leaves to the ignorant vulgar, whom, as an initiate, one who by contemplation has penetrated the *arcana* of the universe, he openly despises. Though he seeks to cover himself by prefatory formulae of orthodoxy – by professing that he repudiates in advance any proposition that is contrary to the Catholic faith and by insisting that his propositions are hypotheses only, 'proposita simpliciter, non edocta' – it is clear that he is, in substance, as heretical as Bruno. Indeed, these pious formulae may have been inserted simply as a necessary protection of the Parisian printer.

Hill also resembles Bruno in another way, for his heresy, like Bruno's, has a certain irenic religious function. Neoplatonism – whether Christian or non-Christian – throughout the sixteenth century, had evaded the new definitions introduced by the Reformation, and had been distrusted, in consequence, by both sides in the sectarian war. Bruno had sought to end that confrontation by preaching a new form of religion which simply ignored Christian theology. Hill makes the same claim: the only difference between Catholics and 'unbelievers', he says, is that the latter reject the traditions of the Church, which, however, are not oppressive, for the Christian religion does not impose firm laws but offers divine nectar to the weak and weary . . . In other words, respect tradition and you may believe what you will. I am not sure that the Catholic Church of the Counter-Reformation would have agreed.

M. Jean Jacquot, the only modern scholar to have looked closely at Hill's philosophy, finds it significant that his book appeared in France just a year after Bruno was burnt in Rome, and he remarks that, although Bruno is only once named in it, it can be seen as a 'tribute to his memory and, in spite of the cautionary preface, as a challenge to the authority that had condemned him.'[46] However, that may not be its only significance. For not all the propositions are concerned with atomism, or magnetism, or the infinite universe, or the plurality of worlds. Some of them are more mundane and some seem eccentric interruptions of the argument; and it is in these, perhaps, that we may discover some traces of the character, and perhaps even the biography, of the author.

First of all, the dedication. The book is dedicated to the author's young son – *filiolo meo Laurentio Hill* – who is also described as *infantulus*, a little infant. At the beginning of the book Hill answers in advance a series of objections which may be made to it, and one of the objections which he anticipates is to this eccentric dedication. Why, the reader may ask, has the author not followed the custom and dedicated his work to some great man instead of to an infant who cannot read it? To this Hill replies, somewhat aggressively, that his friends have allowed him to be denigrated in private discussions, and that he has inferred from this that he must not expect any patronage from them. As for his little son, he will be able to read the book in due course. In the meantime, 'At my age, I owe him something serious, since he, at his tender age, has delighted me with a thousand pretty tricks'. Throughout Hill's writings there runs a strain of irritability. He is a crotchety, angular man, emotionally dependent on his little son. In 1601, it seems, he is smarting from the recollection of a breach with his patrons. They have listened to denunciations of him; and he takes his revenge by ostentatiously dedicating his work to an 'infant' who can give him no protection but can at least cheer his morose and solitary life. If Hill had been dropped by Northumberland and then repudiated, and perhaps forced to flee abroad, because the pliant Sir Robert Basset, frightened by pressure from Popham, had abandoned him and his projects, his language, and his resentment, is intelligible.

A second objection which Hill anticipates is of a more general nature. It might be objected, he writes, that he has included some propositions which do not refer to physical science. To this he replies that 'Nature' is a word meaning existence 'in the most transcendental sense', and thus – he implies – includes everything. But when we look at some of his propositions, even this wide formula hardly seems to justify their inclusion in his book. I think particularly of a group of propositions towards the end of the work. For instance, there is proposition 485, that 'oaths, promises, professions, leagues, oblige men to reticence and command an absolute silence, except when crime or murder is intended'. What has this to do with cosmology or Nature, even in its most transcendental sense? Then there are propositions 487–90: how islands are of all places the easiest to hold against attack; by what means and arguments simple-minded magnates can be persuaded to undertake bold enterprises; how such enterprises can be ruined by venal philosophers, *Graeculi esurientes*, who subordinate great things to their petty purposes;* how in the hour of betrayal it is useless to trust in great men, for the mere discussion of such matters, 'even if you confine yourself to consultation', enslaves you to their command, and 'a man who has been deserted by all his friends is obliged to show abject humility and compliance towards others'. There is a strangely personal edge to these cryptic propositions, wedged, in the closing pages of the book, between protestations of Catholic orthodoxy and assertions of the unity of God and the plurality of worlds.

What is the meaning of these propositions? Once again, we cannot be certain, and we are reminded of Hill's remark, *damnatum esse Luciferi nomen*. But these aphorisms seem to suggest – or at least are compatible with the suggestion – that Hill had urged a certain magnate or magnates to some bold project; that this project had included the seizure of an island; that such an act was not considered by Hill to be criminal or to entail murder, and that therefore the magnate, having discussed it with him under an oath of secrecy, should not have violated that oath by revealing it to other parties; but that in fact he had done so, whereupon Hill's rivals, the 'venal philosophers', had persuaded him to abandon the project, or convert it into a selfish venture; and that Hill, in consequence, had been cast off, isolated and abandoned, and forced to surrender to his fate.

Yet another little detail suggests a connexion between Nicholas Hill the atomist and 'one Hill', the Mephistopheles of the 'gentle' or 'distracted' Sir Robert Basset. Those who have described Nicholas Hill have given the impression of a man of strong emotions and violent language. Ben Jonson, in his epigram which I have quoted, says, of Democritus and Hill, that 'one said, the other swore' that the world consisted of atoms. It must have been Democritus who said, and Hill

---

* The reference is to Juvenal, satire III vv. 77–8:

Omnia novit
Graeculus esuriens: ad caelum jusseris, ibit.

The implication is that flatterers and toadies caused the magnate to sacrifice high ideals for worldly convenience.

who swore. But Hill did *not* swear to his theory in the sense of solemnly pledging his personal credit. On the contrary, he was careful, like Copernicus, to save his Catholic orthodoxy by putting the theory forward as a hypothesis only: in the text as in the title he insists that he propounds nothing dogmatically but allows the reader to form his own opinion.* However, at the end of the original edition of 1601 Hill published a curious and somewhat coarse Latin poem which the editors of 1619 preferred to omit.† On the basis of this poem alone Jonson might well have considered Hill foul-mouthed and used the word 'swore' in that sense. Again, Obadiah Walker quotes Hues as saying that Hill died 'blaspheming and cursing'. Altogether, we cannot say that William Pole's description, of a 'blasphement fellow', is inapplicable to the apparent character of Nicholas Hill; nor would violence of language have been inapposite in a disciple of Giordano Bruno.

If Nicholas Hill, in 1600, was the philosopher advising Sir Robert Basset to establish a utopia on Lundy Island like the utopia which Campanella had sought to establish in Calabria in 1599, and if that project, or fantasy, dissolved, together with the partnership, before Hill published his *Philosophia Epicurea* in France, what happened to the parties afterwards? The history of Sir Robert Basset we know, though only in the vaguest outline. Two years later, on the news of the death of Queen Elizabeth, he went it alone. Resuming his old project, he decided to seize Lundy Island. But this time it was not to set up an utopian commonwealth: it was to stake his own claim as a pretender to the Crown.

An absurd pretence! we may exclaim; but Basset could rationalize it, if he wished. His descent was through the female line, but so was that of every claimant: the King of Scotland, the Infanta of Spain, Lady Arabella Stuart, and at least nine others who, in the words of Thomas Wilson, in 1600, 'gape for the death of that good old princess, the now Queen'.[47] Its great weakness was the taint of illegitimacy; but were not the Tudors technically illegitimate, sprung from the mistress, not yet the wife, of John of Gaunt? and did not the same cloud hang over the Stuarts since Robert II? Of course the attempt was a fiasco, as were all

---

* To those who object 'probabilem huius libelli perniciem', Hill replies 'me nihil proponere dogmatice sed suum unicuique permittere arbitrium'. This repeats the statement in the title, 'proposita simpliciter, non edocta'.

† Possibly it is this poem which caused Donne, Jonson and Hoskyns to associate the name of Hill with the idea of flatulence. Donne and Jonson had both read the 1601 edition of Hill's work, which contains the poem; Hoskyns knew Hill personally and his explosive character.

those other plots, coups and gestures of the old Essexian or anti-Cecilian party which, from 1600 to 1605, successively ruined all who dabbled or could be implicated in them: Essex himself in 1601, Ralegh in 1603, Northumberland in 1605. If Hill was still in England in 1603 he would have known that he would be implicated: Lord Chief Justice Popham would see to that. After all, when Ralegh and Northumberland were charged, their philosopher, Thomas Harriot, would be in trouble. So for Hill as for Basset, escape abroad was a necessity. There is nothing inherently improbable in the story told by Hues that he fled to Holland – the safest refuge in time of danger (as Descartes would agree) even for a Roman Catholic who was not entirely orthodox – that he there practised physic in Rotterdam, and that he commited suicide in a moment of black depression after the death of the little son on whom were concentrated all the affections of this solitary and bitter man.*

Such is an admittedly tentative reconstruction of the curious episode of Sir Robert Basset and 'one Hill'. It rests on shadowy evidence – indirect references, belated hearsay and arcane hints rather than solid documents. The only solid document is Nicholas Hill's one indisputable work, his *Philosophia Epicurea*: that strange and interesting work which fell, as far as we can see, almost dead-born from the press in 1601, but which nevertheless has its place in the history of thought: for it is a contribution – the only contribution by an Englishman – to that 'radical naturalism' which, in the last years of the sixteenth century, so violently broke the old Aristotelian cosmology, leaving the way open to the new methods and new constructions of Bacon, Galileo and Descartes.

When we look at the episode as a whole, and try to see it in its context, the parallel with Bruno and Campanella is obvious, and remains obvious even if the association of Nicholas Hill with Sir Robert Basset should be disproved. It is obvious in their lives and in their ideas. It is also obvious afterwards, in their reputations. Bruno was the greatest, the boldest, as well as the most tragical of the philosophers of Nature who challenged and broke up the old Aristotelean system. After his dreadful fate his name could not be mentioned in Catholic countries. Campanella, after the failure of his 'conspiracy', languished in dungeon after dungeon, furiously writing books which were smuggled out to

---

* The date of Hill's death is generally given as 1610. The only evidence for this is Aubrey's statement 'Mr Henshaw believes he dyed about 1610: he dyed an old man'. These statements are inconsistent: if Hill died in 1610 he would be only forty. But Henshaw's anyway vague evidence cannot be trusted.

Lutheran Germany to be circulated in manuscript, but were not yet printed. Similarly, in Protestant England, though for different reasons, the name of Hill was never mentioned except in terms of ridicule. Atomism had been discredited, there too, by its advocates: politically discredited. Northumberland and Ralegh were in the Tower, charged with treasonable conspiracy. Harriot was suspect as their atheist adviser. Hill had fled abroad.

Twenty years later it seemed that the fortunes of these philosophers had revived. Hill's book was reprinted; Bruno re-emerged, anonymously, in the works of the French 'libertins'* and was attacked, openly, in his own name, by Mersenne. The writings of Campanella began to be printed. Finally, in the 1640s, came the breakthrough. Atomism, thanks to Gassendi, Hobbes, and their circle in Paris, had become respectable. The hour of the 'philosophers of Nature' seemed to have come.

In fact it had not, or it had come only to be overtaken. For the new atomism – the 'corpuscular theory' – was not their atomism: it was a new version whose whole underlying philosophy was different. Neoplatonism was now in retreat; Aristoteleanism had been repaired. Bacon and Galileo, Gassendi and Descartes had substituted a firmer empirical or mathematical base for scientific advance. So the speculative pioneers, whose personal history had been unrecorded in their time, were forgotten – or, if they were remembered, were remembered only as obscure names attached to unread books, or as types of tragedy, satire or farce. After his death in 1639 Campanella would be remembered only as the utopian prophet of Reason of State, the advocate of Spanish world monarchy; for two centuries, all his other works would be neglected.† In spite of his dramatic and tragic history, Bruno would be equally forgotten, and at the end of the seventeenth century the erudite Pierre Bayle could seriously wonder, and even doubt, whether he had really been burnt.‡ As for Nicholas Hill, in the 250 years which separate the account by Anthony Wood in the 1680s from that by Mr

---

* Lasswitz (op. cit. I, p. 480) remarks that Basson, though clearly influenced by Bruno, never mentions him, Bruno's works having been on the Index since 1603.

† Luigi Firpo, *Bibliografia degli scritti di T. Campanella* (Turin 1940), shows that, apart from his *De Monarchia Hispanica*, which was regularly reprinted, almost all the works of Campanella fell into total oblivion from 1638 until the revival of scholarly interest in him in the latter part of the nineteenth century.

‡ Bayle reported the statement that Bruno had been burnt with reservations – and surprise at having to record the uncertainty: 'voilà qui est singulier: on ne sait point, au bout de quatre-vingt ans, si un Jacobin a été brûlé à Rome, en place publique, pour ses blasphèmes. Il n'y a pas loin de l'incertitude à la fausseté dans des faits de cette nature' (*Dictionnaire hist et critique*, s.v. 'Brunus', note B). This is 'historical pyrrhonism' indeed.

McColley in 1939, I know of only one notice of him. It occurred in 1814, when the Rev. H. B. Wilson, writing the official history of Merchant Taylors' School, of which he was second under-master, cites him as a warning example, a bad egg in an otherwise exemplary clutch of old boys. 'Conscious of possessing great abilities', says the good usher, Nicholas Hill 'affected to rise above the common mode of thinking and acting. This led him into many visionary schemes of philosophy and many eccentricities of behaviour. And to this we are to attribute his attachment to some profligate wits who unfortunately admired his humour and flattered him in his conceit. Renouncing the rational religion in which he had been educated, he embraced the absurdities of the Epicurean system, and fell from folly to folly, till at last he lapsed into the faith of a Church that claims to be infallible as a resting place from his errors'.[48] Thus imaginatively was the forgotten English atomist reconstituted as a parson's theme, to fortify the established Church and keep public schoolboys from deviating into that gravest of all their sins: originality.

2
Laudianism and Political Power

The period of the 'personal rule' of Charles I is one of the most disputed periods in English history. Was Charles I a 'tyrant', seeking to set up a new system of government, as his enemies and their whig successors claimed, or did he merely seek to restore the 'conciliar' government of the Tudors, weakened by the Jacobean interlude? His great ministers, Strafford and Laud, saw themselves as conservatives: *stare super antiquas vias* was their slogan; but their opponents, who regarded themselves as true conservatives, defenders of the ancient, historic constitution of England, saw them as innovators, seeking to set up a new, unhistorical form of government. If Charles I was not stopped in his tracks, they said, he would end by establishing an absolute monarchy on the continental model, and the historic institution of Parliament would wither away. To which the supporters of the Crown would reply that it was the parliament-men who were making outrageous new claims, seeking to deprive the monarchy of its historic rights: that they were driving towards the republic to which in fact they would ultimately be driven.

Inseparable from this political problem is the problem of religion. 'Religion it is that keepeth the people in awe', said the parliamentary martyr Sir John Eliot, and certainly the dispute over religion deepened and intensified the struggle, giving it an ideological dimension and thereby involving social classes whose passions were not engaged by mere political issues. So we are brought face to face with the problem of 'Laudianism': the aims and activities of the most controversial Primate in the history of the English Church. Was Archbishop Laud the villain of the piece? Was he (as has been said) the 'one person to whose actions and policies the fall of the Stuart monarchy may be attributed'?[1] Or was he, as others have maintained, essentially a moderate man who merely sought to preserve the dignity and decency of Anglican worship? What was the 'Arminianism' of which he was accused? Was he in fact an 'Arminian'? Is it true, as his enemies insisted, that what they called Arminianism must lead to 'popery'? And what was its relationship to the political aims of Charles I? Did it in fact make the difference between reform and revolution? If Laud had not existed – if Archbishop Abbot had been succeeded by Bishop Williams (who would have been James I's candidate) or by one of those 'moderate' bishops, like Ussher, Morton, Davenant or Hall – would the course of history have been different: would Charles I then either have made no claims to 'absolute monarchy' or have yielded to similarly 'moderate' politicians? Would there have been no civil war?

These questions still agitate the pens of scholars. To Mr Tyacke, as to his contemporary enemies, Laud's 'Arminianism' was an aggressive innovation which challenged the established consensus of the time.[2] To Mr Kevin Sharpe and Mr Peter White he was not an 'Arminian' at all but a moderate advocate of that consensus which his opponents, not he, had undermined.[3] In this essay I wish to suggest answers to these questions by re-examining the central question of Laudianism. I propose to examine it as an intellectual movement within the established Church of England, and to trace the stages whereby that originally academic movement gradually became an essential part of a political and religious synthesis: a synthesis which was judged – and rightly judged – to be a frontal challenge to the political élite of the nation.

In tracing this history I shall begin with the origins of the movement in the universities. I shall then try to show how, in the reign of James I, it became part of a European ecumenical but still essentially academic movement, until the pressure of an international crisis forced it to run in a narrower channel, as the ideology of a party in English politics; and I shall suggest that the movement itself, having been transformed by politics, provided, in the end, the necessary pretext for the onslaught on the political system. In the course of this study I hope that answers may emerge to the questions which I have posed.

I An intellectual movement

However the ecclesiastical history of the early seventeenth century is interpreted, it would be generally agreed that the politics of consensus then gave way to the politics of conviction. Who first challenged the consensus may be disputed, but the challenge is undeniable. The consensus, of course, was the Elizabethan compromise: a compromise both in politics and in religion. Like all compromises, it depended for its success on a certain lack of definition, a permitted ambiguity. Queen Elizabeth herself always refused 'to make windows into men's souls', and in the circumstances her refusal was political prudence: national unity was more important, in her time, than doctrinal uniformity. This policy was applied in the country. It was also applied in the universities, whose normal function includes definition and clarification. But behind the formal toleration, parties were competing for patronage, ideas were gradually solidifying into orthodoxies, and orthodoxies were being challenged in their turn under the pressure of new ideas and, especially, new events.

For our purposes, three distinct but overlapping academic movements can be seen. First, there was the original Erasmian impulse which had been the intellectual inspiration of the English Reformation, at least as it was seen by the educated élite. Secondly, deriving from it, but substantially different from it, there was the disciplined Calvinist system, imported from Geneva. Thirdly, there was the infusion of 'historicist' Protestantism which was brought, from Germany, by the Marian exiles. In England, all these movements converged, and at different times the leaders of one or another of them attempted to dominate the amalgam. These attempts were inseparable from the political circumstances and the political struggles of the time. Central to our subject is the attempt, in the seventeenth century, to reassert, as orthodoxy, the original 'Erasmian' movement, and the fatal involvement of that attempt in the politics of Charles I.

The original Erasmian message, as it came to England under Henry VIII, was tolerant, unsuperstitious, rational and politically uncommitted. It was an appeal to primitive Christianity, as interpreted by the exact scholarship of the Renaissance and by human reason; but it also accepted, in essentials, the continuing historical tradition of the Church. In doctrine it was liberal, professing free will and universal grace. Erasmus himself had a great influence in England, and Thomas Cromwell, the statesman of the English Reformation, was inspired by him. Admittedly, in the storms of the mid-century, his message became blurred and distorted, but Queen Elizabeth and her ministers, having survived those storms, still believed in it and wished to restore it. It was by now a Protestant movement: the Catholic Church, frightened by its implications, had driven it out. So in Protestant

England the *Paraphrases* of Erasmus, his exposition of the Bible, were placed, with the Bible itself, in every parish church.

Erasmianism was no doubt an admirable ideal; but it was an ideal (as Erasmus himself had discovered) for settled times. The mid-century had not been a settled time, and no Protestant could forget the reign of Mary Tudor, when the Reformation had almost been reversed. It had been saved – but how narrowly! – by the death of Mary and the accession of Elizabeth. To the Reformers, therefore, Elizabeth was the saviour of the Church, 'our Deborah', and no praise for her could be too extravagant. Her life must be protected, her throne guarded, her supremacy over the Church recognized. So the cult of the Christian Prince, as the only practical liberator of the Church from the usurpation of the anti-Christian Papacy, received a new impetus and required the support of new arguments – arguments stronger than mere practical convenience or necessity. Such arguments had been elaborated by the Protestant enthusiasts of Germany. They were arguments from history and prophecy. They were now brought to England and adapted to English circumstances. Their classical formulation, in England, was in the works of Bishop Jewel, and, especially, in John Foxe's *Acts and Monuments*. It was a formulation which the Queen and her ministers found very convenient, for it was good propaganda for the Tudor monarchy. So they ordered that John Foxe's work should join the *Paraphrases* of Erasmus in the parish churches of England.

That was all very well for the present but what about the future? Queen Elizabeth was the last of her line. What would happen if the Catholic heir – another Bloody Mary, Mary Stuart – were to succeed and claim the same power to determine the religion of State? This was always a threat, and never more so than in the 1580s when England was at war with Spain and plots to assassinate Elizabeth and place Mary on the throne were hatched under Spanish patronage and blessed by the Pope. In the face of such a threat neither Erasmian liberalism nor consecrated royalism was enough. Royalism indeed could be positively dangerous. So bold and convinced Protestants adopted more radical ideas. If the Protestant Church of England were to survive under a Catholic monarch, they said, it must be independent of the Crown, its patronage, and its nominated bishops. It must rely on its own unbreakable strength. The model for such a Church had been provided in Geneva by Calvin; it had been strengthened there by his successor Beza; and it had shown its revolutionary power in other countries – in France, the Netherlands, Scotland. In the 1580s, while the English Church establishment and its defenders rallied round the indispens-

able Queen, defending her life and her sanctified monarchical authority, other more radical Protestants, apprehensive of the future, sought
to set up, within the framework of the established Church, an
independent Calvinist system, the nucleus of an alternative Church
which, being self-sufficient, democratic and elective, would be proof
against dynastic accident. Queen Elizabeth and her bishops, naturally
enough, did not like this system. Nor did the majority of her subjects.

When the immediate danger was over – when Mary Stuart was out of
the way, the Armada defeated and a Protestant successor in sight –
radical Calvinism lost its political justification, and the Elizabethan
establishment struck back. In 1589 the distinct Calvinist organization
was broken up, and Calvinism, reconciled to the royal supremacy and
episcopacy, was re-absorbed into the Elizabethan consensus. From
now on it would be a moderate, respectable movement, accepting, and
confirming, the established system. It had its internal differences of
course. On one hand there was the 'high Calvinism' of the establishment: authoritarian, élitist, even ceremonious – the Calvinism of
Archbishop Whitgift and, after him, of King James and many of his
bishops. This 'high Calvinism' was perfectly compatible with monarchy
and episcopacy – of a kind. On the other hand, there was the 'Church
Puritanism' of many of the laity: individualist, moralizing, anticlerical
and philistine. Though the terms were often confused in common
speech, there was a difference between Calvinism and Puritanism.*
But these differences were submerged in a common acceptance of the
loosely defined Elizabethan system. The implicit radicalism which had
shown itself in the 1580s had been at least temporarily stilled. Only a
renewed threat of 'popery' could re-animate it; and that threat was not
now visible – at least not yet.

The same change – the same relaxation of ideological tension which
took the revolutionary sting out of English Calvinism – also had
another effect. It enabled the half-smothered spirit of Erasmianism to
reassert itself. That spirit reasserted itself, naturally enough, in the
seminaries of the Church, the two universities. Its re-emergence there is
the beginning of my continuous story.

It appeared first in Oxford. There the acknowledged pioneer was a
Spaniard, Antonio del Corro. His Erasmian pedigree is clear, for he

---

* The difference was noted by Peter Heylyn, the chaplain and biographer of
Archbishop Laud: 'Nor am I of opinion that Puritan and Calvinian are terms
convertible; for though all Puritans are Calvinians, both in doctrine and in practice, yet
all Calvinians are not to be counted as Puritans also; whose practices many of them
abhor and whose inconformities they detest' (*CA*, p. 124).

was one of the avowed disciples of Erasmus who had escaped from the great purge of Spanish Erasmists in the monastery of San Isidro in Seville in 1559. He had escaped first to Geneva and then, via Huguenot France and the Low Countries, to England. There he was patronized by the Earl of Leicester, who, as its Chancellor, imposed him on Oxford University. His presence soon caused scandal in that reluctant institution. 'You cannot imagine', wrote the Anglican Anthony Wood in the next century, 'what fears and jealousies were raised among the old puritanical doctors . . . fully bent to root out the dregs of popery in the university'; and these old puritanical doctors were able to call in powerful allies: the formidable Beza in Geneva, stubborn old Archbishop Grindal at Lambeth, and the leaders of the French Huguenot Church in London. All these were enraged by Corro's irenic views, his rejection of Predestination, and, it must be admitted, his difficult personality. However, thanks to his grand patrons, he survived, and his heretical ideas found listeners in the University. Soon he was to be eclipsed by a far greater man. In 1585, when Richard Hooker was appointed Master of the Temple, his puritan rival there complained that the unsound doctrine of the new Master was 'not unlike that wherewith Corro sometime troubled this Church'.[4]

Hooker also came from an Erasmian background. He had been a student, and then a Fellow, of the most Erasmian college in Oxford, Corpus Christi, and it was there that he had come to grips with the Calvinism which had at first attracted him. As Master of the Temple, the church of the London lawyers, he had to contend with it in a difficult time and an extreme form. Then, in 1590, when the extremists were in retreat, he published the first five books of his great work, *The Laws of Ecclesiastical Polity*. Therewith he supplied the episcopal Church of England with its intellectual justification as a rational, tolerant, reformed but continuous Church, based on Scripture and human reason. Explicitly, his work was a defence against the challenge of the revolutionary Calvinism of the 1580s, but implicitly it was opposed also to the rival philosophy of John Foxe and the 'Church-Puritans'; for it was incompatible with their conviction that the Papacy was Antichrist and with their whole historical thesis: their belief that the Church was justified not by reason or tradition but by prophecy.

Meanwhile, a similar movement was showing itself in Cambridge. Here too the pioneer was a foreign refugee. He was Peter Baro, a Huguenot who had escaped from the massacre of St Bartholomew in France as Corro had escaped from that of San Isidro in Spain. He too came to England, where he became a friend of Corro; and he too found a patron who was Chancellor of a University: William Cecil, Lord Burghley. Thanks to Burghley, Corro was appointed Lady Margaret Professor of Divinity at Cambridge, and there, in 1595, he shocked the Calvinist establishment by publicly declaring, with Erasmus and Hooker, that the human will is free and that all men can, theoretically, be saved. No man was more outraged by these dreadful doctrines, or sillier in denouncing them, than the acting Vice-Chancellor of the University, Dr Some. Dr Baro had been, by then, for over twenty years, a Fellow-commoner of Peterhouse, of which his eldest son was now a Fellow. Dr Some was the Master of Peterhouse. Conversation at the high table of Peterhouse – then, as now, a very small college – may not have been very agreeable in 1595–6.

Of the battle over Peter Baro in Cambridge I will say no more: it has been well and fully described by Dr H. C. Porter.[5] Suffice it to say here that, in the short run, Baro was defeated, and abandoned Cambridge, 'lest I be driven out'. But in the long run he was more successful there than Corro had been in Oxford, for he left behind him disciples who, one after another, began to win over their colleagues, and their colleges, to the new liberalism. The colleges most affected by his ideas were Peterhouse, Pembroke, Caius and Clare; and his most distinguished disciples, when he left Cambridge, were Lancelot Andrewes, Master of Pembroke College, and John Overall, Master of St Catharine's College and Regius Professor of Divinity.

Especially Andrewes. He was a man of vast learning, in discussion with whom Francis Bacon tested his ideas, a great orientalist and patron of oriental studies, an admired preacher. Outwardly he was a supple courtier, all things to all men, prudent even to a fault, respected by all parties in the Church; but under his smooth manner he concealed firm views which he expressed only to his closest friends. By them he was regarded as the undisputed intellectual leader of the new movement which, thanks to them, would first be seen as a Cambridge movement.

Its great enemy continued to be the Master of Peterhouse, Dr Some. In 1599, Some challenged Overall on a number of theological points and then, finding him incorrigible, denounced him to the Vice-Chancellor, Dr Jegon, Master of Corpus Christi College, on whose sympathy he could rely.[6] The controversy rumbled on for a whole year, and in July 1600 it broke out again in public at the annual Commencement: the grand ceremony which closes the academic year. A young Bohemian nobleman, Baron Zdenek Waldstein, a kinsman of the famous Wallenstein, happened to visit Cambridge at that time, and has left an account of that 'tremendous dispute among the professors'. The moderator, he recorded, 'made a most violent attack' on one of his colleagues, showing 'so much animus that the other went quite red with mortification'. The victim of this attack was Overall; his attacker was the Master of Peterhouse who, once again, was Vice-Chancellor, Dr Some.[7]

So the new movement was launched – or, as we may prefer to say, the old movement was re-launched. As yet it had no agreed name. In Cambridge, which was its centre, it was described, somewhat misleadingly, as 'Lutheranism' – presumably because, like the Lutheranism of contemporary Saxony, it was a movement of resistance against the dogmatic Calvinism which, there too, was infecting the established Church. Thus a Cambridge 'Church-Puritan', writing in 1597 – just after the Baro affair – says that 'Lutheranism begins to be maintained', and he records how William Whitaker, the Calvinist Master of St John's and Regius Professor of Divinity who opposed Baro, declared that 'he would stand to God's cause against the Lutherans'.* Others, seeking greater exactitude, associated the movement more particularly with the name of Melanchthon, the German Erasmus.† It would make confusion worse confounded if I were to adopt this transient terminology, so I will continue, for the time being, to be as vague as contemporaries and to treat the movement as a still nameless form of revived post-Calvinist Erasmianism.

So far, I have presented it as a purely academic movement. But academic movements, if they have any vitality, easily acquire political overtones. From the last years of Elizabeth the anti-Puritan theology of the neo-Erasmian movement of Baro, Andrewes and Overall brought it gradually into alliance with another, more practical tendency in the Church. This was the movement for the restoration of clerical and, in particular, episcopal authority: a movement which led to an enhanced ceremonialism in worship and high claims for episcopacy as the indispensable sign of a true Church.

---

* The Diary of Samuel Ward, in M. M. Knappen (ed.) *Two Puritan Diaries* (Chicago 1933), p. 125. The phrase is common at the time: thus the bigoted anti-Arminian Sir Simonds D'Ewes describes Henry, Prince of Wales, whose death in 1612 so distressed the Church-Puritans, as a true Protestant, 'free also from the Lutheran leaven which had then so far spread itself in Germany' (*The Autobiography . . . of Sir Simonds D'Ewes*, ed. J. O. Halliwell, 1845, I, pp. 97–9).

† Thus Heylyn (*CA*, p. 204) refers to Baro's 'Melanchthonian doctrine of Predestination', and Grotius would salute Melanchthon, together with Erasmus, as his master: 'prudens Erasmi simplicitas et dulcissima Melanchthonis anima' (*BHG* I, p. 236) etc.

Between these two movements there was no necessary connexion: it was perfectly possible to combine strong views on episcopacy with 'high' Calvinist theology – as Archbishop Whitgift and, after him, James I would do – or 'liberal' post-Calvinist theology with rejection of high clerical claims – as Hooker and, after him, the Dutch Remonstrants would do. There were many possible combinations which make all simplifications dangerous. But the two movements were brought together, and ultimately welded together, in England by special English developments: by the reaction against the Protestant consensus of the reign of Elizabeth and by the fear of what that consensus had already allowed to happen, and might still bring.

The man who did most to forge this alliance was Richard Bancroft. Like Andrewes and Overall, Bancroft too was a Cambridge man; but he was very different from those urbane and saintly scholars. A masterful man whose hatred of Puritanism has been described as 'paranoid', he had played an important part in detecting and defeating the puritan campaign of the 1580s, and he was determined, after victory, so to build up the episcopal Church that it could never he undermined again. This meant to recover its wealth and power, which had been quietly eroded, to emphasize the outward symbols of its authority, and to give it new guarantees against the uncertainties of politics; for, like the Puritans, he saw that there was an inherent danger in the royal supremacy. Monarchs could be whimsical. The Puritans had feared a Catholic queen. After the death of Mary Queen of Scots there were grounds to fear a Presbyterian king.

In 1588, a year after the execution of Mary, Bancroft advanced the view that episcopacy was not merely a useful human system to be operated by the Crown, but a divinely ordained system with which the Crown could not tamper. In fact, James I, when he came to England, did not tamper with it: he found it too useful. Though he remained intellectually a Calvinist, he hated Puritanism and the Presbyterian discipline, and he made Bancroft Archbishop of Canterbury. While Archbishop, as previously while Bishop of London, Bancroft set out to restore the authority of the Church. The doctrine of the divine right of episcopacy did not, after all, need to be emphasized; like the Calvinist doctrine of the divine right of presbytery, it receded back into the comfortable Elizabethan amalgam; but it had been declared and remained there in reserve: a disquieting element within the Anglican establishment.

Thus anti-Puritanism formed a platform on which the neo-Erasmians of Cambridge and the new clericals of Canterbury could meet and sustain each other. At this stage, they were all Cambridge men who knew each other well, and their combined pressure was felt in their University. It had been felt and opposed, at first, in one small college there, at Peterhouse. Now it was felt, and aroused resentment, throughout the University. The resentment was expressed – but cautiously, in his private diary – by the man who was to be the ineffective oracle of Cambridge 'Church-Puritanism' for the next forty years, Samuel Ward.

Samuel Ward was a product of Christ's College, the most puritan college in the University. He had then moved on, first to Emmanuel, then to Sidney Sussex College, but his heart remained in Christ's. His diaries and notebooks oscillate between two main themes. First, there was the condition of his soul. Was he of the Elect? Could he be in a state of grace? or had he eaten too much at dinner in college last night – had he tucked too freely into those plums, damsons, walnuts, cheese, to which he was so partial? Secondly, there was the condition of the Church, which, as seen in Cambridge, was equally alarming. Puritanism was in retreat. Sinister new 'Lutheran' doctrines were being preached. Royal orders were being promulgated, requiring subscription to new canons. And then there was the new ceremonial, symbolized by the surplice, which was creeping back into college chapels. Ward had seen it come into Emmanuel and Sidney Sussex. It had been sighted in Magdalene. Could the abominable thing be kept out of Christ's? But an intruder even worse than the surplice was the sinister figure of Valentine Cary. He had come to Christ's as Fellow in 1597, imposed by the Crown, no doubt through 'the corrupt practices of the Archbishop'. Ward marvelled at 'the strange workings of God' in allowing such a thing to happen. Twelve years later the working of God was stranger still, for a royal mandate imposed Cary on the college as Master. 'Woe is me for Christ's College!' exclaimed Dr Ward. 'Surely he will be the utter ruin and destruction of that coll!' And indeed he had cause to lament, for the nomination of Cary as Master of Christ's was a turning-point. From now on active Puritanism was in retreat in Cambridge.[8]

Behind all these ungodly innovations, the puritan Fellows of Christ's discerned the secret hand of Dr Bancroft, working first through Archbishop Whitgift, then through King James. Violent sermons against Bancroft were preached in the college chapel. But then, only a year after the nomination of Cary, Bancroft died. On the news of his death, his partisans naturally wished to see his policy continued. 'Some of the bishops and great men of the court', we are told, pressed the claim of Lancelot Andrewes as his successor. Thinking that they had gained their point, they then dispersed. But James I disappointed them. Instead of Andrewes he nominated George Abbot, who had been useful to him in Scotland and had been recommended by a Scotch favourite, recently deceased, the Earl of Dunbar.

For the supporters of the new course the appointment of Abbot as archbishop was to prove a disaster. It was to 'the never enough lamented death of Dr Bancroft' that Edward Hyde, Earl of Clarendon, would ascribe many of the misfortunes which followed. If only Bancroft had lived longer, 'or if he had been succeeded by bishop Andrewes, bishop Overall, or any man who understood and loved the Church', how different the course of history might have been! Peter Heylyn agreed. 'If Andrewes had succeeded Bancroft and Laud Andrewes', he wrote, 'the Church would have been settled on so sure a foundation that it could not easily have been shaken.' For Abbot shared neither the ideas of Andrewes nor the energy of Bancroft. He was essentially an Elizabethan 'high Calvinist', a patron of 'Church-Puritans'. He was also an Oxford man: the first Protestant archbishop of Canterbury to break the Cambridge monopoly. He 'had been Head or Master of one of the poorest colleges in Oxford' (that is, of University College), says Clarendon contemptuously, 'and had learning sufficient for that province', adding, no less contemptuously, that 'he was a man of very morose manners and a very sour aspect, which in that time was called gravity'. This morose sour man would preside over the Church, with dwindling authority indeed, for the next twenty-three years; and in that period all the good work of the last decade would be allowed to slide.[9]

Why did James I appoint Abbot? In retrospect, it seemed an eccentric and mistaken choice, and those who sought to explain it ascribed it to a mere royal whim. But this is perhaps unfair to King James who, though indolent and wayward, was not frivolous: he had certain clear views. Though he detested the Presbyterian discipline of Scotland, and had fallen in love with the hierarchical episcopacy of England, and though he enjoyed the conversation of learned men, regardless of their churchmanship, he remained, intellectually, a Calvinist. He believed, and wrote, that the Pope was Antichrist, and he saw himself as a godly Christian Prince in the style of Queen Elizabeth as seen by John Foxe. He would show this in his choice of bishops. As he liked learned men, he would promote Andrewes, who was a great scholar, and as he liked obsequious men, he would promote Richard Neile, who supported his claims to absolute power. These received bishoprics of dignity. But for the highest posts he chose 'high

Calvinists': not only Abbot as Primate of England, but also Ussher as Primate of Ireland, Williams as Lord Keeper of the Great Seal and archbishop of Canterbury *in petto*.* He would also show it, decisively, in his intervention in the religious controversies of European Protestantism, to which we must now turn.

For the history of ideas can never be confined to a single country. Reformation and Counter-Reformation alike had come to England from the Continent. Corro and Baro had been foreigners. And now the new movement in England was to receive a new impetus, and its course to be diverted into a steeper channel, by developments in Europe, in the United Provinces of the Netherlands: developments which would give that hitherto unbaptised movement a misleading, but a lasting name.

2 England and Europe

The Netherlands had been the original home of Erasmus, and naturally his influence had remained strong there. But there too, as in England, the necessities of politics had transformed it. First the Catholic Counter-Reformation, then the struggle against Spain, had caused that native influence to be overtaken, where it had not been crushed, by the disciplined Calvinism imported into the rebellious provinces by the fighting Huguenots of France. However, in the last years of the sixteenth century, as the strength and security of the new Republic grew, liberal men began, there too, to resent the rigorous doctrine and intolerant discipline that had been forced upon them, and to look back to their own earlier tradition. The man who led them back, the Dutch equivalent of Peter Baro in England, was Jacob Harmensen, or Arminius; and it was he whose name was applied – not indeed in Holland (where they were called Remonstrants) but in England, and there, at first, only by its enemies – to the intellectual movement which we have sought to describe. So, from now on, we can refer to that movement, without further hesitation or apology, by its historically validated but anachronistic name, Arminianism.

---

* I am afraid I am not convinced by the argument of Mr Peter White (see below p. 286 n. 3) that James I was as much an 'Arminian' as Charles I simply because he promoted (or allowed to be promoted) some clergy who held Arminian views. Particular promotions are affected by particular circumstances; a consistent policy must be deduced from wider evidence.

The name has been the cause of much confusion; but we can avoid the confusion if we keep in mind certain essential distinctions. First, we must recognize that in England it denotes, originally, an intellectual, not a political movement: a movement which, though it had a Dutch origin (since Erasmus was Dutch), was already well established in England before the name of Arminius was known there. Secondly, we must recognize that, having once been applied to this intellectual movement, the name Arminianism was afterwards extended to that originally independent movement of clericalism, authoritarianism, ritualism, which had no parallel in Holland, but which, in England, was accidentally associated with it. For the moment, however, it is enough to note that the renewal of the Erasmian tradition within the Calvinism of the Protestant Netherlands, coming when it did, gave encouragement to the parallel but independent movement within the half-Calvinist English Church: an encouragement which is illustrated by the new Dutch name.

As far as England was concerned, the most influential of the Dutch Arminians was not Arminius himself but one of his admirers and supporters, the greatest of all the Dutchmen of that age, Hugo Grotius. Today the name of Grotius is famous in the history of jurisprudence, and when it is celebrated, it is generally by lawyers, who honour him as the founder of international law. But he himself would have been surprised by such a reputation. To him the study of the law – *studia ista arida et inamoena*, those dry, disagreeable studies, as he called it – was at best a secondary interest. He was a scholar, a historian, a statesman. Above all, he was a man of religion. He wished – it was his ruling passion and would ultimately become his obsession – to restore 'the peace of the Church': that is, to go back behind Reformation and Counter-Reformation and reunite Christendom on an Erasmian base. He saw himself, consciously, as the heir of Erasmus, called to complete his work. Again and again in his writings, and especially in his private letters and conversations, he invokes the name of Erasmus. When he went to Rotterdam, his first act was to make a pilgrimage to the house of Erasmus. Erasmus, he declared, was 'the master and teacher of the whole human race', 'the possession of the whole world', an unspeakable human miracle.[10]

Grotius was a layman. Like Erasmus, he believed in a religion for laymen and hated the squabbles of theologians, to which he ascribed the fragmentation of the Church. Like Erasmus, he believed in toleration, and wished to leave insoluble questions in suspense. He was therefore accused of indecent scepticism. Above all, like Erasmus, he was a universal scholar, respected throughout Europe. When Arminius died, in 1609, Arminianism as a theological doctrine was continued by the Dutch theologians Wtenbogaert and Episcopius, but these men wrote for other theologians – Wtenbogaert, indeed, wrote only for Dutch theologians, for he wrote in Dutch. As an intellectual movement in the international republic of letters, it was dominated by Grotius.

The accident of time gave Grotius another advantage over Arminius. In 1609 the war between Spain and the Netherlands, the last remaining war in Europe, was ended by the Twelve Years Truce. War had polarized ideological parties and favoured the extremists on both sides. Peace gave the irenists, the ecumenists, their opportunity. Grotius seized it. In the years 1610–18, when the Netherlands were ruled by his friend Johan van Oldenbarnevelt, the Advocate of Holland, he used his great influence in Europe to preach Arminianism, not as a doctrine for the Netherlands only but as the means of ending the schism in the Christian Church. He believed that it could provide a basis upon which liberal Calvinists in the Netherlands, Anglicans in England, Gallicans and liberal Huguenots in France, could unite leaving the extremists of popery and Puritanism to wither gradually away. He also believed that the leadership in such a movement naturally belonged to England. England was the greatest Protestant monarchy; it had been the head, under Elizabeth, of the Protestant International; and under James I, that most learned of kings, it would surely own its Erasmian inheritance. To Grotius, the court of James I offered hopes comparable with those which the court of Henry VIII had offered to Erasmus.

How fortunate that Grotius now had a reliable agent at that court! Isaac Casaubon, the great Huguenot scholar, had fled from the Calvinist intolerance of Geneva to France, only to find the Catholic pressure in France, though more subtle, equally intolerable; and in 1610, on the assassination of his protector, Henri IV, he accepted the invitation of Archbishop Bancroft and moved to England. There he was at once taken up by James I, who was charmed by his erudite conversation, and loved, after a long day's hunting, and a little tedious business, to relax in his company, discussing nice points of scholarship. Casaubon in turn fell in love with the Anglican Church, so humane and civilized, so free from the intolerance of Geneva and Rome. With such views, and in such a position, Casaubon was, for Grotius, the ideal ambassador at the court of King James, and it was to him, especially, as 'another Erasmus',[11] that Grotius now unfolded his plans for a new united Christendom, with King James as its political head.

Grotius set out his plans in a letter to Casaubon of 7 January 1612. 'I am one', he wrote, 'who, relying on the example of a few others, and especially you, am totally committed to pray and work for the preservation and repair of the peace of the Church so far as that can be done without a betrayal of sound doctrine'. The extremists on both sides made his work difficult, he said, but he would not despair. 'After long thought it seems to me best that those Churches which do not recognize the universal monarchy of the Bishop of Rome should bear witness to their agreement and harmony by a public Confession, leaving in suspense any matter on which there is doubt'. Such a confession would bring in the moderate Catholics, especially when they saw that good works, ceremonies, traditions, were respected. In order to draw up the Confession, a Council must be called, to be attended by delegates of those Churches which repudiated the Council of Trent as a false council. It should be held, ideally, in Britain, and the President and Moderator should be that wisest of kings, King James . . .

Casaubon was delighted by this idea and put Grotius' proposal to the King. The King was at first delighted too; but gradually, as he thought of the implications, his enthusiasm cooled, and Archbishop Abbot, of course, blew upon it with refrigerating breath. However, Grotius did not despair – he would never despair – and next year he had an opportunity to press his project in person. He was sent to England in an official delegation from the Netherlands. The avowed object of the delegation was to make a commercial treaty. The unavowed object, agreed in advance between Grotius and Oldenbarnevelt, was to pursue Grotius' plan for an 'Arminian' General Council of the Church.

In letters from England, Grotius reported his progress to Oldenbarnevelt. King James, he found, was interested but cautious: he was alarmed by reports that the Dutch Arminians were dangerously close to the Socinians (as indeed they were). As a high Calvinist who valued his position as a Christian Prince, James I did not like Socinianism. However, he suspended judgment and invited Grotius to keep in touch with him. Archbishop Abbot, of course, was openly hostile: he cold-shouldered Grotius and clearly sought to prejudice the King against him. However, on balance, Grotius thought, the gains outweighed the losses. Through Casaubon, he had met Andrewes and Overall, whom he believed to be entirely sympathetic. From them he had discovered that there was, in England, a native Erasmian movement with powerful advocates. He had learned about Peter Baro, and on his return to Holland would study the history of Baro's controversy in Cambridge. He had also discovered the work of Hooker which, since it was in English, had presumably been interpreted to him by Andrewes or Overall.* In his letters to his friends he dwelt with enthusiasm on his English experiences: how he had been daily with Casaubon and Sir Henry Savile, the great patron of Greek patristic scholarship, and how he had found, at court, prelates who were not rigid, crabbed, stiff-necked, but cultivated and urbane, distinguished for learning and charity. All in all, he was very satisfied with his visit. The main task now, he thought, was to prevent quarrelsome theologians on either side from inciting the lower orders to disturb the peace while the men of good will got on with the job of regenerating the ecumenical Church.[12]

On their side the English Arminians also took stock of the visit. They were rather more reserved than Grotius, whom they had found too voluble for their taste and somewhat insensitive to the hazards of a foreign court. Why, for instance, had he told the King, when taking his leave, that he was pleased to find Andrewes sympathetic to his own Arminian ideas? The King had not been pleased at that, nor had Andrewes who, as a prudent courtier, was careful not to commit himself in public.† However, it was something to have discovered allies abroad: against international Calvinism they could now oppose an equally international movement, and the support of Casaubon and Grotius enhanced their intellectual stature. The death of Casaubon a year later, in 1614, would be a blow to both sides; but by that time the direct link had been forged: the English and Dutch 'Arminians' would remain in contact – cautious but continuous contact – for the rest of our story.

Nor was it only in Holland that the English Arminians discovered allies. A year after Grotius' visit to England, an Italian archbishop, Marcantonio de Dominis, disillusioned with the Roman Church, conceived a similar idea. Slipping secretly out of Italy into Protestant Switzerland, he there renounced the Pope and then moved on to

---

* Peter Baro's *Summa* was published at Hardewijk in 1613, together with Whitgift's Lambeth Articles, which had been occasioned by the controversy. Grotius found the work circulating in England (*BHG* I, no. 259). After his return to Holland, Grotius sought further information on the subject from an English colonel in the Netherlands who, he discovered, had been a student at Cambridge at the time (ibid., no. 425). For Grotius' discovery of Hooker's work, see ibid., no. 310.

† In 1617 Andrewes was again put out by the use of his name by the Dutch Arminians. The court gossip John Chamberlain reported that, when the matter was raised, Andrewes 'fell into a long speech' of complaint, but – very typically – 'he expresseth not all the while which opinion he inclineth to' (*Letters of John Chamberlain*, ed. J. E. McClure, II p. 111, and cf. p. 138). On the whole episode see P. A. Welsby, *Lancelot Andrewes* (1958), pp. 166–8.

England, where he was received in triumph and made Dean of Windsor and Master of the Savoy. While in England, he published his great work *De Republica Ecclesiastica*, in which he advocated the same policy as Grotius, of an 'Arminian' third Church, between Rome and Geneva, embracing also the Greek Church, with which, as a Venetian, he was familiar. When de Dominis arrived in England, the pro-Puritan party in the English Church was very suspicious of him, and Archbishop Abbot would not see him, but the King referred him to Overall, who easily persuaded him that the Church of England was the ideal leader of a new ecumenical Church. Overall was accompanied, at their meeting, by his secretary, whom he charged to make a record of the conversation. The secretary (who was also his librarian) was another Cambridge man, a young Fellow of Caius College called John Cosin. A learned man, fit to handle scholarly correspondence with foreigners, and a great bibliophile, Cosin was devoted to Overall, whom he would describe all his life as 'my lord and master'. Seven years later, he would write to Grotius to inform him of Overall's death.[13]

Thus by the middle of the reign of James I, in spite of Archbishop Abbot, all seemed to be going well for the Arminians, in England as in the Netherlands. Arminianism, in those years, was intellectually fashionable; and indeed it is easy to see its appeal to cultivated men in a period of peace and restored international civility. Who would not wish to read the serene and limpid work of Hooker, citing reason as the justification of the Church, or listen to the golden voice of Andrewes or Overall, appealing to the cultivated Greek Fathers – Basil and Gregory of Nazianzus and John Chrysostom (newly edited and splendidly printed by Sir Henry Savile) – rather than reiterate the horrible doctrine of 'double predestination' and rummage in unintelligible prophetic books in order to prove the Pope to be Antichrist? King James might not yet have accepted the idea of an ecumenical Council of London to draw up a new Arminian Confession of Faith, but the most cultivated men in Europe were on their side. By 1618 they might well suppose that the future would be with them.

One reason for such confidence was the rapid progress that they were now making in the English universities. Cambridge, where the movement had begun, remained their chief nursery. Here they were helped by a series of Arminian bishops of Ely, including Andrewes himself; for the Bishop of Ely was a force in Cambridge: he was Visitor of three colleges – St John's, Jesus and Peterhouse; he effectively controlled the headships of the last two colleges; and he had convenient local patronage to bestow on college fellows who had earned it. The most active Arminians in Cambridge at this time were Matthew Wren, a devoted pupil of Andrewes, and Leonard Mawe. Wren was now the President (or Vice-master) of Pembroke College, Andrewes's own college, while Mawe was Master of Peterhouse, where the ferment had first begun. These two neighbouring colleges, Pembroke and Peterhouse, would be the twin capitals of Cambridge Arminianism.

Even in puritan Oxford there was now an Arminian nucleus: supporters of the movement could be found in Christ Church and, especially, in St John's College: a Catholic foundation of the reign of Mary Tudor which had stood out against the dominant Puritanism of the University. The champion of Arminianism in Christ Church was John Howson, whom we shall meet again. In St John's it had been preached by John Buckeridge, Fellow and President until 1611. In that year, having been made Bishop of Rochester, he had been succeeded as President by his pupil and nominee, William Laud. It had been a stormy and contested election, for Laud had long been notorious as a trouble-shooter in Oxford; but he had prevailed and soon the college was entirely his.

Such was the position in 1618. To any contemporary observer it might seem that the Arminians were poised for a quiet, gradual assumption of power in the English Church. However, that was not to happen. Once again, as in the 1580s, the motor of events was in international affairs – and once again, the centre of the crisis was in the Netherlands. Now, as then, the struggle of the European powers, about to be renewed, would polarize religious parties in England, forcibly breaking up the Elizabethan consensus, driving Church-Puritans back towards radical Calvinism, leaving 'high Calvinists' high and dry, and transforming the intellectual movement of Baro and Andrewes into the aggressive clerical party of Laud.

This international crisis began in central Europe, where the confrontation of rival religious leagues was sharpened by the revolution in Bohemia; but it was generalized, and transformed into European war, by the struggle for power in the Netherlands as the truce with Spain drew to its term. The leaders in this latter struggle were, on one side, the Stadholder, Maurice of Nassau, the leader of the war party, and, on the other, Grotius' friend Johan van Oldenbarnevelt, the politician of peace. As in England, the Calvinists were the party of radical action: they supported Maurice and war, a holy war against Catholic reconquest, while the Arminians, whose strength was among the patrician oligarchy of Holland, supported Oldenbarnevelt and peace. In 1618, as the storm-clouds gathered in central Europe,

Maurice prevailed in the Netherlands. Oldenbarnevelt was thrown into prison. So was Grotius. They were accused of 'appeasement': appeasement of popery and Spain. Meanwhile the Calvinists exploited their advantage: a national synod was summoned to Dordrecht, or Dordt, to declare the true faith and unite Dutch and European Calvinism in defence of it.

Given the circumstances in which it was called, the result of the Synod of Dordt could hardly be in doubt. Early next year the Arminians, who had throughout been treated not as participants in the debate but as defendants in the dock, were driven out of the Synod, and strict Predestinarianism was declared the orthodoxy of the Dutch Church. Oldenbarnevelt was condemned to death as a traitor – a ludicrous charge – and judicially murdered. Grotius was sentenced to imprisonment for life, and confined in the castle of Loevestein. Thus 'Arminianism' in Holland, its original home, was – at least for a time – totally crushed. Calvinism, in its most rigid form, had prevailed.

The Synod of Dordt was one of the greatest significance for the Reformed Churches – almost as great, in the short run, as the Council of Trent for the Roman Catholic Church. It shut the door against the liberal tendencies which had been at work in Holland and England. To appreciate its impact, we must remember the political background in Germany and the Netherlands. For the Synod was not merely an event in the Dutch Church – although it was the victorious Dutch Calvinists who made the pace. It had been attended by deputies from England and Scotland, the Palatinate and Hesse, Geneva, Basel, Bremen, Nassau. The French Huguenots were forbidden by their government to attend but their most active propagandist, Pierre du Moulin, came from the Calvinist city of Sedan, ruled by the Huguenot leader, the Duc de Bouillon; the Huguenot *grande dame*, the Duchesse de la Trémoille, who behaved as a great power in her own right, attended personally with her chaplain; and the decrees of the Synod would be formally accepted by the French Protestant Church. The English deputies naturally represented the Church of Abbot: they were sound Calvinists in theology – George Carleton, Bishop of Llandaff; Joseph Hall, Dean of Worcester; John Davenant, President of Queen's College and Lady Margaret Professor of Divinity in Cambridge; and his colleague, our old friend Samuel Ward. They were moderate men, and did their best to mitigate the ferocity of the Dutch Calvinists; but they were not successful. The decisions of the Synod, formulated in five articles, were reported by them and received by the English Church, which thus implicitly condemned the whole liberal movement within it.

This result naturally dismayed the friends of Grotius in England. They had envisaged a Council of London to restore the unity of the Church. Instead, they saw a council of their adversaries which had deepened its division and apparently committed the Church of England to an intolerant theology. To Andrewes and Overall this was a great blow. They could be forgiven if they despaired.

One who did despair was the Italian archbishop, Marcantonio de Dominis, who now renounced his Anglican loyalty and went back to Rome, hoping to be received back into favour as a returned prodigal. Like many defectors, he had begun to find the inconveniences of exile; but the adhesion of the English Church to the decrees of Dordt was the last straw. His hopes of a warm welcome in Rome, however, were not realized: he would be arrested on arrival and would die in the prison of the Inquisition. The Church of England, which had made so much of him on his arrival, and was now humiliated by his defection, was no more merciful to his memory. The Puritans positively exulted in the scandal, which seemed to prove their point that Arminianism was half-way to popery. The Arminians, for the same reason, were exasperated against him and denounced him as a traitor. Afterwards, however, when passions had cooled, some of them would be more charitable: 'he was, it appeareth', wrote one of them, 'an honester man than he was taken for'; and another declared that, whatever his personal failings, his great work, *De Republica Ecclesiastica*, was 'unanswerable'.[14]

However, the effect of the Synod of Dordt on the English Arminian movement was not entirely negative. The same shock which drove the Dean of Windsor out, brought others in. Moderate men who had previously supported the established 'high Calvinism' of the Jacobean Church were shaken by the savagery of the Calvinist party in the Synod, especially if they had witnessed it themselves. Bishop Carleton, the leader of the English delegation, had protested against it on the spot. His colleague Joseph Hall, similarly shocked, would begin there his gradual movement to the right: he would end as the defiant assertor of episcopacy. Another who had attended the Synod was John Hales, a learned Greek scholar and Fellow of Eton College, who had worked on Sir Henry Savile's great edition of Chrysostom. He had attended the Synod as the chaplain of the English ambassador at the Hague. Till then, he had been a supporter of the Calvinist party, but his experience at Dordt converted him. The adoption of 'that most extreme and rigid tenent which Beza and Perkins first of all acquainted the world with ' – that is, 'that God should peremptorily decree to cast the greatest part of mankind away, only because he would' – and the 'rough handling of the

Remonstrants', their dismissal 'with so much heat and choler', disgusted him, and from that moment he decided to 'bid John Calvin goodnight'.[15]

The Synod of Dordt, says Mr Tyacke, 'was an event which has never received the emphasis it deserves from students of English religious history'.[16] It polarized the parties in the English Church and thereby so weakened the comfortable consensus of Elizabethan and Jacobean Protestantism that it could never be restored. For the European crisis which had produced it was not settled. It led to general war; an ideological war in which the whole Protestant cause was imperilled. Throughout the 1620s, the armies of Protestant powers and Protestant rebels were everywhere being defeated. It was a process which began with the battle of the White Mountain in December 1620 and would reach its climax in the imperial Edict of Restitution of 1629. In this European struggle, England was sometimes militarily, always emotionally engaged. Against this background it is understandable that the controversies and competition of religious parties in England should be conducted in a less temperate spirit than in the years of peace between 1609 and 1618. This background must be remembered when we return, as we now do, to those controversies and that competition.

3   The struggle for power

We left the English Arminians discountenanced at court but establishing themselves in the universities, and particularly in Cambridge. In 1618 their leaders, Andrewes and Overall, were bishops – Andrewes of Winchester, Overall of Lichfield; but they were uncontroversial bishops, admired for their piety and learning. 'Arminianism' in England was not yet a word of abuse, or indeed a word at all. Even in the Parliament of 1621, the first to meet since the beginning of the crisis, it was never uttered. But in the Parliament of 1624 it was different. It was then that the cry was first raised against 'the dangerous errors of Arminius' and the disciples of Andrewes and Overall were accused, in violent language, of appeasing popery and Spain. It was therefore between these dates – between 1621 and 1624 – that we must place the breakthrough of the new generation of Arminians, the discovery that Arminianism was not merely a permissible, though disputed, tendency within the Church of England but, as in the Netherlands, a new ideology, associated with a particular party and threatening the very existence of the nation. This change coincided with the emergence from the universities and the acceptance at court – not by King James, but

by the Prince of Wales and the Duke of Buckingham – of three men who
had already identified themselves as leaders of English 'Arminianism':
William Laud of Oxford, Matthew Wren and John Cosin of Cambridge. These three men would soon take the limelight. They would
dominate the movement, as they will dominate this essay. But behind
them, in the shadow, stood an older man, their patron, without whom
they would hardly have come to notice: Richard Neile.

Richard Neile,[17] like Andrewes and Overall, was a Cambridge man;
but he was not, like them, at least in his Cambridge days, an
'Arminian'. He had not been touched by the ideas of Erasmus or Baro.
Indeed, he had opposed Baro in writing. Not that he was a scholar
either – he only 'wrote a sheet' against Baro – or an intellectual of any
kind. Essentially he was an authoritarian administrator of the school of
Bancroft, insensitive, tough, thorough, impatient of ideas. He had risen
in the Church by giving practical support to useful patrons: first to
Lord Salisbury, whose chaplain, business agent and secretary he had
been, then, by a natural transition, to the King. But in 1608, being
Bishop of Rochester, Dean of Westminster and Clerk of the Closet, he
had taken Laud as his chaplain, and gradually he had fallen under the
influence of that dynamic little man. He then realized that Arminianism was the intellectual force which would inspire men to continue
Bancroft's work of reconstruction in the Church. When Bancroft died
in 1610, no one suggested that the formidable but abrasive Neile should
be his successor. But if Neile did not succeed Bancroft at Canterbury,
he succeeded him as effective leader of the clerical party in the Church,
and by the early 1620s that party was organized in his household. He
was now – since 1617 – Bishop of Durham; he declared himself an
admirer of Grotius;[18] and he had gathered together, at his London
house, Durham House in the Strand, as his chaplains, a group of young
Cambridge men, enthusiastic not to say aggressive Arminians. These
included John Cosin of Caius College, who had served Overall till
Overall's death in 1619; Augustine Lindsell of Clare College, and
Francis Burgoyne of Peterhouse: a trio soon to become notorious. Laud
too had a permanent foothold in Durham House: he would soon be
recognized as the political activist of the group. So did Wren. So did
others who would afterwards play a part in the story.

Knowing that they had nothing to hope from Archbishop Abbot and
King James, the clergy of Durham House prudently invested in what
would later be called 'the reversionary interest'. That is, they cultivated
the Prince of Wales and, particularly, the royal favourite the Duke of
Buckingham, who now controlled all Crown patronage and seemed to

have acquired as complete an influence over the Prince as formerly over the King. In 1621, thanks to the support of Buckingham, Laud at last acquired a bishopric – and saw to it that he had a reliable successor as head of his Oxford college. It was a poor bishopric in Wales – that was all that King James would consent to – but his influence was not to be measured by his diocese. Next year Grotius was informed that Laud was eager to be in touch with him: he was, Grotius was told, a man of importance, 'in the greatest favour with the Prince of Wales'.[19] In 1623, when the Prince went, with Buckingham, on his famous visit to Spain, the two chaplains who accompanied him were the two Cambridge Arminians, Wren and Mawe, and Buckingham, in Spain, corresponded regularly with Laud. On their return to England, both chaplains would be rewarded. Mawe would be made Master of Trinity College – the greatest preferment in Cambridge. That was a Crown appointment. Wren would succeed him as Master of Peterhouse – imposed on the reluctant Fellows by pressure from the Crown.

Thus by the end of the reign of James I, the Arminian party had strengthened its position at court, in the Church, and in the universities, and with a change of ruler – for in 1624 King James was visibly failing – it was likely that they would strengthen it still further. However, it was already clear that any further advance would be resisted. It was not merely that Neile and Laud, Wren and Cosin, were men of a different stamp from Andrewes and Overall. It was not merely that their tempers had been sharpened, or frayed, under the rule of Abbot. The external circumstances also were very different. The years of peace were over. Just as the imminence of ideological war in 1618 had caused the crisis in the Netherlands in which the Arminians had been destroyed, so now the same prospect faced the Arminians in England. They saw power within their reach; but if they were to grasp it, they must not shrink from a contest. They must renew, in England, the battle that had been lost in the Netherlands. As Laud's chaplain would afterwards put it, the effects of 'those quarrels' in the Netherlands, and of the Synod which so brutally resolved them, would be seen 'when the same points came to be agitated and debated on this side of the seas'.[20] However, when that battle was re-fought, there would be one important difference. The intellectual issues might be the same, but the battlefield was very different. The doctrines which had been republican in Holland, the religion of city patricians, must adapt themselves, in England, to a monarchical society and the absolutist aspirations of a royal court.

In the first four years of the new reign – those years when Charles I found himself locked in conflict with his first three parliaments – the English Arminians fought their great battle for survival and, ultimately, for control of the Church. During those years, the Catholic powers were everywhere successful in Europe, and Protestant fears found hysterical expression. In such circumstances it required some courage to express ideas which had been condemned by an international synod and which almost invariably entailed a charge of appeasement and 'popery'. However, the Arminians had not come so far in order to flinch from the crucial battle: indeed, they went into it with gusto. We can observe that battle, or at least a sector of it, and savour that gusto, through the letters of the man who was now to come forward as the principal troubleshooter of the party, Richard Montagu.[21]

Richard Montagu was yet another Cambridge man – a Fellow of Eton and King's College. Now in his fifties, canon of Windsor, rector of Petworth, rector of Stanford Rivers, he was a scholar whose life hitherto had been of blameless obscurity. As a Fellow of Eton, he was a colleague of John Hales and, like him, had been mobilized by their Provost, Sir Henry Savile, for his great edition of the works of St John Chrysostom. An admirer of Casaubon, he had been employed by King James to complete and publish Casaubon's last work. The study of the Greek Fathers, the example of Casaubon, and, finally, the shocking events at Dordt led easily to Arminianism, and by 1621 Montagu had become one of the Durham House group: 'I give Durham House *jus* and leave', he wrote, 'to use me as they will'. Durham House was prompt to take up the offer, and in 1624 his learning was duly mobilized in the cause. The excuse was the provocation of Roman Catholic evangelists among his parishioners. In answer to them he set out the true doctrine of the Church of England as he understood it – and he understood it in an Arminian sense. He had not, at that time, read Arminius;* but since English Arminianism was of independent origin, that was not necessary. His work infuriated the Puritans, and provoked a heated controversy. Threatened in Parliament, he appealed to the new King, and was saved from parliamentary rage by being made a royal chaplain. This, in the excited temper of the time, created a further scandal: having set out to defend the Church of England against the papists, Montagu was accused of preaching, and Charles I of patronizing, pure popery.

---

* In a letter to Cosin of 12 May 1625, Montagu writes, 'I will now begin to read Arminius' and asks Cosin to help him to find his works. A year later he writes, 'I thank you for your Arminius. I never saw him before. The man had more in him than all the Netherlands.' (*CJC* I, pp. 68, 90.)

The battles which raged around him, and the publicity in which they involved him, both threatened and excited Montagu. Like other clergymen who have suddenly hit the headlines, he acquired illusions of grandeur. The innocent academic scholar saw himself as the master-strategist of the Church, called not only 'to stand in the gap against Puritanism and Popery, the Scylla and Charybdis of ancient piety' but also to direct his party to victory and to distribute, and share, the spoils. For this purpose he allied himself with the three musketeers of Durham House – John Cosin, Augustine Lindsell, Francis Burgoyne. With them, and with the literary assistance of the most formidable of them, John Cosin, he mounted a radical campaign against the politics of consensus and the Church-Puritans who had flourished under Archbishop Abbot.

Poor Archbishop Abbot himself was by now in a bad way. In 1621 he had been so unfortunate, while out hunting with Lord Zouche, as to shoot and kill a keeper instead of a deer. His clerical enemies were prompt to exploit his misfortune. At first, indeed, they were restrained by fear. If the Archbishop were deposed, might not King James replace him by Dr Williams, Bishop of Lincoln, and Lord Keeper of the Great Seal, who reckoned that he had a promise of it? That would be worse even than Dr Abbot. But as soon as King James was dead and this danger past, the Archbishop's enemies were merciless. They simply treated him as non-existent, an unperson. However, even in his eclipse Abbot was not without allies – at least as long as Parliament (and therefore also Convocation) was in session – and his supporters could hit as hard in defence as Montagu and Cosin in attack. In particular, he had his two chaplains, Daniel Featley from Oxford and Thomas Goad from Cambridge.

Long afterwards, at Featley's funeral, the preacher would recall with pride how, throughout those turbulent years, forty-five members of Convocation, 'whereof he was chief, made a solemn convenant among ourselves to oppose everything that did but savour or scent ever so little' of Arminianism.[22] Featley and Goad, like Abbot himself, were firm episcopalians, loyal Church of England men in the old Elizabethan sense; but to Montagu they were no less Puritans for being 'Church-Puritans'. He described them as 'that urchin', 'that ape', 'these hornets'; and his aim was clear and explicit: they must be driven out of Lambeth. How fortunate that he had a secret agent in that palace, who told him what they were up to and leaked documents to him! But even more sinister than the Archbishop's chaplains was the man whom Montagu saw as the manipulator both of them and of the

Parliament: 'that jackanapes' in Oxford, 'one Prideaux'. The mere thought of Dr Prideaux brought a rush of blood to the head of Dr Montagu, for John Prideaux, Rector of Exeter College – 'the Bedlam of Ex' as Montagu called him – Regius Professor of Divinity, Vice-Chancellor, chaplain to the late King, was the most respected figure in Oxford: respected alike for his learning, his moderation, his impartiality; and Oxford, in 1625, in spite of Laud, was still the stronghold of the enemy, the very citadel of English high Calvinism.

'Dr Prideaux, Featley, Oxford, Lambeth . . .', 'I am threatened with wars from Oxford . . .', 'At Oxford they are all on fire . . .' – such was the refrain of Montagu as he mobilized the janissaries of Durham House for the decisive battle. And no ally was closer to him in those days than Bishop Neile's chaplain Dr Cosin. 'I beseech your Lordship,' Montagu once wrote to Neile, 'let Mr Cosin burn all my letters'. Luckily Cosin did no such thing, and so we have a dramatic running commentary on those desperate clerical struggles. Cosin's side of the correspondence does not survive: presumably Montagu burnt his letters; but it is clear that the two men were thick as thieves. Cosin to Montagu is 'good John'; he is the arbiter of Montagu's manifestos – 'what I write', says Montagu, 'I refer all to you'; and he is the essential link between the gladiators like Montagu and the grand strategists, Neile and Laud, who, as all agree, must direct this great battle for control of the Church.

He is also the confidant to whom Montagu unburdens himself and expresses his exasperation with the more cautious politicians of the party. Why, asks Montagu, are these men all so silent? Why does not 'our Gamaliel', Lancelot Andrewes, speak up? More reasonably, since Andrewes was now over seventy, and near to death, why has nothing been heard from his pupil, Dr Wren? Dr White, the Dean of Carlisle, another Cambridge man, he is convinced, is on the right side; but why is he so timid, so frightened of the establishment? And then there are those 'moderate', compromising Jacobean bishops, believers in consensus and a quiet life. It is they, cries Montagu, who are betraying the Church; and yet can they not see that it is they who have all to lose if the Puritans take over? – 'I feel I shall live to see their rochets pulled over their heads'. Sometimes Montagu is near to despair. Why should he fight the battle alone, he asks, only to be let down by his betters who then take the reward? 'I beat the bush and others catch the birds!' Is it worth while, in such circumstances, to persevere? Were it not better done, as others use, to conform, and prosper, with the times? 'Shall I make peace with the Puritans and turn over a new leaf?' And then – oh horror! – can it be true what he has heard: that Dr Prideaux is to be a bishop? Prideaux, the friend of that oracle of the Church-Puritans, Archbishop Ussher, and of the guzzling Dr Ward in Cambridge; Prideaux who (as Cosin has reported) 'hath threatened the first thing the Parliament doth shall be (for they doubtless are at his beck) to burn my book, and why not me?' Against such a disaster, action must be taken at once. 'My Lord of St. David's' – that is, Laud – must be alerted to use his great credit with the Duke of Buckingham and stop it.

The Duke of Buckingham – he was the great man upon whom all seemed to depend in those days. How fortunate that Laud seemed to have captured him! But how securely had he been captured? One could never be sure. The Duke was an opportunist, cultivating now Spanish papists, now French Huguenots. At this moment he was dangerously fascinated by the Master of Emmanuel College in Cambridge, John Preston, a fashionable and supple puritan virtuoso. Luckily, in February 1626, the uncertainty ended. After a carefully stage-managed conference at York House, the London house which he had acquired from the ruined Francis Bacon, Buckingham declared himself effectively for Montagu and Laud. Preston was dropped. With that success, ultimate victory, it seemed, was sure. The party had only to keep together, to back the court unconditionally, and to trust royal patronage to bring them to power.

Three months later, they had a chance to prove their loyalty and further their aim. The King then stated that he wished the Duke of Buckingham to be elected Chancellor of Cambridge University. This was a gratuitous affront to the Parliament then sitting, for the Duke was, at that time, being impeached by it for high crimes and misdemeanours, and responsibility for defeat in war. However the Cambridge Arminians did not hesitate. Four heads of houses, including the two successive Masters of Peterhouse, Mawe and Wren, mobilized their colleges. Cosin, who had been at the York House conference, giving countenance to his friend Montagu, came up to Cambridge from Durham House, armed with letters from the Bishop of Durham, to canvass for the Duke. Passions ran high; a rival candidate was put up (an unheard-of impertinency when the King's wish had been declared) and the Duke's victory was very narrow – a margin of five votes in a poll of 211. But it was enough. Cambridge was now securely linked to the court, and the court to Durham House. Buckingham's first formal act as Chancellor was to incorporate Laud as a doctor of the University.

Within a few months Laud would be intervening in the affairs of both universities. In the summer of 1627 he attended the King on a visit to Woodstock, and there, with the benefit of his advice, the King 'reflected' on the state of the two universities. He gave his orders verbally to the Vice-Chancellor and Heads of Houses of Oxford, who waited on him, and commanded Laud, in the absence of the Duke of Buckingham, its Chancellor, who was abroad in command of the expedition against France, to convey the same orders to the University of Cambridge. Those orders were that the Vice-Chancellors of the two universities were to search for 'all directions, orders, injunctions admonitions or the like, concerning learning or manners' since the beginning of the reign of Queen Elizabeth. Copies of these documents were then to be sent to Laud, for delivery to the King, who would then consider the whole state of the universities and the Church. His purpose was, as Laud wrote, 'that both universities may receive the same rule, go on the same way, and so be the happy mother of piety and union through the Church'.[23] One of the results of this intervention was the introduction at Oxford, on the initiative of Laud, of a 'cycle' for the orderly election of proctors such as had already been established at Cambridge by the statutes of Archbishop Whitgift in 1570. Oxford was to catch up with Cambridge, in discipline as in doctrine: indeed, soon, to replace it as the Arminian university.

For in August 1628 Buckingham was assassinated. There was rejoicing in the country but dismay in the party. Montagu compared 'the dismal blow' to the assassination of Henri IV.[24] Laud was desolated by apparently genuine grief. Wren, in a letter to the King, outdid himself in protestations of sorrow and servility.[25] Forty years later, when all pre-civil war passions were spent, Cosin would go out of his way, in a formal document, to describe this 'untimely death' of the Duke as an event 'ever to be lamented by this whole nation'.[26] Certainly it was a great blow to the party. High hopes had been entertained of the Duke both in Cambridge and at court. In Cambridge there was the prospect of a great new library, to vie with Sir Thomas Bodley's library in Oxford. Successive chancellors had been elected in this hope, but so far without result. Only Buckingham seemed eager to reward the University which had elected him. Now all those hopes were dashed. But at the court, the centre of power, he had already served his turn. Thanks to him, the party was now firmly in control of the Church. Laud was Bishop of London. His supporters had been promoted. Even Montagu was a bishop, and from now on would be silent again, snuffed out by his mitre. In Paris, Grotius heard with delight, and the Huguenots with dismay, that 'the best and most learned bishops and the flower of the university of Cambridge' were Arminians'.[27] Then, early next year, the King took over and, by dissolving Parliament, and keeping it dissolved for eleven years, gave them, at last, security and power.

So the Arminians entered into their inheritance. But at what a cost! That long period of waiting, since Archbishop Bancroft's death, and those last years of desperate struggle, when (as Montagu repeatedly put it) the fate of the Church stood on the razor's edge, had not only left a legacy of resentment: they had also changed the character of the movement. The rational, liberal, civilized, ecumenical Erasmianism of Overall and Andrewes had become wedded to a particular political form and a particular policy, and would be used to consecrate that policy. It was also tainted, not unplausibly since the revolution in Holland – for the Dutch Arminians were now re-grouping in Catholic Antwerp and some of the weaker of them had gone over to Rome – with the smear of 'appeasement'. Arminianism, in the eyes of patriots and Puritans, even of moderate 'Church-Puritans', had become the soul of tyranny and the way to popery. The last debates and manifestos of the House of Commons, before it was summarily and, as he hoped, finally dissolved by Charles I in March 1629, are shrill in their denunciation of 'Arminianism' – and of Laud, Montagu and Cosin, its most notorious advocates. 'An Arminian', declared John Pym's step-brother Francis Rous, 'is the spawn of a Papist . . . and if you mark it well, you will see an Arminian reaching out his hand to a Papist, a Papist to a Jesuit, a Jesuit gives one hand to the Pope and the other to the King of Spain'; and as a logical consequence of this concatenation, the Commons, in their last final protest, demanded that anyone who sought to introduce popery or Arminianism 'shall be reputed a capital enemy to this Kingdom and commonwealth.'[28]

The Arminians, naturally, objected. They had every right to object. They were all convinced anti-papists. Andrewes and Buckeridge had engaged in controversy with Cardinal Bellarmine. Andrewes had also allied himself with Huguenots against Catholic claims. So had Overall and Cosin. Cosin's attitude to Romanism was of 'uncompromising hostility, and by far the greatest proportion of his literary work is expressly directed against that system'.[29] Montagu's controversies had arisen out of his refutation of popery, not of Puritanism. Neile was accused of undue severity towards popish recusants in his bishopric, and had made a violent attack on Marcantonio de Dominis for deserting to Rome. Laud made his name by his refutation of the Jesuit Fisher, and would go out of his way to congratulate a French Huguenot on his refutation of papal claims.[30] None of these men showed the slightest sign of defecting to Rome. Indeed, we can say that whereas Hooker had defined the Church of England on its leftward side, contrasting it with Calvinism, the Arminians defined it on the right, contrasting it with Roman Catholicism. Their crime, in puritan eyes, was that they contrasted it not totally, blindly, rhetorically, but critically; and criticism can be the beginning of dialogue, even respect. How much safer to declare the Pope Antichrist and shut out the critics, as the Calvinists had done at Dordt! Was not that, after all, *mutatis mutandis*, what the Catholics had done at Trent?

But all these arguments were now irrelevant. In 1629 the essential fact was that the Arminans were now in power, and being in power, did not need to argue. There was now no need, for instance, to emphasize the divine right of episcopacy. Once stated, it could be kept in reserve. Meanwhile the royal supremacy, though not admitted in theory, could be exploited in practice. Equally, there was no need to emphasize 'Arminian' doctrines of free will and grace. They too were believed, but why advertise them when they aroused such dangerous public hysteria? So a royal proclamation ordered all public controversy on religious matters to cease. When this was first announced, Montagu was alarmed. Was this, he asked, a swipe at him?[31] But no: it was merely evidence that public controversy was no longer needed. Indeed, it could be counter-productive: 'that great bugbear of Arminianism', as Laud called it,[32] was best kept out of sight: it never emerged without the attendant spectre of popery; and that, of course, could be the beginning of a national scare, distracting men from the real work to be done.

For what was now needed was action: action to undo the damage of the last seventy years. In those years the Puritans had used the Elizabethan consensus to colonize the Church, to draw it, increasingly, towards a Calvinist model – or so, at least, the 'Arminians' believed. Archbishop Bancroft's reign had been too brief to stop the rot, and Archbishop Abbot had allowed it to go on. Laud would put an end to all that. He would use his authority – which at present, since Abbot was still archbishop, was that of the Crown – to reverse the process. He would resume the suspended work of Bancroft. He would dislodge the 'Puritans' who had penetrated the citadels of the Church. He would recover its lands, rebuild its economic base, restore its authority as an estate of the realm. For this purpose he would use every opportunity of patronage and politics. The time for consensus, for compromise, was over. As a high churchman of the next generation would put it, 'Archbishop Abbot's *Yield and they will be pleased at last* was a great miscarriage; Archbishop Laud's *Resolve, for there is no end of yielding* was great policy.'[33]

But how, we naturally ask, was this great policy to be applied? The Church, throughout the country, was honeycombed with 'Puritanism', which the gentry supported. Its wealth had been eroded through neglect, by which the gentry had profited. This process had created vested interests, mental attitudes, prejudices and customs. It was consecrated by a set of ideas which were not, perhaps, very consistent but which contained a useful amalgam of biblical fundamentalism, national sentiment and morality. The Arminians who set out to reverse the process were as yet a small academic party. They professed a different theology and a different philosophy of Church history. They had made converts among university scholars. But as yet they had made little impact on the country. And now the time at their disposal was so short! Andrewes and Overall were dead, Neile and Laud ageing. They had their acolytes of course, their chaplains; but they too, counting their patrons' years, saw that they must make haste. The long process of erosion must be reversed in the period, perhaps brief, when Parliament was in abeyance; and it must be done by an old man in a hurry surrounded by a group of young Turks. In order to see how they set about it, we must turn aside, for a moment, from Oxford and Cambridge, Lambeth Palace and Durham House, Westminster and Whitehall, and see them at work in a diocese which, by a happy accident, was at their mercy: the bishopric of Durham.

4   A model diocese

The diocese of Durham was of course Neile's diocese. In those years of struggle, from 1617 to 1628, Neile played a vital part; for although Laud was the driving force of the new Arminianism, it was Neile who opened the way for its advance. Just as his London house was the headquarters of the movement during the battle, so his diocese was to be the model for the exploitation of victory. He himself had set the example. On appointment to the bishopric, he had at once set out to repair and decorate his two great episcopal palaces, Durham Castle and Bishop Auckland, which he had found in 'great decay', and had so beautified them, we are told, 'that they that saw them could not think that they were the same'.[34] Now, even before the battle for the court had been won, he sent a group of his most active chaplains to colonize the centres of power. To Newcastle upon Tyne he sent Thomas Jackson. Jackson was an Oxford scholar, a very learned man, 'the ornament of the university in his time', who had shed his former puritan views and become an avowed Arminian.* He and his successor would preach sound doctrine in the principal commercial city of the bishopric. To Durham, his cathedral city, Neile sent five Cambridge activists, to be rectors of major parish churches, archdeacons, and canons of the cathedral – for in Durham the bishop had the right to appoint the canons. These five were Francis Burgoyne, Augustine Lindsell and John Cosin – the three musketeers of Durham House – Eleazar Duncon (a Pembroke College man, a lifelong friend and supporter of Dr Wren) and Gabriel Clarke. On arrival at Durham these men found, already installed in the chapter, a colony of Oxford men – Christ Church men, appointed by Neile's predecessor Bishop James, who had previously been Dean of Christ Church. Bishop James was an old Elizabethan, and had no use for Arminianism; nor had his protégés at Durham. The stage was thus set for a battle. The challenger to battle was the undisputed leader of the newcomers, Dr Cosin.

Cosin was the most active, the most extreme and the most aggressive of all the new 'Arminian' clergy. Not for him the simple dignity, decency, even austerity, of Laud's 'beauty of holiness'. He was the master of ceremonies of the new order, prepared not only to attack the ideas but to outrage the senses of the Church-Puritans. He was also imperious, intemperate, and indiscreet. By 1627 this was clear to all. Not only had he been the private collaborator and the public champion of the firebrand Montagu. He had also published a volume of private prayers – 'Mr Cosin's cozening devotions' as they were called – and was attacked in Parliament for tampering with the Prayer Book: always an emotive charge. Meanwhile, in Durham, he and his friends had been at work. Following the example of their bishop, they set out to repair and redecorate their houses and churches. Instead of puritan plainness, so necessary (it was said) to counter the prevalent popery of the North, they sought (as it seemed) to outbid the papists in the external apparatus of worship. Burgoyne at Bishop Wearmouth, Duncon at Haughton-le-Skerne, set their builders to work. Cosin, who – like Neile himself – was always a great builder, completely and splendidly restored his church at Brancepeth.[35] But of course they made the

---

* *AO* III, pp. 664–70. Jackson declared his Arminian views openly in the dedication of his *Treatise of the Divine Essence and Attributes* (1628); which greatly shocked Calvinists like Ussher, Ward Twisse, Prynne, etc. See, for instance *UWW* XV, p. 404, XVI, pp. 462–3; T. Jackson, *Works* (1673) III, p. 177. Jackson was – unusually for a Laudian – a Platonist (see S. Hutton, 'Thomas Jackson, Oxford Platonist and William Twisse, Aristotelian', *Journal of the History of Ideas* XXXIX (1978), 635–52). Laud defended his memory at his trial, as 'a learned and honest man', and his posthumous works were published with the help of Sheldon.

greatest show in their cathedral. Fixed altars in the east end replaced moveable communion tables in the aisle and were served by clergy in rich vestments; there was music – Cosin loved music – instrumental music of organs, sackbuts and cornets, and elaborate vocal polyphony; and a forest of wax-lights and tapers – 340 candles it was said, sixty of them on the high altar, to illuminate that great cathedral at Candlemas. Such things had not been seen in Durham since the Reformation: not even in 1569 when the army of the rebel Catholic earls had entered the city and mass had been sung in the cathedral.

Such outrages could be perpetrated while Dr Neile was Bishop of Durham. But at the end of 1627 Neile was translated to Winchester, to succeed Andrewes in that strategic post, and next year, after the brief three-month reign of Dr Mountain, a new Bishop was appointed to Durham. He was an Oxford man, Dr John Howson, now Bishop of Oxford. His appointment was a sign for Cosin's enemies in the chapter of Durham to strike back.

Bishop Howson was a robust anti-papist. His sermons against the Pope's supremacy, we are told, were unanswerable and 'have made him famous to all posterity'. But he was no Puritan. Indeed, as we have seen, he had been one of the earliest supporters and patrons of Laud, the first to raise the standard of Arminianism in puritan Oxford. He had strongly supported Montagu at the famous conference at York House, and perhaps it was as a reward for this service that next year, though an old man, he was promoted to the rich bishopric of Durham. But he was also a Christ Church man – he had been a canon of Christ Church before becoming Bishop of Oxford – and Christ Church men, as Macaulay has observed, 'wherever dispersed, were as much attached to their college as a Scotchman to his country or a Jesuit to his order'.[37] So, in the summer of 1628, when Parliament was in full cry against both Laud and Cosin, and the new Bishop had not yet arrived in Durham, the Christ Church men in the chapter seized their chance. Their spokesman was one Peter Smart, who, on 28 July, preached in the cathedral on the theme, 'I hate them that hold of superstitious ceremonies'.

Smart's sermon was the beginning of 'the greatest religious controversy of the century in the North of England'.[38] It was an intemperate attack on the whole high-church party for introducing into divine worship 'superstitious vanities, ceremonial folleries, apish toys and popish trinkets', and the preacher singled out for particular abuse the 'schismatical crew of upstart reformers' whom Neile had intruded into Durham. Such an onslaught naturally caused a sensation, and Smart's victims reacted immediately. On the very same day they cited him before the court of High Commission at Durham and themselves sat among his judges. They suspended him from his functions and sequestered his canonry. The case was then referred to the court of High Commission, first at Lambeth, then at York. It was taken up in Parliament. Meanwhile Smart counter-attacked by indicting his accusers at the local assizes. Passions ran high. So did language. Smart, in his legal submissions, repeated and improved the language of his sermon, denouncing the Cambridge canons, and particularly that now notorious trio, Cosin, chief of 'the brain-sick Arminians of Durham', Lindsell, 'a professed disciple of that arch-heretic and enemy of God, Arminius', and Burgoyne, 'next to John Cosin, a principal patron of superstitious ceremonies'. These three, he declared, had 'turned the sacrament into a theatrical stage-play', with pleasant tunes, glittering pictures and histrionical gestures, and had set up images of angels in 'long scarlet gowns, green petticoats, golden wings and gilded heads'.[39]

When the new Bishop arrived in Durham and discovered the storm that had been provoked, he was appalled. By this time Cosin and his friends had managed to alienate the Dean, Dr Hunt, who had originally supported them, but now went over to Smart. The Bishop tried to settle the dispute 'according to the ancient use of that church before the late alterations which bred all these quarrels';[40] but in vain. He was particularly incensed on learning that Cosin and Lindsell had gone up to London, behind his back, and discussed the matter with Laud and Neile. What had the bishops of London and Winchester to do with the internal affairs of the diocese of Durham, which was not even in the same province? He summoned the cathedral chapter, rated Cosin and Lindsell, accused them of turbulence and faction, and threatened to expel Cosin as 'the ringleader of all disorder'.

Cosin and Lindsell had no intention of yielding. They had no respect for the dignity, the age or even the office of their Bishop. They knew where real power lay. They wrote immediately to Laud, stating their case.[41] Thereupon the Bishop received a stiff letter from the King, ordering him 'to desist from meddling with the said Augustine Lindsell and John Cosin, or any other of the prebends of the said Church, till we shall appoint some other to be joined with you' – a clear and wounding indication that the Bishop himself was no longer trusted at court. The King also ordered the Bishop to make haste and institute Yeldard Alvey as vicar of Newcastle.[42] Alvey was a strong Arminian now advanced to this key post in order to cut out an influential local puritan lecturer, Robert Jenison, who took advice from his tutor in Cambridge, our old plum-guzzling friend, Samuel Ward of Sidney Sussex; and the vacancy was caused because Laud had summoned the previous vicar – his special protégé Thomas Jackson – back to Oxford to be President of Corpus Christi College, and 'poison the university of Oxford with his Arminian drugs'.[43] For good measure, the Bishop also received a letter from Strafford, now President of the Council at York, 'of three sides of paper full of like misinformations'.

It is easy to sympathize with Bishop Howson. He was an old conservative, older than Laud, whom he had supported through thick and thin; he had been accustomed to the more open society of Christ Church; and he had gone to this remote province, at the age of seventy-five, 'with great hope' as he put it, 'of a quiet end to a troubled life'. Surely those Christ Church men in the chapter – 'five of my ancient friends and acquaintance of Christ Church' – even those of them who had somewhat puritan views, would welcome their old colleague . . . Instead he had found the place taken over by this aggressive caucus of Cambridge men, whose conservatism was very different from his and who spoke a quite different language. On receiving the letters of the King and Strafford, he set off for London. It was mid-November, and he travelled through 'storms, snow, hail, rains, great winds and high waters'. After thirteen days on the road, he reached Oxford, and in that congenial atmosphere he paused to recover. Thence he sent off a letter to Laud. He protested against the underhand dealings of Cosin and Lindsell. 'His Majesty', he insisted, 'hath been misinformed'. And how, he wondered, had 'these erroneous informations come to His Majesty's ears?' Perhaps, he suggested, through Dr Neile, 'whose chaplains they concern'. (He tactfully concealed his knowledge of the secret meeting at Fulham.) He protested that he had 'suffered more than ever was offered to any bishop of Durham'. Thus he prepared Laud for their expected meeting in London. Whether that meeting ever took place, we do not know. Three months after writing the letter, the Bishop died in London.

Meanwhile, in Durham, Cosin and his friends, confident of support, pushed ahead. Although an unsympathetic assize judge urged them to make peace, they paid no attention to that lay tribunal. This was a clerical matter, they said, and it was for the Court of High Commission to judge. By that court Smart was ordered to make public recantation, suspended from his ministry, deprived of his canonry, fined £400, and, on refusing to pay, imprisoned. He would remain in prison for twelve years. His canonry was promptly conferred upon Thomas Carre, a Peterhouse man recommended by Strafford.

That was in 1632. Next year, the King set out on a ceremonial visit to Edinburgh to be crowned as King of Scotland. Among the courtiers who accompanied him were Laud, as Dean of the Chapel Royal, and Wren, as Clerk of the Closet. On the way he stopped at Durham, stayed with the new Bishop at Bishop Auckland, admired Bishop Neile's improvements to the castle, and visited the cathedral. It was a very satisfactory visit. The official Latin record of it dwells complacently on the details: the red carpet and purple cushions; the canopy of silk embroidered with gold; the orderly procession of chapter and choir; the fine new organs and other instruments; the choral music; the Latin liturgy; the richly decorated altar; the devout standing at the creed; the correct genuflexions. The Dean and canons presented the King with a red velvet cope richly embroidered with gold, silver and precious stones. Having praised its beauty, the King handed it to Dr Laud, Bishop of London, 'who never left his side', with orders to wear it in the Chapel Royal. This Latin record was written, as the ceremony itself had been organized, by Dr Cosin.[44] Then the royal party moved on to Scotland, confident that what had been done in Durham could be done in Edinburgh too. In this, as events proved, they were sadly mistaken.

Could it even be done in other dioceses in England? Durham, after all, was a special case. A particularly determined and energetic bishop had used it as a model and had sent thither a mutually supporting group of like-minded men, with a common loyalty to him and a common background in Cambridge. There they could encourage each other, feeling that they were a band of brothers engaged in a joint enterprise. Elsewhere it was different. A year after the royal visit to Durham, Cosin received a lamentable letter from another old Cambridge friend – a protégé, like himself, of Overall – who had not had the good fortune to be taken up by Bishop Neile. He was Overall's nephew John Hayward, canon of Lichfield, a diocese of which both Neile and Overall had briefly been bishops; but evidently they had achieved little there. The chief town in the diocese, Coventry, was described by Montagu as 'a second Geneva', and the present bishop was notoriously negligent. 'This church and diocese', Hayward wrote to Cosin, 'is Augeas' stable, which I know and see how it might be cleansed and purged'; but lacking local support, he 'must be content to sit down and, like the principal governors thereof' – which I suppose includes Bishop Wright – 'live upon the dung of this stable'. How he longed to be in Durham, with his friend John Cosin, in congenial company! Failing that, he was resolved to retire to Cambridge, to his rectory of Coton, and never again look upon what George Fox the Quaker would call 'the bloody city of Lichfield'.[45]

Clearly, if the new course was to be established through the country, more work was needed. The success in Durham had been spectacular, but it had required a heavy concentration of talent. Almost the whole of Durham House had been emptied into that diocese. If the success was to be repeated all over England, the production of learned, orthodox, committed clergy must be stepped up. A whole generation of Arminians must be formed to take over from the Church-Puritans in possession. For this purpose there must be crash-courses at the universities and the oracles of Church-Puritanism there – Samuel Ward in Cambridge, John Prideaux in Oxford – must be neutralized. We must therefore return to the universities. We have seen that Laud had already been active in both of them behind the scenes. Now he was to take open command.

5   The battle for the universities

To re-orient the universities was not impossible, provided that a movement for change already existed and was backed by power; for all the machinery lay to hand. The turnover of college fellowships was quick, elections to headships and fellowships could often be controlled, and patronage would do the rest. In both Oxford and Cambridge such a movement existed: Arminianism was now fashionable and appealed to the young – at least to the young clergy; and once it was clear that power in both Church and State was behind it, the recruits poured in. All that was needed was to organize the movement and to exploit the opportunities as they arose. That meant, in effect, while keeping the support of the Crown, to understand, and to manipulate, the machinery of university politics.

Until 1628, as we have seen, the Arminian movement had been stronger in Cambridge, its English source, than in Oxford. In general, Cambridge was then the more modern university. It was also closer to the source of power. Most of the great Elizabethan and Jacobean statesmen and churchmen were Cambridge men. James I kept in close touch with the University: he had a hunting-lodge at Royston and on his annual visits to Newmarket he required the Vice-Chancellor and the two professors of divinity to wait upon him and report on academic discipline: discipline which was more easily enforced since Archbishop Whitgift's statutes of 1570 had increased the powers of the Heads of

Colleges. However, in 1628–30 the relative situation of the two universities changed. The assassination of the Duke of Buckingham, their Chancellor, was a great blow to the Cambridge Arminians. They had fought so hard to secure his election, and he had promised so much. Now, only two years after that fierce contest, there was no desire for another such battle, and the University invited Charles I to nominate their new Chancellor. He nominated the Earl of Holland, a courtier whose good looks had made him a favourite first with King James, then with the new Queen, Henrietta Maria, Buckingham's successor as the dominating personal influence on the King. Holland was chiefly concerned to sustain himself by monopolies, pensions, grants, and a rich marriage, while at the same time expressing 'puritan' views and emphasizing his independence of government policy. His chancellorship brought little advantage to the University or to any party within it. He represented the radical chic of the time, and would come ultimately, as such men do in revolutions, to a bad end.

At Oxford, the change was in the other direction. Until 1630, that university, as Montagu had repeatedly complained, was dominated by the Puritans – that is, of course, the Church-Puritans. There were islands of Arminianism in St John's College – particularly after the ten-year presidency of Laud – and in Christ Church; but the dominant character of the place was puritan and the dominant personality in it was Montagu's *bête noire*, the learned Dr Prideaux. However, in 1630 Oxford too lost its Chancellor, the Earl of Pembroke, a grandee who had stood outside, or above, the ideological parties; and Laud was recommended as his successor. Even before Pembroke's death, Laud had made his weight felt in university affairs; his position at court was visible to all; and the young academic clergy, who knew their own interests, formed a strong party behind him. Against him the old establishment put up the new Earl of Pembroke, brother and heir of the late Chancellor. It was a hotly contested election; but Laud won. Three years later, on the death of Abbot, the King fulfilled his old promise and appointed him Archbishop of Canterbury. He thus held two positions which, since the reign of Mary, had been combined in one person only once – and then for only two years: in Laud's hero, Archbishop Bancroft.

The change from Buckingham to Holland at Cambridge, followed by the change from Pembroke to Laud at Oxford, shifted the academic centre of Arminianism. Both as Chancellor and as Archbishop, Laud enjoyed a commanding position in his own university. In each capacity he was Visitor of several colleges, and as Archbishop and chief ecclesiastical adviser to the Crown, he could exercise vast patronage in the Church. In addition, other bishops were visitors of particular colleges. The Bishop of Winchester, for instance, was Visitor of Magdalen, New College, Corpus Christi, St John's, and Trinity, whereby he was 'able to draw a great party after him': how convenient that that bishopric, in 1630, was in the safe hands of the reliable Dr Neile! That made it possible to stuff in the sound and scholarly Dr Jackson as President of Corpus Christi. And when Neile moved up to the archbishopric of York, Laud took no risks. It was 'to make sure work at Oxford', we are told, and to ensure his 'peace and power' there, that he placed Walter Curll in Winchester.[46] Curll was a Cambridge man, a former Fellow of Peterhouse, who had studied under Baro. In Winchester, as in Oxford, he would prove very sound, enforcing 'the beauty of holiness' on his resentful diocese. This he did very success-fully – for a time. But in the end the day of retribution would come: in the civil war his palace would be captured and the aged Bishop would have to escape from his exasperated enemies concealed under a load of manure in a dung-cart.

Of course there were some loopholes in this system. The Warden of Merton College, for instance, Sir Nathaniel Brent, was unsound. He had been Vicar-General to Archbishop Abbot, whose niece he had married. Laud could not remove him, either as Warden or as Vicar-General. Brent's daughter was married to a former Fellow, one Edward Corbet, who was also very troublesome, then and thereafter. But as Archbishop of Canterbury, Laud was Visitor of Merton, and besides, he had his agent there, one Peter Turner, orientalist and mathematician, who kept him informed of all goings-on in the college, and gave himself great airs in consequence, boasting at the high table of his grand contacts.[47] In Trinity College Laud had another private informant in his godson, William Chillingworth, who, while a Fellow there, sent him 'weekly intelligence of what passed in the university'.* Bishop Williams, that incorrigible Jacobean politician who was Laud's greatest enemy in the Church, could well be a nuisance in Oxford: for as Bishop of Lincoln he was Visitor of four colleges – Balliol, Oriel, Lincoln and Brasenose – and as a Welshman he had a personal following in Jesus. Exeter College too was impenetrable: it was the fief

---

* *ABL*, 'William Chillingworth'. Apparently it was on the basis of a report by Chillingworth that Milton's friend, Alexander Gill, an usher at St Paul's School, was haled before the Star Chamber, degraded from the ministry, deprived of his university degree, and sentenced to lose his ears. The unfortunate man had been indiscreet at a convivial gathering in the college wine-cellar: an extreme case of the danger of gossip in academic circles. (See *PMB*, pp. 50–1, 741.)

of Dr Prideaux. But Laud was not seriously troubled by these difficulties. The Bishop of Lincoln would soon be outmanoeuvred and sent to the Tower, and Prideaux was too prudent to expose himself.

By determined use of all the levers of power and patronage, and by his personal influence, Laud soon won over Oxford. He knew what he wanted and lost no time in achieving it. Oxford, unlike Cambridge, had no formal statutes. He supplied them, and thereby ensured that, here too, effective power would be with the oligarchy of college heads, whom ultimately he could manage. In the colleges, the chapels were reformed. Hitherto, we are told, there had been 'no copes, altars or communion tables railed altarwise', no bowing, no crucifixes, 'but such as were either defaced or covered with dust and quite neglected'.[48] Now all that was noiselessly changed. The university church too was improved. A rich Welsh clergyman, whom Laud had made his chaplain, provided it with a handsome porch with elegant spiral columns and 'the image of our lady and a babe in her arms at the top of it'. This annoyed the Puritans but helped the clergyman into a Welsh bishopric. Meanwhile the Archbishop had won support by spectacular benefactions. He had showered the university library with splendid gifts, founded a chair of Arabic, built a new quadrangle in St John's College, and created the university press.

In 1636 Laud decided to celebrate his triumph, and the completion of his new quadrangle, by a royal visit. The King came to present, in person, the new statutes. There were speeches and plays, heavy with ideological content, honorary degrees and prodigious feasting. The whole affair was most satisfactory. Who would have thought that, only seven years ago, Oxford had been the intellectual capital of Puritanism? Now it was, as it would remain, the capital of the High Church party. The achievement of its conversion would long be remembered and admired. Nearly a century later, a reformer who wished to win the universities from apparently ingrained Jacobite to correct Hanoverian loyalty insisted that such conversion was not impossible. As evidence, he cited the achievement of Archbishop Laud, who in a few years had completely changed the character of Oxford, turning it from a Puritan to an Arminian university.[49]

While Oxford was thus transformed, Cambridge, where the new movement had begun, lagged behind. How different it would have been if Buckingham had lived! As it was, Laud had to rely on subordinate agents and intervention by the Crown. The most important of his agents was the Bishop of Ely, because of his local and college patronage: he could be as useful, or as harmful, as the bishops of Winchester and Lincoln in Oxford, and so Laud saw to it that a sound ally was always placed in that see. From 1631 it was Francis White, a confederate since 1622 at least, when they had joined forces to save the Duke of Buckingham from popery. Within the University his most dependable ally was Matthew Wren, now Master of Peterhouse. Like Laud himself, Wren was essentially a college man, a stickler for authority and discipline: he was also a great believer in ceremony and a learned liturgiologist. Wren had been together with Laud in Durham House. In Cambridge he had been the chief strategist of the election of the Duke of Buckingham. As Master of Peterhouse he acted as Laud's agent, reporting on university affairs in order to promote the cause and neutralize its enemies.

One such opportunity had occurred in 1627, when Buckingham was Chancellor. It was the affair of Dr Dorislaus. In 1625 Fulke Greville, Lord Brooke, being now over seventy, decided to do something for his old university, and thought particularly of the study of history. Three years earlier, William Camden had founded a chair of 'civil' – that is secular – history at Oxford: why should Brooke not do the same for Cambridge? When the news reached the Arminian zealots, it was greeted with some misgiving: for the chair at Oxford had gone to one whom they regarded as a Puritan. 'I am glad that the Lord Brooke hath at length begun to remember Cambridge', Montagu wrote to Cosin. 'I hope it will be better employed than the donations are at Oxford'.[50] Secular history was a new subject and not altogether safe, and Lord Brooke, the friend of Philip Sidney, was an old Elizabethan, like Camden, not entirely trusted by the new school.

The scholar finally appointed by Lord Brooke was a young Dutchman, Isaac Dorislaus, and he chose, as the subject of his lectures, the *Annals* of Tacitus. The first lecture passed off well enough, but in the second he justified, or extenuated – with all proper reservations – the Dutch revolt against Spain. For Wren, that was enough. He wrote to the Vice-Chancellor and, very secretly, to Laud, warning them of the dangerous foreign snake that had slid into the Cambridge grass. Dorislaus did not give a third lecture. In Oxford, the Camden chair of history still exists. In Cambridge, thanks – initially at least – to the prompt action of the Master of Peterhouse, chair and subject were extinguished together in 1627.

The affair of Dorislaus is interesting because it illustrates the transformation of Arminianism in England from an independent intellectual movement to political commitment. Dorislaus was an

insufferably pompous and conceited young man* who, long afterwards, became a republican, but there could be no reasonable
objection to him, from an Arminian point of view, in 1627. He had been
recommended to Lord Brooke by Grotius, when Vossius, the Arminian
friend of Laud (and of Wren), had declined. Tacitus was a popular
writer in Catholic, monarchical Europe. The English government,
under Elizabeth, had supported the Dutch revolt, and England was
now, like the Dutch Republic, at war with Spain. The only possible
objection to Dorislaus was that he allowed, in certain cases, the revolt of
subject nations. This had nothing whatever to do with the teaching of
Wren's intellectual master, Lancelot Andrewes. It had much to do with
the aspirations of his political master, Charles I.

In his letter to Laud denouncing Dorislaus, Wren insisted that his
own identity, as informer, be kept secret. He was conscious that the new
movement, in spite of the progress that it had made in certain colleges,
and its access to power through Buckingham and Laud, was not yet
firmly established in Cambridge. Then came the disastrous assassination of Buckingham. But in the following years, even under the
unsympathetic chancellorship of Holland, the high ground was
gradually captured. For this purpose Laud relied not on preaching –
controversial points of doctrine were not, in his view, to be declared
from the pulpit – but on his direct, personal influence with the King.
The Crown nominated two college heads directly – those of Trinity and
King's College – and these were generally sound: two men who had
shown themselves reliable as Masters of Peterhouse – John Richard-
son, the 'fat-bellied Arminian' who had succeeded Dr Some, and
Leonard Mawe, who had campaigned for the Duke of Buckingham –
were rewarded by promotion to the grander and richer Mastership of
Trinity. The Crown also, as heir to the Pope, had power to intervene
directly in university matters: to suspend or dispense with statutes, to
set aside elections, to 'recommend' its nominees as Heads and Fellows;
and this power, hitherto used mainly to gratify individuals, could now
be used more systematically to strengthen a party.[51]

Thus in 1630 Benjamin Laney, a reliable chaplain of Bishop Neile,
was imposed as Master of Pembroke College; in 1632 royal mandates
imposed Edward Martin, Laud's chaplain, as President of Queen's
College and Richard Love as Master of Corpus Christi; and in 1634

---

* See his letter to Grotius of 10 February 1631 (*BHG* III, no. 1582) in which he
expresses his intention of going back to Cambridge to restore its fallen prestige by
leading the minds of young noblemen, now polluted by squalid sophistry, forward to
the fountains of purer philosophy; etc. etc.

another royal mandate made William Beale Master of St John's. Beale
– an out-and-out Laudian – had deserved his promotion by his services
as Master of Jesus, where he was now replaced by another of Laud's
chaplains, Richard Sterne. Jesus College was, of course, a fief of the
Bishop of Ely. This use of royal mandates was often resented. Beale was
only admitted at St John's 'after a struggle of eight or nine months
betwixt the contending parties',[52] and in 1635 a royal nominee, who
was singularly unqualified, was defeated by the anti-Laudian Ralph
Brownrigg at St Catharine's.[53] Some colleges had tried to evade the
danger by holding clandestine elections and announcing the result
before a royal mandate could arrive; but in 1634 this subterfuge was
firmly vetoed by a royal letter.

By 1634, indeed, the Calvinist establishment of Cambridge was in
disarray. Its leader, if it had one, was our old friend Dr Samuel Ward of
Sidney Sussex. He was now Head of his college and Regius Professor of
Divinity, a complacent pluralist, as greedy of distant but profitable
benefices as formerly of cheese and plums. An irremovable old
Jacobean, like Prideaux at Oxford, he felt increasingly isolated as the
headships and chairs of Cambridge fell, one after another, to the
enemy. He had given up his diary now, but he still found a vent for his
doubts and lamentations in his letters to the greatest scholar of the
Church-Puritans, Archbishop Ussher in Dublin. Like Prideaux, too, he
was the academic oracle whom his former pupils in the provinces
regularly consulted. But at best he was a poor man's Prideaux, always
afraid that he would be pushed out of his chair, and meanwhile
impotently repeating his litany of complaint: that he 'never knew the
university in worse condition'; that the success of the Arminians at
court was corrupting university scholars; causing them 'to look that
way'; that every year 'new Heads are brought in'; and that 'we have a
Vice-chancellor that favoureth novelties both in rites and doctrine'.[54]

That Vice-Chancellor was Dr Beale, who now appears as one of the
most aggressive of the Laudians in Cambridge. In his own college he
repaired and refurnished the chapel which had 'been left very naked by
some of his predecessors', in accordance with the new style: fixed and
railed altar, with plate and wax candles; statuary, paintings and
tapestries; organ music, copes and cherubim. Bowing to the altar was
made mandatory, so that 'many godly Fellows and scholars of the
house', we are told, 'left their places to avoid the abomination'. To
replace them, more compliant Fellows were seduced from other
colleges with promises of preferment. As Vice-Chancellor, Beale made
his mark by preaching in favour of the new ceremonies and the duty of

obedience, and by licensing the publication of offensive books. The most offensive was *Five Pious and Learned Discourses* by a deceased Peterhouse man, Robert Shelford, who had written in favour of the doctrine of justification through works, auricular confession, reverence to the altar, and against the identification of the Pope with Antichrist. Puritans naturally found the book 'wholly savouring the spirit of Antichrist'. Archbishop Ussher, who was outraged by its publication, reported that the Jesuits in England sent copies of it to Ireland to confirm Irish papists in their obstinacy. A modern scholar has described its publication as 'a deliberate act of propaganda by the Laudian party'.[55]

The publication of these discourses was almost certainly stimulated from their author's own college, Peterhouse.* For Peterhouse, since the days of Baro, had been a centre, if not the centre, of the new movement in Cambridge. There Matthew Wren was now Master and was declaring his loyalty by building a new college chapel – Laud was insistent that colleges must have their own chapels and not rely on outside churches, as Peterhouse had relied on Little St Mary's, Caius College on St Michael's, and Corpus Christi on St Benet's. Wren contributed personally to the cost of the chapel, organized contributions from others, and saw it built, consecrated and put to use. A great liturgiologist, he introduced a service in Latin, with the correct Laudian ceremonies, but he was content with a simple building and plain glass windows. He was an austere man, a scholar and a disciplinarian, not an aesthete: he left the decorative frills to his successor. They were to be some frills.

In 1634, with Dr Beale as Vice-Chancellor and Dr Ward impotently beating his breast in Sidney Sussex College, Laud felt that he could promote Wren to a bishopric. He sent him, via Hereford, to Norwich, where there was plenty of work to be done, and where he would acquire new fame as the relentless persecutor of Puritanism in East Anglia. There was no difficulty in fixing the succession at Peterhouse. The docile Fellows, out of compliance with their Master, proposed to elect his younger brother Christopher Wren, the father of the great architect. Christopher Wren was an Oxford man, but his brother Matthew had already got round that difficulty by having him incorporated at

* Not only was Shelford himself a Peterhouse man: the volume contained a prefatory poem by Crashaw, evidently written (see Kelliher, cited above, n. 56) just after his migration from Pembroke to Peterhouse; and the inclusion of an attack on it in the diatribe against Wren, *Newes from Ipswich* (1636), suggests that Wren, who had been Master of Peterhouse at the time, may have been responsible for its publication.

Cambridge. However, the Bishop of Ely had other instructions. He duly imposed upon the college the man who could be trusted to realize Laud's 'beauty of holiness' in its most extreme form: John Cosin.

Cosin, of course, was already well known in Cambridge. His part in the election of Buckingham as Chancellor, his controversial book of devotions, the attack on him in Parliament, his well publicized activities in Durham, had marked him out as a trouble-shooter even more extreme, and far more effective, than his old crony Richard Montagu. Joseph Mede of Christ's College was a learned and moderate Anglican, not hostile to Laud; but like Bishop Howson he was shocked by Cosin: 'a most audacious fellow', he exclaimed, 'and I doubt scarce a sound Protestant, and takes upon him most imprudently to bring superstitious innovations into our Church'.* That was on hearing of the 340 candles in Durham cathedral. Now the candles and the other superstitious innovations would come to Peterhouse.

As at Durham, Cosin's first care was to improve the furniture of his church, the formality and outward splendour of its services. The new chapel of the college was completed and decorated without and within. Subscriptions were solicited from old members, and the poet Richard Crashaw, who had moved from Pembroke College to be a Fellow of Peterhouse, wrote two Latin poems which were transcribed and circulated to stimulate the flow.[56] When the chapel was complete, its pavement of polished marble, its stained-glass windows, its carved and sculptured statuary, its coffered ceiling painted sky-blue with a golden sun in each compartment,† and, above all, the rich furniture of the altar, draped in parti-coloured silk, with painted hangings, gilt candlesticks and 'an incense-pot' standing permanently upon it, made it 'the gaze of the university'. Undergraduates from other colleges, it was said, resorted to it 'to learn or practise popery'. There they could see the Anglican service performed in the new style, in baroque elegance, with elaborate organ music and swinging censers. They could also hear sermons very shocking to good Protestant ears.

Like Laud himself, and like so many of Laud's chosen lieutenants,

---

* R. T. Williams (ed.), *Court and Times of Charles I* (1848) I, p. 335–6. Mede was a quiet man of eclectic views. He believed the Pope to be Antichrist, expounded the Apocalypse, and was a friend of Archbishop Ussher and Samuel Hartlib. On the other hand he was a protégé of Andrewes, had Laudian views on the altar and his closest friend was his colleague at Christ's, William Chappell, the 'Arminian' whom Laud chose to be Provost of Trinity College, Dublin (see below p. 142); and Laud made him one of his chaplains. He afterwards became friendly with Cosin, whose interest in music he shared (see his letter in *CJC* I, p. 220).

† I regret to state that the blue and gold ceiling has since been painted over and is now a dull chocolate brown.

Cosin was something of a martinet. While Crashaw, as a religious voluptuary, revelled in the furnishings of the new chapel, Cosin declared the rules.[57] They were clear and strict. All members of the college must attend the services. Latecomers will be deemed to be absent. Entry into the chapel must be decorous. No dirty shoes or ragged gowns will be tolerated. Surplices are to be clean and white, made to measure: reaching to the heels, and billowing out in a circle.[58] When they have been put on, every man must check that his neighbour's surplice is correct. There must be no sneezing or blowing of noses in chapel, no scratching of the head, no yawning. There was to be exact, almost mechanical discipline. This was far more than Laud ever required: his 'beauty of holiness' was simpler, more austere – and more defensible.

As Cosin's Durham had set the pace for other dioceses, so Cosin's Peterhouse set the pace for the other colleges in Cambridge. Some of them strove hard to keep up with it: Laney's Pembroke, Beale's St John's, Queens' under Martin, Jesus under Sterne. Those were the colleges on which Laudian heads had been imposed. But they were a minority. How were the obstinately puritan or merely apathetic colleges to be made to conform: Emmanuel, a notorious puritan seminary now ruled by the Church-Puritan Dr Holdsworth; Corpus Christi, where Dr Love had not lived up to expectations; Sidney Sussex under the moping pluralist Dr Ward? None of these colleges even had consecrated chapels, far less copes and organs, painted statues and choral polyphony. To rectify these abuses, to bring all the Cambridge colleges up to the high standard set by Peterhouse, Laud decided that he must intervene personally, and with power. He would carry out a metropolitan visitation of the University – indeed of both universities, but Oxford being already under his thumb it was Cambridge that was most in his eye.

The universities formally protested. They claimed that they were not subject to the jurisdiction of the Archbishop – only to that of the Crown. But Laud, this time, would not be content with a royal mandate. The universities, to him, were essentially the seminaries of the Church and must not escape his authority. And he was confident of asserting it. Little did the Cambridge Heads know, when they gathered under the chairmanship of the Vice-Chancellor to concert plans of resistance, that the Vice-Chancellor himself was secretly reporting to the Archbishop every detail of their intended defence, so that it might be overcome. The Vice-Chancellor was Dr Beale. Like Dr Wren in the affair of Dorislaus, he was very anxious that his communication with

Laud should not be known, 'as though I laboured to betray the university or upon any occasion were ready to pass by our Chancellor': which, of course, was exactly what he was doing. So well was the secret kept that every historian of his college has defended Beale against the charge of excessive Laudian zeal or time-serving by citing his vigorous public opposition to the visitation which in fact, as we now know, he was secretly promoting. Such a visitation, he assured Laud, was necessary to redress 'our poor . . . and disordered state', but he admitted that the idea was 'so unwelcome to divers amongst us that they labour by all means (under cover of our privileges) to avoid and divert it'. So hard did they labour that on one occasion Beale, in a defeatist mood, advised the Archbishop to gain his ends by conceding the means: to be content to visit the University as a royal commissioner.[59]

Laud would have no such compromise. 'I desire to have my own power', he said; and in December 1635 he sent to the university Heads a stern letter complaining of their procrastination. His patience, he said, had run out: 'If you think by these delays, to make me forget or forgo the business, you will find yourselves much deceived'. So he stood his ground, and in June 1636 the case was finally argued before the King at Hampton Court. There the Archbishop's claim was established. It was soon after this success that he celebrated his triumph in Oxford. A few days after that, he received from Cosin a detailed list of the abuses to be remedied in Cambridge: the unconsecrated chapels, the slovenly services, the profanation of the university church at Commencement, the general indifference to ceremony, the ragged singing of the choristers, the wayward apparel and 'long frizzled hair' of the undergraduates.[60]

In fact Laud never carried out his visitation of Cambridge. More urgent problems intervened and in 1639, in his report to the King, he regretted the still unreformed condition of many colleges there. All could easily have been put right, he said, if he had been able to visit the University as he had intended; but alas, that had proved impossible. So the reform of the University had been left to his agents there, the Laudian Heads of Colleges. These, however, though powerful in their own colleges, provoked resistance from their colleagues in the ruling oligarchy and so could not control the machinery of government. It was all very well when Dr Beale was Vice-Chancellor, but the Vice-Chancellor was elected annually and could not always be relied upon. It was unfortunate that Dr Beale had been succeeded, in the middle of the negotiations about the Visitation, by Dr Smyth, the Master of Magdalene, a stickler for the rights of the University. That had perhaps accounted for the quickening of the Archbishop's always short temper. It was even more unfortunate – and perhaps a sign of the growing opposition – that the high Calvinist Master of St Catharine's, Dr Brownrigg, was elected in 1637, and re-elected in 1638. However, in 1639 the tables were turned. Thanks (it was said) to some sharp practice by Dr Beale,[61] the prize fell to Dr Cosin; and so the model which had been displayed in Durham and in Peterhouse could be pressed authoritatively, not indeed upon the other colleges, but on the institutions and members of the University.

Cosin's vice-chancellorship was, in effect, the substitute for Laud's visitation. It was Cosin who had drafted the programme for that visitation, listing the abuses to be reformed, and it was he who, in his own college, had offered the model of a reformed institution. Now, with feverish haste – for already the cracks in the edifice of royal government were visible – he set out to realize his own extreme version of the Laudian programme. Great St Mary's, the university church, was transformed: altar, screen, steps, pews, services. The parishioners were not pleased but their protests were ignored. Rules of behaviour, like those for Peterhouse chapel, were drawn up and enforced. Even Laud had not been as high-handed as this. Little St Mary's, of course, by now needed no reform: its patron was Peterhouse and Crashaw was its curate. Stern discipline was enforced: a member of the University who ridiculed another for bowing at the name of Jesus received five lashes and was forced to do public penance. On the other hand when a Fellow of Peterhouse – William Norwich, a particular protégé of Cosin – was charged before the Heads for having preached an aggressive sermon in favour of penance, auricular confession, the sign of the cross, etc., and for deriding those who opposed such things, Cosin arbitrarily changed the procedure, overbore and overruled the Heads. He was also accused of covering up the offence of another Fellow of Peterhouse, Richard Nichols, who had offered to procure a fellowship at Peterhouse for an undergraduate of St Catharine's if he would become a Roman Catholic (as Nichols himself would do). On all sides the Vice-Chancellor was accused of despotism. He ceased to consult with the other Heads, as was customary; he gave orders on his sole authority, and with such confidence that they were automatically obeyed; and his orders were always in support, or protection, of the 'Arminian' party.[62]

In all this, Cosin could depend on one firm ally in the University, Dr Beale of St John's. Beale, it was said, was 'the sole encourager of Dr Cosin in his vice-chancellorship to tyrannise in that jesuitical, popish and Canterburian religion'. There was indeed an unfortunate moment in May 1640, when Parliament – the Short Parliament, called perforce to deal with the Scottish troubles – summoned Dr Beale from Cambridge to answer for a heretical and scandalous sermon. This was a terrible affront to his dignity and (as he complained to Cosin) weakened him in his government of his college, which, by now, was 'the orderliest body, for so great a one' (thus he tactfully excluded Cosin's Peterhouse) 'in the university'.[63] However, two days before his attendance was required, the Parliament was dissolved, having proved, as Laud put it, 'peevish'; so the summons lapsed. After the dissolution of Parliament, the Convocation of Canterbury continued to sit and voted a series of canons imposing upon the clergy, among other things, the notorious 'etcetera' oath – an oath of obedience to the government of the Church by 'archbishops, bishops, deans, archdeacons, etc.' The continued session of the Convocation, and therefore the canons which it had approved, were technically illegal; but Cosin was not deterred: he exacted the oath imperiously from all members of the University.

At the same time Cosin sought to emulate Laud as a builder. A great bibliophile himself – he had been Overall's librarian and would create or enrich libraries in Peterhouse and Durham – he decided to fulfil the frustrated plan of the Duke of Buckingham and create a new university library. He actually designed the building. He also hoped to create a new 'Commencement House' – a building for university ceremonies, in order to free the university church, in which they had hitherto taken place, from their profane accompaniments. This was a demand which the Laudians were making at Oxford too. After the Restoration, these projects would be revived. At Oxford, the Sheldonian theatre would be built. At Cambridge, Cosin would renew his plans for a university library. But by then his driving spirit was no longer on the spot; he had returned to the bishopric of Durham, and Cambridge would be without either a new library or a new Commencement House for another century.[64]

For in November 1640, the very month in which Cosin's vice-chancellorship ended, the national counter-attack began. At the beginning of the year Laudianism seemed to have triumphed in both universities. The danger-signs were visible, but the academic clergy, insulated in their comfortable colleges and no less comfortable illusions, continued to behave as if the future was theirs. Even on 5 November 1640, two days after the meeting of the Long Parliament, Joseph Beaumont, Fellow of Peterhouse – a creature of Dr Wren – preaching the regular Gunpowder Plot sermon in the university church at Cambridge, declared that the Scots – 'our brethren of Scotland' as the grateful Parliament called them – were 'more wicked than the Powder traitors': less cunning perhaps, but more impudent and more openly criminal.[65] Six weeks later Laud was formally impeached of high treason. Strafford, by then, was already in the Tower. The day of reckoning had come.

Once they had secured the initiative, the leaders of Parliament set out systematically to undo the whole work of Strafford and Laud. The machinery of their rule was dismantled in the Church as in the State, and war was declared on their whole ideology. That entailed an attack on its source in the universities. Laud, in the Tower, resigned the chancellorship of Oxford. His defeated rival, the Earl of Pembroke, replaced him. Afterwards, when civil war had broken out, and the royal court was established at Oxford, the 'reformation' of the University was halted, or at least postponed; so Laudianism was preserved, or respited, there. But at Cambridge it was doomed. The shocking goings-on in the chapel of Peterhouse were exposed. The right of the Bishop of Ely to nominate heads of colleges was ended. The Bishop himself – now the formidable Dr Wren – was impeached, and, though never tried, would spend seventeen years in the Tower. Dr Smart emerged from prison to claim his revenge. Dr Cosin, declared unfit to hold office in either university or promotion in the Church, would flee first to Durham, then abroad. The other Laudian heads would fare no better. Drs Beale, Sterne, Martin would be seized and imprisoned, Dr Laney ejected. Meanwhile, in their college chapels, exposed to the force of the Parliamentary army, 'Arminianism' would be smashed: literally smashed.

Whenever the Parliament, in its struggle with the King, was defeated or frustrated, it showed its resolution by permitting or encouraging acts of ideological violence. 1643 was a bad year for the Parliament, and in order to show that its spirit was unbroken, that it would never compromise with Laudianism, it authorized a campaign against 'images'. So Cheapside Cross, which had defied many a puritan attack, was at last pulled down, Westminster Abbey and King Henry VII's chapel echoed to the noise of destruction, and at the end of the year, under the authority of the Earl of Manchester, commander of the armies of the Eastern Association, William Dowsing, image-breaker general to those armies, arrived in Cambridge. He had been sent to the University to purge its churches and chapels of Laudian superstition. He began with the most notorious college, Peterhouse. There, he recorded, 'we pulled down two mighty great angels with wings, and divers other angels, and the four evangelists, and Peter with his keys over the chapel door, and about a hundred other cherubims and angels, and divers superstitious letters in gold'.[66] Then his party crossed the road to the next most notorious college, Pembroke. There, after a sharp theological dispute and a brisk exchange of scriptural texts, he accused the Fellows of being 'of Cosin's judgment' and clinched the matter by breaking ten cherubim and pulling down eighty superstitious pictures. So they went on from college to college, and the screech of saws and the thud of hammers and crash of glass was heard as statues and organs and stained-glass fell fragmented to the ground. So ended the Laudian 'beauty of holiness' in Cambridge. A few months later the obstinate Fellows were purged. In Peterhouse all but one were found contumacious and expelled. Just over two years later, Oxford, the last redoubt of royalism, would be taken, and the purge of the universities would be completed.

6   The new synthesis

So ended the attempt to Arminianize the Anglican Church from above. The totality of its collapse has a certain tragic irony. In the reign of James I the episcopal Church of England had been admired in Europe as the model, and the nucleus, of a restored Erasmian ecumenical Church. All that was needed, it was thought, was that the Arminians should direct it. In the 1630s they did direct it – to disaster. By 1647 it had ceased to exist, even at home. Overthrown in Scotland by nationalist Calvinism, driven out of Ireland by revolutionary Catholicism, it had been formally abolished in England by the victorious Parliament. The Archbishop of Canterbury had been publicly executed. The bishops had been driven from their dioceses. Their lands had been put up for sale. The Parliament had not yet decided how to deal with the monarchy. It had no thought of ending the monarchy. It had not yet decided how to remodel the Church. These things were still negotiable. But one thing was not negotiable. All the opponents of Charles I (and some of his supporters) were determined that Laudianism should never return. It must be abolished, irreversibly, before any settlement could be made.

For the Laudians had not only destroyed themselves: they had undermined the whole constitution of the English Church as it had been established at the accession of Elizabeth. Having captured that establishment in 1628, they had shown how easily it could be manipulated, and, in doing so, had fatally weakened it. In 1641 the leaders of Parliament sought to restore, in the Church as in the State, the Elizabethan consensus which they had known, and the Laudian bishops, in self-defence, cowered behind the shields of the 'moderate' 'high Calvinist' clergy whom, for twelve years, they had insulted. Ussher and Williams, Morton and Davenant, Prideaux and Brownrigg, were suddenly brought forward and urged to man the crumbling battlements of episcopacy. Williams, whom Laud had caused to be imprisoned in the Tower, came out to be made Archbishop of York. Prideaux and Brownrigg were made bishops. But it was too late. Those weak ramparts could no longer be defended, and the Jacobean high Calvinists joined the Caroline high Anglicans in a common rout. In the winter of 1641, for protesting against the violence which kept them out of the House of Lords, Williams and eleven other bishops, old and new, joined Laud in the Tower. Laud's chaplain assures us that there was nothing but 'messages of love and consolation' and 'mutual civilities' between them. This is hard to believe.

The sudden and complete collapse of the Laudian system, the unmistakable evidence of the detestation which it had incurred, inevitably raises a number of questions. How was it that a movement which had begun with so fair a prospect, which had seemed so reasonable, and whose leaders had been so generally admired, had, in so short a time, roused such violent and apparently unanimous opposition? Was it, indeed, still the same movement: were Laud, Wren and Cosin in fact 'Arminians' in the same sense as Arminius and Grotius, Overall and Andrewes, or did the same name conceal a different substance? Was it in fact their religious views and practices that provoked the revolution, or did they merely provide the convenient ideological slogan for a revolution that was already brewing and would have broken out anyway? Was the defeat of the movement necessary, inherent in a foredoomed enterprise of lunacy or folly? Or was it a historical tragedy, caused by unpredictable events and human error?

The defenders of Laud and his party, from that day to this, have argued, as he himself did, that he was not an innovator at all, or, in the strict sense of the word, an Arminian: that his theology and his concept of the Church were clearly implied, or at least allowed, long before Arminius, in the formularies of the Elizabethan settlement, and that he merely sought, while keeping within those bounds, to redress the balance: a balance which puritan bigots had disturbed by demanding explicit acceptance of such novel doctrines as 'double predestination' and a historical scheme in which the Pope was Antichrist. So far (they say) was Laud from being a partisan that he actually discouraged controversy: he held that the necessary doctrine of the Church had been set out clearly in its articles, which he caused to be republished, but that these articles allowed a latitude of belief in certain matters which, being unknowable, should not be made matter of acrimonious dispute. As for his 'beauty of holiness', this, we are told, was merely a desire to restore dignity and reverence to divine service. Ceremonies, in themselves, were things indifferent. Many of the ceremonial improvements charged as 'idolatry' against Laud were proved, at his trial, not to have been initiated by him. Some, like the ceremony for the consecration of churches, had been devised by Andrewes, and never then disliked: it had been admitted by the anti-Laudian Prideaux, who had the chapel of Exeter College, Oxford, consecrated by the Laudian Bishop Howson.[67] Others had been introduced by non-Laudian or even anti-Laudian clergy, like Bishop Williams, a great advocate of splendour and decorum in church services. The millenarian Dr Mede, who was so shocked by the un-Protestant ceremonialism of Cosin at Durham, was 'as zealous as his Lord of Canterbury, or rather more' in the practice of bowing to the altar, etc.[68]

With such support it was easy for the Laudians to defend themselves. Bishop Wren's defence, when impeached, was so unanswerable that the parliamentary committee which drew up the charges, having seen it, decided not to go on with the impeachment but to leave him, untried, in the Tower. Even the firebrand Montagu, whose promotion was listed as one of Laud's crimes, was really, behind his vigorous controversial language, a man of moderate views, nowhere inconsistent with the articles of the Anglican Church. As S. R. Gardiner wrote of his most controversial work, 'as far as the matter of the volume is concerned, an impartial judgment will probably consider it as a temperate exposition of the reasons which were leading an increasing number of scholars to reject the doctrines of Rome and Geneva alike'.[69]

Why then, we naturally ask, did this modest religious programme, this orderly return to the *via media* of the Elizabethan settlement, rouse such violent opposition throughout the country, provoking the emotive cry of popery and causing a Parliament of educated English gentlemen to bay for blood? On the face of it, this is a paradox, requiring explanation. Is it, perhaps, because the opponents of Laudianism were the victims of unscrupulous propaganda? Or was the hostility aroused not by the doctrines themselves but either by the implications which they entailed or by the policies to which they gave support?

That the opposition to Laudianism was inflamed by propaganda can hardly be doubted. All through the seventeenth century, political activists – the 'Puritans' of the 1630s and 1640s, the whigs of the 1670s and 1680s – were unscrupulous propagandists. From the reign of Elizabeth onwards an ocean of prejudice had been created, which skilful operators, conjuring with the word 'popery', could rouse into a fearful tempest. If we examine the opposition to Laudianism in the country, we soon realize that such operators were at work: that what seems at first a massive public protest was often merely the organized repetition and multiplication of a few voices. The loudest and most insistent of these voices was that of William Prynne. The outcry against Cosin in 1627 and again in 1641 was almost entirely based on the publicity articulated by him. The fury directed against Wren fed almost exclusively on accounts of his two years as Bishop of Norwich, and these accounts seem to rest largely on the reports of one Samuel Ward, preacher of Ipswich. Ward had supplied the material for the parliamentary attack on Montagu in 1625–7; in 1636 his material was organized and amplified by Prynne and Burton. It was Prynne and Burton who launched the attack on Laud in 1636–7 and Prynne who orchestrated the whole propaganda campaign against him from 1640 until his execution. Launched by the violent publications of Prynne and Burton, abetted after 1638 by the Scottish publicists Robert Baillie and his friends, the propaganda against Laudianism echoed through the counties, ensuring that the gentry who gathered in the Parliaments of 1640 were ready to believe and repeat the worst. A good case can therefore be made for the thesis that the destruction of the Laudian Church was a triumph of organized propaganda.

However, though puritan propagandists inflamed and concentrated the opposition to Laud, it is difficult to believe that they created it. The English laity were not as docile and mindless as that. Therefore we must look further, at the religious and political implications of those doctrines which, to us, seem so innocent and which were defended at the time – truthfully, but in vain – as permissible within the definitions of the Elizabethan settlement.

What were those doctrines? The essence of 'Arminianism' was that God's grace was universal, that Christ died for all men, and that all men, therefore, were capable of salvation: by the exercise of their free will, they could benefit by that freely offered grace. In general, this is a doctrine acceptable to an established Church which is content with conformity. On the other hand a sect, or an infant Church struggling to establish itself, or even a precariously established Church which feels itself surrounded by enemies, requires a less benevolent faith and a more revolutionary spirit; and this, ever since St Augustine mobilized

Roman Christianity against the paganism of African peasants and Hellenist philosophers, has been supplied by distinguishing an élite, predestined to salvation, from a *Lumpenproletariat* of incorrigible sinners foredoomed to destruction. In the early sixteenth century this was the issue which divided the Catholic reformer Erasmus from the radical Luther. In the later sixteenth century the same polarization was renewed within the Protestant world. Where a Protestant society was fighting to establish or preserve itself, it fortified itself for the struggle with the doctrine of Predestination. When that struggle could be relaxed, the more humane doctrine of universal grace broke through.

These opposing doctrines had their distinguishing symbols. Calvinism was a doctrine of conviction. The Calvinist had to convince himself that he was of the élite and to know the exacting rules by which his membership could be tested: he required that Scripture be expounded in this sense, and shown to be applicable to his case. In the Calvinist church, therefore, the essential furniture was the pulpit from which this general doctrine was rehearsed and applied to the particular circumstances of the congregation. To the believer in universal grace this intellectual exercise was less necessary. Salvation, for him, came through membership of a club which was open to all; and that membership was confirmed not by exposition of the distinguishing rules but by participation in mysterious rites. To him, therefore, the most important feature in the church was the altar where those rites were enacted. For these reasons the pulpit and the altar acquired great symbolic importance. To the Arminian, as to the Catholic, the pulpit was a utilitarian feature, secondary to the altar, which was invested with an aura of mystery. To the Calvinist, the order was reversed: the function of the Church was preaching: the altar was the utilitarian feature – often a mere table, brought into the body of the church for the occasion.

For this reason, to claim, as Laud did, that in dignifying and embellishing the altar, in requiring the movable communion table to be fixed 'altar-wise' in the chancel and railed off from profane contact, and in insisting that men should bow before it, he was merely seeking to restore elementary decency to the Church, is somewhat misleading. That, of course, was his defence when he was on trial for his life before a revolutionary tribunal; but in the days of his power he made no such excuse. As he once put it, when William Prynne was in the dock before him, 'the altar is the greatest place of God's residence on earth, greater than the pulpit, for there 'tis *hoc est corpus meum*, this is my body, but in the other it is at most *hoc est verbum meum*, this is my word'.[70] Prynne would remember this when the tables were turned and accuse Laud of preaching transubstantiation: a charge which Laud deflected by quoting Calvin.[71] However it is interpreted, the phrase entails a clear indication of priority: the mystery of the sacrament is more important than the preaching of the word.

In these circumstances it is easy to see how Laud and the Laudians could be accused of seeking to lead England back to popery, how Arminianism itself could be represented as a mere stage on that journey. We know that in fact they had no such intention. Again and again they protested their anti-papal virtue. Had not all of them – Andrewes, Neile, Buckeridge, Howson, Laud, Montagu, Cosin – written against popery and only against popery? 'Never any bishop was so hated by the Church of Rome as I am', Laud would tell the House of Lords, 'I have stayed more going to Rome, and reduced more that were already gone, than I believe any bishop or divine in this kingdom hath done'; and he listed the names of those whom he had thus recovered. But they protested in vain to those who did not wish to hear and who, perhaps genuinely, could see no stability in the central Erasmian position.

That was one weakness of Arminianism. But there was another which, though less obvious – for it had no such visible symbolism – could also be exploited against it. This was its solvent rationalism, even scepticism: a rationalism which also derived ultimately from Erasmus and which laid it open to the most damaging charge brought against the heirs of Erasmus: 'Socinianism'.

Technically, Socinianism was a dreadful heresy: disbelief in the doctrine of the Trinity. No one could accuse the Laudians of that. Laud and Neile had actually been responsible for the burning of such a heretic – the last such victim in our history. Wren, in his long years in the Tower, would write ponderously against Socinianism. But in common parlance Socinianism was little else than the application of reason to Scripture. Since such application undermined not only the doctrine of the Trinity but also some other important truths, it was feared and condemned by Roman Catholics and Calvinists alike. The Roman Church had condemned it in Erasmus. Calvin himself had condemned it in the 'libertine' disciples of Erasmus who had denounced the burning of Servetus: Castellio, Curio, Acontius. Socinus merely gave a belated name to a particular form of Erasmianism, as Arminius too would do.

In the early seventeenth century these two forms of Erasmianism were reunited in Holland. Here again Grotius was a central figure: he began by attacking Socinianism, which then had its capital in Poland, but study of his enemy led him to discover a large area of agreement. Consequently, he found himself denounced alternately as a papist and a Socinian. James I's hostility to the Dutch Arminians was based largely on the smear of Socinianism. So, in the 1620s, when 'Arminianism' was made a charge against the new Laudian clergy, the added accusation of 'Socinianism' was not far behind. While Francis Rous was telling the House of Commons that an Arminian was the spawn of a papist and a creature of the King of Spain, another respectable member of Parliament, Sir Simonds D'Ewes, would describe Arminius as 'an arch-anabaptist, following the steps of Michael Servetus and Sebastian Castellio', and his Dutch disciples as 'that rabble of Jesuited Anabaptists'. D'Ewes himself was a bigoted Church-Puritan, who was continually gratified by the evidence that he was one of the Elect. He regarded the Pope and cardinals as 'saints' compared with Laud and Wren.[72] But the equation of Arminianism and Socinianism was made from the opposite side too. The conservative crypto-Catholic Bishop of Gloucester, Godfrey Goodman, accused Laud and his favoured bishops of Socinianism.[73] It was a charge to which Laud was very sensitive.

Wherein did the 'Socinianism' of the Laudians consist? The term is so elusive that it is difficult to be precise, but essentially it seems to have been applied to their emancipation from dogma. In the spirit of Erasmus, they rejected the old 'superstitions' of Rome; but in the same spirit they also rejected the new superstitions of Protestantism: not only the 'horrible decrees' of Predestination and reprobation but also the whole system of millenarian prophecy, which was the intellectual cement of established Elizabethan and Jacobean Protestantism. Though anti-papist, they did not believe the Pope to be Antichrist, and though royalist, they did not believe in the priestly authority of the Christian Prince.*

* The Laudians were cautious about Antichrist. Laud, at his trial, was accused of implicitly endorsing Shelford's view – which was also the official Catholic view – that Antichrist had not yet come. He replied that 'it was never held by me that the Pope is not Antichrist . . . No assertion in the homilies read this day proves the Pope to be Antichrist. There may be many Babylonian beasts Antichrist, but not yet the Pope'. Montagu maintained, at the York House conference, that Antichrist *could* be either the Pope or the Turk. This was a common and very useful escape-hatch. Sheldon is said to have been the first Anglican clergyman explicitly to deny that the Pope was Antichrist. Laud was equally cautious in disowning the ideas of Foxe, and the Christian Prince; but he disowned them nevertheless. In a private letter to Lord Scudamore (quoted in my *Archbishop Laud*, p. 451) he ascribed the death of Prince Henry to divine disapproval of Henry VIII ('you see his name is gone'); in 1637 he refused to license a reissue of Foxe's *Acts and Monuments* (Rushworth, *Historical Collections*, 1721, II, p. 450); at his trial he criticized Foxe and Jewel as 'two very worthy men in their time, yet everything which they say is not by and by the doctrine of the Church of England'; and in his final sermon he omitted to include Cranmer among the predecessors whom he admired (*WWL* IV, pp. 430–9).

In all these respects – in their rejection of 'double predestination', their belief in the universality of grace, their rationalism, their repudiation of prophetic history – the Laudians can fairly be described as Arminians. Laud himself might avoid the term, which had acquired such dangerous overtones; but his ideas, when he expressed them, declare his position. So do his associations: with Vossius and Grotius in the Netherlands, with Montagu, Cosin, Jackson, his own chaplain Heylyn in England. Altogether, if Arminianism means anything in their time, it is difficult to deny that Laud and his closest allies were Arminians.

However, that admission does not solve our problem, for Arminianism in itself could hardly justify the ferocity of the opposition to Laudianism. If the Laudians were Arminians, so had their predecessors, Andrewes and Overall, been; and no one had whipped up public opposition to them. Indeed, in their hour of trial, Laud and Wren would explicitly defend themselves against the charges of innovation, superstition, popery, etc., by appealing to the example of Andrewes and Overall, who were obviously regarded, even by their accusers, as unexceptionable, saintly men. Even in 1645, that relentless persecutor of bishops, John Milton, would publish a poem he had written, twenty years before, in praise of Andrewes. Moreover, by 1640, although the hostility of the gentry to Laudianism had greatly increased, their specific hatred of Arminianism, which had been so violent in 1629, seems actually to have diminished. It was hardly mentioned now in Parliament.

It is true, there were, even then, certain professional anti-Arminians. The Scotchman Robert Baillie was terrified of any doctrine that might undermine the pure Calvinism established in Scotland. William Prynne was a fanatical anti-Arminian – he had been at it since the 1620s – and since he wrote the first published account of Laud's trial, he naturally rode his old hobby-horse. But Prynne's account was a work of propaganda. The other two, more factual records of the trial – by Laud himself and by Samuel Browne, one of the members of Parliament who managed the prosecution – agree in showing that questions of doctrine in general and 'Arminianism' in particular were of minor importance. Laud was accused of having endeavoured to subvert the fundamental laws of the kingdom and to introduce arbitrary government; and the particular charges were not about altars, ceremonies, free will, but about misuse of power in Council and Star Chamber, exactions of money, denial of law, invasion of property, advising the Duke of Buckingham, opposing the summoning of Parliament, interfering in parliamentary elections, promoting clergy who preached against Parliament, licensing political books. In other words, it was not his theological doctrines which brought him to the scaffold, though these might conveniently be cited, but his political actions, and the support which the Church of England, under his command, gave to the 'tyranny' of Charles.

Thus we come back to the central tragedy of the Arminian movement in England: its association with, and ultimately its commitment to, a particular political system. This association was a historical fact, not the logical consequence of its doctrine. Doctrinally, the English movement was not distinct from the Dutch movement. Laud remained to the end in touch with the Dutch Arminians, and Grotius, to the end, described the Anglican Church of Laud as his ideal;* but historically the English movement ran a different course and became part of a different synthesis. First, by the circumstances of the English Reformation, it was enclosed within an episcopal, not a Presbyterian system. Then, by a historical development, it was associated not, as in the Netherlands, with an Erastian lay movement, but with the clerical reaction represented by Archbishop Bancroft. Finally, the Dutch Arminians rose and fell in alliance with a republican party, the English Arminians through the patronage of a resolute and ambitious King.

For this patronage they paid a heavy price: giving constant public support to royal policy. In 1625–8, when the parliamentary attack on them was most violent, they had been saved by the support of the Crown. Throughout the eleven years of their prosperity, they repaid that debt. They preached obedience. They exalted the royal prerogative. They denied the rights – even the right to exist – of Parliament.† They supported every act of the government: patents of monopoly, ship money, the war against the Scots. So the balance of indebtedness changed. In 1628–9 the King had been criticized for supporting Arminianism in the Church. In 1640–1 the Church was attacked not

---

* Grotius' admiration of the Anglican Church of Laud is apparent in his letters. 'Liturgia Anglicana', he wrote to his brother in April 1645, 'ab eruditis omnibus habita semper est optima'. At the end of his life he told his wife that he wished to die, and her to live, in the Anglican communion. He explained that the only reason why he did not himself attend the Anglican service in the house of Sir Richard Browne in Paris (as she did after his death) was that he regarded such attendance as incompatible with his official position as Swedish ambassador in Paris. See the *testimonia* printed by Jean Leclerc in his edition of Grotius' *De Veritate Religionis Christianae*.

† Laud drew up a paper to show that Parliament had no rightful place in the constitution and that 'the Great Charter had an obscure birth from usurpation, and was fostered and showed to the world by rebellion' (*WWL* VII, p. 627) – a phrase lifted from Sir Walter Ralegh's dialogue *The Prerogative of Parliament*, where it is put in the mouth of a privy councillor in order to be refuted. Beale was accused of preaching in the university church at Cambridge that the King could legislate without Parliament. (*Articles exhibited in the Parliament against William Beale D. D.*, 1641.)

for its doctrine but for its subservience to the despotic aspirations of the Crown.

It has become fashionable to say that it was religion that caused the civil war: that by declaring frontal war on the doctriness which had become the intellectual cement of the previous consensus, the Laudians precipitated a general revolt in which the 'real' Church of England, the Elizabethan and Jacobean Church, was destroyed. But this view begs certain large questions. For it was not only religion which was challenged in 1640: it was also royal power and policy. Can we be sure that there would have been no revolt if Charles I had not given ecclesiastical power to Laud: if (for instance) he had based his authoritarian rule on 'high Calvinism' as the Princes of Orange did in the Netherlands, as Charles I's elder brother, Prince Henry, if he had lived, might have done? And was it really Laud who destroyed the old consensus? Can we say with confidence that that consensus would have lasted any longer if he had never existed? In 1641 its weakness would be exposed and in 1660 it would not be restored: Laudianism, chastened by experience, would then be found to have more staying power. Finally, the collapse of Laudianism in 1640 did not resolve the differences between Charles I and his Parliament. Clearly the problem had many ingredients: perhaps it is rash to place the burden of explanation on only one.

It is better, I suggest, to see Laudianism not in isolation, as a theological system, but as one element in a synthesis: the new political and ideological synthesis which was being evolved, at that time, and not only in England, under the pressure of events in Europe. For those were years in which an old synthesis was breaking down and a new being formed. Princely power was being extended on the basis of religious uniformity: a religious uniformity which no longer depended, as in the sixteenth century, on the personality of the prince but was organically inseparable from the structure and life of the State. 1629, the year of Charles I's breach with his Parliament, was the year of the Edict of Restitution in the Empire, whereby the Catholic Church in Germany, thanks to the victories of Tilly, Spinola and Wallenstein, recovered lands and jurisdictions that it had lost. It was also the year in which Richelieu destroyed the immunities of the Huguenots in France. Charles I was not to be left behind in this process, and the religious movement of Arminianism, which originally had been committed to no political system, but was now, in England, both clerical and monarchical, came conveniently to his aid. Its rationalism, its freedom from millenarian ideology, with its barely contained revolutionary content, appealed to the new age, its 'beauty of holiness' to the sensibility of the royal aesthete. A silent concordat was possible between altar and throne, between a Church that was dignified, civilized, rational, and a monarchy that was legal, authoritarian, modern. Was not this what Richelieu was creating in France: Richelieu who, having defeated the Huguenot grandees, would seek to create, out of national Catholics and converted Huguenots, a united French Church, neither papist nor Protestant but Gallican?

Laud's 'Gallican' aims were noted by contemporaries. Sir Thomas Roe saw him as the Richelieu of England. He was accused of seeking to set up a 'patriarchate' of England, a Catholic system without the Pope. Perhaps the most interesting evidence of his own views is provided by a little incident in 1639. For it cannot have been without a reason that, in that year, he presented, both to the university library and to his own college library at Oxford, magnificently bound copies of a huge two-volume compilation recently published in France on the liberties of the Gallican Church. This work – an arsenal of documentary weapons against the claims and usurpations of the Roman Church in France – had no sooner been published than it was denounced in a circular letter organized by the papal nuncio, signed by the cardinals, archbishops and bishops then in Paris, and addressed to all the bishops in France, warning them that, under a deceptively smooth title, it was a poisonous and deadly weed, planted by the Devil in order to spread schism and heresy, and that it must be utterly cast out. The result was that, in spite of its gigantic bulk, it was eagerly snapped up and all copies were sold within three months.* How two sets came to Laud we do not know, but both were inscribed as his personal copies before being passed on by him to the Oxford libraries, with a warm commendation as being 'most fit to be preserved in the libraries of the Reformed Churches'.[74]

It is unlikely that Laud had read the books. There is no evidence that he knew French. He had no love of France or things French. France to him was represented by Queen Henrietta Maria and her frivolous Catholic coterie at court which he hated and which undermined him: a

---

* The two volumes are entitled *Traitez des Droits et Libertez de l'Eglise Gallicane* and *Preuves des Libertez de l'Eglise Gallicane*. The Bodleian copies are MSS Laud misc. 303–4. I am grateful to Mr Keith Thomas for details of the St John's College copies. A second edition, published in 1651 during the revolt of the Fronde, contains the circular letter of the bishops in Paris and a defence by Dupuy. A third edition was published in 1731 during the contest between the Gallican Parlements and the Catholic clergy. On its connexion with Richelieu's project of a Gallican patriarchate see J. Orcibal, 'Le Patriarcat de Richelieu devant l'opinion', in *Les Origines du Jansénisme* III (Paris 1948), Appendix IV, pp. 108–46.

coterie which had now been dangerously reinforced by the arrival in England of her mother, Marie de Medicis, the former Queen Regent and patroness of the Catholic *dévots*. But this work came from another world. Though published anonymously, it was known to be by the distinguished scholars Pierre Dupuy and his brother Jean Dupuy. Pierre Dupuy had been secretary and librarian of Jacques-Auguste de Thou, the greatest historian in Europe, whose works, for having praised Erasmus and been too friendly to Huguenots, were now on the Index; he was now the centre of an influential scholarly salon in Paris which supported Richelieu's attempt to unite the Catholics and Protestants of France in opposition to the Papacy; and he was the closest Parisian friend of Grotius, now Swedish ambassador in Paris. It is clear that Richelieu's hand was behind the publication. In 1639 Laud's Anglican Church was beset with troubles; but evidently he saw a model for it in the Gallican ideal of Richelieu. If only the Scots – that alliance of malcontent nobles and their Calvinist clergy – could be defeated, as Richelieu had defeated the similar alliance of Huguenot nobles and their Calvinist clergy in France, then perhaps, like Richelieu, he could reconcile the subjects of Charles I to a similar unitary, independent Church, the ideological support of an authoritarian monarchy.

If only the Scots could be defeated . . . if only the summoning of Parliament could be postponed for a few more years . . . if only Charles I had managed affairs differently . . . perhaps then the new system would have been established. It is easy to say that this could not have happened, because it did not: that the personal monarchy of Charles I rested on frail foundations, and was bound to fail. But does not every successful movement pass through a vulnerable phase, before society invests in it and, by investing, gives it lasting strength? Perhaps, if Charles I had been firmer, or more skilful, or luckier, the dangerous moment would have passed. A new generation would then have accommodated itself to a system which seemed likely to last, and England, like France, would have accepted, with variations no doubt, a new synthesis of authoritarian episcopal Church, authoritarian monarchy, and revived, official Aristotelean (or Cartesian) 'reason'.

This is no doubt what Laud had hoped. He had committed his conception of the Church to a modern monarchical State, and once the synthesis was fixed, the elements could not be separated. So, in the moment of crisis, he saw that the only hope was to stand firm in defence of the whole system. Church and State must stand or fall together; and, with courage, they could still stand. But in the moment of crisis,

Charles I lost his nerve. He yielded to pressure, abandoned – at least temporarily – the work of eleven years, sent Strafford to the block. There was a bitter truth in the melancholy comment which Laud recorded in his diary after that last fatal surrender. Strafford's misfortune, he wrote, was that he served 'a mild and gracious prince, who knew not how to be, or to be made, great'.

The Lords and Commons of England saw it similarly. To them too it was all or nothing; and their leaders did not lose their nerve. They were prepared to face every consequence and pay every price rather than allow the firm establishment of the new synthesis. They were also prepared to use every method, fair or foul, in order to discredit the system, put pressure on the King, bring him back into the old Elizabethan consensus. They would encourage rebellion in Scotland. They would exploit rebellion in Ireland. But if they were to strike the political synthesis at its base, they must attack it in England itself. They must mobilize against it not merely the political classes, who had been so easily outmanoeuvred eleven years ago, but a popular force which, by the threat of violence – even, if necessary, of revolutionary violence – could compel an unwilling Charles I to disown and even destroy his 'evil counsellors', as their predecessors had forced the reluctant Queen Elizabeth to allow the execution of Mary Queen of Scots.

How were they to do this? The answer, now as then, was the same. They must appeal to another Elizabethan precedent – perhaps the most powerful, certainly the most lasting force which had been generated in that reign: the Great Fear of Popery. That fear had been fostered by the long struggle against Spain and the Counter-Reformation. It had been fed by the excommunication of the Queen, the claim of the Pope to depose her, and the plots to assassinate her. Since then it had been inflamed by controversy, propaganda and alarmist stories, by Gunpowder Plots and commemorative sermons, the secret intrigues of Spanish ambassadors and Jesuit missionaries. Now it had been reanimated by the ideological war abroad. Thus constantly renewed, it had acquired a momentum of its own. It was the English equivalent of the great European witch-craze, and it would remain formidable for three centuries, a national neurosis which could be awakened again and again: in the myth of the great Irish massacre of 1641 (still repeated, over a century later, by John Wesley),* in the great

---

* Wesley thought that there had never been anything comparable with the Irish massacre of 1641 'from the beginning of the world' and that God might well have a controversy with the Irish 'on this very account, to this day'. *The Journal of John Wesley* (Everyman edition) II, p. 31; cf. III, pp. 10, 232, 380.

scare of the Popish Plot of 1678, in the fable of the Warming Pan in 1688; even, though with dwindling force, in the Gordon Riots of 1780 and the 'Papal Aggression' of 1851.

At a high political level the charge that the Laudians were secret papists was known to be untrue. 'The great contrivers' of the opposition knew Laud personally, had dined with him often, were familiar with his views. They were not Puritans. Almost all of them were episcopalians. They patronized Anglican – sometimes 'Arminian' – chaplains and clergy, and caused the Prayer Book to be used in their private chapels. But in a desperate political struggle, a struggle to defeat a new despotism such as Richelieu had established after breaking the power of the Huguenot nobility in France, all was fair. The cat was let out of the bag by the great scholar and lawyer John Selden – a personal friend of Laud who, however, supported the Parliament. 'We charge the prelatical clergy with popery', he said, 'to make them odious, though we know they are guilty of no such thing'.[75]

Of course they were guilty of no such thing. Not a single Laudian bishop showed any leanings to Rome – for Godfrey Goodman, Bishop of Gloucester, was not a Laudian but an irremovable old Jacobean, thoroughly unsympathetic to Laud. Nevertheless the charge had just enough plausibility to sustain the myth, and no explanation of the collapse of the Laudian movement can be satisfactory unless we examine the charge. To do so, we must place it in its historical context, not only in England but in Europe of the Counter-Reformation.

7　'No popery!'

That the leaders of Parliament were determined, from the start, to raise the emotive cry of 'No popery!' against the Laudians is clear from the part assigned by them to William Prynne. Prynne was a paranoid anti-papist who saw popish and Jesuit conspiracies everywhere, and especially wherever he smelt 'Arminianism'.[76] He and his ally Henry Burton were well known as indefatigable and effective propagandists against the bishops, and they had particular reasons to hate Laud, who had repaid their savage libels with savage sentences. A fortnight after the first meeting of the Long Parliament, they were brought into action. The leaders of Parliament caused them to be fetched from their prisons in the Channel Islands and they made a triumphal entry into London. Branches of rosemary were strewn before them and they were followed by over a hundred coaches, a thousand horses, and a vast crowd on foot. Such a reception argues organization; and indeed it was the beginning of a concerted attack, supported by massive demonstrations, on the 'popish' bishops. It is unlikely that the aristocratic leaders of Parliament had any real sympathy with these rancorous libellers, but they found them useful, indeed essential, in the tense politics of the time.

In 1643, when they decided to put Laud on trial, the parliamentary leaders again turned to Prynne. It was Prynne whom they sent to the Tower to seize his papers, Prynne who selected the evidence to be used against him, Prynne who edited, falsified and published Laud's diary, and whose edition of it was distributed to all the sitting peers, his judges. This edition, and the spate of books which Prynne published at the same time, were all designed to discredit Laud as a papist. In one of his books Prynne claimed to have discovered a dangerous popish plot against the Crown.[77] This alleged plot, said to have been hatched abroad in 1639–40, had been reported to the government at the time and dismissed as fantasy. In 1643, having found the report among Laud's papers, Prynne 'revealed' it to the world and contrived to show that Laud had been one of the authors of a plot designed to assassinate, among others, himself. When Laud was tried, it was Prynne who coached the witnesses. After Laud's execution, it was Prynne who wrote the published account of the trial. The unpublished records show that the central charges were political, but it was the allegations of 'popery' that excited the public, and it was on them that Prynne concentrated and expatiated: indeed, having filled his first volume with them, he lost interest and never published his promised second volume on the other charges.

In fact, we can say that throughout the years 1640 to 1645 William Prynne played the same part that would be played, on a larger scale, a generation later, by Titus Oates. The personalities were very different but the function was the same. Oates too was used by educated 'whig' aristocrats who despised him but who believed that, in so important a political struggle, they could not afford to be squeamish. He too was used to rouse the unthinking mob, pervert justice and destroy their enemies. He too was allowed to parade in triumph as a national hero. And in his case too the cat would be let out of the bag by those who saw through the pretence. The remark of Selden which I have quoted would be echoed forty years later by that most cultivated and sceptical of noblemen, the Marquis of Halifax, who told Sir William Temple that whether the Popish Plot were real or not, it must be treated as real, and that 'unless he would concur in points so necessary to the people's satisfaction, he would brand him everywhere as a papist'. 'So necessary to the people's satisfaction' meant, of course, then as in 1640, so necessary in order to mobilize the people in the public cause.

This indeed was the essential function of anti-popery in England. From the Reformation to the Enlightenment, it was a slogan by which the ruling classes could organize and exploit social radicalism without danger to themselves. In the seventeenth century there was enough social radicalism to frighten those classes: the names of Wat Tyler and Jack Straw were regularly cited during the years of revolution. It is a sign of the determination of the political opponents of the Stuart monarchy that, rather than surrender to its claims, they were prepared to mobilize against it such potentially dangerous forces. How convenient that they could render those forces harmless to themselves by directing them against this stereotype of the national enemy! And how fortunate for them that the application of that stereotype was so plausible that often they were persuaded by it themselves; that sometimes even it was true!*

How plausible was it, or could it be made, in the case of Laudianism? We have seen that, in the strict sense, it was completely untrue: that all the Laudians were openly opposed to 'popery'. Nevertheless, a certain weakness in their case has to be admitted. They were adamant in their opposition to Roman claims of jurisdiction. They opposed certain Roman 'innovations': purgatory, celibacy, monasticism, Mariolatry, 'mechanical devotions'. But the heart of their doctrine, as we have seen, was Catholic. They recognized the central tradition of the Church. They allowed that the Church of Rome was a true Church, though corrupted. The implication was that reunion with Rome was theoretically possible, if Rome would repudiate the Council of Trent as the Church of England would repudiate the Synod of Dordt. Practically, Laud knew that this was impossible, and his aim was to build up an independent Church in alliance with a national monarchy. But theoretically his position was vulnerable. Its weakness was shown in a

---

* It is noticeable that, during the civil war, whenever the Parliament needed to rally its own forces or increase the pressure on the enemy, there were outbreaks of social violence; but these outbreaks were clearly limited – i.e. controlled. In the summer of 1642, when the Parliament was preparing for war, a series of violent agrarian revolts was reported to it by aggrieved landlords. But these landlords were almost always, like Lady Rivers and Lord Cottington, Roman Catholics. Parliamentary grandees like the Earls of Warwick, Pembroke and Northumberland had no trouble from their tenants. Iconoclasm – the destruction of 'popish images' – was another expression of the same tactics: the funeral monuments of royalist families were expendable; those of parliamentary families were spared.

passage of his diary which Prynne naturally seized upon with glee. Laud there recorded how, soon after his elevation to Canterbury, he had twice been approached by a secret emissary of Rome with the offer of a cardinal's hat. His reply, 'that something dwelt within me which would not suffer that till Rome were other than it is', was suppressed by Prynne; but even if he had published it, so conditional a refusal would hardly have satisfied those who saw the Papacy as the Beast of Revelation.[78]

To Laud, discussion of these matters was academic, even harmful. He could see the trouble which Grotius was causing himself through his love of argument. His concern was to build up the authority of his Church, to demand no more than outward conformity, and to discourage all public controversy. The spiritual content – the purified Anglo-Catholicism of Andrewes – could then quietly develop within the secure envelope of an established Church.

Such a policy, in such circumstances, obviously required great discretion. Laud was aware of this. Impatient and intemperate himself, he yet sought to impose discretion on his own clergy. That meant, especially, on the articulate academic clergy, with their busy pens. In Oxford, which he dominated, he had no trouble. Unfortunately there was also Cambridge. There 'Arminianism' had an independent origin; there he could exercise no direct control; and it was his supporters there whose activities formed the most damning evidence of 'popery' at his trial.

Laud's first attempt to impose discretion on his too enthusiastic Cambridge supporters was in 1630. It was in the case of Dr Samuel Brooke, the Master of Trinity College. Dr Brooke had spent fifteen years writing what Prynne would call an 'Arminian treatise' on Predestination, and was confident, as he assured Laud, that it would finally blow up that dreadful doctrine. Laud refused to authorize its publication. This greatly pained the Master, who protested that that doctrine was the root of Puritanism and that Puritanism was the root of all rebellion and disobedience in Parliament and all schism and sauciness in the country and the Church. But Laud remained inexorable. 'I am still where I was', he wrote, 'that something about these controversies is unmasterable in this life'. Thus the central issue in the great religious controversy of the time was left unsolved, in protective mystery.

Laud was able to silence Dr Brooke, as he had managed to silence that other once voluble Cambridge man, Dr Montagu. But when the enthusiasts of Arminianism, Wren, Beale and Cosin, had taken command in Cambridge, it was different. As in Durham, where Laud's old Oxford friend and patron Dr Howson could not control the new radicals from Cambridge, so in Cambridge itself we get the impression that Laud could not control his own most trusted lieutenants. He seems to have been alarmed by Wren's provocative methods, and hesitated to advance him to a bishopric.* By licensing the publication of Shelford's shocking *Discourses* – of which Laud knew nothing† – Beale showed that Laud's policy of restraint had been jettisoned. Then followed other excesses, almost all of them deriving, like Shelford's discourses, from Pembroke College or Peterhouse. In Great St Mary's, John Norming-ton of Pembroke[79] in 1636 and Sylvester Adams of Peterhouse in 1637 preached on the necessity of confession to a priest – and were saved from the inevitable trouble which followed by the influence of Cosin. In 1638, on the day of the Annunciation, Richard Crashaw, Fellow of Peterhouse, preaching in his college chapel, 'turned himself to a picture of the Virgin Mary' saying, 'hanc adoremus, colamus hanc'. Then there was Crashaw's friend Joseph Beaumont, Fellow of Peterhouse, who spoke much, in the same chapel, 'in commending legendary stories and fabulous tales of the virtue of the Cross'. Beaumont was a protégé of Wren, whose rich step-daughter he would marry: a timid creature of profound, not to say abject piety, and like Crashaw, a minor religious poet – Crashaw and water if such dilution can be conceived.‡ As for William Norwich, Fellow of Peterhouse, as late as August 1640, when the writing on the wall was visible to those who could see, he preached in favour of the whole Catholic repertoire: penance, auricular confes-sion, justification by works, the sign of the cross.[80] Norwich's teaching was too much for one at least of his pupils at Peterhouse. John Hutchinson, a young gentleman of Nottinghamshire, was a model undergraduate, who 'loved and reverenced' his tutor, was 'constant at

* 'Our Dean [i.e. Wren, then Dean of Windsor] would fain be any bishop', Montagu wrote to Cosin in November 1628 (*CJC* I, p. 154). In 1633, when Laud was appointed Archbishop, Wren was expected to succeed him in London; but Laud preferred Juxon, his own successor at St John's College, Oxford. Dr King suggests that Laud thought Wren too provocative – as he certainly proved in Norwich (Peter King, 'Matthew Wren, Bishop of Hereford, Norwich and Ely 1585–1667, Ph. D. thesis, Bristol 1969).

† At his trial, Laud said that he had never know Shelford or read his *Discourses*. He evidently supposed that Shelford was still alive: 'if he have said anything unjust or untrue, let him answer for himself'. Shelford, at that time, had been dead for seventeen years. (*WWL* IV, p. 227.)

‡ Certainly there is a great deal of water. Read (if you can) his poem *Psyche or Love's Mystery in XXIV cantos displaying the Intercourse betwixt Christ and the Soul*: an insipid work of nearly 40,000 lines, longer than *The Faerie Queene* or the *Iliad* and the *Odyssey* combined. For his character, see the devastating examination of it by his nineteenth-century editor A. B. Grosart.

their chapel' and delighted in the music there; but in the end rebelled: he would end as a colonel in the parliamentary army, an Independent, and a regicide.[81]

It was too much even for Laud too. At his trial, he would resent the charge that he was responsible for the goings-on at Peterhouse. Those, he said, were the work of Wren and Cosin: 'they are both living, why are they not called to answer their own acts?' He even suggested that he would have restrained such excesses if he could: 'this was not the least cause why I followed my right for power to visit there'.[82] Laud stood here on strong ground. There was a difference between the two universities. Nowhere in Oxford was there such insolent defiance of the Protestant tradition as in Peterhouse, Cambridge.

The devotional excesses of Cambridge extended beyond the University. In 1624 Nicholas Ferrar, a former pupil of Augustine Lindsell at Clare College, abandoning commerce and politics, set up his 'Protestant monastery' at Little Gidding, and soon afterwards George Herbert, public orator of the University, was drawn by him from politics to piety. The influence of Little Gidding spread in the University, particularly in Pembroke College and Peterhouse. The connexion was emphasized when Ferrar Collett was sent to Peterhouse to be the pupil of Crashaw. He was the brother of Mary Collett, who was Crashaw's 'spiritual mother' and presided over the community at Little Gidding. Nicholas Ferrar was presumably his godfather. When Crashaw left Peterhouse in 1643, he handed the care of Ferrar Collett over to his closest friend, Joseph Beaumont.

If the Laudian synthesis had been stabilized, no doubt the Cambridge *dévots* would have found a secure nest within that sturdy frame. But when that frame was roughly demolished, those weak spirits fluttered squawking to a more comfortable home. And where would they find such a home except in the welcoming bosom of the Roman Church? Laud might go unbowed to the block, to which his king would follow him, martyrs for their Church. Wren might sit out his seventeen years in the Tower. Cosin, in exile and poverty, might prefer Geneva to Rome: he would show his contempt for the converts, and disown his own son, who was one of them.* Beale, dying in Spain as chaplain to the royalist embassy of Edward Hyde, would arrange to be buried in secret, deep in lime, to be secure, even in death, from popish hands.[83] Laud's Master of Jesus, Edward Martin, would boldly defy the Parliament and

---

* See his letter to Richard Watson in *The Works of . . . John Cosin* (Oxford 1851) VI, pp. 387–9. He was particularly contemptuous of Crashaw: 'Of Mr Crashaw etc. I know too much.' He had known him, of course – and no doubt the 'etc.' too – at Peterhouse.

after years of prison and persecution, escape to France, firm Anglican to the last.[84] But these were men who had been toughened in the great controversies of the 1620s. The next generation lacked that strength. Having attached themselves to an apparently established cause, they easily slid out in the hour of defeat. The sons of Charles I did not imitate the constancy of their father, or the young Laudians that of their patrons. An ejected Fellow of Peterhouse who visited Rome in the 1640s found there four 'revolters' who had been young Fellows of the college with him in Cosin's time. Among them was Richard Crashaw, now one of the *'seguita* or followers' of Cardinal Pallotta.* Other Cambridge friends of Crashaw were there too. They came from Peterhouse, Pembroke and St John's College – the three most Laudian colleges in the University.[85]

In retrospect, therefore, it is possible to justify the puritan charge that Laudianism led to Rome – at least if one started from Cambridge. However, this would be unfair, because it presupposes the revolution, which no one foresaw. If the revolution had not happened, the defectors (it could be said) would not have defected and the charge, which depends on them, would be false: it was a political accident which made it retrospectively true. Once again, it was a repetition of what had happened in the Netherlands. There too, when the Arminians had been overthrown by a political coup, their leaders had fled abroad. They had taken refuge in Catholic Antwerp, under the protection of a Spanish court, and some of them had gone over to Rome. The greatest of them, Grotius, did not. Pressed by learned Flemish clergy, he stood his ground, and when the pressure became intolerable, moved on to Paris. There the *convertisseurs* again wearied him with their attentions, so that he contemplated flight to 'some corner' of Protestant Germany.[86] The King of Spain even hoped to gain him, by a pension, as an informer against the Dutch 'rebels':[87] an absurd hope. The parallel with the Anglican *émigrés* of the 1640s, struggling to maintain an apparently hopeless position in Catholic Bruges, Paris and Cologne, is sufficiently striking. In each case, it was political collapse, not inherent logic, which led some of them, but some only, to despair of their Church.

* John Bargrave, *Pope Alexander VII and the College of Cardinals*, ed. J. C. Robertson (Camden Society 1867), p. 37. Edward Chaney, *The Grand Tour and the Great Rebellion* (Geneva 1985), p. 387, names the other three revolting Fellows of Peterhouse as Francis Blakiston (a nephew of Cosin), Christopher Barker and Richard Nichols (on whom see above p. 87). Chaney (pp. 364–70) also gives an account of the brothers William and Thomas Knightley, who became 'zealous bigots' in Rome. They had been Fellow-commoners of Peterhouse under Cosin.

However it was not only the admitted Catholic content of Arminianism, or the example of the Netherlands, that fostered suspicion among English Protestants. The evidence is not complete unless we place the Laudian movement in a wider European context. We must remember the new-found strength, and the new spirit of aggression, of the Counter-Reformation, and, in particular, its new tactics of persuasion and its successful exploitation of the idea of corporate reunion.

For the Arminian movement in England came at a time when the Roman Church had recovered its nerve and was regaining lost ground: a period of intense missionary work in Protestant Europe as in pagan Africa and America, Confucian China. In Rome, these activities, which were overseen, since 1622, by the new Congregation *de Propaganda Fide*, were directed through special agencies including colleges for the nations lost through schism: for the Greek East as well as for the Protestant West. The policy was applied in many forms and at several levels, but the greatest successes came through the conversion of prominent individuals. Promising intellectuals were wooed in universities, influential courtiers at royal courts. Young aristocrats with their tutors on the grand tour came to Rome and found themselves courted by urbane cardinals, entertained by the colleges of their nations, guided round the city by scholarly Catholic compatriots and interpreters. Benefices and cardinals' hats were discreetly dangled before powerful clergy. No price was too high to gain a reigning prince.

First the cult of individuals. What vast gains Rome had made by transforming the Huguenot Jacques Davy into the Cardinal du Perron, a convert who was to become the greatest of *convertisseurs* and bring in the King of France himself! To Henri IV, once captured, Rome was willing to grant what it had so fatally refused to Henry VIII of England, a politically convenient divorce. The success in France suggested that England too might be recovered, and discreet approaches had been made to King James I while still King of Scotland only. After the Gunpowder Plot and the King's polemical exchanges with Bellarmine and du Perron, that prospect vanished, but there was always hope of his successor, or of the royal favourite. In 1622 the Roman missionaries were besieging the Duke of Buckingham, and Laud himself was called in to save him. Buckingham remained unconverted, and that was the beginning of Laud's great influence with him, but the priests would make havoc among his kindred: nearly all the fashionable converts at court, in the next reign, were related to him. Having lost Buckingham, Rome relied on Queen Henrietta Maria, who succeeded him as the greatest personal influence on the new King. She had been carefully briefed for her part before leaving France, and would become the patroness of the Catholic missionaries who haunted the court of Charles I, stalking their prey.

The ultimate aim, of course, was the recovery of the lost national Churches. For such 'reunion', Rome was willing to offer, at first, special terms. So, in the fifteenth century, the chalice had been conceded to the laity of Bohemia: a concession which had by now been quietly withdrawn. Since the Reformation, the greatest success of this policy had been in the East. In 1598, at the Synod of Brest-Litovsk, the Greek Orthodox Church in Lithuania and Ruthenia had been won over to form the Uniate Church. Thereafter continuous pressure was applied to individual Patriarchs in the Ottoman Empire, and several of them induced to make personal submission to Rome;* after which their candidature for the metropolitan Patriarchate of Constantinople would be backed by the embassies of Catholic powers. By these means it was hoped – and in the 1630s it seemed likely – that the Eastern Schism would at last be ended and the whole Greek Church subjected to Rome.

It is against this background that we should see the secret offer to Laud, in 1633, of a cardinal's hat. Seen from England, this seems an odd, isolated, rather sinister incident: what other Protestant Archbishop of Canterbury has received so eccentric an offer? But seen from Rome it is part of a consistent policy. Why should not Laud be the Patriarch of a Uniate Church of England, perhaps of Great Britain: the first stage, perhaps, in the restoration of a more perfect union?

There was also the method, or the mirage, of reunion by mutual compromise. This has often been used by the Church of Rome.† Innocent idealists are encouraged to believe that an equal bargain between the Churches can be made: that concession will be matched by concession. Then, as the victim advances, the mirage dissolves, and he finds himself obliged, if he is not to die in the intermediate desert, to swallow whatever water he is given. The hard-liners at Rome – the Jesuits, in particular – disliked even these tactical concessions. Their policy was clear: soft soap was to lubricate the direct route to unconditional surrender. This would be discovered, in the end, by Grotius himself. By 1640 he was prepared to make many concessions for the sake of a general reunion. The final answer from Rome was clear: he must cut the cackle and submit to Rome; once converted, he would be allowed to resume his projects of reunion.[88]

* Thus even Cyril Lucaris, 'the Calvinist patriarch', signed such a submission in 1608.
† Most signally, in our century, in the famous case of the Malines Conversations in 1926.

This method was also used in England. For instance, there was the affair of Christopher Davenport. He had been converted to Catholicism while an undergraduate at Oxford, had then gone to Flanders and Spain, and now returned to England as a Franciscan friar, under the name of Franciscus a Sancta Clara, to be chaplain to Queen Henrietta Maria. In 1634 he wrote a book in favour of the reunion of the Churches. He maintained that the articles of the Church of England were acceptable to Catholics, and that a corporate union was therefore attainable. These views recommended him to some of the English Arminians, and Augustine Lindsell brought him to the notice of Laud. Davenport hoped that Laud would license his book for publication in England: no doubt Lindsell thought that it would reconcile Catholics to Anglicanism. But Laud was not deceived. Davenport, he believed, would never expound the Thirty-Nine Articles 'so as the Church of England would have cause to thank him for it'. So Davenport turned to Rome, and having somehow obtained a licence there, published his book in France, dedicated to Charles I.[89] However, the stalwarts of the Roman Church did not give in. The Jesuits demanded that the book be burnt; in Spain it was put on the Index; and in the end, after an internal struggle, it was banned in Rome, though very unobtrusively, to avoid giving offence to the King of England, of whom great hopes were entertained.[90]

Meanwhile another unofficial missionary had followed in Davenport's footsteps. He was John Jones, who, as an undergraduate at St John's College, Oxford, had shared rooms with Laud. Now, as the Benedictine monk Leander a Sancto Martino, he too thought that he could serve the cause of reunion. So he remembered 'the ancient friendship . . . between my Lord's Grace and me in our younger years', and wrote to Laud asking for leave to pay a private visit to England. Laud did not like the idea at all, but the pro-Catholic or crypto-Catholic party at court – in particular, Laud's former friend and protégé, the Secretary of State, Francis Windebank – saw to it that his request was granted, and he duly arrived in June 1634. 'Leander Jones', as he was called, was also outsmarted by the Jesuits and their allies at Rome and he achieved nothing. He died in England in 1635.[91]

The ostensible purpose of these Catholic emissaries, as of the more official agents who followed – Gregorio Panzani, George Con, Count Carlo Rossetti – was to appease the internecine quarrels of the English Roman Catholics and secure better conditions for them, but they used their opportunities to nose around for likely converts in high places and to report on the prospects of reunion. Leander Jones, in his report, explicitly compared the English Church to the Greek Church at the time of the Council of Florence in 1439, when such a union was formally achieved and the principal Greek bishop was made a Roman cardinal. That union had in fact been repudiated in Constantinople, but Rome still regarded it as legal and the recent creation of the Uniate Church in the East as the delayed and partial realization of it. The papal agents in England courted such Anglican bishops as would receive them and thought that they detected hopeful signs in their conversation. But except for Bishop Goodman, who was converted by Sancta Clara, none surrendered, and Laud refused to see any of them: he preferred to quarrel with the Queen rather than compromise the independence of his Church.

Thus if we look at the matter fairly, we can see that while the Laudian movement was vulnerable to the charge of popery (for it retained Catholic doctrines and traditions, its repudiation of Rome was conditional, not absolute, and it had a weak fringe made conspicuous by damaging desertions), nevertheless its leadership remained firm and self-confident. Even after the national Church had collapsed, the defections to Rome were relatively few, and most of them came from the one institution – Peterhouse, Cambridge – where Laudian practices had run riot. The charge that Laudianism led directly to Roman Catholicism was a charge of guilt by association, and the use of the Great Fear of a Popish Plot by its enemies was in essence the cynical exploitation of public credulity in order to destroy a political system which they believed – rightly – was hardening into political absolutism. For it was the real absolutism which it undoubtedly served, not the speculative popery to which it was alleged to lead, that was the determining cause of the attack on it. As one of the great contrivers, who in 1640 was most outspoken against Laud, would afterwards say, 'it was not for a service-book or for abolishing episcopacy that this war was made . . . it was indeed a war made to destroy the Parliament of England, that is, the government of England, in the very root and foundation thereof; and hereby it appears what it was we defended, and how just and necessary that defence was'.[92] The exploitation of the Great Fear of Popery was part – an essential part – of that just and necessary defence.

8 Conclusion

It is now possible to look at the Laudian experience as a whole and to offer some answer to the questions that it provokes.

First of all, we must distinguish between Arminianism and Laudianism. 'Arminianism' – a vague and loose term, as such terms are – was an intellectual movement which, in England, went back to the time of Erasmus and was carried forward without substantial change, through the Cambridge of Baro, Andrewes and Overall, to Wren and Cosin. Doctrinally it was a permitted option under the carefully ambiguous articles of Queen Elizabeth, and although it was disliked by those who preferred the equally permitted puritan and Calvinist options, it was never regarded either as illegal or as an innovation until the political context around it changed in the seventeenth century. Indeed, it can be said that it was the Puritans, not the Arminians, who were the innovators; but by 1620 their innovations had become quietly established so that they could claim that it was the revival of the older, more liberal tradition that was the 'innovation'.

What was really new in English 'Arminianism' was not the doctrine itself but the alliance of that doctrine, first, under Bancroft, with episcopalian clericalism, then, under Neile and Laud, with royal absolutism. This was Laudianism: Arminianism as part of the new Caroline synthesis of religion and politics which alarmed the political classes and drove them, ultimately, to revolt.

How did this synthesis come about? Not, certainly, through any inherent logic in the ideas. 'Arminianism' was tied to no form of government. In Holland it was republican. In England, under Andrewes and Overall, it was unpolitical. It was only under Charles I that it became monarchical; and the initiative, I suggest, came from the monarch himself.

Not that Charles I, from the start, envisaged such a synthesis: it merely emerged as a response to the pressures and challenges of the time. Charles I had a personal preference for order and authority. He had seen the collapse of his father's uncertain policy, the extremism and the failure of the Calvinist International, the expulsion of his sister from Bohemia and the Palatinate, the humiliations of the years of war. He had also seen the example of the great European monarchies. He did not aspire to 'tyranny' but to a restoration of strong, conciliar government under the law. He did not relish Roman Catholicism: his visit to Spain caused him to hate what he had seen of it there. His sense of order and decorum, his aestheticism, his whole concept of culture, led him naturally towards the Arminian clergy, and from the beginning he gave them his patronage. It was by royal authority that the Arminians achieved power in the Church, and it was in the royal chapels that the model was created which was then imposed throughout England and carried to Scotland.*

The 'Arminians' naturally seized their chance. Now at last they could stabilize the Church to their liking. Royal patronage was the key. Hitherto such patronage had been a whimsical affair. Bishoprics, headships of colleges, had fallen to those whose friends had pressed hardest at court. Now it could be used systematically, in the interest of the party. So the 'Arminians' were advanced – aggressively and defiantly in the turbulent period 1625–8, quietly and systematically thereafter. For this access to power they were happy to pay the price. While reserving the theoretical independence of the Church – for they would not always have a king like Charles I – they preached obedience, defended royal policy, royal taxes, denounced Scotch rebels, English Parliaments, 'moderate' clergy, undertook secular office, voted for secular punishments. Thus gradually, in practice, the synthesis became organic. It took root, threatened to grow stronger, to become the support of a new despotism. Thereby it aroused the fears of the parliamentary classes and united them against it.

How were those classes to secure themselves against that threat? The first necessity was to bring about a new Parliament. Without a Parliament they had no voice, no power. Even with a Parliament they had failed in 1628–9. If they were to succeed, they needed force: force to compel the Crown to call a Parliament, force to preserve that Parliament against dissolution. But where were they to find that force, and how could they apply it? Before 1636 there seemed no answer. But then came the great opportunity: the revolt of the Scots.

As in England, so in Scotland, the cause of the revolt was political: the royal assault on the power of the nobility. That assault had begun with the reign, with the Act of Revocation of 1625; but it was not till 1633, when the Anglican ceremonies first came into Scotland, that the nobility saw the means of effective resistance. From then on, they used the Presbyterian clergy as their tribunes to rouse the people against 'prelacy'. By 1637 the Scottish revolt had begun and the English parliamentary classes had both an example and an instrument of pressure. They could raise the cry of 'No popery' and bring in 'our brethren of Scotland' as their mercenaries, to coerce the King.

---

* Both Laud and Wren defended their ceremonialism as being based on that of the royal chapels, which, however, had been instituted by them, as Dean of the Chapel Royal and Dean of Windsor respectively; and which, in itself, being merely an expression of royal taste, had no legal authority in the country (HMC House of Lords MSS XI, p. 410; see C. Wren, *Parentalia* (1750), pp. 79, 81–2).

It was very convenient because the issue could be presented in impeccably royalist terms. In attacking the Laudian Church, the 'great contrivers' could present themselves as seeking to free the power of the Crown from an arrogant usurpation. In fact, of course, this was tactical hypocrisy, for the Crown, throughout, had been the driving force. Laud had submitted the reports of his bishops to the King and it was the King who, by marginal annotations, had given the final orders for the silencing or deprivation of ministers. It was the King, not Laud, who had insisted on imposing the Liturgy on Scotland – Laud was more cautious than the Scottish bishops whose orders came from the Crown. In Oxford, Laud refused to deprive any academic without a royal order. It was the King who, against the advice of Laud, had insisted that Convocation should continue to sit after he had dismissed the Short Parliament. The King would afterwards admit this; in an attempt to save Laud's life he certified that all the orders had come from himself. But the parliamentary leaders were not concerned with such niceties. Their purpose was to break up the synthesis and they could do this best by pretending, as loyal subjects, that the Laudian Church was denying the supremacy and usurping the rights of the Crown. So Cosin would be accused of denying the royal supremacy, Prynne would write on the *Antipathy of English Lordly Prelacy both to Regal Monarchy and Civil Unity*, and Milton would begin his career as a pamphleteer by pretending to free 'the royal dignity, whose towering and stedfast height rests upon the unmovable foundations of justice and heroic virtue' from dependence on 'the painted battlements and gaudy rottenness of prelatry'.[93]

This was all very well for rhetoric, but how was it to be justified in detail? None of the elements of Arminianism, by itself, was objectionable. Each one of them could be found somewhere in the practice and preaching of clergy who were now being cited with respect: Whitgift, Hooker, Andrewes, Williams, Prideaux . . . The real distinguishing mark of Laudianism was its single-minded systematic support of royal authority. If that authority could not be questioned, any legal case against the Laudians would collapse. In spite of all the propaganda against him, the case against Wren did collapse, and so it was dropped in 1641. The case against Laud himself was carried to a conviction only when the rule of law had been superseded by revolutionary power.

The answer was to raise the cry of popery. It was an essential part of the strategy. What other slogan could have secured monster petitions to the Parliament, brought the London mob to intimidate the King, or the royalist members, persuaded 'many thousands' of Londoners to sign a manifesto condemning the bishops for the publication of a translation of Ovid? Whenever the Parliament needed to rally mass support, the old slogans were brought out: popery and prelacy, bishops and popish lords, images and superstition; but its leaders did not divert their gaze from their true objective: to break up the synthesis which would otherwise harden, as in France, into an absolute monarchy.

They were wise in their generation. At a heavy cost, they broke the synthesis. But paradoxically, by destroying the Laudian Church as an organic part of the State, they forwarded the very process which they pretended to fear. The Laudian synthesis might, in certain circumstances, have succeeded. A little more tact, a little more luck, a few more years, and the critical time might have passed. But once it had failed, the heirs of Charles I, still seeking to re-establish an absolute monarchy, on a continental model, and looking for a religion to consecrate it, turned from the Anglican to what now seemed the stronger Roman Catholic Church.

This chapter of the story began at the court of Charles I – or rather, at that of his Queen, that *femme fatale* of the House of Stuart, Henrietta Maria. She was the patroness of all those Catholic agents and Catholic converts whose activities, tolerated by the King, were so damaging to the public image of Laudianism. Laud himself deeply resented those activities. He felt, as he wrote to Strafford, that he was ground between the upper and the nether millstone, between the Queen's papists at court and the noble patrons of Puritanism in the country. The Queen felt his hostility, and returned it: their relations were cool and distant. The result was surprising, and of far greater significance than she could have guessed. The Queen's distrust, not to say hatred, of Laudianism led to an unavowed alliance, sponsored by her, of Catholics and Puritans: an alliance which would last, with sinister effects, for half a century, and would contribute, as Laudianism did not, to the final ruin of the Stuart dynasty.

The alliance of Catholics and Puritans, never explicit, was largely accidental and opportunist. They agreed on foreign policy: both, for different reasons, supported friendship with France, not Spain; and both Catholics and Puritans felt themselves oppressed by the established Church. Early in 1641, after the fall of Strafford and Laud, the Queen and the patrons of Puritanism at court imagined that, between them, they could create an alternative government; and during the civil war the idea of such an alliance periodically returned, only to dissolve again, dissipated by its own internal contradictions: for each party sought only to use the other. However, it refused to die, even though circumstances changed.

So long as Charles I lived, his queen showed no public disrespect to his religion; but after his execution she openly opposed it. Anglicanism, she was convinced, had failed, and only Presbyterian Scotland (in the first instance) or Catholic Europe (in the long run) could restore the fallen dynasty. Therefore she undermined the Anglicans at the exiled court – Hyde, Cosin, Earle – and sought to convert her sons to Catholicism. In this she was ultimately successful: neither Charles II nor James II would feel any loyalty to the Anglican Church, which both of them would betray. Like their mother, they believed – one indolently, the other earnestly – that established Catholicism was the only religion that could sustain royal power and that, in England, patronage of Dissent was the tactical means of establishing it. So Charles II, having been restored by the Anglican party of Clarendon, would jettison Clarendon as soon as he could in favour of the Catholic-Puritan 'Cabal', and James II, having inherited a throne firmly based on the Church of England, would jettison the sons of Clarendon in favour of an alliance of Catholics and Dissenters: Dissenters, of course, as stalking horses for Catholic power.

Presumably they thought, like their mother, that Anglicanism was a spent force: had not Laudianism ruined their father? But if so, and if the argument of this essay is right, they were mistaken. It was not Laudianism that had ruined Charles I but Charles I who had ruined Laudianism. Admittedly Laudianism had been hated in 1640 for some of its own qualities as well as for its support of royal policy. But the intervening years of persecution had given it a new look, and a new strength; and after 1660 it was qualified, as 'popery' could never be in England, to form part of a new authoritarian synthesis. After the defeat of the Exclusion Bill, and the rout of its whig sponsors, Charles II behaved as if he had at last recognized this fact: though a secret Catholic, he was happy, in 1680–5, to see the old synthesis restored and royal power apparently set firm again on an Anglican, neo-Laudian base. James II, thinking, we must assume, that the panic fear of popery had now blown itself out, sought to substitute a Catholic base, with fatal results. But if he had been content to build on the system he had inherited, can we be sure that the synthesis would not, this time, have been made permanent?

Of course we cannot be sure. But looking back over the whole century we can perhaps risk a generalization. On three separate occasions – in 1641, in 1667, and in 1685 – three successive Stuart kings

– Charles I, Charles II and James II – by repudiating the Anglican synthesis, threw away the chance of stabilizing their monarchy on a firm ideological base. By so doing they missed the chance of creating, in England, a modern, 'despotic' monarchy, on the European model. They showed, each in his turn, that, in Laud's phrase, they knew not how to be, or to be made, great.

3

James Ussher, Archbishop of Armagh

1   A man for all seasons?

James Ussher, Archbishop of Armagh and Primate of All Ireland, is the great glory of the Church of Ireland and of Trinity College, Dublin. He was one of the first alumni of Trinity, was its Professor of Divinity and Vice-Chancellor, and could have been its Provost and Chancellor. At his death he was – though accidentally and obliquely – a great benefactor of it. But he was far more than an Irish worthy. In the words of John Selden, himself one of the greatest of scholars, he was 'that miracle of learning'. He was also an important figure in the background of British politics. No one who studies the history of Britain, or the European world of learning, in the first half of the seventeenth century, can fail to meet him – and indeed to respect him, as his contemporaries did: for in that age of revolution he seemed to rise far above party differences. In the Republic of Letters, he was extolled alike by Catholic and Protestant, Jesuit and Calvinist. In the religious struggles of England, he was courted and praised by royalist and parliamentarian, episcopalian and Puritan. The high Anglican Archbishop Laud, the Presbyterian Richard Baxter, the Independent Oliver Cromwell all paid tribute to him. Even John Milton cooled, for him, his scalding rhetoric. In politics, he was cultivated, and pensioned, in turn by King, Parliament, and Lord Protector. When rebellion shut him off from his diocese in Ireland, the King made him Bishop of Carlisle. When the King was defeated, the Parliament (more usefully) made him Preacher of Lincoln's Inn. He was offered a refuge in Catholic France. And when he died, in 1656, in the house of a royalist countess at Reigate, the puritan Lord Protector ordered for him a state funeral in Westminster Abbey, with the otherwise proscribed liturgy of the Church of England.

A man for all seasons, we may say; and indeed, then and ever since, he has been praised as a 'moderate', the hero of 'moderate' men. If only others had been like him, we are told, the civil war might never have broken out, or might soon have ended: for all men saw in him something to admire, some part of their own philosophy: although it may be that because they found much to admire, they tended to overlook the other parts of his philosophy – perhaps even the essence of it. In this essay I shall attempt to discover and extract the essence of the 'moderate' philosophy which Ussher represented and perhaps, by his massive erudition, obscured. But before doing so it will be convenient to look at the changing face which he has presented to successive generations of admirers, and to see it against its immediate background – that background which has conditioned so much of English history – the politics of the Protestant Church in Ireland.

Let us begin with the preacher of Ussher's funeral sermon in Westminster Abbey, the Rev. Nicholas Bernard. Bernard was a Cambridge man who had gone to Ireland to be ordained and beneficed by Ussher. Soon he had established himself there, a comfortable pluralist: dean of Kilmore; vicar of St Patrick's, Drogheda; vicar of Kildromfarten; chaplain and librarian to the Archbishop. Afterwards, he had returned to England, and being (as his critics said) of 'very accommodating religious opinions', had recommended himself to Oliver Cromwell, who made him his chaplain and almoner. In his sermon, which he afterwards expanded into the first biography of Ussher,[1] Bernard did not say much about Ussher's services to Charles I, Laud and Strafford – these names were now out of fashion – but dwelt on his Calvinist views and puritan associations: his veneration for the Calvinist revolutionary Christopher Goodman, the friend and ally of John Knox; his reverence for the puritan oracle William Perkins; and his 'entire affection' for the fashionable puritan preacher and teacher John Preston, 'the Patriarch of the Presbyterian party'. This was no doubt prudent, since Bernard's book was licensed by the Protector's government. It may also have been true.

Bernard's portrait of the puritan Archbishop did not go unchallenged. Thirty years later another biography of Ussher was published by another of his former chaplains. If Bernard was a Cambridge man who had attached himself to Ussher in Ireland, and wrote during the reign of Cromwell, Richard Parr was an Irishman who had joined him in Oxford, and wrote in the high-tory last years of Charles II. In 1641 he was a Fellow of Exeter College, where Ussher had been given lodgings – in order to be near the Bodleian Library – by the Rector, Dr Prideaux. Once associated with Ussher, Parr remained with him. He accompanied him on his enforced travels during the civil war, and followed him to the royalist haven of Reigate. There he married a rich widow, the patroness of the local living. Having settled into the living, he too found himself a comfortable pluralist; and since he possessed many of Ussher's papers, and could invoke the assistance of an abler scholar than himself in Thomas Marshall, Rector of Lincoln College, he was encouraged by Archbishop Sancroft (who had himself collected many of Ussher's letters) to edit those letters and to write a new life of his former patron as an introduction to them. Parr made good use of Bernard's work – indeed he plagiarized it shamelessly – but his tone, understandably, was different. The puritan associations quietly disappear from the otherwise identical text; we hear no more of Goodman, Perkins, Preston; Ussher's relations with the King are emphasized, while those with the Usurper are omitted or explained away; and instead of the puritan Archbishop we see a character suited to the time of Anglican triumph: an Archbishop, like Sancroft himself, equally firm against popish superstition and puritan enthusiasm.[2]

When Parr began his work, in or just before 1680, the Church of Ireland still remembered its overthrow by the English Puritans, over whom it had now triumphed. When he published it, in 1686, circumstances had changed again. The Roman Catholic James II was now on the throne and the threat came from the opposite direction. Parr himself had difficulties with the censors and his book, as published, bears the marks of their hands.[3] Soon the Church of Ireland would be subverted, once again, as in 1641, by native papists. However, it was not destroyed. Thanks to the Revolution of 1688, it was saved, and throughout the next century its position was secure. In that security, the fame of Archbishop Ussher was allowed to sleep. The eighteenth-century prelates in Ireland were too busy building themselves palaces, or engaging in secular politics, or philosophical speculation, or decorative learning, to bother about theological niceties, or the obsolete polemics of 'the last age', and the greatest historian of England, David Hume, described the course of the Great Rebellion without mentioning Ussher's name. Those who did mention it saw him only as a scholar, and, in particular, as a chronologist: the man who had dated the Creation, and whose dating of it had been accepted by the Protestant Churches in Britain.

The security of the Church of Ireland was undisturbed for over a century. Then it was once again suddenly threatened – and by the same old enemies. On one side, the English whigs, patrons of Dissent, the heirs of the puritan grandees of 1641, on the other, the dispossessed Irish Catholics, heirs of the rebels of 1641, joined in the attack on a rich and alien establishment. By 1840 revolution again seemed a possibility: agrarian revolt had broken out; tithes were being refused to the clergy of the Church of Ireland; whole bishoprics had been abolished by legislation; and the ominous cry of 'disestablishment' was heard in the land. It was in these circumstances that the authorities of Trinity College, the intellectual capital of the threatened Church, commissioned a new biography of Ussher, and an edition of his complete works. For this task they turned to their Regius Professor of Divinity, Charles Richard Elrington.[4]

Elrington was well aware of the topicality of the subject. 'A second time', he wrote, 'the cathedral establishments have been removed . . . The Church is now, as then, placed between the two enemies, Romanism and ultra-Protestantism. Archbishop Ussher was too well versed in these controversies not to perceive that learning was the only human safeguard of the Church . . .' Elrington did not entirely agree with Ussher's politics. He thought him too tolerant of Dissent. He himself believed not in compromise but in defiance. Nor did he agree entirely with his theology. But he agreed with him in thinking that the ultimate triumph over papist and Puritan alike was to be won in the realm of scholarship. It was by superior learning, he wrote – by 'a profound knowledge of the Scriptures . . . a ready acquaintance with history, sacred and profane, a thorough knowledge of Antiquity' – that the Church of Ireland, in the nineteenth as in the seventeenth century, was to refute its critics, command respect, retain an authority which would survive all political changes; and the established Church should keep its endowments intact in order to subsidize 'profound and diversified learning'.[5]

Today we are less favourable to theological controversy, less confident that the religious differences of Ireland will be solved by the arguments of scholars. So perhaps it is not surprising that Ussher's latest biographer dwells less on his erudition than on his conciliatory policy in the public affairs of his time. Mr Buick Knox's conclusion is, however, somewhat defeatist. Unlike Elrington, who supposed that Ussher modified his theological views under the impact of revolution (as who does not?), he supposes that Ussher's views were unchanging but confused: that he had 'no fully integrated policy', 'no clear plan for

meeting the crisis or shaping the future'; in short, that he just muddled
through. He lacked clarity of mind; and like many men who cannot
think very clearly, he made up for the defect by sharpness of temper. If
any one epithet is to be applied to him, it is that used by Dame Veronica
Wedgwood, 'harsh'.[6]

Ussher a harsh man? At first, this may seem surprising. If there is one
epithet that was consistently applied to him in his own time, it was
'gentle'. Strafford wrote to Laud regretting 'the mild and gentle
disposition of the Primate'.[7] Bernard emphasizes his 'most exemplary
moderation, meekness, humility, ingenuity'. Baxter described him as
'the most reverend, learned, humble and pious Primate of Ireland'.[8]
His only fault, wrote Bishop Burnet, was that he had 'too gentle a soul'
for 'the rough work of reforming abuses'.[9] But of course all these men
were Protestants. They saw him within the limited context of English
Protestantism, whose divisions he sought to heal. There indeed he was
a conciliator. But the Protestant unity which he sought had a purpose:
it was for war against an enemy. That enemy was the Roman Catholic
Church – or anything which, to him, smelt of it. There, as Laud wrote
to Strafford, 'the mild man himself which you mention' could be as
fierce as any.[10] His 'gentleness' was relative.

What about his 'muddle-headedness'? Is that also relative? There is
a sense in which all 'moderate' men seem to be muddle-headed to
clear-sighted radicals. But perhaps clear-sighted radicals are not the
best interpreters of history, or of human psychology. Perhaps, in
considering Ussher, we should try to separate him from the parties of a
civil war which broke out when he was over sixty and look at him in the
context of his earlier, more active career. Then we may find him more
consistent: consistent not perhaps within our philosophy, but within
his own.

2   The Protestant philosophy of history

Consider Ussher's early years. He was an Elizabethan, a Protestant,
and an Irishman. He was twenty-two years old when Queen Elizabeth
died, and throughout those years his home had been in an exposed
colonial outpost of English Protestantism, constantly threatened by
that great movement of Catholic reconquest known as the Counter-
Reformation. That movement, in those years, was being carried
forward, ideologically, by the Jesuits and, politically, by the Spanish
branch of the house of Habsburg. In England, this alliance was less

formidable after the defeat of the Armada in 1588, and so the leaders of the Church of England felt free, in the 1590s, to turn their attention from the Catholic to the puritan menace: that was the time of the 'Arminian' revival which would culminate in the high Anglicanism of Archbishop Laud. But in Ireland there was no such sense of security. There the established Protestant Church was a feeble thing. It had been imposed as a state Church; it was accepted only, or mainly, by the official classes and the 'new English' colonists; and although it had legally taken over the endowments of the pre-Reformation Catholic Church, it was unable to preserve them against the greed of its own members, even of its own dignitaries. Such religious zeal as it contained was supplied by the Puritans within it, who had often left England because of their lack of loyalty to the establishment which they were now expected to defend. Around it, not only the native, Celtic Irish, but the 'old English' landowners – the pre-Tudor settlers who by now had gone native and were the natural leaders of Irish society – remained Catholic, and were sustained in their faith by a shadow hierarchy: a hierarchy ready to resume its old position if a Spanish landing were to support a native rising. In 1601, when Ussher was twenty, there was such a landing and such a rising. Both were ultimately defeated; but who could say that the defeat was final, so long as the established Protestant Church was seen as an alien importation, lacking authority or intellectual respectability? It was to give it that authority and that respectability, that Trinity College had been founded in 1591, and opened to students in 1594, when Ussher was thirteen years old.

Planted among the Catholic Irish, as an instrument of conversion and defiance, Trinity College was, of necessity, a 'puritan' foundation, and its early provosts and fellows were generally regarded as Puritans within the Church. But they were also Puritans of a special kind. Intellectually, they were 'Ramists' – that is, they had accepted the pedagogic doctrines, fashionable in their generation, of the French Huguenot Pierre de la Ramée, or Petrus Ramus, who had been murdered in the massacre of St Bartholomew in 1572. The Ramists were austerely intellectual humanists but without too much humanity, and somewhat priggish. Contemptuous of literature and philosophy, of the rhetoric of Cicero and the hierarchical values of Aristotle, they preened themselves on the rigour of their logic and the 'analytic' method by which they pared away the irrelevancies, disposed of the inconsistencies, and extracted the meaning of their chosen texts; by which, in the end, they were imprisoned: voluntary prisoners of their

own linguistic philosophy. Socially, they saw themselves as a merito-
cratic élite, and they trained their disciples to form such an élite,
outside the traditional, but to them irrelevant, hierarchies of society. In
the 1590s Ramism dominated the Calvinist universities of Scotland; in
England it found a congenial home in Cambridge (always a high-
minded University); and when the counter-attack began in Scotland
and Cambridge, its advocates found a welcome in the new college in
Dublin. 'During the first thirty years of its existence', says Professor
Kearney, 'Trinity College was a Ramist foundation'.[11] Those thirty
years were the years which Ussher spent at the college, first as a
student, then as Professor of Divinity.

Ussher himself came of an 'old English' family, settled in Ireland
almost since its conquest in the twelfth century. But it was also an
official family and, as such, had become Protestant at the Reformation. His maternal grandfather and his paternal uncle had been
prominent in the founding of Trinity College, and he himself was one
of its first pupils. But the family's Protestantism was not very firm
and there had been relapses. Ussher's maternal uncle, Richard
Stanyhurst, had been converted to Catholicism in England by the
Jesuit Edmund Campion and had withdrawn to Louvain. There he
became a Spanish agent, and a prolific writer in the Catholic cause.
Stanyhurst's two sons, Ussher's first cousins, became Jesuits, and his
sister, Ussher's mother, would also later be converted to Catholicism.
At Trinity, Ussher naturally studied the controversies which thus
divided his family. He read the works of his uncle Stanyhurst. He also
read, and was impressed by, another Catholic work, the *Fortalicium
Fidei*, by the English Catholic *émigré*, Thomas Stapleton. This had been
published in Antwerp in 1565 and was the most powerful work of
Catholic propaganda addressed to the English-speaking Protestant
world. Its author, who, like Stanyhurst, lived under Spanish protection, was regarded as 'the most learned Roman Catholic of all his
time'.[12]

Both Stanyhurst and Stapleton had historical interests. Stanyhurst
wrote a history of Ireland and of St Patrick. Stapleton translated the
Ecclesiastical History of the Venerable Bede. St Patrick had converted the
Irish to Rome; Bede recorded the conversion of the Anglo-Saxons by
the Roman missionary St Augustine of Canterbury. These were topics
which would interest Ussher all his life. But he did not accept the
Catholic arguments of Stanyhurst and Stapleton. This was partly due
to the influence of another work which had an even greater effect on
him, the *De Quattuor Summis Imperiis* of the German Protestant Johann

Baptist Philippi, known as Sleidan. This work, which had been published in 1556, set out the Protestant scheme of history, as divided into the four successive great monarchies foretold by the Prophet Daniel and the Book of Revelation, and looked forward to the Fifth Monarchy of Christ on earth. It was widely read in England and has been described as 'the text book of English chiliasm'.[13]

These books by themselves indicate the nature of Ussher's early interests at Trinity College, and indeed throughout his life. He was concerned with the historical basis and justification of the Christian Church. Which of the two Churches into which Western Christendom was now split had the warrant of history? Which of them had been foreshadowed by the prophecies of the Old Testament as the means of their fulfilment in the great cosmological drama of the divine purpose? Which of them was truly continuous with primitive Christianity and which a deviation from it? The Catholics pointed to the obvious fact of the Roman supremacy. Had not Christ given his commission to St Peter? Was not St Peter the first Bishop of Rome? Had not his successors ruled the Church, and determined its doctrine and tradition, ever since? The Protestants, however, had by now developed an alternative thesis. Indeed it was more than a thesis. It was a universal historical system, firmly based on Scripture and Scriptural prophecy, buttressed and fortified by modern science and held to be irrefutable.

This Protestant system had been formulated in Germany in the 1540s and 1550s – by Sleidan himself, and by the so-called 'Centuriators of Magdeburg' – and it had been carried to England by Englishmen – John Bale, John Jewel, John Foxe – who at some time had been exiles in Germany. The essential elements in it were the millennium – the thousand-year period during which Satan was bound; the reign of Antichrist, during which he was let loose again; and the final triumph of the Saints in the 'fifth monarchy', the monarchy of Christ on earth. By Ussher's time, all these elements had been accommodated into a coherent scheme, with only marginal variations. The thousand years were reckoned to have begun in the time of Christ and to have run to the eleventh century. This was the great age of the Church, in which (in spite of occasional setbacks) it had grown and prospered. Constantine, the Christian Prince, had given it authority throughout the Roman Empire, and paganism had retreated before it. Even after the fall of the Empire, the Church had extended its sway, winning over its barbarian successors. However, even in that happy age, there were hints of trouble to come. In about 600 AD – the time of Pope Gregory the Great and Mohammed – Antichrist had been born, and in the eleventh century, being fully grown, he had performed his destined role: he had unlocked the gate of the pit and released Satan from his bonds.

Who was this Antichrist? His identity was not certain. To some he was the conquering power of Islam, personified first by the Arab, then by the Turkish conquerors. But good Protestants had no doubt that he was the Papacy which, in the eleventh century, had taken over the Church, usurped the authority of the Christian Emperor, the successor of Constantine, and transformed religion throughout Christendom. Thanks to him, for the next five centuries Satan had raged furiously and true religion had almost been extinguished. Happily, in those dark centuries, while the oppressed saints waited to be rescued by a new Constantine, a visible Church had been maintained by a succession of persecuted witnesses to the truth: Berengar of Tours, the Waldensians, the Poor of Lyon, the Albigensians, Wyclif and Hus. Then, in the sixteenth century, had come Luther and the German Reformation. That was the breakthrough: the beginning of the great struggle which would end, at some time to be exactly calculated, with the Fall of Antichrist, the conversion of the Jews, the rule of the Saints, and the Second Coming of Christ.

Such was the scheme of history, as proclaimed by Protestants throughout Europe. It was a general scheme; but within it, English Protestants discovered that a special role was reserved for the Church in Britain. For in Britain, they insisted, Christianity had always been pure, scarcely touched by the virus of Rome. It is true, the pagan Anglo-Saxons had been converted by St Augustine of Canterbury, a Roman missionary. But why begin with the Anglo-Saxons? What about the ancient Britons? Long before the arrival of the Saxons, the British King Lucius had professed an authentic, uncorrupted Christianity which went back, perhaps, to the time of Christ himself; for had it not been brought by Joseph of Arimathea, the disciple who had come personally to Britain? Had not Constantine himself – 'our English Constantine' (born, it was claimed, of a British princess in York)* – derived his Christianity from Britain? And it was this sound native British Christianity, not the imported Roman kickshaws of St Augustine of Canterbury, which had supplied the real substance of the Anglo-Saxon Church: a Church which, though superficially respectful to Rome, showed its real independence by retaining its vernacular

---

* Constantine was in fact born in Nish, now in Yugoslavia, and his mother was his father's local concubine. The British myth was rejected by Camden in his *Britannia* (1586) and by Ussher in his *De Britannicarum Ecclesiarum Primordiis* (1639).

language and its own laws. Only with the Norman Conquest and the Hildebrandine Papacy – the precursors of the Habsburgs and the Counter-Reformation – had the Roman Antichrist extended his power to the British Isles; and even so, his dark empire had never closed over them; for had not successive English kings resisted papal aggression? Had not Henry II stood up to the insufferable Becket? Had not John, however unsuccessfully, opposed the most formidable of all Popes, Innocent III? Was not Wyclif, 'the morning star of the Reformation', an Englishman? And had not Henry VIII, and now Elizabeth, boldly resumed their legitimate 'imperial' power?

This Protestant framework of history, which gave to England, and to its monarchs, a special part in the unfolding of the divine plan, was the orthodoxy of Elizabethan England. It was made popular, above all, by Bishop Jewel's *Apology for the Church of England*, by the successive editions of John Foxe's *Acts and Monuments*, and by nationalist poets and antiquaries like Edmund Spenser and Michael Drayton, Archbishop Parker and John Dee.[14] There were variations of detail, of course, and in the seventeenth century these variations would develop into rival systems. Puritans would then push the captivity of the Church back into the fourth century, repudiating the Emperor Constantine and his 'imperial' successors. Radical preachers would move the millennium forward into the future, after the fall, instead of before the rise of Antichrist. These new doctrines, which released the radical implications of Tudor Protestantism, would become formidable in the 1640s, but for the moment we need not consider them. In the reign of Queen Elizabeth, when Ussher was young in Dublin, the historical philosophy of English Protestantism was essentially conservative, and the radicalism of the Ramist discipline which he there both learned and taught,[15] while giving to that philosophy a firm logical structure, was also contained by it. It was directed outwards, against the Roman Catholics, who, of course, totally rejected the whole Protestant historical scheme.

In his student days, in Dublin, Ussher convinced himself that this historical philosophy was true, and that the Roman Catholic historians, and particularly Stapleton, had only been able to contest it by falsifying the evidence. They could therefore be refuted if the evidence was fairly set out. This evidence consisted not only of the central documents of the early Church – of the Fathers and the Councils – but also of the half-buried local records which would demonstrate the continuous existence, even in the darkest centuries, of the true Church.

In 1603, when he was a young Fellow of his college, Ussher was sent to London to buy books for its library. It was the first of several such visits. In London he was taken up by the group of English scholars, headed by William Camden and his friend and pupil Sir Robert Cotton, who had created the Elizabethan Society of Antiquaries. These men were delighted to recruit an enthusiastic young scholar who could interpret for them the antiquities of Ireland, and Ussher became a lifelong member of their circle. He supplied papers on medieval Irish history and institutions comparable with the English papers which they had read at their meetings, and in 1607, when Camden published the last edition of his *Britannia*, he included in it a section on Ireland, for which he expressed his debt to 'the diligence and labour of James Ussher . . . who in various learning and judgment far exceeds his years'.

Ussher was, above all things, a scholar. Later in life he was drawn, reluctantly, into administration; later still, into politics. But always his first choice was for scholarship. However, no scholarship is entirely 'value-free', and Ussher's scholarship, vast and various though it was, operated, like any other, within a world-picture, a cosmology, which it was designed to illustrate. Any account of his life which ignores this central fact seems to me abortive from the start and, in the strictest sense of the word, preposterous: for it inverts his own priorities and removes the essential motor of his work. Ussher's multifarious learning staggered his contemporaries; but they at least could see its unity and its purpose, for they understood its basic philosophy. To us, who do not share that philosophy, to whom the very idea of a synthesis of prophecy and history is unacceptable, all that erudition may well seem, at first sight, a chaotic miscellany, a wasteful dispersal of intellectual energy into unrelated subjects. Only if we recognize its connecting philosophy can we see the unity, the intellectual cohesion, which, in his own time, it possessed.

Ussher's devotion to scholarship, his preference for scholarship over administration, and his determination to use sound scholarship as an ideological weapon, is obvious from the start of his career. He refused to follow his father into the law. When his father died, he renounced his inheritance, reserving to himself only a small allowance and relying for his support on his fellowship at Trinity College. At Trinity he refused the provostship in 1609, just as he would refuse the chancellorship in 1633, 'fearing that it might prove a hindrance to his studies'. When he accepted the bishopric of Meath in 1621, and the archbishopric of Armagh in 1625, it was not, I think, with any expectation of arduous diocesan duties. Those, after all, were still the years of James I, in which bishoprics were given as endowments for scholars whose doctrines pleased the King. Nobody believed, at that time, that the Church was heading for a crisis, that episcopacy itself would have to be defended in fact as well as in theory, and that its most formidable enemy would be not on the Right but on the Left – not mutinous Irish papists but revolutionary English Puritans.

As Bishop of Meath, Ussher did not entirely neglect his diocese. Indeed, his account of it in 1622 is a valuable document, showing his conscientious interest in it when required.[16] However it is clear that his heart was not in it. Nor, for long periods, was he. As Fellow and Professor of Trinity College, he had been accustomed to make regular visits to England to buy books, to converse with English scholars, and to study in English libraries, and he did not see why, as a bishop, he should alter his habits. Even when he was in Ireland, he preferred Dublin, which was in a different province, to his episcopal residence in Trim. This did not please his metropolitan, Dr Hampton, the Archbishop of Armagh, who wrote to him rather severely on the subject, urging him to 'spend more time in your own diocese', and recommending him to entertain his Catholic neighbours in Meath rather than denounce their doctrines in Dublin: 'in this way', wrote the Archbishop, 'such as will not hear your doctrine may be drawn to love and reverence your Lordship for your hospitality and conversation'.[17] The rebuke does not seem to have disturbed Ussher, for a year later he was still not to be found in Meath. He was not even in Dublin. He was in England, visiting his learned friends, buying books, studying in libraries. In these activities he was encouraged by King James, who favoured antiquarianism in the Church as much as he distrusted it in the State. Secular history, as studied by Camden and Selden, tended to prove the rights of the subject, which was inconvenient. Ecclesiastical history, as studied by Ussher, demonstrated the subordination of the Church to the Crown, which was far more satisfactory.

Ussher was still in England nearly two years later, when Archbishop Hampton died and King James appointed him as his successor. Even so, he did not hurry back to Ireland. Ignoring the appeals of his fellow bishops, he left the metropolitan see of all Ireland in the hands of his predecessor's officials, and for another eighteen months quietly continued his studies in England. Then he returned in time to give a lead to the Irish bishops on the one topic which could stir him into action: the menace of popery. This seemed to him necessary because King James was now dead and Charles I was preparing, at a price, to grant toleration to his Catholic subjects in Ireland. To Ussher this was a dreadful betrayal. So he rallied his brethren and together they signed a petition against such a treaty with the Devil. 'The religion of papists', their document ran, 'is superstitious and idolatrous, their faith and doctrine erroneous and heretical, their Church, in respect of both, apostatical. To give them therefore . . . a toleration is a grievous sin'.

Ussher's hatred of popery was fundamental to his life and work. Though he corresponded courteously with Catholic scholars, he would never compromise with their doctrines. How could he, when he really believed that the Pope was Antichrist? The phrase, to him, was no mere Scriptural metaphor, but the expression of a scientifically established conviction. At Trinity College, his lectures were described as 'polemical' against the Church of Rome. As Bishop of Meath his 'new persecutions' of the local Catholics raised 'murmurings' from their co-religionists in England, and the sermon with which he welcomed the new Lord Deputy to Dublin in September 1622, on the text 'he beareth not the sword in vain', caused an outcry even from the Protestant establishment.* He had to explain that he was not actually proposing the extermination of the King's Roman Catholic subjects. His surviving sermons are as violently anti-papal as those of any puritan fanatic. He was always quick to see Jesuits under the bed, even in the most unlikely circumstances. So in the later 1620s, when Charles I had trouble with his early Parliaments, Ussher ascribed it all to 'priests, friars and Jesuits, and such like popish agents sent out from their seminaries beyond seas', disguised as Puritans. Jesuits disguised as Puritans would be his stock explanation whenever things went wrong.

Immediately, popery must be resisted, politically defeated. On this all good Protestants were agreed. But if it was to be destroyed finally, Ussher believed, it must be refuted intellectually, and this could only be done if the true religion were set up against it on a firm intellectual base. This he believed that he could do. It was to be his life's work. For eighteen years, we are told – from the age of twenty to that of thirty-eight – he carried out a systematic programme of study. He read through all the early Fathers of the Church and arranged the records of the Church Councils in chronological order. His purpose was not mere erudition, 'bare curiosity', but 'to refute the arrogance' of the papists. But that was only a beginning. His ultimate intention was to write a great *Bibliotheca Theologica*, a massive documentary compilation which would display the Protestant truth, firmly based on three unshakeable

---

* *UWW* XV, pp. 174, 180–4. It was this sermon which elicited the rebuke from Archbishop Hampton. As Elrington remarks, it is odd that both Bernard and Parr, 'who must have been acquainted with the whole transaction', never mention the episode but 'preserve a most mysterious silence upon the subject' (*UWW* I, pp. 58–60).

pillars: correct Scriptural texts, exact chronology, accurate history. That done, argument, he believed, would cease: the Protestant truth would be obvious to all, and the frivolous and fraudulent hypotheses of popery would simply wither away.

3 The organization of research

This was the ultimate aim; but before it could be achieved, how many problems presented themselves! Texts had to be found and interpreted, preliminary controversies resolved, specialist studies undertaken. How could it be otherwise when all the secular sciences were new or being revised, when each one of them depended on the findings of another, and the subdivision of labour, so necessary to progress, had hardly begun? Even to find the necessary books was difficult: it involved visits to libraries, begging letters to noble owners and to other scholars, employment of copyists. Lord William Howard had a great library, but it was far away, in Cumberland. Archbishop Parker had left a splendid collection of manuscripts to Corpus Christi College, Cambridge; but then, as now, it was hard to penetrate. The Bodleian Library at Oxford was in its infancy, and there was nothing like it at Cambridge. Luckily Ussher soon established good relations with that great collector, the Earl of Arundel and his Dutch Librarian Francis Junius; Sir Robert Cotton's splendid library was always at the disposal of approved scholars; through Cotton and Camden he was now a friend of the other great Jacobean scholars in London – John Selden, Sir Henry Spelman, Sir Henry Bourgchier, afterwards Earl of Bath, and many others. Soon his network of correspondents would extend abroad, to Holland, France, even to Italy.

To find the texts was only a beginning. After that came the great problems. For instance, there was chronology. If world history was to be related to a divinely ordained plan, it was essential to begin by establishing the order of events, even in the remotest ages. But how could that be done? The Old Testament was an authoritative text; but it gave no dates: only the generations and ages of the Patriarchs, in years. And what kind of years were they? Lunar? Solar? And how exactly were they measured by Egyptians, Babylonians, Jews? The only canons of certainty in these difficult matters were Scripture and the established regularities of astronomy. But the language of Scripture was often figurative and vague and scientists – even the greatest of them – differed in their findings. The magisterial chronology of Scaliger was questioned by Ussher's protégé, Thomas Lydiat, and in astronomy (as the mathematician Henry Briggs assured him), Kepler 'hath troubled all and erected a new frame' for the motion of the planets.[18] The meaning of Daniel's seventy weeks was disputed by the theologians, the dates of the Persian monarchy by the orientalists. Calculations might indeed be quickened by Napier's useful new invention of logarithms;[19] but what if the evidence itself was contradictory? How was one to reconcile the astronomical Canon of Ptolemy with the historical narrative of Thucydides, the presumably contemporary evidence of the prophet Daniel with the presumably authentic history of Xenophon's *Cyropaedia*? Perhaps the evidence of the Muslim East could be brought in to resolve the discrepancies of the Judaeo-Christian West. But that, of course, required oriental manuscripts, oriental languages. Ussher collected the manuscripts and wrestled with the languages. He had mastered Hebrew and Syriac, but that was not enough. He struggled with Arabic – his brother Ambrose, who died young, was a considerable Arabist – and he corresponded with the most distinguished of English Arabists, William Bedwell; but in the end he found the effort unrewarding: there was 'little fruit to be gathered of exceeding labour', he said, and he regretted the great loss of time.[20]

Even in more modern times there were unresolved problems: for instance, concerning the Waldensians and the Albigensians. If these were to be presented as the only true Christians in the age when Satan was let loose and Antichrist raging, it was important to be sure of their doctrines; which was not at all easy. Here the great Huguenot scholar, Isaac Casaubon, might be able to help.[21] For Casaubon, who had lived in both Geneva and Montpellier – that is, in both Waldensian and Albigensian territory – had come to London after the assassination of Henri IV and was now engaged, under the eye of James I, in refuting the Catholic *Annals* of Cardinal Baronius. But alas, in 1614 Casaubon died: a great loss. Perhaps then one should fall back on British Antiquity: the independent origins of the British Church, so improperly challenged by Stanyhurst and Stapleton. Here at least the sources were close at hand: the Elizabethan antiquaries had worked well; their Jacobean successors were eager to help; and Irish and Welsh were easier to learn than Persian and Ethiopic.

It was an immense task, and it kept Ussher busy all his life. Periodically he published his findings, but publication never ended any line of research: his studies continued, in every direction, expanding all the time. Their first important product was published in 1613. It was a Latin work on the continuity of the true Christian Church, and its purpose, as summarized by Dr Parr, was 'to prove from authors of unquestionable credit and antiquity that Christ has always had a visible Church of true Christians who had not been tainted with the errors and corruptions of the Roman Church . . . and that these islands owe not their first Christianity to Rome'. As a corollary to this thesis, it demonstrated, from history and prophecy, that the Papacy, at least since the eleventh century, was the Antichrist foretold in the Book of Revelation, and that the Protestant Church of England was the truest representative of that continuous and visible, if sometimes subterranean Church. Ussher dedicated his book to King James, whose views on the identification of Antichrist were known to be sound. In his dedication he urged the King to apply strong medicine to *pestis pontificia*, the popish plague.

Ussher's book *De Christianarum Ecclesiarum . . . continua successione*, as published, consisted of two out of a promised total of three parts. The first part covered the thousand years during which Satan was bound. The second described the loosing of Satan in the eleventh century and the tyranny of his agent, the popish Antichrist, down to 1370. Those three centuries had been his heyday; thereafter the Great Schism had sapped his strength and the true Christians, whom he had persecuted, had asserted theirs. The third part, which was to complete the work, was to cover the period from 1371 to 'the restoration of evangelical liberty' in modern times – i.e. to the Reformation.

In fact, this last part was never published. When the first two parts appeared, they were read by Ussher's Roman Catholic uncle, Richard Stanyhurst, now an *émigré* in Flanders. Stanyhurst was so outraged by the work (and particularly by the dedication) that he published an open letter to his heretical nephew, castigating him as an indiscriminate historical glutton, who shovelled into his book, 'as into a stinking sewer', all the anti-papal dirt that he could find; and he promised that he would shortly publish a conclusive refutation of the theory that the Pope was Antichrist.[22] On reading this letter, Ussher decided to hold up the third part of his book in order to meet and answer his uncle's challenge; which, however, never came.* So his own work ceased, somewhat abruptly, at the end of the second part, with the destruction of the Albigensians and their dispersal eastwards to Bohemia, Poland, Livonia. However, the last words point the way forward: 'others turned west and found a refuge in Britain'. So the stage was set for the appearance of Wyclif and his disciples, and the emergence of England as 'the elect nation'.

* *UWW* XV, p. 148. Stanyhurst died in 1618, but Ussher continued to wait for some years, expecting a posthumous publication.

This first major work of Ussher, incomplete though it is, sets out the plan of all his later writings. It is a work in which real historical scholarship is used in order to document an apocalyptic scheme revealed to Moses and the Prophets and still in process of orderly realization. But massive though it was, it was still only a sketch, leaving many gaps to be filled, many new lines of research to be pursued. One such line, and one for which Ussher had particular qualifications, was the early history of Christianity in Ireland. For since Britain was an empire, now united under James I, it would be useful to show that Ireland too had shared its history of religious independence: that its Christianity, from the beginning, had repudiated the claims, and been uncontaminated by the abuses, of Rome.

The result of this specialist study was Ussher's next important historical study, his discourse on 'the Religion anciently professed by the Irish'. In this work he sought to show that until the twelfth century – that is, in that happy millennium 'before the Devil was let loose to procure that seduction which prevailed so generally in these late times' – the Celtic peoples not only had resisted the novelties pressed upon them from Rome but had professed a religion substantially 'the very same with that which now by public authority is maintained': in other words, they had been good Elizabethan Protestants. It was only in the twelfth century, 'in the raging times of Antichrist', that false doctrine and idolatrous ceremonies had been established there. Thus the present Protestant establishment in Ireland was nothing less than a restoration of the true, original, Christian tradition, and Irish history confirmed, in detail, the thesis set out in Ussher's work on the perpetual succession of the Church.

Ussher published his discourse – or at least the first version of it[23] – in 1623, at the beginning of his three-year stay in England. That long absence may not have been to the advantage of his diocese or the Church of Ireland, but it was certainly a great stimulus to his scholarly work. It was then that he mobilized the great machine of research which he would continue to drive, and be driven by, for the rest of his life, then that he established himself in the Republic of Letters of the Protestant world. What a task he then set himself! Always there were new texts to be discovered: texts of the Scriptures, of the Fathers, of 'the Rabbins and the Talmud', of the Venerable Bede and the Saxon chronicles, of the Dark and Middle Ages. But before such texts could be used, their accuracy had to be established. Many of them were unpublished, or, if published, distorted in the interest of parties, or 'castrated by the Roman knife'. Many were inaccurate, defective or obscure. So a great preliminary labour was necessary: textual collation, source-criticism, historical comparison. Otherwise, as a correspondent wrote, 'vain will be our labour in writing of the visibility of the Church when we shall rely upon such sandy proofs'.[24]

Fortunately, in so good a cause Ussher had many collaborators. One of the most enthusiastic was Sir Thomas Bodley's first Librarian at Oxford, Thomas James. James was a Fellow of New College and a very learned man. He shared Ussher's patristic and antiquarian interests. Among other things, he had established, to his own satisfaction, that the Britons and Scots, like the Irish, had preserved their independence of Rome in the Dark Ages: that they had been 'averse and heretical (as they are called) to the whole world, almost till the time of St Bernard' in the twelfth century. This was most useful: it clearly supported Ussher's theory. Even more useful was James's offer to organize a battery of Oxford scholars to transcribe texts. He had already made a beginning and was confident that, with another twelve men in his work-force, he would 'drive the papists out of all their starting-holes'. 'But alas, my Lord', he added, 'I have not encouragement from our bishops!' Ussher supplied the encouragement. Urged on by him, James mobilized other allies: Dr Goad and Dr Featley, Archbishop Abbot's chaplains at Lambeth; Caesar Calandrini, the minister of the French church in London; country gentry with houses conveniently near Oxford. He proposed a similar factory in Cambridge too: if only the heads of colleges there would mobilize their resources, he thought, it 'would do more for the profit of learning and true religion than by building ten colleges'; and he tried to divert Dr Sutcliffe from his 'college of controversy' in Chelsea to this more useful project. Ussher was delighted to find such willing support and Thomas James worked hard to organize his team. When Ussher was appointed Archbishop of Armagh, Dr Morton, the Bishop of Lichfield, was put in charge of 'the whole direction and managing of this business'; but even if he was absent in Ireland, Ussher was to remain its patron and inspiration: 'Good my Lord', James wrote to him, 'what can be done by your Grace, let it be done to the uttermost. The work is in a manner yours: to God the glory'. Its completion, he added, would be as great profit to the Church of England as anything since Erasmus' time.[25]

Ussher did what he could. Thanks to his assured position in the Jacobean intellectual establishment – his status, his reputation, his contacts – he was able to rake in the necessary manuscripts. All his friends were alerted. Wherever a library was for sale, they must be ready to pounce. The great library of Dr Dee, the famous Elizabethan scholar and magus, who had died in 1608, was still unsold in 1624, owing to lawsuits: could it not be obtained? What had happened to the books of Hugh Broughton, the eccentric rabbinical scholar, who had died in 1612? How maddening that the books and matrices of the Dutch orientalist, Thomas Erpenius, who died in 1624, had been nabbed by his publisher! Luckily his manuscripts at least were secured: the Duke of Buckingham – tipped off by Ussher's friends – got them for Cambridge University, of which he was Chancellor. It was a question of watching the obituary lists of the Republic of Letters. While there was death there was hope. As his work progressed, Ussher would build up an international agency to discover, purchase, consult and copy books and manuscripts. He would obtain catalogues of the Libraries of the Vatican and the Escorial and of the great library of the French historian Jacques-Auguste de Thou, and find local agents who would look up the books there – for the world of learning did not heed sectarian differences. A travelling Danish scholar would devil for him in Rome, the Grand Duke's English numismatist in Florence, his own Dutch physician in Paris. Ambassadors had standing orders to look out for books published abroad; the scholarly Sir Henry Wotton in Venice, the magnificent spendthrift Earl of Carlisle in France, the great bibliophile and patron of science Sir William Boswell in the Netherlands. And then there were the barely tapped resources of the East: not only Persian and Arabic astronomical texts, but Syriac, Chaldean, Ethiopic versions of Scripture used by the Eastern Christians, which might stem from older texts and preserve truer readings. Fortunately Ussher had his agents there too. In Aleppo the chaplain of the English Factory, Thomas Davies, was eager to help in the cause, to bring, as he put it, 'a little goats' hair or a few badgers' skins to the building of God's tabernacle'. Through the Maronite patriarch on Mount Lebanon, the Abyssinian colony in Damascus, and the Nestorians in Iraq, Davies sought out manuscripts for Ussher and obtained for him a Chaldean Old Testament and a copy – the first of several – of the Samaritan Pentateuch, which was thought (at first) a great find.* Later, Ussher would use the German orientalist Christian Rave as his agent in Constantinople and the Oxford scientist John Greaves would scour for him, as for Archbishop Laud, the monasteries of Egypt and the Levant.

* The Samaritan Pentateuch is mentioned by some of the early Fathers, but no copy of it reached Europe till 1616, when Pietro della Valle acquired a complete text from the Samaritans in Damascus. It was first published in Paris in 1631. By that time Ussher had obtained six copies (some of them incomplete) in the East.

It was while he was engaged in this scholarly activity that Ussher was appointed by King James to the archbishopric of Armagh. No doubt he accepted it in the spirit in which it was given, as a means to continue his scholarly activity with enhanced authority and resources. How unfortunate that this was to prove the last Jacobean appointment! Only four days after signing the patent, King James died, and a very different reign began. Charles I, unlike his father, did not enjoy controversy. He was uninterested in scholarship or patristic learning. The change was apparent at once. In the Convocation of Canterbury which met at Oxford during the first Parliament of the new reign, Thomas James sought support for his project, but found the bishops even more lukewarm than usual. Ussher had no greater success with the heads of Oxford colleges. When he returned to Ireland in 1626 the project faltered. Three years later, together with its author, Thomas James, it died. In the same year, 1629, in Church as in State, a new course began.

It was the period of 'Thorough', the personal rule of Charles I. Gone now were the easy Jacobean days of learned absentee bishops pleasing the King by controversial virtuosity. A royal order commanded bishops to reside in their dioceses and mind their proper business. Gone too were the doctrines of 'high Calvinism' within an episcopal Church. Geneva now replaced Rome as the prime ideological enemy. In any case, the emphasis henceforth was to be on conformity, not argument. Religious opposition was stifled. Religious controversy was commanded to cease. Nor did this new course apply only to England. As the trusted adviser of the King of Great Britain Laud was able to impose his will on the Churches of all three kingdoms. Archbishop Abbot had already discovered this in England. Soon Archbishop Spottiswood would discover it in Scotland. Archbishop Ussher would discover it in Ireland.

4   The new regime in Ireland

For the next eleven years – 'the eleven years' tyranny' of Charles I, as they used to be called – Ussher was confined to Ireland. The King had no great love of his opinions, nor had the Archbishop been very tactful in expressing them. Preaching at the opening of the second Parliament of the reign, in February 1626, he had urged the King to repress 'the Arminian faction', now basking in court favour. His 'puritan' friends were delighted. 'God's blessing be upon you for this good service so opportunely performed!' exclaimed their Cambridge oracle, Dr Samuel Ward. 'I pray God His Majesty may have a true apprehension of the ensuing danger'. His Majesty, however, had no such apprehension, and by 1629 that was only too clear: the 'Arminians' were then in power in England. Soon they would be creeping into Ireland too.

The high Anglican biographers of Ussher are eager to assure us that, in spite of the statements of contemporaries – and in particular of Laud's chaplain and biographer Peter Heylyn[26] – there was no difference between the views of Ussher and those of their own heroes, Strafford and Laud. They dwell upon the civilities which the three men maintained in their public relations, and the private compliments which they exchanged. Ussher, they point out, laboured to have Laud elected as Chancellor of Trinity College, and Laud tried to persuade Ussher to accept the thankless task instead of himself. Clearly, we are told, 'the utmost cordiality existed between them'.[27] But this is to place too much weight on the language of courtesy and the necessities of politics. If we wish to know their true feelings about each other, we must look not at the formal letters exchanged between them but at their less inhibited correspondence with their personal friends: the secret ciphered letters which passed between Laud and Strafford on one side, and Ussher's private correspondence with his scholarly friends in Oxford, Cambridge and London on the other. Then we shall find a somewhat different picture.

Certainly both Strafford and Laud respected Ussher. They deferred to his seniority, both in years and in status. They admired his learning. They recognized that, as Primate of a legally independent Church, he could not be commanded: he must be consulted, courted, humoured. They agreed with him on some practical matters. But they could not see him as a real ally. He was learned and honest, Laud admitted, but was that enough to make a good bishop? And he answered, emphatically, No. At one time he described Ussher as a 'shrew', of whom he would gladly be rid. 'I have long assured myself', he wrote in 1637, 'that no man can easily be found more unfit for government than the Primate'. Strafford agreed. Ussher's proceedings, he wrote, 'were not open and free to those ends I had my eyes upon'. In the end, they forgave him much because of his admitted virtues. Ussher's behaviour might have been devious, Strafford wrote to Laud, but 'he is so learned a Prelate, and so good a man, as I do beseech Your Grace it may never be imputed unto him'; and Laud, reluctantly, conceded that 'some men's weaknesses must be borne for their worth's sake'.[28] Ussher, on his side, was deeply suspicious of Laud. He saw him as the head of a party which was seeking to undermine the established orthodoxy and the ancient independence of the Church of Ireland.

The particular issue which most exasperated Strafford and Laud was Ussher's deliberate obstruction of their plan to replace the 'Calvinist' articles of religion, accepted by the Irish Church in 1615, by the Thirty-Nine Articles recently republished in England to justify Laudianism. But their complaints were not confined to particulars. Both complained of Ussher's unco-operative spirit: his neglect of business, his omission to answer letters, his lack of commitment to their forward policy, his compliance with the Anglo-Irish Protestant laity who were eating up church endowments. On a visit to Ussher at Drogheda, then the capital of his archbishopric, Strafford admired the fine house which Archbishop Hampton had built for himself, but was shocked to find 'not so much as a communion table in the chapel, which to me seemed strange: no bowing there, I awarrant you';[29] and in Dublin he was dismayed to discover that Ussher had authorized, and still defended as 'a very great ornament to the Church',[30] the gigantic private monument with which the Earl of Cork, the most rapacious of the new colonists, had obstructed the east end of St Patrick's cathedral. However much he respected Ussher's learning and character, Laud knew well that it was not through him that the Church in Ireland would be delivered from the predators and the Puritans.

Therefore he used other agents: forceful men, imported from England, who would circumvent or cut out the unhelpful Primate and get things done. In order to push through his policy at the centre, bully the bishops, control the clergy, he would rely on the Lord Deputy Strafford. In order to obtain exact information on the state of the Church in the provinces, to restore its buildings and recover its property, he would rely on the energetic John Bramhall, newly appointed Bishop of Derry. It was Bramhall who blocked Ussher's attempt to confirm the Irish canons in 1635: 'I was the means to stay it', he claimed.[31] In order 'to have an eye to the press', Laud relied on the saintly Dr Bedell, who had shown his quality as Provost of Trinity College, 'which sheweth', as Laud's chaplain would write, 'that Ussher was not thought fit to be trusted in it'[32] – and indeed he was not, as his own publications would show.

The most direct confrontation between Laud and Ussher came in the affairs of Trinity College, of which Laud was Chancellor and Ussher Vice-Chancellor. Ussher's candidates for the provostship of the college included the Puritan Richard Sibbes and the millenarian scholar Joseph Mede, neither of whom would have been very agreeable to

Laud. They agreed on Bedell, but that proved a mistake by Ussher. In 1629, when Laud promoted Bedell to the bishopric of Kilmore, Ussher was warned by his agent in London that a plot was being mounted: 'someone deeply tainted with the Arminian tenets' was scheming to succeed him at Trinity. On that occasion Laud, new to power, was conciliatory. 'I am engaged for none', he assured the Primate. 'I heartily love freedoms granted by charter, and would have them maintained'. So he allowed the election of Robert Ussher, a kinsman of the Primate. Eight years later, when Robert Ussher had been removed as incompetent, Laud's love of free elections had evaporated. The college, he said, was 'as ill governed as any other in Christendom, or worse', and he told Strafford that this time there was to be no mistake: the next Provost must be William Chappell, dean of Cashel, a sound Arminian in doctrine and a sound disciplinarian in practice: he has earned fame in literature for having, while at Cambridge, corporally chastised the insufferably priggish undergraduate John Milton. Strafford obediently played his part. He met the Fellows of Trinity in the college and told them that they would not be allowed to leave till they had elected Chappell. 'They are all willing', he reported with satisfaction, 'so as on Thursday next he will be Provost, and your Grace shall not need to trouble the King about it'.[33] Chappell was duly elected and soon 'begot a mighty reformation' in Trinity College.[34] Ussher detested him, but Laud supported him, and having secured his promotion to the bishopric of Cork, insisted, in defiance of the college statutes, that he keep the provostship of Trinity. That also was very painful to Ussher.

Strafford, Bramhall, Bedell, Chappell – these men were all very different from Ussher. All of them were determined to restore authority, to reform abuses, to preach Laudian ideas. None of them being Irish, they looked with dismay on the greed, faction and corruption of Anglo-Irish society, and were not afraid to challenge it. Ussher was not merely a scholar who (as Bishop Burnet would put it) 'was not made for the governing part of his function':[35] he was also an Anglo-Irish Protestant who took that society for granted and showed very little desire to change it. So, when he was defeated by Laud and Strafford, he worked off his frustrations on Chappell, and on Bedell. His feud with Chappell became a public scandal, giving indecent pleasure, as Laud complained, to the 'Romanists who swarm there'. As for Bedell, now Bishop of Kilmore, Ussher would censure him, in very petulant terms, for learning Irish and preaching to the natives in the only language that they knew. Here, as Elrington sadly admits, Ussher showed that he shared the prejudices of his class as well as the ideas of his generation. 'In direct opposition to the principles of the Reformation', he opposed the translation of the Scriptures into a vernacular which, as a member of a colonial élite, he wished to see extirpated.[36]

These were differences of temperament, of politics, of social background. But there were also deeper, ideological differences which made it impossible for Ussher and Laud to agree except on the narrowest strip of ground. Both believed in the Protestant episcopal Church; but Ussher, defending it primarily against Rome, saw no enemies on the Left, and made, sometimes, impermissible surrenders to Calvinist bigots in Ulster, while Laud, defending it primarily against the Puritans, could be remarkably indulgent to the extremists on the Right. In Laud's eyes, Ussher, to buy puritan support, was prepared to sacrifice some of the essentials of episcopacy; to Ussher, Laud, in his campaign against Puritanism, was sacrificing some of the essentials of Protestantism. Nor was it merely a matter of facing different enemies. Each was defending a distinct concept of the Church. Ussher, the heir of Jewel and Foxe, traced the true Church through the medieval heretics, the Albigensians and the Waldensians. To him the Papacy was Antichrist, absolute evil, and the modern 'Arminians' were papists in disguise. Laud was the heir of Hooker and Andrewes, though he went beyond them in his high view of episcopacy by divine right. He saw the Christian Church as a continuous institution, vindicated by tradition and reason, of which the Roman Church, though at present corrupted, was a true part. He had no use for Waldensians or Albigensians, and not much for Jewel and Foxe.*

Since the two men faced opposite ways, they could generally avoid frontal collision. It was to their interest to avoid it. But their philosophical differences ran deep, and were reflected most strongly, naturally enough, in the University in which both were interested. At Trinity College, Ussher, with his Ramist dislike of Aristotle and traditional hierarchy, faced Laud, who at Oxford declared Aristotle paramount and who sought to strengthen hierarchy in Church and State. The direct confrontation was between Ussher, supported by the

---

* Laud's chaplain and biographer, Peter Heylyn, is particularly contemptuous of the idea that 'the visibility of the Church must be no otherwise maintained than by looking for it in the scattered conventicles of Berengarians in Italy, the Albigenses in France, the Hussites in Bohemia, and the Wicliffites among ourselves' (*CA*, p. 51). The 'Arminian' Richard Montagu similarly poured scorn on the 'lineal deduction from, and extraction out of, Wiclef, Huss, Albigenses, Pauperes de Lugduno, of a visible Church, though never so reverently preached or authoritatively printed' (*CJC* I, pp. 45–6). For Laud's attitude to Jewel and Foxe, see above, p. 196 fn.

Dublin establishment, and Provost Chappell, supported by Strafford and Laud. Strafford and Laud won, as they generally did, 'by the strong arm of power', and crowned their victory by imposing new statutes on the college. When Strafford sent his own son to the college, to be under the care of Chappell – 'I purpose not', he wrote, 'to have him one of Prynne's disciples' – it was clear that the puritan, Ramist domination was over.[37]

5   The Protestantism of the ancient Irish

This philosophical difference between Laud and Ussher emerged clearly in the historical works which Ussher published during the eleven years of Laud's rule in the Church. In them he discharged the immense scholarly energy which he had accumulated during those years of study in England. All of them illustrated his general philosophy – his belief in the visible continuity of the Protestant Church; but all of them also reflected his special interest in the early history of his own country, Ireland.

In the course of his work on the early Christianity of Ireland, Ussher had found himself faced by a very inconvenient historical fact. Although he had established to his satisfaction that the Irish, during the first millennium of Christianity, had been good Protestants, even Calvinists, he had to admit that the purity of their faith had been tainted, again and again, even then, by 'the poison of the Pelagian heresy'. This was a heresy which was particularly odious to good Calvinists, for it denied Predestination and professed free will and the possibility of universal redemption. It was also undeniably British in origin: its founder, the fourth-century heretic Pelagius, was British – a Welshman called Morgan, it was supposed – and his principal disciple, Celestius, was Irish. Pelagius himself had been routed in his own time by St Augustine, who had fixed upon the Church his rigid doctrine of Predestination, but the protean heresy had not been finally defeated. It had broken out again in Ireland in the seventh century, and in the ninth century an Irish *émigré* in Paris, John Scotus Erigena, the most learned man of that dark age, had, with other Romanizing clergy, preached 'semi-Pelagianism' as the official doctrine of the Catholic Church.

To see the pure 'Protestant' faith of ancient Ireland repeatedly corrupted by such a heresy was sufficiently embarrassing to Ussher. What made it worse was that 'Pelagianism', in his time, was once again a live issue. To good Calvinists, it was synonymous with the new

'Arminianism' which had convulsed the established Church of the Netherlands after 1610 and which, though condemned at the international Calvinist Synod of Dordt in 1618, was now reasserting itself in the Church of England under the patronage of Laud. Moreover, it was painful to admit that now, as in the ninth century, some of the greatest scholars seemed willing to defend this deplorable heresy. Such were Hugo Grotius, now an exile in Paris, and his friend, G. J. Vossius, professor at Leiden. In 1618, on the eve of the Synod of Dordt, Vossius had published a scholarly history of Pelagianism which Calvinists regarded as a defence of the doctrine.[38] Both Grotius and Vossius had friends and disciples in England – as, of course, had their Calvinist adversaries. The controversy was thus carried to England, and was most intense in the later 1620s when the English 'Arminians' were challenging the Calvinist control of the Church.* These were the circumstances in which Ussher decided to celebrate a newly rediscovered anti-Pelagian protomartyr, Gottschalk.

Gottschalk, or Gotteschalcus, was a Benedictine monk of the ninth century, who had challenged the fashionable semi-Pelagianism of his time and defended, against it, an extreme form of Predestination. He was thereupon accused of various heresies, cited before the Council of Mainz, and condemned to solitary confinement in a distant monastery. His book was burnt; he himself was tortured; and having refused to recant his opinions, he died in prison, and was refused Christian burial. After that, his name and opinions were forgotten until the controversies of the early seventeenth century and the researches of Vossius restored this lost chapter of history. Vossius, of course, disapproved of Gottschalk. Ussher, led to him by Vossius, saw him very differently. So he too took up the subject, and having acquired the two confessions of Gottschalk, which had been found in the monastery of Corvey and obligingly supplied to him by the French Jesuit scholar Jacques Sirmond, he resolved to set the record right.

By this time, 'Arminianism' was established in the Church and Laud had secured a royal order banning the publication of works of controversy concerning Predestination. He did not want those embers stirred. The order was impartially enforced: the high (very high) Calvinist Dr Downham, Bishop of Derry, on one side, the 'Arminian' Dr Brooke, Master of Trinity College, Cambridge, on the other, fell

* See, for instance, Daniel Featley, *Pelagius Redivivus, or Pelagius raked out of the Ashes by Arminius and his schollers* (1626). The writer declares that Arminianism is 'plausible to corrupt reason', but that holy Scripture, 'to which, natural reason must bow and strike sail', gives no support to 'this new model of God's counsels fram'd in man's brain'.

equally under the ban. But Ussher was not deterred. In 1631 he boldly published, in Latin, and in Dublin, his 'History of Gottschalk and the controversies of Predestination occasioned by him'. In it he presented Gottschalk as a loyal follower of St Augustine, another martyred witness to the true faith, a precursor of the Waldensians, the Albigensians, Wyclif and Calvin.

Theoretically, having stirred the forbidden embers, Ussher too should have come under the ban; but in fact no move was made against him. No doubt he was considered too grand to touch; and perhaps the Latin language, and the Dublin printing, were a protection. Ussher dedicated the work to Vossius, as one scholar to another – as such, they had the friendliest relations, and Ussher sought to bring Vossius to Ireland as his dean of Armagh[39] – but it was clearly intended not as a tribute, but as a challenge. 'He is stirring up a controversy with Vossius', wrote Grotius; and Ussher's puritan friends hoped that his book might 'occasion Mr Vossius to revise his story'.[40] Ussher also sent a presentation copy of the work to Laud, who, predictably, was not pleased by it. Neither Vossius nor Laud revised their views on account of it.[41]

Having put Pelagianism in its place as a popish corruption of Christianity, Ussher returned to the pure Christianity of the early Irish. First, he republished, in an extended form, his work on that subject. It appeared in 1631, the same year as the 'History of Gottschalk'. Then he turned specifically to the problem of Pelagianism in Ireland. For this purpose, he brought forward two Irishmen, old heroes of his, 'Sedulius and Claudius, two of our most famous divines', who had resisted the heresy. His first intention had been to publish the letters of Sedulius, an *émigré* Irishman of the ninth century, like Erigena, known (to distinguish him from the earlier poet Caelius Sedulius) either as Sedulius Scotus – 'Sedulius the Irishman' – or as Sedulius of Liège (for he taught at Liège). Unfortunately, these letters, which had been cited by the abbot Trithemius a century and a half ago, could no longer be found; but Ussher's search for them enabled him to compile another work, no less satisfying to Irish pride. This was a collection of letters, most of them previously unpublished, illustrating Irish history from the sixth to the twelfth century.[42] He published them in 1632. They showed that in those centuries, while its Christianity was uncorrupted by Rome, Ireland had been a beacon of light for the Western world, a land of saints and scholars, to which the Anglo-Saxons from England had resorted in troops in search of literature and pure doctrine. Its people was also, as Bede had written in the eighth century, 'a harmless nation, always very friendly to the English'.*

Ussher had scarcely sent his Irish letters to the press when he began another major work of history. This was his *Britannicarum Ecclesiarum Antiquitates*, an impressive work of scholarship which would be praised by Gibbon as containing 'all that learning can extract from the rubbish of the Dark Ages'.[43] It is a massive compilation of all the evidence concerning the Christianization of England, Scotland and Ireland from the beginning of the process until the sixth century AD – i.e. before the arrival of the Roman missionary St Augustine of Canterbury – and including, once again, the early history of the Pelagian heresy. Although Ussher declined to commit himself to belief in all his sources, the sceptical spirit of which he made a great parade in his dedication is not always exercised in the text. The work, like all his work, has a polemical purpose. By sheer weight of matter it imposes upon the reader the firm conclusion that the British Isles were thoroughly Christianized – perhaps by the Apostles themselves – long before the Bishop of Rome acquired his primacy in the Church, and that their Christianity was the orthodox predestinarianism of St Augustine of Hippo, challenged but not defeated by the heresy of Pelagius. That, as Ussher's friend Dr Prideaux wrote, would 'put a period, I trust, to the troublesome fancies which of late have been set on foot': in other words, to Laudian ideas. The book, according to Ussher, had been commissioned by King James, so it too had originated in those years of gestation, the early 1620s, when Ussher was in England. King James, of course, had been fascinated by these learned controversies. But it seems that Ussher did not start serious work on it till 1632, and it was not ready for the press till 1639.[44] It was therefore dedicated to King Charles, whose interest in ancient Britons, antiquarian research and the niceties of theology was very limited.

Ussher's *Antiquities* was his last historical work and the last work which he would write in Ireland, and so, at this point, we may make a general comment on his contribution to Irish history. Whereas he idealized the Irish of the Dark Ages, as maintaining Christianity in its primitive purity, his interest in them, it seems, ceases altogether in the twelfth century and is then transferred to his own Anglo-Norman ruling class. It is that class, he implies, not the barbarous Celts, who, in his own time, are the true heirs of the ancient Irish Protestants. On the

---

* It was left for Milton to add the graceless comment: 'a harmless nation, saith Beda, and ever friendly to the English; in both which they seem to have left a posterity much unlike them at this day'. *History of Britain*, in *CPW* V, p. 222.

face of it, this is odd; for according to his own scheme of history the Anglo-Norman conquest, blessed by the Papacy, was an expression of the raging of Antichrist. Moreover, the contemporary account of that conquest, recently published by Ussher's friend Camden, showed that the religion of the native Irish, at that time, was very far from pure: that it was compounded of semi-pagan superstition and gross immorality.[45] As a scholar, Ussher might well have found these facts embarrassing. No doubt he would have been able to 'save the phenomena': the evidence, it could be said, came from a tainted source. But could the evidence be altogether ignored? . . . Perhaps it was easier to switch his interest from the Celtic to the Waldensian and Albigensian opponents of Antichrist, who presented no such problems. The ancient Irish could then, like the ancient Hebrews and the ancient Greeks, be pickled in their ancient virtue, to which their modern descendants – unless they followed their English conquerors back to their forgotten origins – could make no claim.

A few months after publishing his *Antiquities* in Dublin, Ussher obtained his release from Ireland, to which he had now been confined for fourteen years.* Early in 1640 the rule of Strafford and Laud began to crumble. In April the King was forced to summon Parliament, and although he dismissed it after three weeks, it was clear that he had lost the initiative. It was in these circumstances that Ussher accepted an invitation to revisit England. He was invited, according to Bernard, 'by some eminent persons upon the occasion of the then differences between the late king and parliament'. Since we find him, on his arrival in London, lodging at Warwick House, it is fairly clear who those eminent persons were. Warwick House was the London house of the Earl of Warwick, and the Earl of Warwick, the friend of Pym and Cromwell, was the greatest patron of the Puritans in the Church and one of the most active of those 'great contrivers' who sought, through Parliament, to bring down the regime of Strafford and Laud.[46]

To all those men, Ussher, though absent in Ireland, though so discreet, so outwardly deferential to present power, had been a hero, perhaps the only hero in the Church hierarchy. Was he not an old Elizabethan, the last bishop to be promoted – and that only just in time – before the new reign? All through the rule of Laud, the frustrated defenders of Elizabethan Protestantism – Dr Prideaux in Oxford, Dr

* Parr, op. cit., p. 40, says that 'about the end' of 1631, Ussher was in England; but he explicitly deduces this conclusion from the fact that Ussher's book *On the Religion anciently professed by the Irish and British* was published at that time in London; which does not necessarily entail that consequence.

Ward in Cambridge, and their pupils throughout England – had seen him as their spiritual leader; he was venerated by Pym and Hampden; he was a patron and friend of foreign Protestants; and since he was not only the greatest of ecclesiastical scholars but also an Archbishop, the Primate of an independent Church, he was able to stand on his own feet and even (in the safe language of scholarship) to express his own views. If Laud were to be toppled – or cut out, as Archbishop Abbot and, before him, Archbishop Grindal had been – no man was better suited to replace him as effective leader of the established Church, guiding it back to the Elizabethan model, than the Primate of Ireland; and we can hardly doubt that this thought was in the mind of the Earl of Warwick and his friends when they summoned him to England.

Whatever the leaders of Parliament may have hoped, and whatever his own sympathies, it is unlikely that Ussher would have involved himself actively in their politics. If John Pym was 'much with' him, Ussher was also 'often with His Majesty, and well used',[47] and Laud, perhaps somewhat maliciously, persuaded the King to offer him lodgings in the Deanery of Westminster – the Dean, Laud's defeated enemy Bishop Williams, being still a prisoner in the Tower. But Ussher's aims were not political. He had come to England, and brought his family over, intending, we are told, to stay 'a year or two, about his private affairs': in other words, to resume his learned researches. Soon he was in Oxford and had gone to ground in the Bodleian Library: on the eve of the meeting of the Long Parliament, we find him 'almost totally buried among the manuscripts there'.[48] However, he emerged to preach to the Parliament against popery on the anniversary of the Gunpowder Plot. He was still in England a year later, when the Irish rebellion broke out. That settled his future. He would spend the next fifteen years in England and would never see Ireland again.

6 The civil war

So we come to the last phase of Ussher's career: the period by which he has so often and so variously been judged. In the controversy over episcopacy in 1640–1, precisely because he was untainted by Laudian extremism, he was pressed into service, and he who, for so long, had recognized no enemy except on the Right now had to turn about and defend his order against his former allies on the Left. This did not entail any inconsistency, only a narrowing of terrain. Ussher had never believed in high-flying episcopacy, episcopacy by divine right, but he had always believed in the institution, as a rank, not a distinct order, in the Church,[49] and no man was better qualified by learning to defend its antiquity: he could draw on all that vast reading, all those massive 'collections' of the Fathers and the Councils. Thereby he drew into action an antagonist who was, though in a different way, hardly less learned than himself – and far more eloquent: John Milton.

Milton would afterwards crow that he had challenged the giant whom no one else dared to tackle – though he was disappointed that the giant did not notice the challenge.[50] Of course the controversy settled nothing. But it illustrated, very vividly, the intellectual crisis of the Church in 1641, the obsolescence of the Elizabethan consensus. The Laudians, under royal patronage, had attacked that consensus from the Right. They had discarded the radical, prophetic content of the Tudor Church, rejected the religious imperialism of Henry VIII and Elizabeth, the Protestant messianism of Cranmer, Jewel and Foxe, and had replaced it by a new clericalism justified by reason and tradition. Now that they had failed, the heirs of the Elizabethans, the bishops and scholars of James I – Ussher and Williams, Davenant and Morton, Prideaux, Ward, and their friends – expected, under parliamentary patronage, to resume their rule. Had not Charles I himself, in his disarray, protested that he would happily settle, in all things, for the system that had prevailed in the time of Queen Elizabeth?

They were sadly mistaken. The system which the Laudians had undermined from the Right was no longer strong enough to withstand an opposite attack from the Left, and Milton was the eloquent articulator of the attack. In vain Ussher marshalled his prodigious learning to demonstrate the existence of bishops in the early Church. In vain he quoted the Fathers and Councils. Those who had been exasperated by Laud were not prepared to restore the enfeebled relics of a system which the Laudians had so easily captured and transformed. They too now rejected the Church of Jewel and Foxe – not for its radical but for its conservative content. They would have nothing to do with a golden first millennium of the Church, with Constantine or any other Christian Prince. They were no longer interested in 'Antiquity' or the Fathers. Milton wrote contemptuously of 'that undigested heap and fry of authors which they call Antiquity'. And who anyway, he asked, were the Fathers? 'Whatsoever either Time or the heedless hand of blind Chance has drawn down to this present, in her huge drag-net, whether fish or seaweed, shells or shrubs, unpickt, unchosen, those are the Fathers'. It was a devastating dismissal of Ussher's whole programme of a *Bibliotheca Theologica*.

In the first year of the Long Parliament, the year in which Charles I seemed willing to compromise with its leaders, Ussher was often consulted by him. He was consulted in the great crisis over the life or death of Strafford, and gave an honourable reply. He was consulted on the reform of the Church and attended the committee set up for that purpose under the serpentine Bishop Williams, now set free and installed again in his Deanery of Westminster. Unlike Williams, whom nobody trusted, Ussher commanded the respect of both sides. The solution which he suggested was the 'reduction of episcopacy to the form of synodical government' – that is, the limitation of the power of the bishop, in every diocese, by a 'synod' of the lower clergy. However, it was never put to the test. When first offered, the King refused to consider it: he preferred the risks of civil war. Seven years later, when he had lost the civil war, Ussher would offer it again, but this time the leaders of Parliament would refuse it: they preferred the total abolition of episcopacy. As Ussher himself would express it, 'as the King would not when the others would, so others would not when he would'.[51] So long as Ussher lived, his proposed compromise was kept secret; but after his death it was published by his chaplain Bernard, and it would be proposed again, by the nonconformists, at the Savoy Conference of 1661, but with the same result. It was a compromise which was invariably grasped by the weaker party, to save something from defeat: it was never acceptable to the party which felt, at the time, the stronger.

Ussher's proposed compromise has been much praised by 'moderate' historians. It was praised at the time by Richard Baxter, who declared, rather smugly, that he and Ussher, left to themselves, could have settled the Church, on this basis, in half an hour. On the other hand, Ussher's high church biographers, embarrassed by this lapse by their hero, play it down as a tactical necessity. 'It was certainly a very great concession to popular clamour', says Elrington, who then somewhat desperately suggests that the form in which it was published may have been cooked in order to satisfy 'the anti-episcopal prepossessions of Dr Bernard'. In fact, the project does not need such extenuation.* It is entirely consistent both with Ussher's positive views on 'primitive episcopacy' and with his own character. Nor, indeed, does it deserve Baxter's praise: for it failed as much through its inherent defects as through the pressure of political circumstances.

* Baxter says that he asked Ussher explicitly 'whether the paper be his that is called *A Reduction of Episcopacy to the Form of Synodical Government*, which he owned, and Dr Bernard after witnessed to be his' (*Reliquiae Baxterianae*, 1696, p. 206).

Its fundamental defect was that it was a purely clerical compromise. It might suit Ussher, an episcopalian clergyman of Calvinist views, and it might suit Baxter, a Calvinist clergyman, episcopally ordained. But the civil war was not merely between the clergy, and it was not for them alone to make the peace. Neither Clarendon nor Selden, nor Cromwell nor Milton would have been satisfied with such a result: a combination, at the expense of the laity, of new Presbyter and old Priest.

Ussher's high church biographers assure us that he was trusted by the King throughout the civil war. However, it must be said that the King, so long as he was a free agent, always preferred the 'Arminian' clergy, Hammond and Sheldon: it was only when he was on the defensive, and obliged to seem conciliatory, that he allowed Ussher to be wheeled into action. If Ussher spent the period of civil war in Oxford – for which he was censured in London[52] – that was due rather to the lure of the Bodleian Library than to that of the court. It is remarkable that Clarendon, who was with the King at Oxford throughout this time, and was the leader of the party of conciliation, and was himself a scholar and a friend of scholars, never, in his great *History of the Rebellion*, mentions Ussher. Evidently he regarded him as irrelevant, and his schemes of religious compromise as unrealistic.

As indeed, by that time, they were. For Ussher's whole philosophy – that Tudor amalgam of apocalyptic theory, providential history and underground continuity which had been the unifying force behind all his intellectual activity – was by now out of date. It was not merely that present politics had polarized its constituent elements. Episcopacy itself had acquired a new philosophy and no longer needed the old justification. Hooker, Andrewes and Overall had liberated theology, Camden, Bacon and Selden had liberated history, from such fundamentalist conceptions. Grotius was the prophet of a new, more rational, more sceptical 'Arminian' Church, and it was his disciples – Hammond, Sheldon, Clarendon – who now declared Anglican philosophy. The events of the 1640s might force Ussher to modify some details of his credo. There is evidence that, in the course of his life, he came to doubt absolute predestination.[53] But his basic philosophy remained the same: how could he change a whole system of belief to which he had committed himself by the study and writing of forty years? To the end he believed that the scheme of history was laid down by God, and revealed in prophecy; that the Pope was Antichrist; that the true Church had been continued, at first, through the independent Churches of Britain and Ireland and thereafter by the persecuted heretics of the Middle Ages; and that the established Protestant, episcopal

Church of England and Ireland, under the patronage of a Christian Prince, marked the culmination of this process. These were not views that were held, or could be held, by intelligent Anglicans in the mid-seventeenth century. Such men had contracted out of the old synthesis, leaving its decomposing remains to be the sustenance, for another century, of reactionary Puritans.*

But Ussher lived on, an impressive magazine of accumulated erudition – 'a walking concordance and living library' as the unfriendly Heylyn described him – wedded to his obsolescent philosophy, unwearied in his pursuit of facts and manuscripts to support it. When the episcopal Church of England was being destroyed by the Puritans, the real enemy, he still believed, was popery – the popery which, in Ireland, had now risen in revolt against his Church and his class and threatened to destroy both. It also threatened to destroy his life's work: for when he came to London in 1640, he had left his great collection of manuscripts in his house at Drogheda in the custody of his chaplain Dr Bernard. In the winter of 1641–2, when Drogheda was besieged by the rebels, the library was in great jeopardy: according to Bernard, 'the priests and friars without talked much of the prize they would have of it, but the barbarous multitude of burning it, and me with it'. In fact, the siege was raised and the library would ultimately be shipped over to Chester and thence to London, but it would be several years before Ussher recovered it. In these circumstances it was naturally with dismay that Ussher, at Oxford, became aware of a sinister new development. While the Parliament was becoming more radical, the King was turning for support to the ultimate enemy, the Irish papists.

In the spring of 1644 the agents of the Roman Catholic Supreme Council in Ireland sent a delegation to Oxford to seek from the King, as the price of their support, freedom of worship and an independent parliament. They were followed by a rival delegation from those few Anglo-Irish Protestants who were prepared, but also on terms, to support the Crown. Their terms were severe. A Protestant historian has described them as 'the harshest and most brutal assertion of Protestant ascendancy and of the right of the alien minority to enslave the children of the soil'.[54] Ussher naturally supported these claims. When the King preferred the Catholic offer, Ussher went to him and sought to dissuade him: a toleration, he once again insisted, was a thing most dangerous to the Protestant religion and he was therefore always opposed to it.[55] When the King nevertheless plumped for the Catholic party, Ussher decided to abandon England and emigrate to France.[56]

* I am thinking, in particular, of Richard Baxter and John Wesley.

The choice of France was curious, but presumably he had received some offer. Parr tells us that Richelieu had sent him a gold medal in recognition of his book on the antiquities of the Irish Church, and that Ussher had responded by sending the Cardinal 'a handsome present of Irish greyhounds, and other rarities which that country affords'. That must have been in 1639–40. According to Bernard, Richelieu invited him to France after the Irish rebellion of 1641. At this time, Richelieu was contemplating a Gallican 'patriarchate' independent of Rome, and perhaps he saw Ussher's work on the independent Irish Church as useful intellectual justification.* By 1644, Richelieu was dead, but the Gallican party remained strong and a few years later Ussher would receive another invitation to France – this time from the Queen Regent, Anne of Austria.[57] At any rate, there can be no doubt that his present intention was serious; he obtained a letter of introduction from Dr Williams, now Archbishop of York, who happened to be at Oxford at the time, to the Huguenot scholar and lawyer Didier Hérault, then living in Paris.[58] Williams was also, at that time, preparing to leave the sinking ship: he was about to set off to his native Wales in order to take up arms for the Parliament and thereby, in Clarendon's sour phrase, 'the better enjoy the profits of his own estate which lay thereabouts'.[59]

In fact Ussher did not go to France. He stayed in Oxford and fought the battle against popery there: his Gunpowder Plot sermon before the King on 5 November 1644, we are told, caused offence.[60] Then, next year, after the battle of Naseby, when the fall of Oxford seemed likely, he withdrew to Cardiff, where his son-in-law, Sir Timothy Tyrrell, was royalist governor. A year later, Cardiff being no longer safe, he again contemplated emigration, to France or Holland; but in the end he retreated further into Wales, to the protection of the recently widowed Lady Stradling at St Donat's castle. On the way, he was held up and 'plundered by the rude Welsh in Glamorganshire', who broke open his trunks and carried off all his books and papers. He soon recovered most of them, but two manuscripts which he particularly valued were irretrievably lost. They were on the history of the Waldensians. Naturally he suspected that 'a priest or Jesuit in some disguise' – disguised presumably as a rude Welshman – was responsible: no doubt having stage-managed the affair in order to stifle, once again, those

---

* The Roman Catholic controversialist John Sergeant afterwards wrote, 'I remember how Bishop Usher (as I was told) had bin willing to become a Catholick, had Cardinal Richelieu yielded to give him £600 a year to be his Antiquarius, at which kind of knowledge he was excellent' (quoted in Edward Chaney, *The Grand Tour and the Great Rebellion* (Geneva 1985), p. 385). The story of Ussher's willingness to be converted is obviously fantasy, but the connexion with Richelieu is confirmed.

ancient witnesses to the Protestant truth. Similarly, when the King was executed, Ussher lamented, not that puritan fanatics would now complete the destruction of the episcopal Church, but 'that thereby a great advantage was given to popery, and that from thence forward the priests would with greater success advance their designs against the Church of England and the Protestant Religion in general'.[61]

Such ideas seem grotesque to us, but they flourished in the mental climate of the time: a panic fear of popery was the neurosis of the age, and any disaster could awaken it. Good Calvinists – Prynne, Baxter, Peter du Moulin and others – repeated a story that, when the King was executed, Queen Henrietta Maria's Catholic chaplain had been seen on horseback, disguised as a Cromwellian trooper, waving a sword in triumph as the axe fell.[62] 'Jesuits in disguise' were a particularly common phenomenon: the early Quakers – even Milton (in retrospect) – were seen as such.[63] Those who lived in Ireland were, of course, particularly liable to these fantasies. Even the Laudian Bishop Bramhall believed (like the Huguenot du Moulin) that over a hundred 'Romish clergy', trained abroad and disguised as Presbyterians and Independents, had been sent to England to penetrate the Parliamentary army and then, in secret collusion with Catholics in the royal army, promote revolution and regicide for the advantage of their Church. Bramhall would afterwards report this as a known fact to Ussher, who was no doubt glad to have such confirmation of his own views.*

If the *pestis pontificia* was so dangerous, clearly it was more than ever necessary to develop the antidote. In spite of all interruptions and diversions, in spite of ecclesiastical administration, politics, civil war, Ussher never lost sight of his ultimate aim – that aim which he had formulated in Dublin in the first years of the century and for which he had mobilized all those resources on his visits to England in 1619–21 and 1623–6: the compilation of a great *Bibliotheca Theologica* which would demolish the historical foundations of Roman Catholicism. It was for this purpose that he had built up his great 'collections' of material, and it was to extend these collections that he had come to England in 1640. Unfortunately, first the outbreak of the Irish rebellion, then the civil war, had severed him from his collections and so, at Oxford, he had been diverted once again into specialist studies, in which indeed he had done valuable work: he had distinguished the

---

* Bramhall to Ussher 20 July 1654, in *UWW* XVI, pp. 293–6. Even in the mid-nineteenth century these stories were believed by Professor Elrington (*UWW* I, pp. 263–6); but he too was a Protestant in Ireland, breathing the hallucinogenic air of Dublin.

authentic from the spurious letters of Ignatius – one of the major achievements of critical scholarship – and had established the origins of the Creeds. Even when he had returned to London, made his peace with the victorious Parliament, and settled down, as Preacher of Lincoln's Inn, in the Countess of Peterborough's home in St Martin's Lane, it was some time before his library, which by now was impounded in London, was returned to him, and by that time he had embarked on a new work of scholarship. So the *Bibliotheca Theologica* was once again postponed while he wrote yet another subsidiary study. This was the work by which he is best remembered, although his successive biographers are surprisingly reticent about it: his attempt to establish an exact chronology of world history.

7　The date of Creation

Both as a historian and as a theologian, Ussher had always been interested in chronology; for how could the 'synchronism' of history and prophecy be proved without the framework of established dates? Already at the age of fifteen he had drawn up, in Latin, 'an exact chronology of the Bible up to the Book of Kings', from which, we are told, he did not much deviate afterwards:[64] further evidence that, though his erudition grew, his mind was only filled, not changed. In the early 1620s, during that long stay in England, he had pursued the subject further, seeking to control the written records of Antiquity by the astronomical evidence supplied to him by John Bainbridge, the Savilian professor at Oxford. On his return to Ireland in 1626 this chronological work had been suspended. It would have been different, perhaps, if he had succeeded in persuading his Cambridge friend Dr Mede, the greatest expert on the millennium, to come to Dublin as Provost of Trinity College.* But Mede would not leave Cambridge, and Ussher, confined to Ireland, concentrated on another part of his great plan: the study of Irish antiquities and the history of Pelagianism. However, after 1640, being back in England, he was able to resume his work on chronology, which now became the principal subject of his study.

Ussher's chronological scheme was based, largely, on that of the great Huguenot scholar, Joseph Scaliger. Scaliger, like Ussher, had commanded a vast range of erudition – linguistic, mathematical,

* Mede's great achievement was his harmonization of prophecy and history, published in his *Clavis Apocalyptica* (1627). His views were very sound: he identified the appearance of the Waldensians with the first blast of the angelic trumpet (Rev. 8: 6–7).

scientific; but he was a far more original thinker, supremely confident of his own genius and, at times, fanciful in its exercise. His great innovation was the invention of 'the Julian Period' – a purely notional period of 7980 years within which no day ever had exactly the same position in the three cycles by which time was measured: the solar cycle of nineteen years, the lunar cycle of twenty-eight years, and the Roman civil cycle or Indiction of fifteen years.* By an elaborate calculation, Scaliger posited the beginning of the Julian Period in BC 4713, and then proceeded, by a brilliant display of philological, mathematical and astronomical virtuosity, to reduce all the calendrical systems of the past to one frame, and place all the major historical events of Antiquity in their proper relationship to each other within it. The essential hinges were supplied by the reigns of Nabonassar in Babylon, from whose accession on 26 February 747 BC Ptolemy dated his astronomical observations; of Nebuchadnezzar, where the Babylonian computations could be linked with the events recorded in the Bible; and of Cyrus the Great in Persia, which could be linked with Greek history. Incontestably accurate dates were supplied by recorded and mathematically verifiable eclipses. Thus the conclusive link between the ancient chronology of East and West was supplied by Alexander's victory over Darius at Gaugamela, which could be pin-pointed by the lunar eclipse of 29 September 331 BC: a date which 'remains the cornerstone of later Greek history'.[65]

This system was all very well as far as it went – as far back, that is, as Nabonassar (if he could be correctly identified).[66] But what about the period before that? There Scaliger's only source was the Old Testament. That of course was always authoritative. Unfortunately it was not always clear. The period of the Kings of Israel, from Solomon to the last King Zedekiah, was of particular obscurity, with joint reigns, overlapping reigns, regencies, interregna, all imperfectly defined: what man of sense, exclaimed Scaliger, could ever find a sure foothold there?[67] But if the chronologer could thread his way through that Serbonian bog, the going gradually improved, and ultimately, as he waded ashore on the far side of Noah's Flood, he would be cheered by the beckoning figures of the long-lived pre-diluvian Patriarchs whose regularly recorded ages and generations provided accurate milestones back to the Creation. There, since the Old Testament often specified

---

* Scaliger is generally credited with the invention of the Julian Period (which he so named, as he himself explains, because it is reckoned in the years of the Julian calendar); but Ussher ascribes the original idea of this 'artificial epoch' to Robert of Lorraine, the eleventh-century Bishop of Hereford, who epitomized the chronicle of Marianus Scotus, though he concedes that it was adapted to the purpose of chronology by Scaliger (*UWW* VIII, p. 6, XV, p. 557).

the days of the week, Scaliger was able to be very exact. The day of Creation, he concluded, was Sunday 25 October in the year 764 of the Julian Period, or, in the vulgar system of the Christians, which that 'most elegant period' had now replaced, 3950 BC.

From Scaliger, Ussher adopted the device of the Julian Period, and many other features. But he was determined not to be dazzled by his great predecessor, and he insisted on re-calculating the calendrical equivalents of Antiquity. So he began again the measurement of the ancient year. For this purpose he sought the text of a work by the Greek astronomer Hipparchus in the libraries of the Escorial and the Vatican. He called on the assistance of his Oxford friends. John Greaves, now Bainbridge's successor as professor of astronomy, undertook to hunt for astronomical manuscripts in the East, and Gerard Langbaine, the learned Provost of Queen's College, would help him with medieval sources. In 1648 he published a tract on the Solar Year, and its adoption and refinement in Antiquity: a learned treatise to which he added numerous tables showing, *inter alia*, the lunar and solar cycles and making it possible to find Easter for ever. Without any evidence, he insisted – an 'outrageous insistence', says Professor Barr[68] – that the ancient Hebrews used a solar year more or less identical with the unreformed year of his own time. Other problems too he solved in an equally convenient way. The lives of the Patriarchs, for instance, were longer in the Greek Septuagint than in the Hebrew text of the Old Testament, so that the whole time-scale accepted by the Greek Church was longer. Which text was Ussher to follow? As a scholar, he admitted that the Hebrew text was as liable to corruption as any other,[69] and he eagerly sought out other early versions, but he ended by plumping for 'the Hebrew verity'; which certainly suited his purposes. He even published a treatise showing that the Greek text of the Septuagint was little better than a forgery. This however convinced nobody, then or since.[70]

Having thus cleared the way, Ussher was able to proceed to his detailed chronology of the ancient world. In 1650 he published the first volume, as *Annals of the Old Testament*. It extended from the Creation to the reign of Antiochus Epiphanes in the second century BC. Four years later came the second part, which carried the chronology down to the Destruction of the Second Temple of Jerusalem by Titus in AD 70. This was the last of his works to be published in his lifetime. An appendix to it, his *Chronologia Sacra*, was published soon after his death by his son-in-law Sir Timothy Tyrrell.*

* It was put out by Thomas Barlow, then Bodley's Librarian, to whom Tyrrell had entrusted it. See Barlow's dedication of the published text to Tyrrell.

Here let me record my personal gratitude to Archbishop Ussher. When I was a child I was taken regularly, on Sundays, to our local parish church, from whose formal proceedings I fear that my attention was inclined to wander. Happily, it found a rival attraction still within the holy circle of orthodoxy. The prayer books supplied in the pews contained a series of tables which, I now realize, came ultimately from the Archbishop: tables of fascinating complexity which enabled the reader to work out, via the Epact and the Golden Year, the date of Easter in any year, past or future. I never discovered what the Epact and the Golden Year were, but many a mechanical litany, many a dull sermon, formed a comfortable continuo while I conjured with these fascinating tables, checking that they worked and applying them to random years in the past and the future. Moreover, the Bibles provided in the same pews had in their margins (as my own Bible had not) the dates of every event: the Creation in 4004 BC, the Deluge in 2349 BC, the Exodus from Egypt in 1492 BC, etc. This information, which gradually became, for me, the main pleasure of church-going, gave to my knowledge of the Old Testament a valuable sense of historical continuity, and although the detail have since been revised here and there, I can say, with Gibbon, that in my early years, though indirectly, 'the *Annals* of Ussher . . . distinguished the connection of events and engraved the multitude of names and dates in a clear and indelible series'.* But I do not recollect that the marginal summary in that Bible recorded the refinement of detail which gives the Archbishop's work such a nice sense of chronometrical precision: the statement that the Creation took place not merely in 4004 BC – which Elrington, in 1847, thought very probable (it was, he observed darkly, 'a very remarkable astronomical epoch')† – but on Sunday 23rd October; and that the machinery was set in preliminary motion on the previous day, at about 6.00 pm.[71]

---

* Gibbon, *Memoirs* (World's Classics), p. 33. Gibbon afterwards discarded Ussher as a guide, preferring 'the system of M. de la Nauze . . . as it appears to me far more probable than that of archbishop Ussher' (*The English Essays of Edward Gibbon*, ed. P. B. Craddock, p. 110). Louis Jouard Monbroux de la Nauze (1696–1773), a French academician, supported, in general, the system of Newton.

† *UWW* I, p. 266. The remark is evidently based on that of the Rev. William Hales, *A New Analysis of Chronology and Geography, History and Prophecy* . . . (1830) I, p. 228 n. Hales wrote that 'the year BC 4004 was a remarkable epoch when the great axis of the earth's orbit coincided with the line of the equinoxes, and consequently the true and mean equinoxes were united. This curious discovery was announced by the great French astronomer La Place, in his *Mécanique Céleste* tom. III, 113'. Hales, like Elrington, was an Anglican clergyman in Ireland and a professor of Trinity College, Dublin.

Ussher was able to be so precise because the Bible was explicit and infallible, astronomy was an exact science, and Scaliger had supplied him with a universal calendar. It was known that the Creation had taken place on a Sunday; it was deducible that it was the first Sunday after the autumnal equinox; and that day could be identified with the aid of the Julian Period. The only problem was to find the year, and this could be done by counting backwards from Nebuchadnezzar and Nabonassar. In all this, Ussher followed the method of Scaliger: if he differed from Scaliger (like his Jesuit rival Petavius), it was simply in detail. While the magisterial Scaliger, *aquila in nubibus* as he was called, wheeled above the clouds, glorying in his own magnificent versatility, the more pedestrian Archbishop, like a sure-nosed basset-hound, kept close to the holy ground of his text. He was thus able to convict his predecessor of a vulgar error in supposing that Abraham had been born when his father Terah was only seventy: on the contrary, Ussher skilfully showed that Terah had been one hundred and thirty years old at the time:[72] Scaliger had failed to notice that Terah was twice married and that Abraham's mother was the second wife. This, says a nineteenth-century clergyman, was 'the most brilliant and important of Primate Ussher's improvements in chronology'.[73] Inevitably it threw out Scaliger's date for the Creation, which, both agreed, was 1949 years before the birth of Terah's eldest son. Ussher showed the same scrupulous care in his astronomical calculations: he did not forget that the sun had twice been irregular in its motion, having stood still for a whole day over Gibeon at the command of Joshua, and gone back ten degrees on the sun-dial of Ahaz for the benefit of Hezekiah; but he concluded that these irregularities were somehow absorbed by the ultimate regularity of the solar system.[74]

Ussher's chronology was, for its time, a useful work of scholarship; but we cannot fail to notice that its utility consisted partly in the support that it gave to that historical (or meta-historical) philosophy which Ussher, throughout his life, sought to prove. According to Jewish tradition, the world had a life-span of six thousand years: two thousand years of Nature before the Law given to Moses, two thousand of the Law, two thousand of the Messiah. This tradition suited the Christians, and when they had dated the birth of Christ, and based a new system of chronology on it, 4000 BC became the ideal date for the Creation. But now Scaliger had upset that system. He had proved that Christ could not have been born in the year assigned to him – at least not if the story of the massacre of the Innocents was true – and so his birth had to be put back to 4 BC, to give Herod his chance. This meant that the ideal date of the Creation also had to be put back four years. How convenient that the Archbishop's nicely calculated steps through the chronological morass of the Jewish kingdom, combined with his emendation of the birthday of Abraham, had led him to precisely that result! This, as Professor Barr says, was 'a major triumph'. Scaliger would no doubt have given Ussher's chronological deviations short shrift, as he gave short shrift to those of Ussher's *protégé* Lydiat.[75] But then Scaliger, in spite of his Calvinism, was a free spirit: he did not seek to subordinate chronology to ideology.[76] Ussher, for all his citizenship of the Republic of Letters, was not, and did.

Ussher's chronology lasted as long as his ideology, perhaps even longer. Sixty years after his death, the English orientalist Humphrey Prideaux described his *Annals* as 'the exactest and most perfect work of chronology that hath been published';[77] the great Neapolitan historian Pietro Giannone accepted it as his surest guide through those dark centuries;[78] and if it would afterwards be undermined by that of Isaac Newton, it has to be admitted that Newton's system, though more critical in detail, rested essentially on the same combination of astronomical exactitude and ancient myth: of the precession of the equinoxes, the celestial observations of the centaur Chiron, and the literal truth of the Old Testament.[79]

8 The inheritance

The labour of his chronology, though a useful support for his philosophy, was a diversion of Ussher's energies, already distracted by politics and war, and when he died, at the age of seventy-five, he had still not produced his intended *magnum opus*, his *Bibliotheca Theologica*. The burden of completing his life's work therefore fell to his surviving friends. His manuscript 'collections' were left to Gerard Langbaine, the Provost of Queen's College, Oxford, to edit and publish. Langbaine transcribed them and did what he could to restore the damaged text ('the quotations in the margins being much defaced with rats'). However, he did not complete the task: a winter's hard work in the Bodleian Library 'in a very severe season' was too much for him and he 'got such an extreme cold as quickly . . . brought him to his end'. The learned Dr Fell, Dean of Christ Church, then took over the work but soon gave up. Langbaine's incomplete copy remains in the Bodleian Library. Ussher's original has passed to the British Museum. The industrious Elrington examined it there, but blenched at the sight: it was, he wrote, 'a folio of about 600 pages, written so closely as to be read with great difficulty, every atom of paper covered with interlineations and marginal notes lying in every direction'. After a long and laborious collation, he too gave up: the work, he decided, was unpublishable.

Various other works of Ussher survived in manuscript. Some of these were printed by Bernard, who, says Elrington drily, 'would have consulted much better for the reputation of the archbishop' if he had left them unpublished – adding gratuitously that Bernard had no doubt tampered with the text, ascribing 'to his patron his own false and mischievous opinions'. Others came ultimately into the hands of Archbishop Sancroft, who caused them to be published. Among them was a substantial but unfinished work on the vernacular Scriptures. In this Ussher showed that for six centuries after the death of Christ the Scriptures had been read in the vernacular language: it was only in the seventh century, with the birth of Antichrist, that Roman imperialism sought to subject the whole Church to the Latin language; and he was pleased to show that one of the last to resist this process, until the Waldensian revolt five centuries later, was an Englishman, the Northumbrian poet Caedmon, who, as Bede tells us, wrote his biblical history 'in his own, that is the English, tongue'.[80] No doubt it was this polemical interest which had caused Ussher to acquire the only manuscript of the Anglo-Saxon poem ascribed to Caedmon. This was published, in Ussher's last year, by the Dutch scholar Francis Junius, to whom he had given it. Other writings by Ussher – learned footnotes to his unwritten *magnum opus* – remained in manuscript till the nineteenth century. They were then published, with unconcealed misgivings, by Elrington, who concluded that they only showed 'that we must rest the character of the archbishop, and our hopes of information, upon the works which he published himself'.[81]

Thus Ussher's great work, towards which he had been studying for fifty years, and which was to be the final, incontrovertibly documented, historical vindication of the Anglicanism of Elizabethan England – that amalgam of apocalyptic prophecy and providential history and continuous episcopacy – was never completed, and indeed, by 1660, when Anglicanism was restored in Ireland as in England, it was already out of date. Already, by 1630, the Elizabethan theology, like the Elizabethan compromise which sustained it, had been wearing thin. Now that it had been first undermined by Laudianism, then shattered by revolution, the next generation would not wish to reassemble it and the long-prepared intellectual infrastructure which was to secure it came too late for its purpose. So there remained of Ussher's work only the spin-off from that still formless nebula, the periodically detached particles which had solidified into distinct, and perhaps permanent contributions to European learning: the documents which he had printed, the manuscripts which he had collected, the occasional scholarly problems which he solved. It would, I fear, have pained Ussher to know that his ambition, so closely related to, and indeed driven by, his hatred of popery, would be realized, for posterity, not by a single Protestant scholar but by the collective efforts of Catholic clergy: that his chronology, and that of his Protestant successors, would be finally replaced by the great *Art de vérifier les dates* of the Benedictine monks of St-Germain-des-Prés and that the *Bibliotheca Patrum*, having been begun in his own time by the Jesuit Fronton le Duc and continued by the same Benedictines, would be finally published in the nineteenth century by the entrepreneurial genius of the Catholic abbé Jacques-Paul Migne.

Ironically, Ussher's most permanent legacy is one which he himself did his best to dissipate: his manuscripts. Unlike Archbishop Parker, who took care to secure his great manuscript collections by leaving them to his old University, Ussher left his whole library, as a marketable asset, to his only child Elizabeth and her husband Sir Timothy Tyrrell. The Tyrrells promptly decided to market it, and it would undoubtedly have been scattered, or sold abroad, had not Oliver Cromwell intervened, first to stop the sale, then to secure the library – at the expense of the pay of his soldiers in Ireland – not for Trinity College but for his projected new 'puritan' university in Dublin. The fall of the house of Cromwell frustrated that project; the new university was not founded; and Charles II, finding himself the possessor of the library, presented it, more appropriately, to the Archbishop's own university. There it remains still, a magnificent collection of books and manuscripts, an accidental but permanent and worthy monument to its creator, who thus, once again, after death as in life, was seen to be honoured by both sides in the great debate: revolutionary and traditionalist, Puritan and Anglican, usurper and King.[82]

Looking back over Ussher's whole career, we naturally ask, what was its significance in the intellectual and political history of his time? His erudition was impressive, even by the standards of that time, which was a heroic period of European scholarship, and he rescued much of the evidence of the dark age of Irish history: indeed, the reconstruction of early Irish history on a solid base begins with him. But he was not a historian of the calibre of 'the Jacobean giants': of Camden, the creator of English 'civil history', of Spelman, the discoverer of feudalism, of

Selden, who placed Church history in its institutional context. These
men, whatever their own religious views, sought the springs of history
within history itself: they were, in the eighteenth-century sense of the
phrase, 'philosophic historians'. Ussher, blinkered by his Ramist
training, had no such philosophical range; and he was limited, as well
as stimulated, by his Irish context: by his exposed position in that
colonial world in which Protestant ideas had to assert themselves
defiantly, aggressively, in order to be heard above the voices of the
Catholic gentry, who still dominated society and Parliament, and the
sinister unintelligible babble of the priest-led Celtic peasantry behind
them. He had his philosophy, of course; but it was a philosophy
conditioned, and perpetuated, by these constraints: the obsolescent
philosophy of the Elizabethan and Jacobean divines from which, in
England, a new generation of laity and clergy, scholars and divines,
was seeking to escape.

Ussher was not alone in these convictions: they were the inheritance
of his generation. But he was, by general consent, the most distinguished of all those who, in his time, articulated them: the acknowledged
leader of all those Jacobean clergy who, in the reign of Charles I, found
themselves suddenly excluded, or extruded, from authority. The
question therefore arises, could these men, as has so often been claimed,
if they had been promoted instead of the Laudians, have prevented the
catastrophe of the Puritan Revolution? The answer to that question is
necessarily speculative, and begs many other questions which it would
be rash to answer. Could Charles I have been other than he was? Is it
conceivable that, with his political and religious views, he might have
continued the Jacobean tradition of high Calvinism in the Church?
Even if it is – or if we could suppose that his elder brother had lived to
reign – is it certain that 'high Calvinism' would have been a continuing
bond between the King and his subjects, whom Laudian clericalism
divided? Might not that high Calvinism also have been found
compatible with royal autocracy? After all, James I found 'high
Calvinist' bishops ready to support his claims to divine right, and in
Holland it was the Calvinist party which would support the attempt of
William II to make his dynasty absolute, the 'Arminian' party of
Amsterdam which would frustrate it. If we believe that it was not
religion but politics which created the crisis of 1640–2, we cannot
assume that a difference of religious doctrine, combined with the same
politics, would have prevented it. What we can say is that if Charles I
(or Henry IX, had he lived) had sought to sustain an 'absolute'
monarchy on the basis of an Elizabethan high Calvinist episcopal

Church, his opponents would have found it less easy to mobilize against him the primitive emotions of anti-popery which proved so useful to them in their attack on Laud. The struggle would then have lacked something of its ideological ferocity. Perhaps – who can tell? – through that lack, the King would have won it; though whether, in such a victory, the same Church system could have survived, is another question.

For Ussher and his supporters were not really 'moderates'. Their religion was not a muddle-headed compromise between opposite intellectual systems. It was an ideology in its own right, the central ideology of the reformed Tudor Church, preceding both Laudianism and sectarian Puritanism. Clearly defined, unyielding to puritan pressure, aggressive against popery, it had been formulated by the Marian exiles, accepted by Elizabethan bishops, solidified by the dramatic events of the 1580s. James I found it entirely congenial. But in the changed intellectual climate of the 1630s, it no longer persuaded a new generation of educated men. As a coherent intellectual system, it was maintained chiefly by a wasting generation. In a moment of crisis it could be re-inflated by the vulgar fear of popery, but it had lost its own dynamism. In the crisis of 1640–2, both sides protested that they wished to revert to the Elizabethan political system. If that could have been done, no doubt the Elizabethan orthodoxy would have been restored too. But what if those protestations were mere lip-service, or if the Elizabethan political system was no longer viable? Then there was no place for the Church of Ussher. Which was what happened in fact. Surprisingly, the Church of Laud, once it had been divorced from a particular political system, had more inherent strength.

4

The Great Tew Circle

1 Falkland and his circle

We have all heard of the Great Tew circle – the group of young men (they were nearly all young men) who lived together in a kind of continuing seminar or reading party at the Oxfordshire house of Lucius Cary, 2nd Viscount Falkland, in the 1630s, those halcyon years before the storm of the civil wars and revolution. We have several contemporary accounts of that circle. John Aubrey, who knew many of its members, wrote one of these accounts. It occurs in his *Brief Lives*, originally written as raw material for his friend Anthony Wood's *Athenae Oxonienses*:

> 'My lord much lived at Tue, which is a pleasant seat, and about 12 miles from Oxford; his lordship was acquainted with the best witts of that University, and his house was like a Colledge, full of learned men. Mr William Chillingworth, of Trinity College in Oxford (afterwards D.D.), was his most intimate and beloved favourite, and was most commonly with my lord; next I may reckon (if not equall) Mr John Earles, of Merton College (who wrote the Characters);* Dr [George] Eglionby, of Ch.Ch., was also much in esteem with his lordship. His chaplaine, Charles Gataker, (*filius* [Thomae] Gataker of Redriff, a writer), was an ingeniose young gentleman, but no writer.†

* I.e. *Microcosmographie, or a Peece of the World discovered in Essayes and Characters* (1628). The book was published anonymously.

† In fact Charles Gataker appears to be the author of *Five Captious Questions, propounded by a Factor for the Papacy, answered by a divine of the Church of England*. This was published in 1673, together with a letter from Falkland addressed to the same 'Factor for the Papacy'. Falkland's letter is dated 1636, which is probably the date of composition of the pamphlet. The author signs as 'C.G.', whom a manuscript note on the Bodleian copy identifies as Charles Gataker.

For learned gentlemen of the country, his acquaintance was Sir H. Rainesford, of . . . neer Stratford-upon-Avon, now . . . (*quaere* Tom Mariet); Sir Francis Wenman, of Caswell, in Witney parish; Mr [George] Sandys, the traveller and translator (who was uncle to my lady Wenman); Ben. Johnson (vide *Johnsonus Virbius*, where he haz verses, and 'twas his lordship, Charles Gataker told me, that gave the name to it); Edmund Waller, esq.; Mr. Thomas Hobbes, and all the excellent of that peaceable time.[1]

But the best-known account is by the most famous member of the circle, whom Aubrey does not name, but who was an intimate friend of Falkland, and is, of all his friends, the most permanently associated with him: Edward Hyde, Earl of Clarendon. In both his *History of the Rebellion* and his *Life*, Clarendon describes the idyllic, intellectual life at Great Tew which made that house seem 'a college situated in a purer air' than Oxford, 'a university bound in a lesser volume'. Well known though they are, it is tempting to quote Clarendon's accounts in full, but I must resist that temptation.[2] Clarendon's style is too ample for extensive citation in an essay, and I must be content to select and to summarize.

Clarendon describes how Falkland, having been excellently educated at Trinity College, Dublin (his father being Strafford's predecessor as Lord Deputy of Ireland),* returned to England to inherit the two estates of his maternal grandfather, Sir Laurence Tanfield, a successful and close-fisted judge, at Burford and Great Tew. Coming from Ireland, he was 'unentangled with any [English] acquaintance and friends, which usually grow up by the custom of conversation, and therefore was to make a pure election of his company, which he chose by other rules than were prescribed to the young nobility of that time'. In other words, he chose them for their intellectual interests and conversation. At first he lived in London, which, on account of that conversation, was 'the place he loved of all the world'. Unfortunately, in his mother's London house he found one great inconvenience. The old Lady Falkland, a woman 'of a most masculine understanding, allayed with the passions and infirmities of her own sex',[3] had recently declared herself a Roman Catholic,† and with the zeal of a convert, had herself become a great *convertisseuse*. She began with her maid, who was

---

* Falkland was entered at St John's College, Cambridge, in 1621, but migrated to Trinity College, Dublin, in 1622 when his father was sent to Ireland as Lord Deputy.

† She had previously been a high Anglican, cultivating the 'Arminian' clergy of Durham House. (*UWW* XV, p.356.)

an easy prey, having been over-exposed to Presbyterian preachers in Scotland;* then she went on to her five surviving daughters; and by the time she had finished, she had converted her two youngest sons too.[4] Her eldest son found this pressure intolerable and so he retired to the country. He shut himself up in his house at Great Tew and there resumed 'his severe course of study', adding Greek to his previous languages and reading all the Greek historians, Homer and the Church Fathers.

Isolation in the country, in the seventeenth century, could be isolation indeed, even in a great house. Even at Chatsworth and Hardwick the sociable Hobbes (who was one of the visitors to Great Tew) found the conversation thin, and his understanding growing 'mouldy' through lack of exercise. But Falkland found a way of avoiding the tedium of rural life: he had all his friends to stay. In the intervals of these intellectual house-parties, he studied his books, which were numerous and recondite. He was a great collector of books, and his famous library was designed for use, not ostentation. 'How often', says one who lived in his house, 'have I heard him pity those hawking and hunting gentlemen' who, because they were strangers to literature, did not know what to do with themselves if confined indoors by the weather![5] When he was alone at Great Tew, Falkland was a voracious reader. But when his chosen friends came to stay, then, says Clarendon, he turned from reading to discussion:

> He looked upon no book, except their very conversation made an appeal to some book; and truly his whole conversation was one continued *Convivium Philosophicum*, or *Convivium Theologicum*, enlivened, and refreshed with all the facetiousness of wit, and good-humour, and pleasantness of discourse, which made the gravity of the argument itself (whatever it was) very delectable. His house where he usually resided (Tew, or Burford in Oxfordshire) being within ten or twelve miles of the University, looked like the University itself, by the company that was always found there. There were Dr Sheldon, Dr Morley, Dr Hammond, Dr Earles, Mr Chillingworth, and indeed all men of eminent parts and faculties in Oxford, besides those who resorted thither from London; who all found their lodgings there, as ready as in the colleges, nor did the lord of the house know of their coming or going, nor who were in his house, till he came to dinner or supper, where all still met;

---

* She had been with Lady Falkland's eldest daughter Katherine, now deceased, who had been married to the Scottish Earl of Home.

otherwise, there was no troublesome ceremony, or constraint to forbid men to come to the house, or to make them weary of staying there; so that many came thither to study in a better air, finding all the books they could desire in his library, and all the persons together whose company they could wish, and not find, in any other society. Here Mr Chillingworth wrote and formed and modelled his excellent book against the learned Jesuit Mr Knott, after frequent debates upon the most important particulars; in many of which he suffered himself to be over-ruled by the judgment of his friends, though in others he still adhered to his own fancy, which was sceptical enough, even in the highest points.[6]

Chillingworth's 'excellent book' was, of course, his famous work *The Religion of Protestants*, which caused such immediate concern to the hitherto triumphant Catholic propagandists, and gave – in the words of Hobbes – 'some shrewd back-blows' to his own party. It was published in 1638 and is the greatest intellectual contribution of the Great Tew circle. Well might the devout, not to say abject, Catholic converts of the Cary family wring their hands in anguish at the very thought of the detestable Chillingworth who, in their view, had treacherously seduced the head of their family and undone all, and more than all, the pious achievements of their evangelizing mother.

For if Falkland was the patron, Chillingworth was the intellectual motor of the Great Tew circle. He had come thither in curious circumstances. At the end of 1628, as a young Fellow of Trinity College, Oxford, he had been converted by the famous Jesuit missionary, Thomas Piercy, alias Fisher. He had then gone abroad to the English seminary at Douai, but within a few months had returned to England a disillusioned man, still outwardly a Catholic, but inwardly already doubtful of Catholic claims. His doubts were known to his godfather, Archbishop Laud, and to other members of the Anglican establishment, who promptly took steps to recover him, as they ultimately succeeded in doing, for the Anglican Church. They were not known, apparently, to old Lady Falkland, who saw in him only a fellow convert, perhaps even a fellow *convertisseur*. For Lady Falkland, an insufferable blue-stocking – she claimed to have taught herself Hungarian, and to read the Bible in Irish (which seems a tall story)[7] – was particularly eager to convert 'the scholars of Oxford and Cambridge', for whose benefit (since they 'do not generally understand French') she was translating the works of the most famous of French converts and converters, Cardinal du Perron. At all events, Lady

Falkland received him into her house in London as an ally. She soon discovered her error, for one night she overheard him not fortifying but undermining the Catholic faith of one of her carefully converted daughters. She promptly expelled him from the house, but was mortified to learn that her eldest son, who had already fled from her tedious preachings, had received him at Great Tew and appointed him tutor to his two youngest brothers. The formidable dowager was not daunted. By a skilful stratagem she contrived to steal the two boys away and send them abroad to be brought up by Catholic priests. This episode confirmed Falkland in his dislike of the Catholic Church and its missionaries, and in his friendship with the renegade Chillingworth.[8]

If Clarendon was Falkland's greatest friend among politicians, Chillingworth, all contemporaries agree, was his closest intellectual friend. These three sat at the very centre of the Great Tew circle, and thought alike on many topics. Others were no doubt more casual visitors, and although it may be possible to disengage a general philosophy, it would be unreasonable to look for identical positions in all of them. The very freedom of discussion which characterized their debates, and which made Great Tew a welcome refuge from the conformity of Laudian Oxford, ensured that opinions were various and that no orthodoxy reigned. In fact, all who came there were in some way heretics: they came, says Clarendon, 'not so much for repose as study, and to examine and refine those grosser propositions which laziness and consent made current in vulgar conversation'; and it was this taste for heresy, this willingness to dissent from received opinion, rather than any common opinion received by them, which united the whole circle, in varying degrees of intimacy, around their host.

Of the members of this wide circle Aubrey and Clarendon between them give a long list. But even that list is not complete. As each says, there were others: 'all the excellent of that peaceable time'; 'indeed all men of eminent parts and faculties in Oxford' – and in London too. Among these others Clarendon himself elsewhere notes the fastidious poet Sidney Godolphin, and 'the ever-memorable John Hales of Eton', 'who had sure read more, and carried more about him in his excellent memory, than any man I ever knew, my Lord Falkland only excepted'. The poet Sir John Suckling remembered chiefly the poets.[9] Anthony Wood adds Thomas Triplet, 'a very witty man of Christ Church', who would return to Great Tew after Falkland's death to educate his sons and edit his writings, and Hugh Cressy, of Merton College, of whom we shall hear more. Thomas Barlow, afterwards Bishop of Lincoln,[10] who knew Falkland well, both at Great Tew and afterwards at the royal court at Oxford, includes among those who, like him, enjoyed his 'friendship and frequent conversation' the poet Abraham Cowley; the lawyer John Vaughan of Trawscoed, afterwards Lord Chief Justice; the 'father of chemistry' Robert Boyle; and Boyle's sister Lady Ranelagh.*

Books and conversation, the freedom of that great library, the animation of those long debates, the warmth and friendship of that collegiate life in a hospitable country house – this was what all the members of that circle would always remember. It was Falkland's wonderful capacity for friendship – he was 'the dearest and truest friend that through the whole course of my unhappy life I ever had the happiness to meet with' – combined with the intellectual stimulus of his company that Thomas Triplet would afterwards recall: 'this it was that made Tew so valued a mansion to us; for as, when we went from Oxford thither, we found ourselves never out of the university, so we thought ourselves never absent from our own beloved home'.[11] John Hales wrote of the 'gaiety of spirit' which he always found there. John Earle, 'who was very dear to the Lord Falkland' and spent with him 'as much time as he could make his own', used to say 'that he had got more useful learning by his conversation at Tew . . . than he had at Oxford'.[12] The debt of Chillingworth to those debates is emphasized by Clarendon. On the other hand Bishop Barlow, who was himself a great bibliophile (he would be Bodley's Librarian on the way to his bishopric), declared that although Chillingworth was Falkland's closest friend, his greatest debt was to the library at Great Tew.[13]

How often all these men, in retrospect, returned to the 'happy and delightful conversation' of Great Tew. They were bound together, in part, of course, by the personality of their host. That little man, with his unrefined features, ungraceful gait and unmusical voice, no sooner spoke than his 'untuned tongue and voice easily discovered itself to be supplied, and governed, by a mind and understanding' of marvellous power and enchantment, 'and his disposition and nature was so gentle and obliging, so much delighted in courtesy, kindness and generosity, that all mankind could not but admire and love him.'[14] This universal respect was extended from Falkland himself to the friends whom he

* Those named by Barlow as friends of Falkland were not necessarily members of the *convivium* at Great Tew. Abraham Cowley, according to his biographer, Bishop Sprat, met Falkland at Oxford in 1642–3. Robert Boyle, born in 1627, was too young to have been of the party at Tew. He clearly admired Falkland. Since Barlow names him, he may have been brought into Falkland's circle through his elder sister Lady Ranelagh, who was born in 1615 and is known as the friend not only of Falkland and Clarendon but also of Milton.

chose. As Anthony Wood wrote of George Morley, afterwards Bishop of Winchester, he 'first became known as a friend of the Lord Falkland, and that was enough to raise a man's character'.[15] Clarendon himself, as Sir Charles Firth has said, had a genius for friendship, and his friendship with Falkland was clearly the great friendship of his life.[16] It was 'a most entire friendship, without reserve, from his age of twenty years, to the hour of his death'. In private life and in politics they were inseparable. Until 1642, when they left London for York, it was noticed that they always sat together in the Long Parliament. In 1642–3, at York and at Oxford, they worked in combination. The death of Falkland at the first battle of Newbury, on 20 September 1643, was to Clarendon an emotional shock of which we hear the reverberations whenever he recalls it.

For Falkland died a defeated man. The civil war had destroyed his world. All his attempts to shorten that war had failed, and he could see no end to it. As the King's Secretary of State, he had incurred the censure of more robust Cavaliers for his passionate desire of peace: they had thought him 'so enamoured on peace that he would have bought it at any price; which', says Clarendon, 'was a most unreasonable calumny'; and in the end he had exposed himself to a certain death which could hardly be distinguished from suicide.

In 1647, when Clarendon, in the island of Jersey, was writing his *History of the Rebellion* and came to the battle of Newbury, he resolved (as he wrote to John Earle) to 'enlarge upon the memory of our dear friend that perished there; to which I conceive myself obliged, not more by the rights of friendship than of history, which ought to transmit the virtues of excellent persons to posterity'. So he wrote the first of the two famous sketches of Falkland from which I have quoted. At one time he thought that he might 'enlarge it into the whole size of his life' and publish it separately, ahead of his *History*, as 'Tacitus published his life of Julius Agricola before either his *Annals* or his *History*';[17] but in the end he left it in his *History*, where it is the most eloquent and most moving of the 'characters' for which that work is famous. How can anyone, writing of Falkland, forbear to quote the beginning and the end of that marvellous piece? The beginning:

> In this unhappy battle was slain the lord viscount Falkland: a person of such prodigious parts of learning and knowledge, of that inimitable sweetness and delight in conversation, of so flowing and obligingly a humanity and goodness to mankind, and of that primitive simplicity and integrity of life, that if there were no other

brand upon this odious and accursed civil war than that single loss, it must be most infamous and execrable to all posterity.

and the end:

Thus fell that incomparable young man, in the four-and thirtieth year of his age, having so much despatched the business of life that the oldest rarely attain to that immense knowledge, and the youngest enter not into the world with more innocence: and whosoever leads such a life need not care upon how short warning it be taken from him.

Twenty years later, in his autobiography, Clarendon wrote a second account of Falkland, as long and as vivid as the first. Between them, the two accounts form, as Sir Charles Firth wrote, 'an incomparable portrait': 'twice over he draws it at length, and each time the long, involved periods glow and throb, and one feels behind the words the sense of irreparable loss and undying affection'.[18] That same sense is evident from other sources. In 1647, before writing his first account, Clarendon wrote his will, and in it he enjoined his sons, then young children, always to live in friendship with the sons of Lord Falkland;[19] and six years after writing his second account, the last work which he wrote, only a year before his death, would be inspired by the desire to vindicate the memory and the philosophy of 'that unparallel'd Lord'.[20]

Such was the character of Falkland, the central figure of Great Tew – or at least, such was the impression he made on those who came into his circle. And yet how little we really know of him! Had it not been for Clarendon, he would hardly be remembered. For today, all trace of him has disappeared. No contemporary monument marks his grave at Great Tew. His descendants died out in 1694. The house itself disappeared in the eighteenth century, and no picture of it is known to me. His personal papers are lost. His 'frequent letters' to his friends, which Clarendon mentioned, have all apparently disappeared. His unpublished writings, whatever they were, perished within a few years of his death: already in 1651 they were described as 'long since involved in the common loss':[21] a planned biography of him was never written.*

* Sir Peter Pett, Fellow of All Souls, proposed to write such a biography for an edition of Falkland's works, and to use the evidence of Falkland's friends, including Cowley, Waller, Robert Boyle, Lady Ranelagh and Lord Chief Justice Vaughan. But it came to nothing – perhaps because the surviving 'works' were so few (*The Genuine Remains of Thomas Barlow*, 1693, pp. 327–33).

His 'incomparable library', so praised by the scholars who used it, so filled with rare and suspect works, was sold by his wastrel son for 'a horse and a mare';[22] and although it seems to have been rescued by Falkland's friend, Archbishop Sheldon, and placed in All Souls College, of which Sheldon had been Warden, that incurious institution heedlessly scattered it, in 1925, as a parcel of 'obsolete books' only to be 'got rid of'.[23]

It may be argued that the loss is not, after all, very serious. Falkland himself was not an original thinker. His personality may have been – must have been – powerful, but his mind was not. His poems, mainly dedicatory poems in other men's books, are slight. His published prose works are few and thin. Apart from two speeches in the Long Parliament in 1641 – one on episcopacy, one on ship money and the judges – and the draft of a second speech on episcopacy, they consist only of his *Discourse of Infallibility* and his answer to a reply to that discourse by an anonymous Roman Catholic Controversialist.* The *Discourse* was circulated in manuscript during his lifetime but not published till 1645, when the text came to the hands of the university printer in Oxford. One of his Catholic critics called it 'Chillingworth's book in little and an embryo of his larger volume grown up after'; and his defender, Henry Hammond, admitted the truth of the charge: Falkland's work, he wrote, was an 'epitome' of Chillingworth's *Religion of Protestants*, 'useful and gainful to supersede the trouble of reading the larger book'.[24] Altogether, in literature as in politics, Falkland himself emerges as a lightweight: which makes the devotion and admiration of Clarendon, who surpassed him in both, all the more personal. To us the interest of Great Tew is not, ultimately, in the person of its owner: it is in the group of men who gathered there and for whom their membership of that Oxfordshire country club was to be, I believe, a formative influence throughout their lives.

I know that this has been disputed. The Great Tew circle has been represented as a mere casual miscellany of dilettanti, accidentally immortalized by Clarendon's panegyric of Falkland: a fair-weather house-party soon to be dissipated by the harsh realities of civil war. In his book on the *Intellectual Origins of the Puritan Revolution*, Mr

---

* In the 1660 edition of Falkland's *Discourse*, the reply to it (which is there reprinted) is ascribed to the well-known anti-Jesuit Catholic controversialist Thomas White, *alias* Blacklo; but Bishop Barlow says explicitly that it was written by the Jesuit Guy Holland (*AO* II, p. 569), This reply, which was answered by Falkland, is often confused with the (unprinted) 'Exceptions' to the same *Discourse* which were answered by Hammond (see below p. 220), and which are therefore also sometimes ascribed to White. Certainty being unattainable, I have judged it prudent to leave all these Catholic objectors in the anonymity which they clearly preferred.

Christopher Hill never refers to them. In his book on *The Age of Charles I*,²⁵ Archbishop David Mathew devotes a whole chapter to Great Tew, but only to dismiss it as 'an over-written episode': the only intellectual influence which he discovers behind it is that of the Catholic St François de Sales, for which he gives, and I know, no evidence, and though he may seem to strengthen his case by ascribing the Catholics Wat Montagu and Sir Kenelm Digby to the group, I know no evidence for that ascription either.* The intellectual influences which dominated Great Tew are, I believe, perfectly clear, and I shall come to them in due course.† Meanwhile I shall say why I consider that the group deserves consideration.

First of all, there is its quality. Let us admit that the Great Tew group was a somewhat esoteric graduate reading party in the country. Even so, the graduates are rather remarkable. They included a future Archbishop of Canterbury; a future Lord Chancellor who was also the greatest historian of his time; 'the father of English biblical criticism';²⁶ the most original political philosopher of the century; and the most influential English philosopher before Locke. I refer to Sheldon, Clarendon, Hammond, Hobbes and Chillingworth. Even the less famous members of the group are not obscure. Morley, Earle, Barlow all became bishops. Waller and Cowley are remembered as poets, Hales as a scholar. A small private circle which contained all these men, before any of them was famous, at least argues that their host's 'election', in Clarendon's phrase, was very discriminating.

Secondly, I would point to the remarkable cohesion of the group. For it is not true, as is so easily supposed, that the Great Tew group was ineffectual, or that it was permanently shattered by the impact of the civil war. Far from it. When we think of the other groups and parties of those revolutionary decades — of their kaleidoscopic mutations and

---

* David Masson, *The Life of John Milton* (1859–94) I, p. 686, seems to be the first to state that Sir Kenelm Digby was intimately associated with the Falkland set, but he gives no evidence for the statement. Digby's cousin George, Lord Digby was a friend of Clarendon and Falkland, with whom he voted in 1640–1 and whom he recommended as ministers in 1641, and, like Falkland, an admirer of Chillingworth and Daillé (see *Letters between the Lord George Digby and Sir Kenelm Digby Kt. concerning Religion*, 1651); but Kenelm Digby preferred Chillingworth's Catholic adversary Thomas White, *alias* Blacklo. Falkland wrote a letter to Wat Montagu on his conversion to Rome (published in the 1651 edition of Falkland's *Discourse*); but it is an open letter, replying to Montagu's letter to his father the Earl of Manchester, which had been published, and does not of itself argue personal friendship, or even acquaintance.

† The most perceptive account of the intellectual interest of the Great Tew circle seems to me B. H. G. Wormald, *Clarendon, Politics, History and Religion* (Cambridge 1951), part III.

fragmentations – we must be impressed rather by the perseverance and cohesion than by the dissolution and failure of this intellectual society.

Admittedly, they failed in their first hopes, and therefore it is easy to say that their hopes were unreal, politically unattainable. In revolutions, those who do not ride the storm are easily accused of incompetence. 'Hyde and Falkland', writes Dame Veronica Wedgwood, echoing the accepted view, 'may justly be respected for their ideals and pitied for their misfortunes; they cannot be praised for their political judgment'.[27] But if success is the criterion of political skill, who, in those tempestuous years, could claim it? Could Pym, who saw all his work ruined and died in the wreckage of it? Could the 'Presbyterians', who failed either to defeat the King, or to prevent the revolution, or to control the Restoration? Could the Levellers, who at one time seemed to drive the whole revolutionary machine and then, within two years, were totally destroyed and forgotten? Could the Republicans, who twice held power and were twice thrown aside by the army which they could not command? Could Cromwell himself, who, for a few years, ruled the three kingdoms but whose whole empire, at his death, dissolved in ruin? If it was naïve to hope for a new political and religious settlement in 1641, it was a *naïveté* widely shared at the time. The Puritans too believed that they were within sight of a bloodless victory. John Milton and Samuel Hartlib, Stephen Marshall and Jeremiah Burroughes, all celebrated in those days the triumph of their cause. Their rejoicing was premature. For twenty years every victory was barren; only the last victory, that of Clarendon and his friends, proved the basis of permanent settlement.

Let us glance at the men of Great Tew as a group in the revolutionary decades. Bound together in the 1630s by personal friendship and common interests, they were highly critical of the government of Charles I. In 1640 several of them went into Parliament – Clarendon,* Falkland, Waller, Godolphin. Hobbes would have been a member if he could, although by then he had already begun to go his own way.† In Parliament, Clarendon, Falkland and Waller worked together as a reforming group. Between them they attacked every aspect of the 'Eleven Years Tyranny': the royal encroachment on 'liberty and

---

* Since he entered this essay as the historian, the Earl of Clarendon, I shall, for convenience, generally name him thus, although he was, throughout Falkland's life, a commoner, Edward Hyde; but to chop and change would be confusing.

† Hobbes evidently tried to represent the borough of Derby in the Short Parliament of 1640, as the nominee of his patron, the Earl of Devonshire, but the electors absolutely declined to accept him (HMC Earl Cowper, II, p. 251).

property', the subservient judges, the Laudian bishops, the unpar-
liamentary taxes, the 'prerogative' courts.* Their clerical friends,
Morley and Hammond, were appointed to the Assembly which was to
reform the Church.† Later, when Pym and Hampden moved, or were
driven, from reform to revolution, and the Parliament was split, the
Great Tew group continued to work together. When Clarendon was in
danger of arrest on a charge of high treason, it was his old friends who
organized his escape. Morley, in London, discovered the danger and
warned Falkland, who immediately sent word to Clarendon. Clarendon, who was staying with Lady Lee at Ditchley near Oxford – two
miles from Tew – at once arranged to flee to the King at York. Since he
was unfamiliar with the roads, and feared arrest, he sent for Chillingworth from Oxford. That night, his horses were sent on to the farm of
Chillingworth's brother, near Coventry. In the morning, with Chillingworth as his guide, he set out in Lady Lee's coach-and-six. From
Coventry, Chillingworth guided him by safe byways to York.[28]

In the spring and summer of 1642, Clarendon and Falkland played a
large part in creating the new royalist party which rescued the King from
his political isolation in England. They provided him with propaganda
which won over half the country. The propaganda was belied by
events: the King would fight, and die, for sovereignty, not 'mixed
monarchy'; but they believed that, in the end, they could make it true.
In this they were no more mistaken than their opponents; for Pym also
professed that he was contending for 'mixed monarchy', which he
believed he could make true, but afterwards he would be found to have
fought for parliamentary sovereignty and military dictatorship. Even

---

* On 6 July 1641 Falkland spoke in the House of Commons against the ship money
judges who had sought 'the transformation of this kingdom from the estate of free
subjects . . . into that of villaines' (*The Lord Falkland his learned speech . . . touching the Judges
. . . 1641*). At the conference with the Lords on the same day, speeches were made by
Clarendon and Waller, who had carried up the impeachments of the judges (*Mr Edward
Hyde's speech at a conference between both Houses on Tuesday 6 July 1641 . . .; Mr Waller's speech in
Parliament at a conference of both Houses in the Painted Chamber, 6 July 1641*).

† The assembly, which ultimately became the Westminster Assembly, was
appointed in April 1642: the clergy were nominated by members of Parliament, two
per English county, one per Welsh county. Almost all so nominated were accepted
unanimously. The Lords then added a further fourteen names. Hammond was one of
those added by the Lords, but the Commons objected against him. However, after a
conference, at which the Earls of Pembroke, Holland, Bristol, Leicester and
Northumberland – all of them, at that time, 'popular peers' – insisted that he was
'learned and orthodox', the Commons allowed him. (*Lords Journals* V, 84, 95–7;
Commons Journals II, 595; BL MS Harl. 163, fo. 141v.) The Assembly did not meet till
1 July 1643: it was by then an illegal body, resting on a parliamentary ordinance only,
and neither Hammond nor Morley took part in it.

after the civil war had broken out, and the group seemed divided, its members continued their co-operation. Chillingworth wrote pamphlets advocating settlement[29] and Clarendon and Falkland in Oxford worked together with Waller in London. 'Waller's Plot' of 1643, concerted between them – for Waller 'held constant intelligence and intercourse with the Lord Falkland' – was a plan for peace on the principles of Great Tew.[30] At any time until the summer of 1643 the hope of settlement depended on the success of their policy; and if settlement had been achieved, they would have determined its form.

Thereafter, indeed the pattern changed. The exposure and exploitation of 'Waller's Plot' by Pym was the first great blow to the party of peace in both camps. Then came the parliamentary alliance with the Scots: those fatal allies of whom Pym had so skilfully disembarrassed himself two years before, but who were now disastrously re-introduced into an English quarrel. No wonder Clarendon hated the Scots: their intervention in English politics, on whichever side, invariably wrecked his plans, indeed all plans, for an English settlement. The year 1643–4 was anyway a climacteric period for the Great Tew group, which then suffered a series of personal losses. First Waller, after the failure of his 'plot', narrowly escaped execution in London. According to Aubrey, he had to bribe the whole House of Commons to survive. Luckily, he was rich enough to do so. Having survived, he fled to France, discredited by his betrayal of his friends – although, in Clarendon's phrase, his company remained acceptable even where his character was odious.[31] Then Falkland himself, sleepless from 'the very agony of the war', exposed himself to a soldier's death at Newbury. Soon afterwards Chillingworth, captured at Arundel castle, was 'so barbarously used' by the parliamentary soldiers that he died within a few days at Chichester. Meanwhile Sidney Godolphin had been killed by a chance shot as he pursued the enemy through Chagford, 'an obscure village in Devonshire'. In the same year George Aglionby died at Oxford 'of the epidemique disease then raging'.[32] Thus within a few months the policy of Great Tew seemed in ruins and four of its members, including its leader, were dead.

Nevertheless, the survivors did not despair. At the royal court in Oxford, Clarendon continued the struggle. It was in those same months that he persuaded the King to bring the uncommitted members of Parliament to Oxford and, through them, to work out a formula of conciliation. He was encouraged to persevere by his surviving friends. Morley and Sheldon were with him constantly at Oxford, the former as canon of Christ Church, the latter as Warden of All Souls College. In

1643 they had been joined by Hammond, fleeing from his living at Penshurst with a price on his head. These three, all in contact with Clarendon, would attend the King constantly as his chaplains. Clarendon clearly saw himself as the political heir and executor of the dead Falkland. Others saw him so too. Lady Ranelagh, the blue-stocking sister of Robert Boyle, whose family were on the parliamentary side, wrote to him explicitly in that capacity: as the closest friend of Falkland she urged him to continue his work for peace;[33] which indeed he did, although the shattering loss of his friends, the political and military disasters of 1644, and the intrigues at court conspired to ruin his efforts. By 1645 a peace of compromise was clearly unattainable and a peace of conquest would not realize any of the aims of a party which now seemed discredited and broken beyond repair.

2   The circle after Falkland

For fifteen years, from the battle of Naseby to the Restoration, it was 'the Puritans' who dominated English politics. Nevertheless, throughout those years, the surviving members of the Great Tew circle preserved their solidarity and their philosophy. Clarendon was now the dominant figure among them, at least in politics. When he left Oxford with the Prince of Wales, Earle accompanied him, while Sheldon, Hammond and Morley remained as the chaplains and companions – when he was allowed to have them – of the King. After the execution of the King, Earle and Morley would go with Clarendon into exile: Morley would live for three years in Clarendon's house while Sheldon and Hammond acted as his allies and informants in England. All five would remain in close and regular correspondence. Between them they would plan the ultimate return both of the monarchy and of the Church, and determine the form which it would take. They would be the royalist architects of the Restoration, and it was their ideas which would triumph after 1660.

Moreover, all of them still remained bound together around Great Tew. After Falkland's death, his widow had continued his patronage,* and at her own death in 1649 she appointed four of his circle – Sheldon, Morley, Earle and Hammond – as overseers of her will and guardians

---

* For Lady Falkland's good works see John Duncan, *The Return of Spiritual Comfort and Grief in a Devout Soul* (1649): a collection of imaginary letters to her by a sequestered parson whom she had harboured at Great Tew; also Thomas Triplet's preface to Falkland's *Discourse* (1651).

of her children. Sheldon and Hammond, in England, looked after the encumbered estate of Great Tew while Morley and Earle, on the Continent, received the successive heirs and struggled to provide for their education in France and Holland. The communication between these two groups was handled by Thomas Triplet, the former tutor at Great Tew: he had a weekly connexion with Earle and, through Earle, with Clarendon, who was a close personal friend.

In the correspondence of this severed group, the affairs of the ruined monarchy and broken Church are mingled with the no less disordered affairs of Great Tew. The first of Falkland's sons to be sent abroad was Lucius, third viscount, who died in France in 1649. Then his next brother, Henry, fourth viscount, took his place: a weak, unstable spendthrift, whose follies exasperated his guardians. It seemed beyond hope, wrote one of them, that 'this mercury' would ever 'become a man some way answerable to his name, title, and our desires'. He had scarcely arrived in France when he wished to return to England. His grandmother, Lady Morison, supported him, but the Great Tew group united to resist the pressure. Morley, who watched over the young Falkland on the Continent, urged that he be kept there for some years as the only means to prevent him from ruining his estate and to give Hammond and Sheldon, together with his father's executors, time to clear it of debt. Between them they succeeded in keeping him abroad till 1656.* It was no doubt after his return, in that year, that he sold his father's library, and that Sheldon intervened to save it.

It was not only Falkland's sons who engaged the attention of his surviving friends. After 1649, the mercurial fourth viscount being unmarried, Falkland's younger brother, Patrick Cary, became heir-presumptive to the title and the estate. He was the elder of the two brothers who had been 'stolen away' from Falkland's house and sent by their mother, first to France, then to Italy, to be brought up as Roman Catholics; after which Falkland, in indignation, had declined all correspondence with them. Patrick Cary made some study of the law, but seems to have made no use of it: he preferred writing poetry. For a time he lived on the charity of Queen Henrietta Maria, who gave him a secret pension, and of Pope Urban VIII who, at her instance, added 'an abbey and a priory *in commendam*': both, it seems, sinecures, Cary being a layman. But with the poverty of the Queen and the death of the Pope, these sources dried up, and when the English estates of his family came

---

* The activities of the guardians, and their problems with the young Lord Falkland and his estate, are recorded in the correspondence in BL MS Harl. 6942, on which see below, p.295 note 135.

within his reach, he began to waver in his Catholic loyalties. He turned towards the English friends of his late brother and hinted, at the same time, that he might be recovered for Protestantism.

Among others, he approached Clarendon. He used as intermediaries his own sisters, the nuns of Cambrai, whom Clarendon, out of love for their brother, visited in their cloister. Then he wrote direct to Clarendon, who by that time was in Madrid as ambassador for Charles II. After dwelling on Clarendon's known love of 'my brother Falkland', and describing his own life-history and misfortunes, he came slowly to the point. Could not Clarendon use his influence with the court of Spain to secure 'an express effectual order' to the authorities in Flanders to grant Cary an office of profit or a pension there? A canonry would not do, unless it were without obligation to take orders, 'a thing I am less willing to do since my poor nephew Falkland's death': i.e. since he became heir to the peerage. In view of that prospect, he was thinking of marriage and heirs: in which he was wise, for his descendants would in fact afterwards inherit the title, and still hold it.[34]

On the face of it, the letter was not happy, either in content or in timing. Cary was a stranger to Clarendon to whom he now presented himself as a drifting parasite, without firm loyalty or convictions. He had been a creature of the Queen, whom Clarendon hated, believing that she had ruined Charles I and was seeking to ruin Charles II. Now he was asking not to serve but to sponge. And he made this application to a man who believed, above all, in active virtue: who despised Catholicism and its converts, and had himself accepted poverty, exile and hardship rather than surrender his principles or compromise his loyalty. Objectively, we would expect Clarendon to feel contempt for Cary's letter: contempt such as he would express, in olympian, sardonic tones, for so many feckless royalists who preferred ease and plenty to strenuous loyalty.

So we might expect. But in fact we would be wrong. The magic of Falkland's name dissolved all antipathies, and Clarendon replied to the begging letter at length, and in tones of real warmth. 'Since the unspeakable loss of your excellent brother', he wrote, 'I have rarely felt so great a pleasure as the first sight of your name to a letter gave me'. It reminded him of 'that conversation I was once more blessed with than other men'. Although there was no hope of a pension from Spain, Clarendon promised his good will and wrote to Secretary Nicholas in Brussels to see whether he could help.[35] The help was evidently insufficient. Cary was reduced to taking the habit at Douai, which, feckless as ever, he discarded within a year. He then declared himself dissatisfied with the Roman Church, went to England, married, and obtained letters from Speaker Lenthall 'to all in power in Ireland for some place there'. His father having been Lord Deputy in Ireland, his thoughts had often turned thither. He had previously had letters from the Queen to the Marquis of Ormonde, the royalist commander in Ireland, for the same purpose, Catholics being then 'by the articles of peace made capable of bearing office in that kingdom'. That application had been fruitless, but now, as a Protestant, he fared better. He became Clerk of the Pells in Cromwellian Dublin and died there in 1657.[36]

Thus the links between Falkland's friends and Falkland's family were gradually weakened. But in May 1660 a little episode re-affirmed them. The House of Commons of the Convention Parliament, having resolved to send a delegation to the Hague to invite Charles II to return to England, included among them the mercurial young Lord Falkland, who had been elected as member for the city of Oxford. As no other qualification is apparent, we may suppose that he was chosen as a compliment to the King's chief adviser, the successful negotiator of the Restoration, Clarendon. As Clarendon wrote in 1662, when securing a military commission for him in Ireland, 'I would think myself happier to oblige his father's son than in compassing anything for my own'.*

For the rest of his life, Clarendon remained faithful to the surviving members of that group and honoured the memory of those who had died. In the time of his greatness, the portraits of Falkland, Chillingworth, Hales, Sheldon, Morley, even Waller, would hang in his gallery in Clarendon House.[37] In the time of his disgrace and second exile, he would write the sympathetic characters of them all in his *Life*. At his death, they were his most trusted friends. It was to Morley and Sheldon that he would bequeath the manuscript of his *History*, by their judgment that it was to be published or suppressed.

This strong and lasting emotional solidarity among the members of the Great Tew group is illustrated also by the attitude of Clarendon towards the two of them who most signally deserted and, as he thought, betrayed their common ideals. These were Thomas Hobbes and Hugh Cressy.

Of Thomas Hobbes there is no need to say much here. Here we are

---

* Falkland had been involved in an abortive Cavalier rising in Oxfordshire in 1659, and had been imprisoned in the Tower from August to November 1659. The royalist conspirators generally found him hot-headed and uncontrollable – as his guardians had done. See David Underdown, *Royalist Conspiracy in England* (Yale 1960); and cf. *History of Parliament, The House of Commons 1660–1690* (1983), pp. 18–19.

only concerned with his relations with the Great Tew group. They were evidently close. We know that Hobbes visited Great Tew, and we know that Falkland was 'his great friend and admirer'.[38] His early works were circulated in manuscript among members of the group, and he was a close personal friend of many of them – Chillingworth, Waller, Clarendon, Godolphin, Sheldon, and others. As tutor to the Prince of Wales from 1647 to 1651, Hobbes was a member of the exiled court, and so continued to enjoy regular contact with Earle, Morley and Clarendon. It is clear that their views diverged, but this divergence does not seem to have disturbed their personal relations. Hobbes was at least a royalist, indeed a high-flying royalist: if his views alarmed his Great Tew friends at that time, it was rather because of their ultra-royalism than because of any radical content.

In 1650 that radical content began to appear. Early in that year, one of those friends, Robert Payne, an extruded canon of Christ Church, Oxford, now living privately in Abingdon, wrote to him urging him to publish his own translation of his early work *De Cive*, of which an unauthorized version had appeared in English.[39] Hobbes replied (as Payne reported to Sheldon) that he had no time for such an enterprise: 'he hath another task in hand, which is Politiques in English, of which he hath finished thirty-seven chapters'.[40] Hobbes' account of his new work alarmed his friend. Soon afterwards, in Paris, Hobbes showed the completed text of his new work to Clarendon. It was *Leviathan*. Clarendon was aghast at the doctrine which it contained and protested at the thought of such inopportune publication. But Hobbes replied, in effect, that it was most opportune: 'the truth is, I had a mind to go home'. Soon afterwards, *Leviathan* was published in England and Hobbes duly went home. In *Leviathan*, he had made it clear that he accepted an effective *de facto* government.

Hugh Cressy's defection from the Great Tew group was in a different direction. He was a young Fellow of Merton College, Oxford, who had spent some time in Ireland as chaplain to the Earl of Strafford, and had been rewarded by him with several Irish benefices. But the patron to whom he was most devoted was 'his most honoured lord, Lucius Viscount Falkland', 'his most beloved Lord Falkland', 'my noble dear lord, Lucius Lord Falkland', whom he visited whenever in England. Falkland took him into his household on his final return from Ireland, and later, when Secretary of State, secured for him a canonry of Windsor. But after the disasters of 1643–4, Cressy lost the hope which had once sustained the Great Tew fraternity. He saw the English Church ruined at home and no base for it abroad; he listened to the gleeful boasts of the Catholic propagandists who declared that all was now over with that schismatic Church; and in his despair, like many other weak brethren, he crept into the warmer bosom of the Church of Rome. In 1646, at Rome, he publicly recanted his Protestantism, and next year, in Paris, he published his best-known work. It was entitled *Exomologesis*, and was an explanation of the motives of his conversion. Like Newman two centuries later, Cressy had discovered that the Church of England had been rotted from within by heresy and compliance with heretics; he had decided that it was about to sink; and he had scrambled for safety into a guaranteed, unsinkable lifeboat. For the next thirty years, he was an indefatigable Catholic propagandist, asserting, with diminishing plausibility, that the Church of England no longer existed.

Cressy's *Exomologesis* was a famous book in its day. Like Hobbes' *Leviathan*, it was a body-blow delivered at a reeling institution; for just as Hobbes, the ultra-royalist of 1640, suddenly (as it seemed) inverted his own theories in order to legitimize the regicide usurper, so Cressy, the high Anglican clergyman, suddenly turned round and savaged his own faltering Church. 'This *Exomologesis*', wrote Anthony Wood, 'was the golden calf which the English papists fell down and worshipped. They bragged that book to be unanswerable, and to have given a total overthrow to the Chillingworthians, and to the book and tenets of Lucius Lord Falkland'. But even in his conversion, Cressy did not entirely escape from the memories of Great Tew; for his first post, as a Benedictine priest, was as confessor to the English nuns of Cambrai, among whom were the four perverted sisters of Lord Falkland.[41]

Both Hobbes and Cressy were intimate friends of Clarendon. In his old age, Clarendon described Cressy as 'an old friend . . . with whom I have been acquainted nearly fifty years', and he described how, as undergraduates at Oxford, they had gone together to hear a famous sermon preached by Thomas Lushington in the university church.[42] Hobbes similarly was to Clarendon 'my old friend', 'one of the most ancient acquaintance I have in the world'. In the 1640s, when Clarendon read Hobbes' early works in manuscript, he recorded his dissent, but he remained his friend: he exerted himself to secure a legacy for him and begged him to continue sending him his works.*

---

* Clarendon read Thucydides in Hobbes' version (as is shown by the page-references in his commonplace-book, BL MS Clar. 127, fos. 50–4). He also read Hobbes' *Elements of Law* in manuscript and asked Hobbes to send him his *De Cive* (*Clar. SP* II, pp.322, 340–1, 350). In his 'Memorabilia', written in 1647 (MS Clar. 126, fos. 150–5), he cites Grotius 'against Mr Hobbes his absolute power of kings and confounding the right of property', and cf. Clarendon, *A Brief View and Survey of . . . Leviathan* (Oxford 1676).

Equally, when Cressy deserted the English Church, Clarendon did not disown him. He deplored his 'odious alteration (for methinks apostasy is too cholerick a word towards a friend)',[43] but he protested that they were friends still. The men of Great Tew made a cult of friendship and civility and always protested their respect for intellectual differences. Hammond equally refused to oppose Cressy after his conversion, 'that he might give no disturbance to a person for whom he had so great a value' and whose conversion, all agreed, was disinterested.[44]

What finally shattered Clarendon's friendship with both Cressy and Hobbes and drove him to make public attacks on both of them was not their religious or political 'alteration': it was their blasphemy against the saints of Great Tew. In 1651, when Hobbes published his *Leviathan*, Clarendon was of course shocked by the argument – or at least by the application of it, for he had read the argument before. But he was even more shocked by the dedication. For this infamous book was dedicated, in fulsome terms, to the memory of one of the Great Tew circle – the poet Sidney Godolphin who, like Falkland himself, had been killed in 1643. Clarendon himself had introduced Hobbes to Godolphin, and it was Godolphin's legacy of £200 to Hobbes which Clarendon had sought to secure for him. To dedicate such a work to such a man, in such circumstances, seemed to Clarendon a heresy worse that *Leviathan* itself.

Then, in 1672, Cressy went further still. In the contortions of religious controversy he declared not only that the Church of England had been rotted from within, but that he himself had witnessed the process: for the corrosive ideas had been injected into it from the laboratory of Great Tew. It was his own patron Falkland, and Falkland's evil spirit Chillingworth, he wrote, who had spread the poison; and he added that he spoke with knowledge, because it was he himself, all unwitting, who had supplied it to them.[45] The poison was a book, the *Traicté de l'employ des saincts pères* by the French Huguenot pastor Jean Daillé, published in 1631 – the germ of Chillingworth's *Religion of Protestants*.

This was too much. Old and exiled in a foreign country, without books, uncomfortable and alone, Clarendon reached for his pen and, in drastic excoriating sentences, excommunicated both the heretics. The incomparable Falkland was cleared of all heresy. Cressy, said Clarendon, had got all his facts wrong. Daillé's book had been read and discussed at Great Tew long before Cressy's arrival from Ireland; nor could Cressy pretend to relate his conversion to it: he had never dreamed of conversion 'till long after the death of the Lord

Falkland and Mr Chillingworth, not till the same rebellious power that drove the king out of the kingdom drove him likewise from the good preferments which he had enjoyed in the Church'; which economic loss, added to 'the melancholic and irresolution in his nature, prevailed with him to bid farewell to his own reason' and plummet into popery.[46] As for Hobbes, it was an insult, said Clarendon, to dedicate a pernicious and erroneous book like *Leviathan* to Godolphin, 'whose untimely loss in the beginning of the war was too lively an instance of the inequality of the contention, when such inestimable treasure was ventured against dirty people of no name'.[47]

So even their quarrels illustrate the solidarity of the Great Tew group. When we consider that solidarity, so firmly preserved through years of political disaster and ideological confusion, we must ask ourselves what was the charm which held them together. It cannot have been merely the personality of Falkland, who perished so soon. It cannot have been merely the shared experience of youth, for that did not preserve other groups from division. It must have been to some extent, at least, a set of beliefs held in common. In the remainder of this essay I shall try to isolate those common beliefs, and thereby give some intellectual substance to a group of men which has been too often dismissed as a mere coterie, but which, I will suggest, had its part in the real intellectual development of the seventeenth century.

3   The 'Socinian' tradition

The first and most obvious fact which must strike any reader is that Falkland himself, and most of his friends, were widely accused of being 'Socinian'. Falkland, says Aubrey, was so exasperated by his mother's attempts to convert him to the Romish Church 'that he settled and rested in the Polish (I mean Socinianism). He was the first Socinian in England'. His *dévote* sister put the same point somewhat differently. Her brother, she says, had for some years 'good inclination towards religion' – that is, of course, towards Roman Catholicism – but then, 'meeting a book of Socinus, it opened to him a new way'. That and the dreadful Chillingworth, she said, were his undoing. Cressy makes the same charge: Socinianism, he says firmly, was the corrosive poison which Falkland and Chillingworth had so fatally injected into the Anglican Church.

Chillingworth, in particular, was regarded as the villain of the piece; he was recognized, perhaps rightly, as Falkland's seducer. When Chillingworth was known to be writing his great work, the Jesuit

Edward Knott, against whom it was directed, tried to forestall the attack by denouncing him in advance as 'a downright Socinian'.[48] Knott's fellow Jesuit Guy Holland, who answered Falkland and declared him a Socinian, added that the veins of that poisonous doctrine 'are observed to run branching throughout all Chillingworth's works'.[49] From the opposite side, the same charge was made, even more ferociously, by the intruded rector of Petworth, Francis Cheynell. Cheynell was a bigoted Presbyterian who railed and sneered at those 'rational Lords that have such vast possessions' – i.e. at Falkland. When Chillingworth was dying, this fanatical anti-Socinian persecuted him with a strict Calvinist questionnaire; then, when the unrepentant Chillingworth was dead, the minister of Christ threw his book after him into his grave, bidding the heretic and the heresy rot together. After which he would publish two tracts for the times: first *Chillingworthi Novissima*, 'The Last Days of Chillingworth', then *The Rise, Growth and Danger of Socinianism*.

The other members of the group were accused of the same errors. Henry Hammond, who defended Falkland's religious views, was regularly accused of Socinianism by his critics.* The same charge was made against Hales, to whom two anonymous Socinian tracts were (though wrongly) ascribed. 'Leave Socinus and the Schoolmen', Sir John Suckling urged him,[50] thus clearly suggesting that he read Socinian books – as he clearly did, for in one of his letters he regrets that he cannot lend his copy of a book by the German Socinian Crell since he has already lent it to 'my good friend Mr Chillingworth'.† According to Aubrey, Hales 'was one of the first Socinians in England: I think the first'.[51] Suckling himself, as he admitted, was liable to the same charge.[52] Falkland's chaplain, Charles Gataker, who was one of Aubrey's informants, had himself been brought up in a tainted home, for his father had defended the Socinian Antony Wotton and had a library of Socinian books.[53] Thomas Barlow, whose own views were, or became, much more conservative, collected Socinian books both for himself and for Falkland.[54] Altogether it is unquestionable that Falkland's whole circle was widely regarded as 'Socinian', and Falkland himself as the chief patron of Socinianism.

* See below, p.220.
† *The Works of the Ever-Memorable Mr. John Hales of Eaton* (hereafter Hales, *Works*), ed. Lord Hailes (1765) I, pp. 199–200. Crell, or Crellius, was the German Socinian whose views had interested Grotius. His works were well known to the Great Tew set and their friends. Sir Philip Warwick, sending a message to Sheldon through Hammond, quotes Crell as if his writings were well known to all three (BL MS Harl. 6942 no. 28).

What was this dreadful heresy of Socinianism which the orthodox of all the established religions so vigorously denounced and which seemed to have thrust its strongest root into the soil of Oxfordshire? It is important to realize that the single word covers two different things. There is Socinianism in the wide sense, which is the use of human reason generally in matters of faith – hence Cheynell's sneer against 'rational Lords'; and there is Socinianism in the strict sense, which is the application of that reason to a particular article of faith, namely the doctrine of the Trinity, with the inevitable result that the doctrine dissolves and the ancient heresy of 'Arianism' reasserts itself. When a man is accused of Socinianism, 'the sting of the libel', as the lawyers say, is in the suggestion that he is a strict Socinian – i.e. an Arian, a unitarian. But not every Socinian is a Socinian in this strict sense: a man may be able to defend himself against the charge of unitarianism and yet he may still be a Socinian in the wide sense. That is, even if he does not follow human reason into the abstruse and forbidden mystery of the Trinity, he may still accept it as a guide in religion: the only guide in those areas where direct Revelation is not available. It is by reason of this linguistic confusion that the charge of Socinianism, in the seventeenth century, is so difficult to define or to establish, and that so many persons who themselves disowned the name were nevertheless branded with it. So, when we hear the charge we must ask in what sense it is preferred, and in what sense rebutted. We shall then generally find that it is preferred in the wide sense and rebutted in the narrow: that the defendant repudiates the particular charge of unitarianism but might well plead guilty to the more general charge of rationalism. This distinction would not have satisfied the accuser, for whom rationalism was the greater crime although Socinianism was the more convenient, because the more emotive name for it.

When we apply this test to the Great Tew group, the answer is clear enough. Neither Falkland nor Chillingworth nor Hales nor Hammond nor any other member of the group was a strict Socinian, a unitarian. All believed, or believed that they believed, in the Trinity. But in the wide sense, all of them, even Clarendon himself, were Socinians. They took to themselves the liberty to doubt. They were ready to consider any objection, any reason. They read forbidden Socinian books. Falkland's library was (till All Souls College broke it up) one of the earliest and most complete Socinian libraries in England.[55] The distinction is nicely made by Clarendon himself in his controversy with Cressy. Cressy had called Falkland a Socinian. If Socinianism consists in disbelief in the Trinity, retorted Clarendon, his friend could easily be freed from that 'odious reproach'. But if it consists in 'the having read Socinus, and the commending that in him which nobody can reasonably discommend in him, and the making use of that reason that God has given a man', in order to interpret the Scriptures, then 'the party will be very strong in all churches'.[56] This was not an argument which Cressy would have accepted – especially since Falkland had explicitly admitted, in his *Discourse*, that he would follow reason wherever it led: 'I profess myself not only to be an anti-Trinitarian but a Turk whensoever more reason appears to me for that than for the contrary'.[57] However, it seems that that moment had not yet arrived for him.

If the Socinianism of Falkland and his friends was general rather than particular, the cult of reason even in religion rather than the unitarian heresy, how did that cult express itself? In order to answer this question, let us look at the authors whom they regularly cited and seek to identify the ideas which were common to them. We shall then be able to see the Great Tew circle as the culmination, in England, of a European tradition, and to put their views in a wider intellectual context; and we shall be able to ask why their 'Socinianism' was particularly significant in their time.

The intellectual forebars who are most clearly and explicitly cited by Falkland, Clarendon, Hales, Chillingworth and even Cressy are not the strict 'Socinian' writers (whom they undoubtedly read) but the writers in what I have called the wide Socinian tradition. These writers are, first of all, Erasmus; then the 'libertine' continuators of Erasmus – Castellio, Acontius, Ochino, Cassander, Socinus himself; then the liberal Protestant thinkers of the turn of the century, and, in particular, the French Huguenot and Platonist Philippe du Plessis Mornay, the Anglican Richard Hooker and the Dutch Arminian Hugo Grotius.

Erasmus, the founder of this tradition – the father of Socinianism in both the wide and narrow sense – is cited by all the Great Tew writers. To Falkland, Erasmus was, 'though no martyr, yet one who may pass as a confessor, having suffered, and long, by the bigots of both parties'.[58] Chillingworth, after his reconversion to Protestantism, quoted 'that great Erasmus' as one of his masters.[59] Clarendon also cites him against the bloodthirsty clergy of the civil war: 'those ministers of the Church who, by their function being messengers of peace, are the only trumpets of war and incendiaries toward rebellion';[60] and he would keep portraits of Erasmus and More in his gallery at Clarendon House.

The continuators of Erasmus, who were persecuted by both sides for persevering in his tradition, and who took refuge in Switzerland,

England or Poland, are equally familiar to the Great Tew writers: indeed it was their dependence on these heretics, who preached the sovereignty of natural reason, which caused them to be attacked as 'Socinians'. Falkland, in his *Discourse*, claims 'that liberty of choice practised by such spirits as those of Cassander and Melanchthon'.[61] Chillingworth acknowledged the influence on him of Cassander and Castellio.[62] Even Cressy, after his conversion, in order to attack Calvin, finds himself defending Calvin's victims, whom in his Great Tew days he had learned to admire, Cassander and Castellio.[63] All admitted that they had read Socinus.

A particular favourite of the Great Tew group was Acontius: that is the Italian reformer Giacomo Aconcio, a disciple of Castellio, who had fled from Italy to Switzerland in 1557 and then, *via* Alsace, to England. In England he had been patronized by the Earl of Leicester and had served Queen Elizabeth as an engineer, designing for her, with another Italian, Giovanni Portinari, the new fortifications of Berwick-on-Tweed.* In England he had written his famous book *Stratagemata Satanae*, dedicated to Queen Elizabeth in 1565, and published at Basel. This book, a proclamation in favour of toleration, scepticism and liberty of conscience, contributed greatly to the 'Socinian' tradition, and parts of it appear almost verbatim in the first Confession of Faith of the Polish Brethren published nine years later.[64] It was a favourite book at Great Tew: Christopher Potter, the Provost of Queen's College, Oxford, published an edition of it at Oxford in 1631.[65] Potter was a former Calvinist who had been converted to Arminianism in 1629: he was a close friend of Hales, Hammond, Sheldon, and, particularly, Chillingworth. It was to defend Potter against Knott that Chillingworth wrote his *Religion of Protestants*. In that work Chillingworth explicitly refers the reader to Acontius. 'This persuasion', he wrote – the persuasion that the human mind should be free to interpret Scripture – 'is no singularity of mine, but the doctrine which I have learned from divines of great learning and judgment'; and he refers the reader to the seventh book of Acontius' *Stratagemata Satanae* and the last oration of Zanchius.[66]

But above all, the Great Tew group looked back to their more immediate predecessors, through whom the Erasmian tradition was transmitted to them. Of these the first was Philippe du Plessis Mornay, the Huguenot statesman, soldier and scholar who served Henry of

---

* On Acontius' fortifications see Lynn White Jr, 'Jacopo Aconcio as an Engineer', *Amer. Hist. Rev.* LXXII (2 January 1967). He also offered to drain the marshes of the Thames Estuary.

Navarre as counsellor and propagandist throughout the French Wars of Religion and who, after his master's triumph and abjuration, became the leader of the Huguenot party at the French court. Du Plessis Mornay was a prolific writer, and the pressure of politics and controversy sometimes drove him into extreme positions; but his mind had been formed in the Erasmian tradition, and it always retained that formation. In his youth he caused one of Castellio's works to be translated into Dutch;[67] he always advocated freedom, and free discussion, of religion; and in his later years he founded the famous 'Arminian' academy of Saumur which would be the continuing centre of liberalism among the increasingly defensive and bigoted French Huguenots. After his death, Mornay's works were edited by the sceptical Huguenot, so admired by Falkland, Jean Daillé. The work of Mornay which was cited by the Great Tew group was his treatise *De la vérité de la religion chrestienne*, written in Antwerp in 1579–80 and published there next year: an unsectarian work which sought to prove the truth of Christianity by natural reason and so convert 'atheists, epicureans, pagans, Jews, Mohammedans and other infidels'. The book was widely read, by both Catholics and Protestants. Mornay himself published a Latin translation of it, and an English translation, begun by Mornay's friend Sir Philip Sidney, was completed, after Sidney's death, by Arthur Golding. Mornay's work would be explicitly recommended by Falkland, Chillingworth and Hammond.[68]

A more powerful influence, because a profounder thinker, than du Plessis Mornay, was Richard Hooker. Hooker's influence on Chillingworth, as Mr Orr has shown, was all-pervasive. 'Mr Hooker, one of the most learned judicious writers that ever that Church [of England] had', remained an oracle to Cressy, even after his conversion.[69] Hales 'loved the very name of Mr Hooker'.[70] Earle was a great admirer of Hooker: during his exile in Cologne, from 1654 to 1656, he would translate Hooker's *Laws of Ecclesiastical Polity* into Latin, so that its message might be understood in Europe. He did not publish his translation – the Restoration and the cares of a bishopric intervened – but on his death in 1665, Clarendon would send his son, Lord Cornbury, to Mrs Earle with instructions to rescue the manuscript of so important a work. Clarendon himself clearly venerated Hooker. He quoted Hooker in the declarations which he wrote for the King on the eve of civil war,[71] and the first paragraph of his *History of the Rebellion* is deliberately modelled on the beginning of Hooker's great work. Thereby he implicitly declared his aim: his *History of the Rebellion* was to be the secular counterpart of Hooker's *Laws of Ecclesiastical Polity*.[72]

But the greatest of all influences on the Great Tew group was that of Hugo Grotius, the Dutch scholar, statesman and philosopher. This was not only an intellectual influence, communicated through books: it was also – since Grotius was their contemporary, and engaged in the same struggle, though in a different theatre – direct, even personal. For Grotius was the Erasmus of the seventeenth century: in him, Erasmus lived again. Grotius himself always avowed his intellectual descent. Again and again he cites Erasmus, to whom 'we Hollanders can never be grateful enough'.[73] Grotius also admired Cassander: he wrote a poem in praise of Cassander and would republish, with a commentary, Cassander's work. He also admired Mornay, whom he knew personally[74] and from whom he borrowed the title of his most popular work. It was perhaps through Grotius that Falkland and his friends came to Mornay and other precursors.

Grotius, whether named or not, is everywhere at Great Tew. He was its immediate tutelary spirit, the father-figure who had taught both Falkland and Chillingworth and would survive them both. In 1632, when Chillingworth, having returned from Douai to England, and settled in the Falkland household in London, was pressed by Laud and Juxon, Bishop of London, to rejoin the Church of England, it was not they or their arguments that could convince him. 'A great desire he expresseth still', Juxon reported to Laud, 'to go over and confer with Grotius',[75] who was then back, temporarily, in his native Holland. Thereafter the works of Grotius began to be printed in England, and his arguments reappear in Chillingworth's writings.[76] In 1639 George Sandys, the poet of Great Tew, translated Grotius' early tragedy *Christus Patiens*, and Falkland himself wrote a dedicatory poem in praise of Grotius for it. In the same year Grotius' most important religious work, his *De Veritate Religionis Christianae*, was published in Oxford. Hammond, as we shall see, was a devotee of Grotius. So was Clarendon, who, in his exile in Jersey and France would read and annotate Grotius' works and send to Holland for his posthumous publications. To him he was 'the great Grotius, who may justly be esteemed as good, if not the best scholar that age brought forth'.[77]

4   The philosophy of Great Tew

Erasmus, Acontius, Castellio, Hooker, Grotius . . . these very names define a clear tradition. Let us first seek to extract that tradition. Then we can see how far it was adopted by Falkland and his circle.

Politically, it was a conservative tradition. Though they were often denounced as heretics, none of its advocates can be described as radicals. All of them wished to preserve the form of society which they had inherited. Erasmus disclaimed any desire to disturb the structure of Church or State, though he sought reform in both. Hooker was the eloquent defender of the Elizabethan settlement. Grotius accepted the established Calvinism of the Netherlands, just as Erasmus had accepted its established Catholicism. One of his favourite quotations is the phrase in which Thucydides expressed the same conviction: 'whatever form of government we have received, that we should keep.'[78] '*Republica*', he would write in his exile, '*contentus fui qualem acceperam: in ecclesia mitia ac benigna duris ac rigidis praetuli*'.[79]

They were opposed to radical change because it involved violence and war, which they detested. Erasmus denied the whole concept of the just war. 'War is not absolutely forbidden', he wrote, 'but it is better to be killed than to kill'. In some of his most famous works – in his *Complaint of Peace* and in his bitter satire against the bellicose Pope Julius II – he eloquently denounced the wars of princes in which the patient labours of generations were consumed, and he directed his sharpest irony against the wars of religion. The post-Erasmians, being victims of persecution, had even stronger reasons to hate it. In the French Wars of Religion, du Plessis Mornay, though obliged to be a soldier, was a constant advocate of peace. In the crisis of the Netherlands in 1618, Grotius and his fellow Arminians were accused of 'appeasement'. The purpose of his greatest work, *The Law of Peace and War*, was – as he wrote to the German Socinian Crell – 'to assuage, as far as I could, that savagery, unworthy of Christians, and even of men, in making and waging war'; the savagery which he saw all around him in the early stages of the Thirty Years War.[80]

To avoid such violence, all these men preached tolerance, especially in matters 'indifferent'. Erasmus was the first writer to make the distinction between *fundamenta*, or essential doctrines, and *adiaphora*, on which men could agree to differ; and to increase the list of *adiaphora* in the cause of tolerance was the constant aim of his successors.[81] Tolerance, indeed, was their watchword. The burning of Servetus, the first of the 'strict' Socinians, by Calvin – an act of which even Melanchthon had approved – disgusted them and provoked their most famous work, Castellio's *De Haereticis an sint Persequendi* (1554). The same doctrine of toleration would be regarded as the hallmark of the seventeenth-century Socinians: at the end of the century the bigoted Calvinist Pierre Jurieu would describe it as 'ce dogme socinien, le plus dangereux de tous ceux de la secte socinienne'.[82] The Socinians, of course, needed it: they were a small, defenceless sect who could only survive by tolerance. But it had been advocated from a position of strength, by Hooker. The Church, he had insisted, did not consist of the 'Elect', or the 'godly', only: it included papists, who are not to be classed as 'malefactors', and even heretics whom we must acknowledge to be 'though a maimed part, yet a part of the visible Church'.[83] Grotius similarly advocated toleration: in an unpublished work, *Meletius*, now lost, he expressed views on toleration which gravely shocked the orthodox.[84]

With tolerance goes scepticism. The scepticism of Erasmus was notorious and exasperated his adversaries on all sides; but he persevered in it. 'Human affairs', he wrote, 'are so obscure and various that nothing can be clearly known. This was the sound conclusion of the Academics [i.e. the Greek Academic Sceptics], who were the least surly of the philosophers'.[85] It was a conclusion which could be applied to Christian doctrine too. The doctrine of Predestination, for instance, 'cannot be resolved till the day of judgment; so why not suspend judgment?' Erasmus would have been content to leave many problems in suspense and he urged his contemporaries to turn aside from controversy about indifferent or unknowable things and concentrate upon essentials: upon 'the philosophy of Christ' which was so clear and simple and could so easily be extracted 'from the purest sources of the evangelists and apostles and their most approved interpreters'.[86] His successors continued his tradition. Castellio, in 1563, wrote a work *de arte dubitandi* and Acontius' *Stratagemata Satanae* put all dogma in question. Grotius, with the other Dutch Arminians, was regularly accused of scepticism; and he did not reject the charge.[87] In his book *De Veritate Religionis Christianae* he hailed, among his predecessors, with Vives and du Plessis Mornay, Raymond de Sebonde, the fifteenth-century philosopher of 'natural theology' who had inspired the scepticism of Montaigne.[88] The same list would be taken over by Falkland, who would add the names of Charron and Grotius himself;[89] and Chillingworth would add that of 'that noble writer Michael de Montaigne'.[90] Scepticism, they all believed, was compatible with Christianity – was even necessary to it. 'It shall well befit our Christian modesty', wrote Hales, 'to participate somewhat of the sceptick'.

The cult of reason, political conformity together with reform, hatred of violence and war, toleration of dissent, intellectual scepticism – these are virtues (if they are virtues) which appeal to laymen; and most of their advocates were themselves laymen, or relied on the laity, or lay governments, for support. But they also had their theological counterpart. In particular there was the doctrine of universal redemption – the theoretical possibility that all men might be saved without subscribing to particular theological tenets, even (in certain circumstances) without profession of Christianity, by a mere moral life. This doctrine entailed the freedom of the will. Erasmus had defended free will against Luther and had refused to deny salvation to any man, even to the pagans who had not heard of Christ: indeed he came near to canonizing some of them: did he not once exclaim, *Sancte Socrates ora pro nobis*. – a shocking blasphemy? The Dutch and English Arminians believed firmly in universal redemption and free will and cited texts which clearly justified them. Of course they were accused by the strict Calvinists of 'Pelagianism'. It was in order to justify their position, and end all controversy on the subject, that the most learned of the Dutch Arminians, G. J. Vossius, the friend of Grotius and of Laud, wrote, with the encouragement and assistance of Grotius,[91] his *Historia Pelagiana*.

Finally, on the basis of such a philosophy, there was the ideal of the reunion of Christendom, split apart by Reformation and Counter-Reformation. Such reunion had been the aim of Erasmus, and although, by the end of his life, it seemed further away than ever, it was not forgotten. It was advocated, in particular, on the Catholic side, by the Belgian George Cassander and the French Claude d'Espensée; then, as the Wars of Religion became more savage and divisive, the mirage dissolved. However, at the end of the century, when a new era of peace began, it returned, in a modified form. In the France of Henri IV there was a movement for the union of Catholic and Huguenot Churches on a Gallican base. In England the idealized *via media* set out by Hooker offered a more concrete model, rejecting alike the superstitious innovations of Rome and the pedantries of Protestantism, and firmly based on the twin pillars of correctly understood Scripture and human reason. Of course, by now, the interests which opposed it were entrenched. Calvinist Protestantism had become identified with nationality, and Catholicism had been reinvigorated by the Counter-Reformation. The former repudiated, the latter sought to exploit the ecumenical idea. As this became clear, the English model seemed the most promising, and the European heirs of Erasmus looked to it as the nucleus of a third Church which would point the way to an ultimately reunited Christendom.

One of the ablest propagandists of this idea was a favourite pupil of Hooker, Edwin Sandys, whose brother, George Sandys, would become the translator of Grotius and the poet of Great Tew. Both the brothers,

Edwin and George, travelled widely, and both, in their travels, showed a particular interest in questions of religion. Edwin Sandys travelled through Italy, Germany and France at the end of the century, and his travelling companion was another favourite pupil of Hooker, George Cranmer: it was to Cranmer and Sandys that Hooker had submitted the manuscript of his great work, for their opinions. On his return, in 1599, Sandys submitted to the Archbishop of Canterbury the manuscript of a short book, the fruit of his travels, his *Relation of the State of Religion*.[92]

In his book, Sandys, like Hooker, avoided polemics: his quest was not for sectarian victory but for a Church that could, by transcending sectarianism, reunite Christendom. If Catholics would discard their superstitious observances, if Protestants would 'abate the rigour of certain speculative opinions', then, he believed, a new 'centre party' could be re-created out of those men 'of singular learning and piety' who, in all countries, sought to re-establish the peace of the Church. Spain indeed must be left to the Moors and Jews who had corroded its Church. Italy was ineligible unless it could disembarrass itself of 'popery' – perhaps the Pope should be allowed to transform himself, as so many other abbots, bishops, Grand Masters had done, into a purely secular prince. But in France – the France of Henri IV and the *politiques* – Sandys saw the possibility of a non-popish Catholicism that could coexist, indeed merge, with moderate Protestantism. In such an ideal Church a place could also be found for the Greek Christians who had been the first to reject the Roman claims, and who now languished under Turkish tyranny. To Sandys, as to Hooker, the nearest approximation to this ideal Church was the Church of England. By its continuity with the medieval Church, by its peaceable and orderly reformation, by the secular authority of its prince, the Church of England, 'concurring entirely with neither side, yet reverenced of both', was not only the pattern for others to imitate but also the fittest of all to be the umpire between them and to lead them gradually to unity with the same 'general and indifferent confession and sum of faith, an uniform liturgy, a correspondent form of Church-government'.

Sandys' book was printed in 1605, six years after it had been written. It ran quickly through three impressions. Then, suddenly, it was suppressed – probably in consequence of the Gunpowder Plot, which made any such plea for coexistence with Catholicism inopportune. It was not published again in England during the author's lifetime. But within a few years it was translated into Italian and French. The Italian version was annotated by that great Catholic supporter of Protestantism,

Paolo Sarpi. The French version was read by that great Protestant supporter of Catholicism, Hugo Grotius, who urged that it be translated, as an excellent book to dispel prejudice, into Dutch.[93]

Throughout his life Grotius sought – perhaps above everything – the reunion of Christendom; and he sought it in exactly the same form as Hooker and Sandys. His ideal Church was to be based on Scripture and Reason: Scripture interpreted by Reason, cleaned by exact scholarship and protected by toleration and scepticism. It was also to embrace both liberal Catholics and liberal Protestants, rejecting alike the extreme papal claims and extreme Protestant fundamentalism. And its natural centre was to be in the 'Arminian' Church of Jacobean England. In 1613, when he visited England, Grotius had high hopes of realizing the ideal set out by Sandys. Enchanted by the discovery of like-minded English clergy – especially Lancelot Andrewes and John Overall – he envisaged a general council to meet in London under the presidency of King James. It was to begin as a Protestant Council, but ultimately moderate Catholics would be brought in, and perhaps also the Greek and Asiatic Churches. Its end – if only the quarrelsome theologians could be silenced – would be the restoration of an ecumenical, national, universal Church.

Vain dream! Scarcely had Grotius returned to Holland when the *scabies disputandi* of the theologians set all, once again, on fire. Against the background of an impending European crisis – the resumption of war by the Spanish monarchy and the Counter-Reformation – the mirage vanished. When the General Council of Protestantism at last met, it was not in England, presided over by a lay ruler, in a time of universal peace, but in Holland, threatened by a war of extinction; it was dominated by Calvinist extremists; and it resulted in a political revolution in the Netherlands. Grotius himself was a victim of that revolution. Imprisoned in the fortress of Loevestein, he consoled himself for political defeat by turning to literature and scholarship. To practise his scholarship he translated the Greek poets. He resumed his long disused study of law and laid the basis of his most famous work, *De Jure Belli ac Pacis*. But he did not abandon his hopes. It was in his fortress-prison that he began what was to be, in his own time, the most influential of all his works. This is the book which was first published in Dutch in 1622, but is best known in its later Latin translation, entitled *De Veritate Religionis Christianae*. This little book, which recalls Erasmus' *Enchiridion Militis Christiani*, was to be a bestseller. Robert Boyle, the father of chemistry, would have it translated into Arabic as an evangelical work. Its purpose, like that of du Plessis Mornay's work with the same title, was to unite all Churches, and reconcile non-Christians to Christianity, by placing Christianity clearly on the base of non-sectarian, universal human reason.

When Grotius escaped from prison, he fled to France. Others of his friends stopped in Flanders. In France and in Flanders the Catholic Church fished among the wreckage. 'Arminianism', the Erasmian *via media*, 'Socinian' rationalism, said the emissaries of Rome, had proved impossible to sustain: if Protestants wished to escape from the Scylla of Calvinist bigotry, their only hope was to allow themselves to be sucked into the Charybdis of Rome. Rome, even Counter-Reformation Rome, was the only real ecumenical Church; Rome alone had the authority to define a truly universal faith; Rome also, in those years, was carrying all before it in the Thirty Years War. Faced by this universal triumph of Rome, the Protestant Churches of Europe retreated into Calvinist extremism. In Venice, the Catholic friar Paolo Sarpi declared his support for the Calvinist International. In England, James I yielded to the party of Puritanism and war. The Arminian bishops went into eclipse. Sir Edwin Sandys himself moved over to the puritan opposition. If 'Arminianism', in those years, was unable to survive in England, what chance had it among the broken, isolated, exiled 'Arminians' of Holland?

So, one by one, they surrendered. Peter Bertius, Grotius' friend and fellow exile, was converted to Rome. So was his chaplain François d'Or. So was Willem van Oldenbarnevelt, the son of the executed Grand Pensionary of Holland. And of course, attempts were made upon Grotius himself. The Flemish Jesuit Andreas Schott wrote to him urging him to read the signs of the times and accept the Roman supremacy. So did Dr Hemelaer, the canon of Antwerp who had helped him on his flight to freedom. Rumours of his conversion were always in the air. The King of Spain offered him a pension. Even his closest friend, G. J. Vossius, thought him in danger. But Grotius stood firm: he would move neither to Left nor to Right. Finally, to escape the pressure, he would leave France, 'for I am weary of this pressure to go to mass'. He would retreat into Germany, and then into Swedish service, and remain, to the end of his life, a preacher of rational, Erasmian Christianity based, ideally, on an 'Arminian' Church of England.

If we now turn from the tradition which Falkland and his friends acknowledged to the philosophy which they expressed, we find all the same distinctive characteristics. All of them believed in political continuity. As Clarendon put it, they 'wished to live under the same government they were born'.[94] All of them believed passionately in peace, holding that violent change led to self-destruction. Nothing troubled Hales so much as 'the brawls which were grown from religion'.[95] Hammond, according to his biographer, both preached and practised 'that great fundamental doctrine of peace and love'.[96] Chillingworth passionately deplored 'carnal' methods of controversy 'such as are massacres, treasons, persecutions and, in a word, all means either violent or fraudulent'.[97] 'He did really believe all war to be unlawful', says Clarendon.[98] It was his hatred of this 'unnatural war' that reduced Falkland to despondency and made him 'with a shrill and sad accent ingeminate the word, *Peace, Peace*'. Clarendon himself detested war, foreign no less than civil. He would write bitterly of the Franco-Spanish war of the 1650s and 'a war wantonly entered into, without the least pretence of right and justice';[99] and no less bitterly of the 'bare-faced war against the Dutch' into which Charles II would allow himself to be driven.[100] He was as scathing as Erasmus (whom he quoted) about militant clergy, and believed that 'no reformation is worth the charge of a civil war'.[101] In religion, all believed in universal redemption and free will. Falkland admitted that, in some respects, he would rather be a Pelagian than a Calvinist; and he cited with approval Erasmus' view that even some pagans could be saved.[102] All advocated intellectual toleration and hoped, by enlarging the category of 'things indifferent', to restore the unity of the Church. All believed in the positive function of scepticism – though some of them were prepared to carry scepticism further than others; for they were not a school but a group of men who discussed their ideas together: who were drawn together by a basic community of interest but could and did vary in their particular conclusions.

Such was the general philosophical outlook which the men of Great Tew held in common. But as they were not merely academical men, they wished to apply their views in action. So the question which we must now ask is, how relevant were these views to the intellectual and political situation in the 1630s: the years in which Europe was convulsed by the Thirty Years War and England, at peace, was being ruled by Charles I, Strafford and Laud?

5 Chillingworth

In their cult of reason, their ecumenism, their scepticism, the men of Great Tew were in a well established intellectual tradition; but it was a tradition which, by their time, was on the defensive. The years from

1618 to 1625 were a watershed in the intellectual as in the political history of Europe. The advance of the Catholic Counter-Reformation, the triumph of intolerant Calvinism at Dordt, the outbreak of European war, and the Catholic victories of the 1620s all caused an ideological polarization which threatened to engulf the ideals of the previous generation. In the renewed wars of religion what room was left for the ideas of Erasmus and Grotius? Such ideas were eroded from both sides, and those who clung to them found themselves in intellectual difficulties. This was the situation which has been described as 'the crisis of Pyrrhonism'.

Pyrrhonism was the philosophy of scepticism, so named after its founder, the Greek philosopher Pyrrho of Elis. The crisis occurred because, by 1620, the operation of natural reason threatened to undermine Christian doctrine just at the time when the orthodoxies of its rival parties were being hardened by events. In the previous century, this danger had been less apparent. Protestants had then used natural reason to undermine Catholic doctrine and Catholics – in particular the Jesuits – had sought to retaliate in kind. By now each had succeeded to such an extent that even the agreed central truths of Christianity were at risk. These central truths were symbolized by the incomprehensible doctrine of the Trinity: hence the united front against 'Socinianism'. The problem for Christians was how to find a basis from which to reason which reason itself had not already undermined.

One solution to the problem – the simplest for indolent minds – was to reject reason altogether, to accept 'authority' and allow it to demand unquestioning faith. This, of course, was the solution recommended by the Catholic Church. The Roman missionaries, who were so active everywhere in these years, exploited scepticism in order to show the limits of human reason; then they offered perplexed intellectuals an escape from 'the moving sands of natural reason'[103] to the firm rock of Peter. The infallibility of the Roman Church, they said, provided a base – indeed the only base – upon which reason, otherwise so self-destructive, could build a solid philosophy of the world.

This argument was used very effectively by the Jesuit John Piercy, *alias* Fisher, who reappeared in England in the 1620s and began his spectacular series of conversions. In 1622 he converted the Countess of Buckingham and nearly crowned this triumph by bringing her son, the all-powerful favourite, after her. William Laud was one of those called in to save him, and this was the beginning of his spectacular success at court. From the account that Laud published afterwards, it is clear that Fisher had exploited the argument from scepticism.[104] A few years later

Fisher was in Oxford, and it was there, in 1628, that he converted Chillingworth, then a young Fellow of Trinity College. Next year, Lady Falkland announced her conversion and set to work on her household and family. That the arguments used were the same is clear from Falkland's own later reaction. It is also implied in the remark of his younger brother, Patrick, when he began to wobble back towards Protestantism. 'Mr Patrick Cary's conversion', Hammond then wrote to Sheldon, 'is rather from the Romish than to the Protestant religion. A seeker he saith he is, and unravels and questions all, that he may build infallibly'.[105]

But if conversion to popery was one way out of the discomforts of scepticism, it was not the only way. Protestants had their fundamentalism too, a belief in Prophecy and divine Providence which pointed exclusively to their Church as the true Church. That fundamentalism now rested especially – and somewhat ironically, since the early Reformers had questioned its authenticity – on the Book of Revelation. Thus the famous biblical scholar Joseph Mede, of Christ's College, Cambridge, a man of enormous and varied erudition, was for some time lost in 'the troublesome labyrinths of the Pyrrhonists' before he found his way out by discovering (as he thought) the key to the Apocalypse.[106] Christ's College, in Mede's time, was a centre of the new millenarian certainty which stabilized the uncertain thinking of many a country clergyman, Puritan and Anglican alike: for such millenarian doctrines, though implicitly rejected by the followers of Hooker, the 'Arminians' and the Laudians, were accepted by 'moderate' Elizabethan and Jacobean Anglicans. Mede himself was such an Anglican; and one of the Great Tew circle, Dr Walter Ralegh, is described by Aubrey as 'a millenarie (his tract on that doctrine is lost) but . . . conformable'.[107]

Others who were baffled by the 'Pyrrhonist crisis' sought to fortify a faltering religion by the external certainties of science. Thus the Minim friar, Marin Mersenne, wrote his great polemical work on scientific truth (as its title shows) to defeat the Pyrrhonists.[108] Soon afterwards the young Robert Boyle, while on the Grand Tour, suffered a Pyrrhonian crisis. Standing before the monastery of la Grande Chartreuse in 'the wild mountains' of Dauphiné, he suffered from 'such strange and hideous thoughts and such distracting doubts of some of the fundamentals of Christianity that . . . nothing but the forbiddenness of self-dispatch hindered his acting it'. After languishing for 'many months in this tedious perplexity', he gradually found his way out, through mathematics, 'the bravest science in the world (after divinity)' to a rational Christianity.[109] Sir Thomas Browne, who had studied at Oxford under the 'Socinian' tutor of Pembroke College, Dr Lushington – the same Lushington whose too avant-garde sermon had been attended by Clarendon and Cressy – also suffered from the Pyrrhonist crisis: from 'sturdy doubts and boysterous objections, wherewith the unhappiness of our knowledge too nearly acquainteth us'. He tells us how the Devil, in the form of natural reason, 'played at chess with me, and yielding a pawn, thought to gain a queen of me, taking advantage of my honest endeavours; and whilst I laboured to raise the structure of my reason, he striv'd to undermine the edifice of my faith'.[110] Like Boyle, Browne too was brought, by scepticism, to the verge of suicide. He overcame it by rearing his bizarre architectural folly of *Religio Medici*, a dazzling, unrepeatable, fairy palace constructed out of Platonism, Hermeticism, witches, natural science, and the gaping cracks of the Elizabethan compromise papered over by magniloquent phrases, its towers lost in an *O Altitudo*.

These were the devices whereby some men escaped from the burden of scepticism. Bolder spirits took more radical courses. In 1629 Descartes began his quest for a new basis of constructive philosophic thought. He wanted, as he said, 'esbahir les Pyrrhoniens', to dish the Pyrrhonists, by finding some axiom 'si ferme et si assurée que toutes les plus extravagantes suppositions des Sceptiques n'estoient pas capables de l'esbranler', a foundation upon which to base 'toute la certitude humaine'.[111] The result was the new Cartesian scholasticism, which would ultimately merge with Catholic orthodoxy. In the same year, 1629, Thomas Hobbes discovered the certitudes of geometry, and in 1634–6, on a visit to France, it dawned upon him that they could be applied to morals and politics too and provide for both a permanent protective system. Thanks to this new certainty Hobbes could resist all the blandishments of the Roman *convertisseurs*. 'Begone', he told them as they clustered hopefully round his sick-bed in France, 'or I will detect all your cheats from Aaron to yourselves'.

Still others sought a more practical form of escape. Allowing that there was no end to scepticism, they repudiated the whole process of 'contemplation' and substituted for it the ideal of the active life. To the medieval saint, 'contemplation' had been an end in itself. But that contemplation had been within a firm, closed metaphysical system. Once that system had been broken contemplation could only reveal its cracks and fissures and thus weaken instead of strengthening the mind. So strenuous spirits rejected the whole process. Milton, whose early poems show such love of nature, turned consciously away from 'a cloister'd and fugitive virtue, unexercised and unbreathed, that never sallies out and seeks her adversary' and preached instead the gospel of public spirit, of action, of 'involvement' in the affairs of his time. In *Paradise Lost* he would express his disdain of the philosophers who debated the insoluble problems.

> Of Providence, Foreknowledge, Will and Fate . . .
> And found no end, in wand'ring mazes lost.

Andrew Marvell, who had so loved the exquisite gardens of Nun Appleton, showed again and again, in his poems – those haunting amoebaean dialogues between the Mower and the Garden, the Resolved Soul and Created Pleasure – the tension between that ideal of cultivated reflexion and the demand, to which he must ultimately yield, of restless activity and public virtue: the activity that will

> tear our pleasures with rough strife
> Thorough the iron gates of life

the public virtue that would call a Cromwell from the contemplation of 'his private gardens' to fight his way to empire and

> cast the kingdom old
> Into another mould

It is against this background of the Pyrrhonist crisis, I believe, that the philosophy of the Great Tew group was formulated. Nearly all the members of that group were exercised by the problem of scepticism. Falkland himself had refused to accept the easy way out offered by his mother and embraced by his brothers and sisters. Chillingworth had accepted that solution only to be disillusioned by his experience at Douai. He there discovered, as others have discovered since, that the Catholic Church, which can look so liberal to the potential convert, shows a very different face once he is inside: a discovery which Clarendon would afterwards rub into the later convert Cressy.[112] While he was a Roman Catholic, Chillingworth hoped to convert Sheldon; so it is reasonable to suppose that Sheldon – whose early days are so ill-documented – was also in a promising state of doubt. Cressy's scepticism and need of certainty is clear from his history and from his apologia – which indeed is little other than a long descant on the pains of a scepticism which his mind could not resist but which his soul could not endure, until 'like Noah's dove, wearying myself with flying up and down and finding no rest for the sole of my feet, I was at last forced to return into the Ark': the Ark of the Catholic Church.[113] Of Clarendon's reaction to the 'Pyrrhonist crisis' of the 1630s I shall have something to say later in this essay.

Scepticism was not the only reason why Chillingworth had yielded to the seductive arguments of the Jesuit Fisher. There was also that other aspiration of the intellectuals of the time: ecumenism, the desire for a reunion of Christendom. To the heirs of Erasmus, ecumenism and scepticism went together: scepticism reduced the area of controversy and the Church could be reunited on the basis of a rational Christianity. This was the argument of Grotius, whose system of natural law was to be universally valid 'even if it were allowed that God did not exist'[114] – and was to transcend sectarian differences if He did. However, this desire for reunion could also be exploited by the Roman Church. If unity was so desirable, its propagandists argued, a central authority was necessary in order to define the limits of reason; and where could this authority be placed, or found? Protestantism was now divided; the idea of unity under Arminian leadership had been shattered at Dordt; the attempt at Calvinist leadership had been destroyed on the battlefield; only Rome, universally victorious, it seemed, could be the centre of unity. In the East as in the West, against the Greek Church as against Protestantism, it was pressing its claims. In its hour of triumph, it too could speak the language of reason: reason based on authority, reason leading to authority. So the Jesuit Schotte fished from Antwerp among the defeated Dutch Arminians, and the Jesuit Fisher plied his net among the disoriented scholars of Oxford.

That this was the lure so effectively cast before Chillingworth has been shown by Mr Orr. Chillingworth, in 1628, was not merely a doubter seeking certainty and accepting infallibility. He was also a disciple of Hooker and Grotius. He was 'concerned with the overriding need to restore the Christian unity that had been shattered by the Reformation'. But he insisted that this comprehensive Church must be rational, that it 'must respect its members' intellectual integrity'.[115] He was assured that the Roman Church would meet both conditions: indeed that the logic of Hooker led to it. This was the logic that had converted the blue-stocking Lady Falkland: her doubts had begun, she said, through 'reading a Protestant book, much esteemed, called Hooker's Ecclesiastical Polity', which, she found, 'left her hanging in the air; for having brought her so far (which she thought he did very reasonably) she saw not how, nor at what, she could stop, till she returned to the Church from whence they were come'.[116] The same logic, pressed by Fr. Fisher, carried Chillingworth to Douai.

At Douai he discovered his mistake. There he learned that the convert, once secured, was expected not to think but to obey. The Church which, from outside, had seemed so liberal and so rational now showed itself very different. It too, like the Protestant Churches, was not universal but sectarian. He had been inveigled into conversion, he now felt, by half-truths. So he decided to return to England and consider freely where, if anywhere, a rational, non-sectarian, comprehensive Church was to be found. His godfather, Archbishop Laud, was of course eager to reclaim him. Laud, Juxon, Sheldon all worked on him. But Chillingworth was in no hurry to jump from one sectarian Church into another. He would refuse for some time to subscribe to the Thirty-Nine Articles, or accept a proffered living in the Church of England. It was at this time that he wished to go over to Holland and consult Grotius. He did not do so; but in the end he did as Grotius would have advised him. He accepted the Church of England as the nearest approximation to his ideal. He left the Catholic household of Lady Falkland and migrated to the 'rational', 'Socinian' household at Great Tew. There, in that cultivated house, in that well-stocked library, and with the advantage of constant discussion with acute and interested friends – for Chillingworth needed constant discussion: he would have agreed with the *cri de coeur* of Grotius in prison, that study without the commerce of scholars is crude and flavourless[117] – he would write his great work *The Religion of Protestants*: a work of controversy indeed, but a work which rises above the controversy around it; for who now remembers Knott and Fisher, Floyd and White, Holland and Lacey and Rushworth, the troop of Catholic controversialists whose only historical distinction is their entanglement with him?

Chillingworth's book emerged from those discussions at Great Tew. Together with Falkland, he sought a canon of certainty from which natural reason could operate in religious philosophy as an alternative to the acceptance of an infallible authority, which both rejected. Together they explored the works of the early Fathers – those whose authority was accepted by Catholics and Protestants alike. Falkland, says Clarendon, 'had read all the Greek and Latin Fathers . . . for in religion he thought too careful and too curious an enquiry could not be made' among such uncontested authorities.[118] However, they soon decided that the Fathers did not provide such a canon. They were helped to this view by the work which Cressy, in retrospect, and wrongly, saw as the source of their pernicious ideas and which he blamed himself for introducing to Great Tew: the *Traicté de l'employ des saincts pères* of the Huguenot pastor of Charenton, Jean Daillé.

Daillé, by a learned and careful examination of the Fathers, showed that, whatever their value as historical commentators, they certainly could not provide an agreed basis of doctrine. As Chillingworth put it, he showed 'some Fathers against others, the same Fathers against themselves, a consent of Fathers of one age against a consent of Fathers of another age'.[119] The result of his work was to increase, rather than diminish, the area of scepticism: to push the sceptic further back in search of a secure basis for reason.

It pushed Chillingworth back to Grotius and Hooker. Allowing that absolute certainty is unattainable, rejecting alike the infallible authority of Rome and the rigid dogma of the Calvinists, and yet seeking a solid base on which to build, he settled for a lesser degree of certainty, 'moral certainty' which is attainable by natural reason: for religion must have a moral foundation, and natural reason is itself an emanation of the moral order written by God in the hearts of man. Such natural reason, recognizing its own limits, is essential to faith as to knowledge. It is the only means to interpret Scripture as well as to eliminate error, 'the last resolution unto which the Church's authority is but the first inducement'. It is not infallible – there is no infallibility anywhere – but it is the only criterion we have: probability is the most to which we can aspire. Rationally vindicated probability, not a 'vain and arrogant pretence of infallibility', is the answer of a robust spirit to the seventeenth-century 'Pyrrhonist crisis'.[120]

Like Hooker, like Grotius, like Laud, Chillingworth allowed that the Church of Rome was a genuine Church, though corrupted. The true Church – or the nearest to it – was the Church of England. The Church of England, he concluded, was, 'in its constant doctrine, so pure and orthodox that all in it shall be saved', and 'there is no error in it which may necessitate or warrant any man to disturb the peace or renounce the communion of it'. But the quality of that Church, to him, lay essentially in its non-theological character: its simplicity, its rationality, its historical claim to preserve the essential, ecumenical Christian philosophy. To the Jesuits who accused him of destroying belief, Chillingworth replied that his criticism was not destructive of the essence of Christianity, 'for Christian religion is not now to be built, but only I desire to have the rubbish and impertinent lumber taken off, which you have laid upon it, which hides the glorious simplicity of it from them which otherwise would embrace it'. Whereas the unnecessary additions of the Roman Church were imposed on men's belief by the claim of infallibility, the simple truths of Anglicanism could be accepted by natural reason and a man could therefore take the moral responsibility of believing them and acting upon them. Being thus rationally and morally acceptable, they could be the doctrines of the whole Church; for it was not the English Church which was in schism but the Church of Rome, 'for imposing upon the faith of Christians doctrines unwritten and unnecessary, and for disturbing the Church's peace, and dividing unity for such matters'.[121]

Such was the conception of Anglicanism accepted, after his spiritual travels, by Chillingworth. It helps us to explain the somewhat ambivalent relationship between the men of Great Tew and the Anglican establishment of the 1630s. For although all of them were Anglicans and Arminians, all of them looked somewhat ambiguously on the Anglican, 'Arminian' Church of Archbishop Laud. Falkland himself defended Arminianism in Parliament but 'he had', as Clarendon admits, 'unhappily contracted some prejudice to the archbishop' and he made a famous and fierce attack on the Laudian episcopate.[122] Clarendon, who revered Laud personally, deplored his faults and criticized the illiberalism of his rule, both at home and abroad. Hammond, Morley and Sheldon were all, in one way or another, distrusted by Laud and none of them received promotion under him. Hales was summoned and questioned by Laud for the tract on Schism which he wrote for Chillingworth. Chillingworth's book was censured by Laud: and he himself maintained a discreet but perhaps suggestive silence about his godfather, who had personally reclaimed him from popery, and who dominated the Church while he was writing his defence of it.[123] Earle, Hammond and Morley were all appointed to the Assembly of Divines by the Parliament which had condemned Laudianism and imprisoned Laud. Altogether the whole group, whose survivors would do so much to restore a 'Laudian' Church in 1660, seem to have stood at a certain distance from Laud himself, and to have been suspected by him.

The explanation is, I think, clear. It can hardly have been their 'Socinianism' which offended Laud, for he himself was tolerant in theology: indeed he was explicitly accused of promoting 'Socinians' in the Church. But in two respects the 'Arminians' of Great Tew differed sharply from the 'Arminians' in the ecclesiastical establishment.

First, the men of Great Tew disliked clericalism. It was because the Laudian bishops were a clerical interest, claiming divine right, and despising the rights of the laity, that Falkland attacked them in Parliament in 1641; and he emphasized the point three months later by defending episcopacy itself, as distinct from the Laudian form of it, against the clerical claims of Scotch Presbyterianism.[124] Clarendon was no less anticlerical. That great Anglican, the defender and restorer of the Church, would make sharp observations on the English clergy, Anglican as well as puritan, in opposition as well as in power; he too hated the Scotch Presbyterians for their clericalism, preferring the English Independents, radical though they were, for their Erastian tolerance; and he would write a whole book on the invasion of the civil power by ecclesiastical pretensions over 1600 years.[125]

Secondly, the men of Great Tew were affronted by what they saw as the narrowness of the Laudian Church. Following Sandys and Grotius, they wished to see the Church of England as part – even head – of an international Church, and in that Church they would include foreign Protestants and foreign Catholics. Among foreign Catholics, they respected, in particular, the French and Venetians who resisted the papal claims. Among foreign Protestants, they allowed the non-episcopal Churches of France, Holland and Germany. Anglican episcopacy, they believed, was the best and purest form of Church-government; but they made no exclusive claims for it – it was a human system only, and as it had been praised, for England, by Calvin and Beza, and allowed by Knox, they willingly returned the compliment and admitted that the non-episcopal Protestant Churches of the Continent were also branches of the true Church. These differences of Church-government were, to them, 'indifferent', the deposit of history and political events. As such, they should be respected, not condemned. This was very different from the attitude of Laud, who forced the foreign Protestants in England into conformity and cut off communications with the Protestant Churches abroad. To the men of Great Tew this was an affront: Laud, they believed, in spite of the liberal ideas which he had inherited, was narrowing the Church of England, making it too a sect.

Thus Chillingworth and Falkland wished to bring the Church of England back into the Arminian tradition from which, under the Laudians, it had deviated. They wished to preserve its middle position, its 'Arminian' doctrine, its basis in reason, but to release it from clericalism, and reassert its ecumenical claims. Was this an impossible aim? It was an aim which, when advanced by Grotius, had foundered in the Thirty Years War. But England, in the 1630s, was at peace. Thanks to a 'blessed conjuncture', it enjoyed – as Clarendon afterwards recollected – 'the greatest measure of felicity that it had ever known'. If only those years of peace could have continued . . . However, they did not, and by the end of 1643 civil war was raging, Falkland and Chillingworth were both dead, and the philosophical discussions at Great Tew must have seemed, as they have seemed to historians since, a distant episode, privately remembered but finally closed. Chillingworth's book was their sole visible product. However, as we have seen, the survivors remained in constant touch. Their philosophy too was continued – in different circumstances and different places.

6   Clarendon

When Falkland was killed, his mantle, as Lady Ranelagh stated at the time, fell upon Clarendon. Since the beginning of the crisis in 1640, Clarendon had been the closest ally of Falkland in politics. Like Falkland, he had opposed the discredited regime of Strafford and Laud. He had helped to destroy the instruments of their rule. Then he had sought to preserve the monarchy on a reformed base. When civil war had broken out, he had sought to keep the King to moderate courses and had worked for peace. When all his efforts failed, he did not lose sight of his aims, but returned to intellectual life. He began his great *History of the Rebellion*. In doing so, he drew on his former days at Great Tew.

Clarendon was a historian before unexpected events made him the historian of the Rebellion. History was one of the subjects discussed at Great Tew. Falkland himself studied it deeply: after mastering the Greek tongue, according to Clarendon, he 'accurately read all the Greek historians' – and indeed, in his published work he quotes some of the most recondite of them.* Hobbes began as a historian: his first work was a translation of Thucydides, and it was perhaps this translation, which was published in 1620 and read by Clarendon, that brought him into the Tew circle. Clarendon, all his life, was a reader of history – not merely contemporary English history: there is not a historian of repute, ancient or modern, whom he did not at some time read, annotate and criticize. Even Cressy would take to the writing of history in defence of his conversion, dedicating to Catherine of Braganza, the Catholic Queen of Charles II, his history of the early English Church.

---

* E.g. Anna Comnena, the imperial Byzantine historian of the early twelfth century, whom he quotes in Greek. Since the first complete edition of her work was not published till 1649, he had presumably read the epitome of it published by D. Hoeschel at Augsburg in 1610.

But if history was studied at Great Tew, it was history of a particular kind. It was 'civil history', history as an empirical science, containing its own rules, which could be deduced from it and applied in practice. This 'civil history' had been introduced to modern Europe by the great Florentines, Machiavelli and Guicciardini, who had sought, through it, to explain the revolution of their time, the destruction of Italian independence; it had been continued by the French historian Jacques-Auguste de Thou, and the Venetian Enrico Davila, who were concerned with the civil wars of France, and by Paolo Sarpi, the champion of Venetian independence against the Counter-Reformation Papacy; and its English founder was William Camden who, in 1625, established a chair of 'civil history' in Oxford, as Fulke Greville, Lord Brooke, attempted to do in Cambridge. Both Sarpi and Camden wrote their historical works as material for the great *Historiae sui temporis* of de Thou. The change from literary or moral to 'civil' history was accompanied by a change in the popularity of the ancient historians: Livy and Plutarch, the uncritical commentators of ancient national virtues, were overtaken by Thucydides, Polybius and Tacitus, the advocates of historical explanation. Polybius was admired for his philosophical exploration of profound causes: a well-known sentence of his, 'Take away from history the questions how and why, and what is left but mere entertainment, pleasant enough to read, but of no lasting value?', was chosen by Camden as the epigraph for his own *Annals*. Tacitus was admired as the statesman's historian, the critical anatomist who laid bare the secret springs of policy; and his modern imitators showed their admiration by entitling their own works, like his, *Annals* and *Histories*.

The men of Great Tew, as a group, were interested in this 'civil history'. Their master, Hugo Grotius, was himself a practitioner of it, although his *Annals* and *Histories* of the Dutch Revolt, begun long ago (also as material for de Thou), had not been published in their time. The theory of the new history was expressed by Grotius' friend and fellow Arminian G. J. Vossius in his *Ars Historica* (1623) and his work on the Greek and Roman historians (1627). That it was this kind of history which interested Hobbes, till he was seduced by the apparent certainties of mathematics, is suggested by his decision to translate Thucydides, and by the dedication which he prefixed to that work: for he there recommended to his patron the study of 'history and civil knowledge' as 'profitable instruction' for politicians. Another member of the group, John Hales, wrote a short treatise on 'the method of reading profane history'. In this he divides the task of the historian into three layers: the collection of facts; the rational arrangement of facts;

and, finally, 'that Penelope which you must woo', historical explanation. The great master of historical explanation, to him, is Polybius who, in examining the actions of a State, is not content 'as it were, to cast its water, but looks into its bowels and shews where it is strong and where diseased'.[126]

It was in this tradition that Clarendon studied. His historical reading is known to us from his references, from his writings about history, and from his own manuscript notes. He took copious notes on Thucydides, Tacitus, Machiavelli, Sarpi, Camden, as well as on other historians, ancient and modern. He regarded Polybius as one of the best of historians. He revered Camden, whose portrait would hang in his gallery. When he came to write his *History*, his chosen model would be Davila; but John Evelyn, reading the newly published *History of the Rebellion* in 1702, would find it most 'like that of the noble Polybius, leading us by the courts, avenues and porches into the fabric'.[127]

The breadth of Clarendon's reading, his critical use of the great historians, his perpetual interest in the problems of history, as shown in his notebooks and minor works, sufficiently refute the judgment of Ranke that he was essentially an insular historian. The more modern view of him as an old-fashioned, backward-looking historian, an 'Ancient' who did not understand the 'Moderns' of his time, is even less justifiable. Clarendon was a conservative indeed: like all the men of Great Tew, he saw history as continuity, not radical change. But he was also, in his own time, a 'modern'. His modernity is implicit in his reading and in his writing. While the favourite historian of the Puritans, Sir Walter Ralegh, sought the explanation of historical events in divine providence, Clarendon would begin his *History* with a firm declaration that the causes of the rebellion were 'natural', such as could be traced in the history of other nations. Like Gibbon, he paid lip-service to Providence; but having done so, he concentrated his attention on 'second' or secular causes. He also, like Camden, thought that 'the growth and improvement of the arts and sciences' was among 'the most proper subjects of history'.[128]

In his notebooks Clarendon gave explicit expression to his modernity. The opinions of the ancients, he there wrote, should not receive 'stupid reverence', but they were entitled to 'a temporary belief and a suspension of our own judgment till we are fully informed of all the grounds and motives which have induced a conclusion'. To deny such conditional assent shows 'want of that modesty which is essential to the being and growth of knowledge'. On the other hand, 'having with due reverence weighed what Antiquity hath discovered', we should seek to advance knowledge by 'observation and experience': the way of 'the most accomplished Viscount of St Albans', 'the incomparable Viscount of St Albans', Lord Chancellor Bacon. Hence 'the improvement of the science and art of navigation in this last age' and of astronomy 'by Galileo's glasses' which have discovered new stars.[129]

'Suspension of judgment', the ἐποχή of Pyrrho of Elis – the phrase leads us back to the 'Pyrrhonian crisis' which so vexed the members of the circle at Tew. Clarendon too, it seems, was touched by that scepticism, aware of that problem. But his answer was not that of Chillingworth, nor that of Hobbes, nor that of Cressy. Rather it was that of Milton and Marvell. Like them, he solved the problem of human uncertainty by the active pursuit of public virtue, and he looked to history for intellectual guidance in that pursuit.

Always, in Clarendon's life, we can detect the tension between the cult of friendship and uncommitted literature and the call of public duty and strenuous action. In his autobiography, written long afterwards during his second exile, he looked back with nostalgic delight to his early life among poets and men of letters. His account of those leisured hours at Great Tew, of that enviable rural tranquillity and companionship in the halcyon days before 1640, 'so happy that it was hardly capable of improvement', is written from the heart. Again and again, in his letters and papers, he returns to the theme of lettered rural ease and friendship: the idyll which was so rudely shattered by the civil war. Even in defeat and disaster, he felt its solace. In 1646–7, when the King had been defeated and captured and he himself was lingering in Jersey, the last unconquered outpost of royalist England, writing his *History*, he could recapture some of that old pleasure. There we are surprised to find him, enjoying 'wonderful contentment', reading and writing, annotating Thucydides, Tacitus and Livy, reorganizing his notes on Machiavelli and Commines, Bacon and Grotius, positively relishing the delights of retirement, the sense of daily improvement in knowledge. It is as if he were back in Oxfordshire, and the intervening years of political struggle and civil war had been a dream.[130]

And yet, could it last? Was it real? Was it right? Like Milton, Clarendon believed that man had a moral duty to spurn delights and live laborious days. In Jersey, even while he relished his days of study, he was always thinking of the ultimate restoration of royal authority in England. When his friend from Great Tew, John Earle, thought of giving up the struggle for the sake of rural peace among his friends at his old parsonage of Bishopstone, Clarendon was shocked. 'Can you believe', he asked, 'the company and presence of your friends there . . .

would have the same relish it used to have?' 'How could you and I live in any tolerable degreee of happiness in a place where all conversation must be snares and all commerce reproaches?' And then, as if one thought led to another, his mind went back to the vanished felicity and open conversation of Great Tew, and he wrote of Falkland, Sidney Godolphin and Thomas Hobbes: in particular, of Falkland, 'of whom, in its place, I intend to speak largely, conceiving it to be so far from an indecorum that the preservation of the fame and merit of persons, and the deriving the same to posterity, is no less the business of history than the truth of things'. And he asked Earle to send him his own tribute to Falkland, which he had once read to him at Dartmouth.[131]

In all his writings, Clarendon showed not only his love of rural retirement and contemplation but also his contempt for those who valued its delights above the call of public duty. When the royal cause seemed lost, many of his old friends thought of giving up the struggle, of 'compounding' for their estates and living quietly upon them. Clarendon would never make or approve any such compromise. To compound, he wrote, was inexcusable: 'innocence is the best wealth'; and he would write with withering scorn of those great aristocrats and upstart courtiers who preferred their wealth and ease to their duty. So when civil war flared up again, in the spring of 1648, he suspended work on his *History*. Henceforth, for twelve years, he would have no time to write. He would be the active politician of the exiled royal court, the unwearying animator of the royalist underground in England, the patient architect of ultimate royal restoration.

However, throughout those years he continued to read; and his reading illustrated his continuing interest in the ideals of Great Tew. In his enforced leisure in Jersey he had followed the example of Grotius in his enforced leisure at Loevestein. As Grotius had solaced himself by reading the Greek poets, writing his book on rational Christianity, and annotating the New Testament, so Clarendon taught himself Greek, read the ancient historians, began his *History*, and – like du Plessis Mornay also in his hour of defeat and dejection – meditated on the Psalms. He read and re-read the works of Grotius and his own notes on Grotius. Later, in his pinched, uncomfortable exile in France or Flanders, he would send for Vossius' work on historiography, enquire 'what books of Grotius are now printing at Leiden or Amsterdam', and welcome the long-delayed publication of Grotius' *Annals*. When all his schemes had at last borne fruit and Charles II had returned to his throne, Clarendon, in his greatness, would plan to re-create, in his new country house in Oxfordshire, that delicious rural retirement which he remembered from the past. There he intended to live as Falkland had lived, among his friends. There his family was to succeed him, enjoined to constant friendship with the neighbouring family of Falkland. There he hoped to complete his own great *History*.

His hopes were rudely disappointed. Before his country house was finished, a sudden 'gust of envy' had cast him from power and driven him once again into banishment. Although he would continue, by correspondence with his son, to oversee the building of Cornbury he would never return to that England which he had so reluctantly left in 1647 and to which he had so gladly returned in 1660. His monumental *History* would be completed not in the rural peace of Oxfordshire but in exile in Montpellier and Moulins. That exile, which sharpened his once equable temper, would sharpen also his nostalgic recollection. He would hurl his anathemas against the apostates Cressy and Hobbes, and in his own *Life* he would recall the delightful days of retired study in the 1630s.

There also, in his *Essay on an Active and Contemplative Life*, he would set out his philosophy of history and life: his conviction that scholarly retirement is of value only as part of 'magnanimous activity'. Even the study of history, he insisted, required such involvement. All great historians have been men of action, for only by participating in events can one understand them. Contemplation is indeed necessary; but contemplation divorced from worthy matter of contemplation – that is, from the real, active world – is barren and circular. That pleasant 'garden of contemplation' (and the metaphor brings us once again back to Marvell at Nun Appleton) breeds only night-flowers which close at sunrise: 'we have very little testimony, very few records, of any notable fruit gathered from this dry tree of solitude . . .' Clarendon was attacking the monkish historians of the Middle Ages, but it is easy to see the modern monk who was in his eye: the academic theorist and apostate, Hobbes.

Thus Clarendon found his own way out of the 'Pyrrhonian' crisis of his time. By alternating between political action and historical study he resolved the old debate between *vita activa* and *vita contemplativa* which had exercised the Greek philosophers and had been transmitted by Cicero to the men of the Italian Renaissance. But meanwhile what of the religious ideals of the Great Tew group? In order to answer this question we must go back to the year of regicide and the establishment of the Republic, 1649.

7 Hammond

In 1649 the Church of England was, by all appearances, extinct. Its hierarchy had been abolished, its liturgy proscribed, its lands sold. There seemed no future for it. The Roman Catholics smugly referred to it as 'the late Church of England', dismissing it as a brief, forgettable episode in Christian history, like the Donatist Church in fourth-century Africa. To the temporarily exultant Scotch Presbyterians it was 'a non-entity, or a thing that hath not so much as any being': a decaying relic of which the Stuart court must disembarrass itself if it were ever to return.

The Stuart court seemed only too ready to agree. It is sometimes assumed that the restoration of the monarchy in 1660 logically or necessarily led to the restoration of the Church. But this is too easy an assumption. At the exiled court of Charles II, there were many who regarded the Church of England as a liability. It was his loyalty to that Church (they said) that had ruined Charles I. Therefore, if his son was to be restored, he must seek the alliance of a Church that had real power, not this mere phantom. In other words, he must either take the Covenant and re-enter England as the puppet-King of Presbyterian Scotland, or yield, as so many of his exiled subjects had yielded, to the comfortable embrace of Roman Catholicism and enlist the armed support of France or Spain.

Against these arguments, the members of the Great Tew circle at the exiled court – Clarendon, Earle and Morley – fought a continuous battle. They were supported by John Cosin, the Laudian Master of Peterhouse and Dean of Peterborough, whom however they somewhat distrusted – he had been too extreme a Laudian, too clerical and ceremonious – and by Sir Richard Browne, the royalist 'resident' in Paris, who fitted up an Anglican chapel in his house: indeed it was said that the Church of England, at that time, had no existence except in that house. But all the influence of the Queen and her courtiers was against them, and as they watched the defections around them they must often have despaired of success. And anyway, what would success at court avail them if, when the King was restored, the Church of England had ceased to exist in England? To prevent such a situation it was essential that that Church be kept alive there too. The question was, who would organize that now shadowy Church and sustain it in the catacombs?

The natural leaders of the Church were its surviving bishops.

Unfortunately the surviving bishops, elderly men overwhelmed by the torrent of events, showed very little desire to lead. Their natural head, now that both archbishops were dead, was the Bishop of London, Dr Juxon, Laud's particular protégé, whom he had made Lord Treasurer. But Dr Juxon had made it clear, at the very beginning of the troubles, that he had had enough. He then (in the indulgent phrase of Clarendon) 'wisely withdrew from the storm, and enjoyed the greatest tranquillity of any man in the three kingdoms throughout the whole boisterous and destroying time that followed': that is, he lived as a country squire in the Cotswolds, hunting a much-admired pack of hounds. The other bishops similarly kept out of trouble. Even Bishop Duppa, the least inactive of them, likened himself to a tortoise, tucked safely under his shell, and wrote defeatist letters about 'the expiring Church'. Some of them, like Bishop Skinner of Oxford, conducted furtive ordinations in their houses, but none of them accepted any risk. 'Indolence and pusillanimity' were the qualities ascribed to them. The most formidable of them, Bishop Wren, was in the Tower, sullenly scribbling unreadable treatises against ancient heresies, and awaiting deliverance by divine Providence rather than through any exertion by his colleagues.

Since the surviving bishops were so unhelpful, Clarendon and his friends abroad looked for other clerical allies at home, and to whom should they turn but to their old friends from the Great Tew circle, Hammond and Sheldon?

Hammond and Sheldon had both been at Oxford during the first civil war, Hammond as canon and sub-dean of Christ Church, Sheldon as Warden of All Souls College, both as chaplains to the King. When the King slipped out of Oxford to give himself up to the Scots at Newark, he left his chaplains behind; nor was he allowed, either by the Scots or by the English Parliament, when he became their prisoner, to enjoy their services. Hammond and Sheldon, it was explained, had not taken the Covenant, and therefore they were unfit to minister to the King of covenanted nations. So the King was obliged to listen to Alexander Henderson, when among the Scots, and to Stephen Marshall among the English, until he rebelled against these intruded clergy, preferring 'to be his own chaplain in his bed-chamber, where he constantly used the Common Prayer by himself'.

When cornet Joyce carried the King off from Holmby House, and he became the prisoner of the army, his condition at once improved. He was then allowed his own chaplains, and he sent for Hammond, Sheldon, Morley and Robert Sanderson, another Oxford man closely associated with them. The Presbyterians in Parliament protested; but the Independent rulers of the army ignored their protests, and Hammond and Sheldon continued with the King until his flight to Carisbrooke at the end of 1647. There they rejoined him briefly, but soon they were once again removed from him, and returned to Oxford. They were promptly summoned before the Visitors sent by Parliament to purge the University of 'malignant' or uncovenanted persons. Refusing to acknowledge the Visitors, both were imprisoned and, on their release, forbidden to come within five miles of Oxford or of the King. After the execution of the King, both lived obscurely in the country, protected by royalist families. Sheldon lived first at Snelston in Derbyshire, the guest of the widowed Mrs Okeover of Okeover, then at Bridgeford in Nottinghamshire, under the protection of another widow, Lady Savile, of Rufford Abbey. Hammond lived first with Sir Philip Warwick at Clapham, Bedfordshire, then, from 1650 till 1660, with Sir John Pakington at Westwood, Worcestershire. It was Westwood that was to be their intellectual centre.

Sir John Pakington, the owner of Westwood, was a wealthy baronet with estates both in Worcestershire and in Buckinghamshire, where his family controlled the most notorious of rotten parliamentary boroughs, Aylesbury. He himself had sat as MP for Aylesbury, until he was 'secluded' as a royalist, and replaced, ultimately, by the most vocal of the regicides, Thomas Scot. However, it was not so much Sir John as his wife, and her family, who provided the link between Westwood and Tew. For Sir John Pakington, who had inherited his estates at the age of four, had been brought up by a guardian appointed by the Court of Wards; and this guardian, whose daughter he had afterwards married, was a neighbouring Worcestershire landowner, Thomas, Lord Coventry.

Lord Coventry, who died in 1640, had been for fifteen years Lord Keeper of the Great Seal. According to Clarendon, who was grateful to him for encouragement at the beginning of his legal career,[132] he was 'a man of wonderful gravity and wisdom' who 'understood not only the whole science and mystery of the law . . . but had a clear conception of the whole policy of the government both of Church and State, which, by the unskilfulness of some well-meaning men' – i.e. of Laud and his friends – 'jostled each other too much'.[133] Three of Coventry's sons – William, Francis and Henry – had been at Queen's College, Oxford, under Chillingworth's friend Christopher Potter; Henry had gone on to be a Fellow of All Souls under Sheldon; Francis and Henry were both friends of Chillingworth;[134] and Francis was the first English translator of Grotius' *De Veritate.** Thus already in the 1630s the Coventry family was associated with the Oxford friends of Lord Falkland; and this association was strengthened in the 1650s when Coventry's two daughters, Dorothy, Lady Pakington and Anne, Lady Savile, became, at Westwood and Rufford, the hostesses of Hammond and Sheldon.

It was from these houses of refuge that the policy of Great Tew was resumed after the disasters of the Civil War and Revolution. The surviving letters of that now scattered group, and particularly those of Hammond to Sheldon,[135] show them at work. There we see them not only looking after the wayward heirs and entangled estates of Lord Falkland and corresponding secretly with Hyde, Earle and Morley abroad, but also securing the survival of the Anglican Church, preparing it to resume its old position, and seeking, by scholarship and controversy, to establish its credentials against both its Catholic and its puritan enemies.

In this partnership, the burden of organization probably fell mainly on Sheldon. He was essentially an administrator rather than a scholar. At Great Tew he had been singled out as the future Archbishop of Canterbury, as indeed he was to become. Now, in consultation with Hammond, he worked to secure the continuity of episcopal succession and ordination, to concert the policy to be adopted in the face of the divisive tactics of the puritan government, to raise money for impoverished clergy, to encourage the faithful, and to plant chaplains in royalist houses and thereby rebuild the Church on a lay basis and correct the friction of Laudian times. This was in itself an arduous business, full of frustration. The frustrations began at home.

Mrs Okeover's daughter was married to Sir Robert Shirley of Staunton Harold, a young baronet whose indiscreet royalism was continually putting him in prison. Sheldon complained of his 'great mutability and unsteadiness'. Even more disconcerting was the attitude of Lady Savile's son, Sir George Savile. He was devoted to Sheldon, but carried his rationalism and scepticism to alarming

* *True Religion Explained and Defended . . . 1632* (STC 12400). The name of the translator is not printed, but it is recorded in the Stationers' Register (28 July 1631) as 'Francis Coventry esquire', and his identity was known to Grotius, who wrote to his brother that the translator was 'Coventrii, viri illustris apud Anglos, filius', 'viri praenobilis Coventrii filius' (*BHG* VII, pp. 461, 616; VIII, pp. 2–3). Presumably Grotius had learned this from his English friends who were in a position to know. Such evidence seems conclusive. I cannot think why the editor of the *Briefwisseling*, B.L. Meulenbroek, should say that Grotius was mistaken and that the translator was the Franciscan friar Christopher Davenport (on whom see above, p. 112) who, having been born at Coventry, occasionally used the name Franciscus Coventriensis. There is neither evidence nor probability for such a suggestion.

lengths, being attracted to the 'heathen principles' of *Leviathan* which so excited 'the looser sons of the Church and the King's party'. All the efforts of Hammond and Sheldon could not bring Savile into line: his increasing scepticism would outrage the increasingly conservative Clarendon.* Later, as Marquis of Halifax, he would be famous as the Trimmer. But Shirley proved a generous patron to the Anglican clergy recommended by Hammond, and displayed his loyalty by a unique gesture. Perhaps the most splendid memorial to the work of Hammond and Sheldon in those dark years is the delightful church which Shirley built at Staunton Harold with its defiant inscription.

> In the year 1653
> When all things sacred were throughout the land
> Either demolished or profaned,
> Sir Robert Shirley, baronet,
> Founded this church,
> Whose singular praise it is
> To have done the best things in the worst times
> And hoped them in the most calamitous.

Three years later Shirley died – once again a prisoner in the Tower.

If Sheldon was the organizer, Hammond was the philosopher and propagandist of the underground Anglican Church. The philosophy which he expressed has often been described as Laudian. But it was Laudianism with a significant difference. Arminian indeed in doctrine, rational in method, ecumenical in its ultimate aims, it was also conciliatory, not authoritarian, and respectful of lay reason and lay interests. In fact, as we would expect from the persons, it was the Arminianism of Erasmus and Grotius, of Andrewes and Overall, before it had been subordinated to the clericalism of Laud and the policy of Charles I. Afterwards – after 1660 – it would be convenient to speak of the restoration of the Laudian Church. Laud, after all, like Charles I, had been a martyr. But in the 1650s such language was not used. The name of Laud is not mentioned in the surviving correspondence of Hammond. The continuity of ideas, as of persons, runs not through Laud and his bishops but through Falkland's Great Tew.

Hammond's position as the intellectual heir of Falkland and

---

* After the Restoration, when Clarendon had quarrelled with Sir William Coventry, he would be particularly hostile to Savile, whom he would describe as 'a man of very ill reputation amongst men of piety and religion, and was looked upon as void of all sense of religion, even to the doubting, if not denying, that there is a God' (*Life* II, p.168).

Chillingworth was quickly established. A Fellow of Magdalen College, Oxford, he had held the living of Penshurst in Kent, presented by the Earl of Leicester – an opponent of Laud. In 1643, just before Falkland's death, he had returned to Oxford, and next year, at the instigation of his friend and admirer, Christopher Potter, Provost of Queen's College, he had published his *Practical Catechism*. The book soon brought him into trouble. A group of Presbyterian ministers in London denounced it for 'unsound opinions, abominable errors, damnable heresies and horrid blasphemies, destructive to the very fundamental truths of Christianity', specifying particularly the 'infamous and pernicious error' that Christ died for all and not only for the Elect.[136] When the Puritans established themselves in Oxford, the Presbyterian controversialist Francis Cheynell, who had fulminated against the 'Socinianism' of Chillingworth, denounced Hammond from its pulpits for the same heresy: in that whole Catechism, he said, there was no mention of the Trinity. Hammond's reply, that in a practical catechism there was no need to refer to 'that speculative mystery', only served to deepen the suspicion. In 1645 Falkland's *Discourse on the Infallibility of the Church*, which had previously circulated in manuscript, was published at Oxford. This was presumably a printer's venture: it does not seem to have issued from the Great Tew circle.* Next year, a more official text was printed in London. It had a preface, which the previous edition lacked, and was followed by an answer to some anonymous 'objections' by 'a Romanist' which had circulated in manuscript. The preface and the answer were both by Hammond, who was presumably responsible for the publication.

Next year, 1647, having published his refutation of 'the Chillingworthians and Lucius Lord Falkland', Cressy sent a copy of it to Hammond, whom he clearly regarded as their present representative. Hammond was unimpressed by the work but declined to enter into controversy with a former friend. Probably about the same time, he was approached by his friend John Fell who proposed to him an authoritative edition of the Fathers. In the general context of Hammond's work, the intention seems clear: a critical, scholarly edition taking note of Daillé's work which meant so much to the Tew circle, and which had not yet been exploited, or translated into English or Latin. But

---

* I assume this for two reasons: first because the edition lacks any preface, explanation or other indication of authority – as if the printer had nothing but the manuscript to go on; secondly, because it was evidently unknown to Clarendon, who, in his character of Falkland, written in March 1646–7, expresses regret that Falkland's *Discourses* are unpublished. Clarendon had left Oxford in March 1645, but he would surely have known if the *Discourse* had been published by authority, and by his friends.

Hammond declined this task too. He doubted the vendibility of such a work, and he was at that time fully occupied, attending the King, supporting him in print, and defending his own *Practical Catechism*.

After the execution of the King and Charles II's ruinous surrender to the Scotch Presbyterians, the Church of England was at its lowest ebb. The year 1651 has been marked as the worst period of defection to Rome. In that year, two Cambridge men appeared as champions of Falkland and Chillingworth. It was the first sign of support from that university, and both men were friends of Hammond. The first of them was Thomas Smith, of Christ's College, who published a translation of Daillé's work. In his preface, Smith mentioned Falkland's respect for Daillé and showed detailed knowledge both of Falkland and of Falkland's unpublished manuscripts. Since he had been only nineteen when Falkland was killed, this knowledge must have been supplied to him by a friend of Falkland. Smith also refers to a hitherto unprinted treatise by Falkland 'shortly to be publisht', and quotes from the preface to be attached to it by 'the learned J.P.'. This was the second of our two Cambridge men, John Pearson, of King's College, a former pupil, at Eton, of John Hales, whose *Golden Remains* he would afterwards edit. He was now living privately in the country. The new treatise by Falkland which he published was a second discourse in answer to the criticism of the first. It was published in 1651 in the third edition of Falkland's original discourse. In his preface to it, Pearson referred to Cressy, who was stung to reply in a second edition of his own apologia.

It is tempting to see the hand of Hammond behind these related publications, both of which reflect his known interests and both of which depend on a knowledge of Falkland's work and papers. Moreover, both Pearson and Smith soon re-emerge in connexion with Hammond. For this revival of interest in Falkland and Chillingworth provoked once again their original enemy, the Jesuit Fr. Knott. In 1652 Knott, now seventy years old, published at the Hague yet another attack on Chillingworth. It was entitled *Infidelity Unmasked*. Thereupon Thomas Smith wrote to Hammond to enquire whether he would reply to it. Hammond replied that he would not: nor, he thought, would Jeremy Taylor. He had little respect for Knott, whose book, he afterwards told Sheldon, was 'so very tiresome that I cannot read much in it'. To Smith he suggested that, for a rejoinder, he apply to 'Mr I. P.' – i.e. John Pearson.[137] Evidently both Smith and Pearson were directed by Hammond and deferred to him. In the end Smith himself replied to Knott. At the same time he published a translation of another work by Daillé – his *Apology for the Reformed Churches*. He had made this translation some years ago, he wrote, 'at the urgency of some learned friends'. He had been unwilling to print it then; but now, when the Papists were exploiting the ruin of the Church of England, its publication seemed seasonable.

So far, it might seem, Hammond, since 1646, was eager to keep out of the controversy raised by Chillingworth and Falkland. All that time he had been very busy, first in serving and defending the King, then in sustaining the relics of the episcopal Church, of which, as his adversary John Owen wrote, the whole weight seemed to have fallen on him. Perhaps, like Thomas Smith, he thought his own vindication of Falkland 'unanswerable', so that he could now leave that controversy to be managed by younger men. Meanwhile, he was working more constructively to provide the Church of England with a solid intellectual base. That base was not to be the quaking ground of the Elizabethan settlement, which the high Calvinists and the Puritans had captured, and were now endlessly disputing with each other, but, as Falkland and Chillingworth had argued, Scripture and Reason. This led him, and leads us, back to the presiding genius of Great Tew: Hugo Grotius.

Grotius himself was now dead. He had died in 1645. The European war, in protest against which he had written his most famous work, was then still raging. So was the English civil war. All his hopes now seemed in ruin. The Dutch Arminians were still a defeated and proscribed party. The English Arminian party, of whom he had once hoped so much, had been destroyed. His particular English disciples were dead. In his last years, living in Paris as ambassador of Queen Christina of Sweden, he had pinned his fading hopes for 'the peace of the Church' on the Gallicanism of Richelieu. But in 1643 Richelieu had died. In the spring of 1645 Grotius had been summoned to Stockholm and given his discharge. He was then sixty-one years old. Returning by sea, he was shipwrecked in the Baltic, rescued, and taken, in an open coach, through vile weather, to Rostock. There, on 28 August, he died of exhaustion. It was the year of Naseby. Never can the cause of European ecumenism, as he saw it, have seemed more hopeless.

However, in the years which followed, Grotius acquired a new fame, or notoriety, in England, and it was largely through the survivors of the Great Tew circle, and particularly through Hammond, that he acquired it. In his last years he had followed the example of Erasmus and studied the whole Bible thoroughly, not as a theologian but as a humanist scholar, seeking to extract its true meaning, without presupposing divine inspiration, and to relate it to its historical context.

The result was his *Annotations of the Old and New Testament*, published in successive instalments from 1641 to 1650. These annotations pleased neither Catholics nor Protestants. Grotius denied several books of the Bible to their supposed authors and implicitly undermined both the doctrine of the Trinity and the whole Protestant eschatology: for he argued that all the prophecies of the Apocalypse, in so far as they related to public affairs, were to have been fulfilled long ago, within a few years of their utterance, and were quite irrelevant to later history.

Grotius' *Annotations* were eagerly read by the Great Tew circle. Clarendon, in his exile, wrote to his friend Edward Nicholas to find him a copy.[138] 'Have you seen Grotius on the Revelation and the Epistles of Peter, John and Jude?' Hammond wrote to Sheldon in 1650.[139] Hammond was at that time finishing his book *The Reasonableness of Christianity* – a link in the chain from the works of du Plessis Mornay and Grotius to those of Locke – and was planning a similar set of annotations. At first he was disconcerted by some of the 'wide conjectures' of Grotius, but on the whole he was enthusiastic: 'Grotius' notes on the Revelations I find of good use to me, for he is on a scheme almost perfectly all one with mine'.[140] Hammond would publish his own annotations in 1653. Though less radical than Grotius, he agreed substantially with him – indeed his critics would accuse him of plagiarism – and Puritans and millenarians would regularly lump them together, deploring the ruin of their own labours by 'the new way of Grotius and Hammond'.

The renewal of interest in Grotius and his English disciples is illustrated by a series of publications, in 1651–3, by Clement Barksdale, an Oxford clergyman, now chaplain to the royalist Lord Chandos of Sudeley Castle, Gloucestershire. In a slim volume of religious poetry, Barksdale included three poems in praise of Grotius and one on Hammond. He hailed Grotius as an irenist

> studious how to reconcile
> This and that Church in mild Cassander's style

and Hammond as the defender of 'noble Falkland' and episcopacy.[141] In the same two years, Barksdale published translations of two works by Grotius, a short life of Grotius, and an account of a religious 'disputation' between himself and a group of local puritan gentry and clergy, in the course of which he had cited Hooker, Grotius and 'that great ornament of the English Church, the learned and pious Dr Hammond'. These citations did not please the other disputants, and were interrupted by the parrot-cry, 'an Arminian! An Arminian!'[142]

All this inevitably revived the charge of 'Socinianism' – a charge to which the puritan government happened at that time to be particularly sensitive. For now Socinianism was appearing as a dangerous heresy within Independency itself, threatening the puritan consensus. Early in 1652 the Council of State ordered the seizure of a pamphlet setting out, in Latin, 'the Racovian catechism', the confession of faith of the Polish Socinians: a publication authorized by the offical licenser, John Milton. The puritan establishment was alarmed. John Owen, Cromwell's clerical favourite and permanent Vice-Chancellor of Oxford University, with fourteen other Independent ministers, petitioned Parliament, demanding action. Parliament duly condemned the work as 'blasphemous, erroneous and scandalous' and ordered that the whole edition be burnt.[143] That affair died down, but Owen, once aroused, and egged on by the most bigoted of Dutch Calvinists, resolved to crush, once and for all, this 'hydra of Socinianism'. He did so by hurling at it a heavy volume, bristling with theological learning, his 'Diatribe on Divine Justice'.

He reckoned without the irrepressible John Bidle, 'the father of English Socinianism', who had been behind the publication of the Racovian catechism. Bidle was a Puritan – unlike Grotius and his disciples, he believed the Pope to be Antichrist. For several years he had been in and out of prison. Now, in December 1654, he returned to the charge with a particularly offensive publication. He was haled before Cromwell's Parliament and, once again, imprisoned. The affair caused a great stir in the Protestant world: England, it was now said, had become the metropolis of Socinianism, and Owen, now recognized as its most formidable enemy, was requested by the Council of State to defend the national honour by destroying the heresy. He responded with another learned work, even heavier than the last: over 700 pages. Bidle was the immediate enemy, but Owen recognized that it was not enough to crush the puritan head of the hydra: 'the great obstacle' which impeded the triumph of orthodoxy was not an obscure if irritant sectary but that 'giant in all kinds of literature', 'the learned Grotius', whose most formidable English defender was Hammond.

The controversy between Owen and Hammond over the Socinianism of Grotius would last two years. In treatise after treatise, Owen would attack, and Hammond would defend, the works, and in particular the *Annotations*, of Grotius: his rationalism, his scepticism, his apparent indifference to the doctrine of the Trinity, his 'gnostic' tendency to allegorize the more incredible parts of Scripture, his rejection of that prophetic scheme upon which the ideology of Puritanism rested. Then, as the controversy widened, and other writers came in, it would be overtaken by another, and the attackers would switch from the alleged Socinianism of Grotius to his alleged 'popery'. The director of this new attack was Richard Baxter.

Baxter was a moderate English Presbyterian but a fanatical anti-papist. Like William Prynne, whom he admired, he saw papist conspiracy everywhere: Jesuits in the background, Jesuits in disguise, Jesuits under every bed. As a moderate man, he hoped to form an alliance with the 'moderate' Anglican clergy, but as an anti-papist he was quick to smell the Beast among them. So he divided them into two classes, 'the old episcopal divines' of whom he had hopes – that is, those who clung, as he did, to the old Elizabethan system, the disciples of Jewel and Foxe – and 'the new episcopal divines', the 'Arminians' who rejected that system, rationalizing away its ideological base and defining their relationship with Rome. These latter clergy he would describe as 'Cassandrian Grotian papists', for 'under the name of episcopal divines' they 'do prosecute the design of Cassander and Grotius to reconcile us to the Pope upon certain abatements and reformations of the Romanists'. Having watched Hammond's controversy with Owen from the wings, Baxter entered the fray in 1658 with his work, *The Grotian Religion Discover'd*. His challenge was not to Hammond, an enemy whom he respected and personally admired, but to Hammond's friend and protégé Thomas Pierce.* Later he would continue the controversy with other adversaries. The gist of his argument was that Grotius was not a Socinian but – need it be said? – a Jesuit disguised as a Socinian.[144]

These controversies were still being pursued when the English Republic faltered and the various clerical parties saw that they must jostle for position under a restored monarchy. The strongest parties were the Presbyterians, who had opposed the Republic and were now seeking to bury it, and the Anglicans who, as consistent royalists, hoped to be restored to authority with the King. Neither side could be sure of success: the Presbyterians were uncomfortable about their past and the Anglicans could not be certain of the King. Much therefore depended

---

* Pierce, like Hammond, was a Fellow of Magdalen College, Oxford, of which he would become President in 1661. Hammond was godfather to his son and he wrote Hammond's epitaph in the parish church of Hampton Lovell, Worcs. In his acrimonious controversy, mainly with Baxter's ally William Barlee, his most important work is *The New Discoverer Discovered, by way of Answer to Mr Baxter's Discovery of the Grotian Religion* (1659).

on political initiative, political skill. Here Clarendon and his friends had an advantage, for they knew their own minds and purpose, they had kept together, and they had contrived to maintain their position both at the exiled court and in the country.

The danger was clear to the most sharp-sighted, but not the most sensitive, of Presbyterians, the Scotchman Robert Baillie, to whom a firm Presbyterian establishment in England seemed the only guarantee of Presbyterian domination in Scotland. Baillie, who regarded all moderate men (and especially those on his own side) with contempt, urged his friends to go straight for the enemy's jugular. While the English Presbyterians still held, or seemed to hold, bargaining power, he believed, they should act decisively: they should send a petition to the King at Breda, demand the immediate dismissal of Clarendon, and hasten to employ 'some serious and judicious pen' to expose and destroy 'that high, proud, malicious, and now very active and dangerous party' around him. His particular enemies were Hammond, Pierce, Heylyn and Jeremy Taylor, who, he said, had not only fully confirmed everything that he had ever said about the Laudian bishops, but had 'gone beyond them to all the Tridentine Popery of Grotius'. Baxter (he added), with his half-baked ideas of compromise, was doing great harm. He should be put in his place: told 'either to be silent, or simply regulate in his writings by those brethren who are wiser than himself' i.e. who agreed with Professor Baillie.[145]

It was no good, or it was too late. The old party of Great Tew was determined to capture the key positions at once, in the Church as in the State. Sheldon, Hammond, Morley, Earle were all to be bishops. Hammond was to have Worcester – the diocese in which Westwood lay. There was mumping among the torpid old bishops. Bishop Skinner of Oxford, who had once been Chillingworth's tutor, raised 'little trifling objections': rich bishoprics, he said, should not go to whipper-snappers of fifty-five, who had not even been deans, but to those who (like himself) had been waiting long in poorer sees . . .'[146] There was also, among the old bishops, a dread of Socinianism, which perhaps lurked behind those objections. The only personal request that the bishops made to Charles II, while he was still at Breda, was that he should not receive back, as his chaplain, the high Anglican clergyman Thomas Lushington, who was suspected of that terrible heresy.[147]

However that may be, the objections were ignored. Hammond's position was unshakeable so long as the Great Tew group had influence. But he was never consecrated as Bishop of Worcester nor saw the restoration of King and Church. Like Moses, he only glimpsed that

Promised Land. Seeing it, from his deathbed, he also foresaw trouble to come: would the party which had held together in adversity preserve its integrity in power? 'I must confess', he said, 'I never saw that time in all my life wherein I could so cheerfully say my *Nunc dimittis* as now. Indeed I do dread prosperity: I do really dread it'. He died on 25 April, the very day on which Parliament met to receive the restored King. The bishopric then went to Morley, and, three years later, when Morley moved to Winchester, to the still hungry Skinner, who had not, after all, waited in vain. By that time the Restoration was complete. The Presbyterians had been ditched. Baillie could not understand how it had happened. This 'overturning of the Reformation in England', he wrote, was 'very strange and grievous, and I suppose we know not yet the bottom of the mystery'.[148]

8 Conclusion

In this essay I have tried to look at the Great Tew circle not only in its flourishing years, so eloquently commemorated, but over the whole period from its first formation in 1634, through its dispersion in the 1640s and 1650s, to the reassembly of its surviving members in positions of power after 1660. By so doing, I have shown, I hope, that it was not a mere ephemeral house-party but a remarkably coherent group of men with clear and consistent ideas. Those ideas were formed in the 1630s, in the years of peace, but in opposition to the established orthodoxy of that time. In politics, the members of the circle were ambivalent about Charles I: they were royalists, but critical of his personal rule. In religion they were ambivalent about Laud: they were Arminians who opposed his clericalism. They looked back from the political Arminianism of the Laudians to the intellectual Arminianism of Andrewes. In philosophy they were rationalists, sceptics; but sceptics who grappled with the problem of Pyrrhonism and sought to find, in constructive reason, a firm basis for belief. They were also irenists; for if such a basis could be found, they believed that ideological disputes would become irrelevant and religious unity be restored. In all this they were the heirs to a discernible tradition: the tradition of Erasmus, du Plessis Mornay and Hooker. Their immediate master was Grotius.

In 1640–1 they all supported the party of reform in both Church and State. The failure of reform was a defeat for them. When civil war broke out, they all supported the King, but still sought a settlement on the terms of 1640–1. Here too they were defeated, and after 1643, with the failure of 'Waller's Plot', the aggravation of the war, and the successive deaths of Falkland, their patron, and Chillingworth, their intellectual leader, it has seemed to historians that they were finally dissipated. However, in spite of some defections, this was not so. Held together by strong personal friendships, by a sense of responsibility to the family of their patron, and by a shared political and religious philosophy, the survivors of the circle remained remarkably united. Clarendon succeeded Falkland as their political leader; Hammond succeeded Chillingworth as their philosopher. In exile, Clarendon, Morley and Earle kept the exiled King, with difficulty, loyal to the Church; at home, Sheldon and Hammond kept that now disestablished Church, with difficulty, alive. Meanwhile, they maintained the intellectual claims of their party: Clarendon set out its historical philosophy in the spirit of Hooker, Hammond its theology in the spirit of Grotius. Finally, in 1660, they achieved their triumph. Crown and Church were restored on something like the terms which they had advocated in 1641: a Crown that was in harmony with Parliament, without prerogative courts and prerogative taxes, a Church that was episcopal in form, 'Arminian' in doctrine, but strengthened by lay support.

That was its short-term victory. It was not a predestined or predictable victory. It was not what General Monck, the apparent engineer of the Restoration, had intended – if indeed he knew what he intended; for in Clarendon's sardonic words 'the whole machine was infinitely above his strength . . . and it is glory enough to his memory that he was instrumental in bringing those mighty things to pass which he had neither wisdom to foresee, nor courage to attempt, nor understanding to contrive'.[149] It was not what the English Presbyterians had intended. They had invited the King back and naturally supposed that they would have a voice in the settlement. They may not have expected, like Baillie, a Calvinist Church and a covenanted King; but they looked back, no doubt, to the ideals of 1646 and 1648, to the abortive Propositions of Newcastle and Treaty of Newport: a monarchy under their control and 'a lame erastian Presbytery' in the Church. It was not what Charles II himself would have chosen: an easy-going absolutism and toleration (at least) for Dissenters, especially Catholic Dissenters, was his ideal. It was not what the old royalists or the old bishops wanted: their aim was straightforward re-possession and revenge. Clarendon would write contemptuously of the greed and vindictiveness of the old bishops, and the old Cavaliers would speak bitterly of him. That it nevertheless happened, that the restored monarchy represented the political ideals of 1641 and – more remarkable still – the 'Arminianism' of the Laudian Church, was, to say the least, surprising. It was not an accident, nor was it a historical necessity. It was the achievement of a party with a consistent philosophy which it was prepared to translate into action. Perhaps it was the only means by which a bloodless restoration could have been achieved; but a bloodless restoration was not a historical necessity either.

Of course no settlement can be permanent: we are all at the mercy of our successors. History, as the statesman Clarendon saw, is continuing life: it cannot be controlled, as the academic Hobbes would have liked to control it, by static models. The years after 1660 were full of movement and the 'Restoration settlement' would be eroded on all sides. But some elements in it had a long life. The monarchy and the established Church may be very different now; but we have them still.

The most distinctive contribution of the Great Tew group was the restoration of the Anglican Church not merely as an institution of State, in a particular form, victorious over Calvinism, Puritanism and the sects, but also with a particular philosophy. Though its form was the same as in the past, its content had changed. It was not now the Elizabethan and Jacobean Church, so cried up in 1641, with its 'high Calvinist' doctrine and its Tudor ideal of the Christian Prince, the successor of Constantine and Theodosius, fulfilling an almost messianic role. Equally it was not the aggressive, clerical Church of Laud, armed with power, an inseparable, organic part of an authoritarian new monarchy. What distinguished it was its emancipation from prophetic history (which was the emancipation of history too), its acceptance of critical reason and humanist scholarship as the interpreter of its own documents – and, of course, its new base in the laity.

That too could not be permanent. Nothing in history is permanent except its human content and the human spirit which drives it. The Pyrrhonian crisis was not stayed on the provisional basis supplied by Chillingworth's probability any more than by the more systematic models of Descartes and Hobbes. The same sceptical reason which Falkland and his friends had used to undermine the authority of the Fathers and fall back on the Bible would be used by the Roman Catholic abbé Richard Simon to disintegrate the Bible and return to Tradition. Thus the rationalism which seemed established within the restored Church, and which would cause its highest prelates to be accused of 'Socinianism', would lead insensibly to the Deism which threatened to undermine it altogether; and the tribunes of orthodoxy, in their alarm, would once again call for rejection of reason and a return to an unquestioned 'authority'. So Dryden, like Cressy, would slide through scepticism into a comfortable (and timely) Catholicism, and in the next century Chillingworth, who had once seemed to fortify the Protestantism of the Church of England, would be respected as an intellectual precursor by the deist Gibbon.[150]

This spectacle would worry the Tractarians of the nineteenth century. Reacting against the deism of the previous century, they looked back to the high Anglican 'Caroline divines' as their true precursors and were disconcerted to find the greatest of them tainted with the very rationalism and scepticism which they deplored. Their answer was to dismiss these heretical tendencies as marginal deviations and themselves to take refuge in defensive ritualism and obscurantist theology: in other words, effectively to disown the central beliefs of their alleged masters.* Looking at the past more historically, and with fewer commitments, we do not need these evasions, and we may well prefer the robust sense of Falkland, Chillingworth and Hammond, who dared to tread the *via media* in its most perilous terrain, not merely in the narrow defile between the high, enclosing walls of opposing bigotries but along the precipitous, crumbling ledge between faith and reason.

---

* I am thinking particularly of the remarks of Nicholas Pocock (see below, p.295 n.135) a learned Tractarian who was the first scholar to use the Hammond – Sheldon correspondence. He was shocked by the rational and sceptical 'crochets' of Hammond and sharp in his censure of Jeremy Taylor, whose 'controversial works ... do not entitle him to the appelation of an orthodox divine'. It is instructive to compare the rational biblical criticism of the 'Laudian' Hammond with the troglodyte obscurantism of (say) Dr Pusey's exposition of the book of Daniel. And yet Pusey was no less learned a man.

5

Milton in Politics

I Milton and the Revolution

John Milton cannot be separated from the Puritan Revolution. That revolution filled his central years. It drew him away from literature, to which he had resolved to devote his life, distorted his career, and transformed his poetry. It made him famous in Europe, and has made it difficult for posterity to judge him even as a poet. He was twenty-one when the process began: for it was in 1629 that Charles I, in scenes of ideological passion and personal recrimination heightened by defeat in war, repudiated the Elizabethan inheritance, decided that the Elizabethan compromise was no longer workable in State or Church, and began that system of government which its strongest proponents – Strafford and Laud – described as 'Thorough', and which whig historians afterwards named 'the Eleven Years Tyranny'. Those eleven years were the incubatory period of the political Puritanism which was to show itself so explosive a force. He was thirty-two when the still incomplete system of royal absolutism cracked under the impact of the Scottish revolt and the 'great contrivers' of opposition set out consciously to restore the old compromise. The attempt failed, and its failure led to twenty years of civil war, revolutionary republic, military usurpation, ending in political disintegration, the return of the monarchy, and the ruin of all his political hopes.

Up to the crisis of 1640 Milton had been a poet: a poet whose achievement, however posterity has valued it, did not adequately fulfil his own ambition; for he aimed high, was conscious of great abilities, had immortal longings in him, knew that his work, 'by certain vital signs that it had in it', would live, and was not afraid to say so.

Nourished on the great poetry of the past, and some of the less great poetry of modern times – on the Bible, the classics, the high, Neoplatonic allegory of Spenser, and the now forgotten but once so popular Protestant cosmogony of Sylvester's du Bartas – he was determined to compete with it. With what infectious, uninhibited enthusiasm he described his plans, in 1638–39, to the sympathetic friends whom he had discovered on that liberating grand tour in Italy! But all those plans were pushed aside when the political crisis broke out. In 1641–2 the energy, the eloquence, the literary power were still there; but immediately they took a new form and a new direction. Diverted from poetry into prose, they were put to serve an increasingly radical revolution.

For the next twenty years, as the revolution ran its untidy course, Milton's poetry all but dried up. The great epic poem of which he had spoken so freely was addled within him. Only a few personal sonnets, and those sometimes crabbed and dry, crept from his costive pen. Instead of poetry, he was now busy writing propaganda: first religious, then personal, then political: pamphlets against bishops, pamphlets in favour of divorce, pamphlets against censorship, on education, against monarchy, vindications of regicide, of the Republic, of himself, State papers for a military usurper, instructions for a dying Republic.

In 1660, when the revolution had finally collapsed, Milton was fifty-one years old, defeated, dispirited and blind. He had spent his life, and lost his sight, in a sterile and often discreditable career of violent and, in the end, futile polemic. Lucky to be alive, but ungrateful for his survival, complaining – there is something shocking, in the circumstances, in his complaints – of having fallen on evil days and evil tongues (what right had he, Dr Johnson pertinently asked, to speak of evil tongues?), he became an 'internal *émigré*', shrunk into himself and his multiple private heresies. Only his power over language remained as marvellous as ever; and now it could be redirected back into poetry. But once again it was transformed. When his great poem at last appeared, it no longer bore any relation to the national epic which he had once envisaged and so enthusiastically promised. It was that stupendous literary fossil, whose 'grand style' so bewitched the next century, straining feebly after the lost ideal of 'the sublime', but which, as Dr Johnson would write, no man wishes were longer, *Paradise Lost*.

It is easy to regret Milton's deviation into politics: to lament the loss of the poem which he had envisaged in 1638, in the vigour and freshness of his genius, and for which he had prepared himself so carefully, but which was now sacrificed to the dreary trade of a revolutionary propagandist. But such lamentation is a vain exercise. For to Milton his two functions, as poet and propagandist, were inseparable. The public ideals which he expressed – so rapturously in 1641–2, so vindictively in 1648–55, so sourly in 1659–60 – were an authentic expression of his philosophy, of his whole personality: just as authentic and essential as the poetry which was being transformed within him by the same events. Behind the publicist, as behind the poet, stands the same coherent but perplexing character, isolated, even before his blindness had cut him off, by heroic illusions and almost megalomaniac egotism.

'Isolation', 'illusions', 'egotism' – some may regard these as strange words to use of one who spoke so much of public spirit, public duty: who cut short his visit to Italy (according to his own account) in order to take part in the battle for English liberty; who explicitly rejected 'a cloistered and fugitive virtue'; and who would be claimed by a series of whig or radical writers as a founding father of whig or radical traditions. But can we really deny or doubt it? Milton was a lonely genius, supremely conscious of his own gifts, and of the mission to which it was his duty to dedicate them. All his life, even when he was most eloquent in protesting his involvement, he lived in mental isolation, recognizing few, if any, equals among his contemporaries. If he descended into the arena of politics, his aim was not to participate in great events, but to dictate them. At times he was a prophet, magniloquently declaring the philosophy which he had discovered in solitary study, at times a propagandist, the shrill and blinkered scribe of a revolutionary party. But at moments of political crisis, at least until the last crisis of all, when the whole revolution was about to be reversed, he offered no advice. He retreated into the clouds, or into himself, became the divine poet, misunderstood and traduced by an unworthy, uncomprehending world.

I realize that not everyone would agree with this statement. Dr Christopher Hill, reacting (not unreasonably as it seems to me) against the comfortable, conservative portrait of Milton so lovingly drawn by Mr W.R. Parker, protests that Milton was 'and remained to the end, a profoundly *political* animal' – was indeed 'a practical politician'.[1] Unlike Dr Parker, 'for whom the word "radical" has an ugly sound',[2] he sees Milton as an active radical operator whose high professions of austerity and aloofness are a mere smokescreen and whose real life was spent not reading books but picking up ideas at second-hand in London alehouses, 'in permanent dialogue with the plebeian radical thinkers of the English Revolution'.[3] These radical friends of Milton, we are told, represented 'a lower-class heretical culture'; gathering in taverns, they expressed progressive democratic views 'with which we still have not caught up'; and they forestalled us in other ways too: they took tobacco 'as a means of heightening consciousness, akin to drug-taking in our own society'.[4] Much though I enjoy the thought of our severe, olympian poet – that poet whose chief characteristic, as Dr Johnson wrote, is 'gigantick loftiness' – basking in radical pop-culture on a tavern-stool, like a Balliol undergraduate (class of 1968) holding forth in the King's Arms, I have to admit that I cannot find, even in Dr Hill's richly documented book, any concrete evidence for it; nor do I recollect any passage in his works in which he speaks of taverns except with contempt, as the home of debauched Cavaliers.* No doubt Milton did see himself and all his own actions through an ennobling retrospective haze, but although we may suspect him of exaggeration when his statements are improbable and unconfirmed, we cannot simply sweep good evidence aside in favour of pure suppositions.†

Nevertheless I share some of Dr Hill's reservations about Dr Parker's portrait of Milton. In all Dr Parker's work – a work of monumental scholarship – one dimension seems to me to be lacking. Dr Parker's Milton is the whig Milton, radical indeed in politics but ultimately rather conventional: the kind of whig who was acceptable after 1688 when whiggism was established and patrician and its original enthusiasm, even messianism, had been expurgated from it. During the long period of whig ascendancy, that new version was orthodox. More recently all such images have crumbled. Locke, Newton, Penn, all have lost something of their old patina. Thanks to Mr Worden, we now see a very different Edmund Ludlow from the 'wooden' Ludlow known to Carlyle, S.R. Gardiner and Sir Charles Firth.[5] That wooden Ludlow was created by the deist John Toland, who also wrote the classic early life of Milton: the Milton who was accepted by Macaulay as 'the martyr of English liberty' – that is, of whig liberty. Dr Hill's radical Milton at

---

* I think of Milton's descriptions of the 'obscene and surfeited priest' who 'paws and mammocks the sacramental bread as familiarly a\ his tavern biscuit', and of the royalists as 'the ragged infantry of stews and brothels, the shipwreck of dicing-houses and taverns'. 'Tavern-haunting' he explicitly associates with 'laziness' and 'neglect of all sound literature'. In *Defensio Secunda* (1654) Milton objects that, if universal suffrage were established, 'turbulence and gluttony would soon exalt the vilest miscreants from our taverns and brothels'.

† As far as I can see, the sole evidence that Dr Hill gives for Milton's bohemian life in London taverns is his nephew's statement that he sometimes kept a gaudy day with two sparkish young lawyers, his friends. All the rest is surmise: 'I see him' (p. 5); 'I suspect' (p. 8); 'we may assume' (p. 98); 'I suggest' (p. 99); 'I would guess' (p. 109); etc. The inconvenient absence of supporting evidence can then be ascribed to 'a conspiracy of silence' (p. 99).

least is a change from this. But still something is missing. What we miss is the ideological force which, at least for a time, gave to his 'whig' ideas their historical, even metaphysical power and inspired his greatest eloquence, and the weakening of which left him, in the end, like so many of his generation, disillusioned and sour. In this essay I shall try to re-insert into Milton's politics this necessary ingredient.

2 Egotism, humanism, prophecy

Let me begin with what seems to me the most obvious, indeed the fundamental trait of Milton's character: his egotism.[6] Has any great poet, in any language, been so totally self-contained, so magnificently, so contemptuously self-assured? The point was made, and cogently illustrated, by Dr Johnson in his famous essay in *The Lives of the Poets*: that 'hastily penned and hostile biography', says Parker; that 'wicked essay', says Denis Saurat, who nevertheless concedes that 'for all his wickedness, Johnson was not deficient in penetration'.[7] 'It appears in all his writings', says Johnson, 'that he had the usual concomitant of great abilities, a lofty and steady confidence in himself, perhaps not without some contempt of others; for scarcely any man ever wrote so much, and praised so few. Of his praise he was very frugal; as he set its value high, and considered his mention of a name as a security against the waste of time, and a certain preservative from oblivion.' It is difficult to dissent from this judgment. In his writing Milton drops great names to which he can add no lustre – Grotius, Galileo, Selden, Cromwell – but recognizes no small debts; which is one of the many problems of his biographers.

On the other hand his own ego is seldom absent. Encouraged by his father to believe that he was reserved for great things, he easily convinced himself that he was one of the Elect, entitled to dictate, and that it was unpardonable for any lesser man to contradict him. In his early pamphlets his lyrical account of the new and glorious era about to dawn is regularly accompanied by the claim that he will be there, harp in hand and robes flowing about him, as its divine poet. In his later pamphlets the cause which he sets out to defend to the educated world of Europe is as regularly involved with personal abuse and personal justification. His demands for freedom of divorce, of printing, of worship, are all generalizations from his own particular predicament. He had no sympathy with, or understanding of, or wish to understand, other men. As Saurat writes, he had to be 'not one single individual, but the norm, the rule, the law to all'.[8] His poetry tells the same tale. *Lycidas*, the critics agree, is a lament not for Edward King but for John Milton. How different, in this, is Shakespeare! Shakespeare created characters who still have an independent and vigorous life while their creator remains unidentifiable in the shadows. Milton created only two heroes, rebellious Satan and blind Samson; and both are himself.

This insulating egotism was essential also to Milton's public life. Even in the midst of revolution, he appears to live in an abstract world, a world created for him not by immediate practical needs, but by reading: by literature and philosophy. This isolation began after he left Cambridge, in the six years which he spent in his father's house, first at Hammersmith, then at Horton in Buckinghamshire. In those years, which seem to us so delightful – the years which produced *Comus* and *Arcades*, *L'Allegro*, *Il Penseroso* and *Lycidas* – he was, as he tells us, 'wholly dedicated to studious labours'. He read deeply, systematically, with a purpose. He was seeking, through literature, a philosophy not of literature only but of life, history, religion. And in due course he found it. It was the philosophy which was to dominate his life and whose fragmentation against the rocks of revolutionary politics would be the tragedy of his life, distorting his poetic genius.

The philosophy which he discovered was a blend – a unique blend – of two traditions, one classical, pagan and humane, the other biblical, theological, prophetic. Let me begin therefore by summarizing these two traditions.

The classical tradition was the tradition of ancient freedom: political freedom as the public expression, and the guarantee, of an internal freedom of mind. This ancient tradition, a tradition of active public spirit in good times, of stoic self-discipline in bad times, of broad culture always, was essentially aristocratic. It presupposed an aristocracy of 'virtue'. When expressed in politics, it was naturally republican, and a republic was its ideal political form; but it was not a necessary form: virtue could thrive under an enlightened or virtuous prince – a Pericles, a Marcus Aurelius, a Cosimo di Medici, or, as in Venice, 'the mild aristocracy of elective dukes'. Defined and expressed in pagan Antiquity, its ruling concept had been revived in Renaissance Italy by the great Florentines, who defined it as *virtù*: that *virtù* which was the property of no particular country but which, historically, had passed from ancient Greece to republican Rome, from Rome to Renaissance Italy, and which, in their time, was already passing from Italy to northern Europe.

In Renaissance Italy, *virtù* had retained its essentially pagan character. How Machiavelli had despised the effeminacy, the abject, debilitating character of Christian teaching and ritual compared with the robust, even sanguinary, national ceremonies of pagan Rome! Later, in northern Europe, the Protestant humanists had christianized the concept, converting it into the aristocratic Christian freedom of the French Huguenots: of Agrippa d'Aubigné or Philippe du Plessis Mornay or the duc de Rohan: those self-contained, self-disciplined heroes, '*princes qui règnent sur eux-mêmes*'. However, though these last may seem the closest parallels to Milton, Milton himself did not pay tribute to them. He had, says his nephew, 'no admiration for the manners and genius of France';[9] and the Huguenots, for all their dissenting virtue, were very definitely French. He preferred to acknowledge his debt to Antiquity and to modern Italy. In Italy, even in the 'corrupt' pagan Italy of the Renaissance or the popish Italy of the Counter-Reformation, he recognized, in individuals if not in society, the continuing tradition of *virtù*.

The second tradition was very different. It was not Greek but Jewish, not pagan but Christian, not humanist and republican but theocratic and, in Heaven at least, monarchical, even despotic. It also entailed a peculiar conception of human history, as the realization of ancient prophecy within a theologically determined scheme. This scheme, which had been accepted by the first, radical Christians before Constantine, and had never been quite forgotten since, had now become an orthodoxy of established Protestantism. As applied to more modern history, it entailed the doctrine of the binding of Satan, the Millennium, the rise and fall of Antichrist, and the Last Things. Its main sources were the prophetic books of the Bible, particularly the books of Daniel and Revelation.*

By 1600 the essentials of this doctrine had been, as it seemed, firmly established. It was then generally agreed that, some time after the birth of Christ, Satan had been bound and cast into a pit, and that while he languished there, the true Church had flourished for a thousand years; but that this happy state had been checked by the birth of the monster Antichrist who, on reaching maturity at the end of the thousand-year period, had released Satan out of the pit and allowed him to rage against the Church. However, ultimately all would be well. Amid great convulsions and 'shakings',[10] Antichrist would fall and Christ would

---

* The most valuable work on Milton's eschatological and historical views seems to me to be Michael Fixler's *Milton and the Kingdoms of God* (1964); a work not mentioned by W.R. Parker, *PMB*, and cited, but not noticeably used, by Christopher Hill, *Milton and the English Revolution* (1977).

then return to set in motion a new scenario, culminating in the bodily resurrection of all flesh, the Last Judgment, and the end of time.

Within this general framework there was room for manoeuvre and learned dispute. Was Satan bound at the very birth of Christ or later – perhaps as late as the early fourth century when the Emperor Constantine established Christianity as the religion of the Roman Empire? Were the thousand years to be understood literally or figuratively? What events in the history of the Church corresponded with the appearance of the various apocalyptic animals, the sounding of the successive trumps, the outpouring of the successive vials? Who, or what, were the ten horns of the fourth Beast, or the locusts which rose from the bottomless pit? Infinite ingenuity was exercised on such arcane questions, but there was general agreement that Antichrist was the Papacy which, after the establishment of Christianity, had captured the Church and had thus continued, in a new form, the old persecuting Roman Empire.* Fortunately, even after that, the true Church had managed to survive. The oppressed heretics of the Middle Ages – the Waldensians or Vaudois of the Swiss valleys and the Albigensians of southern France – had prepared the way for the decisive break-through of the Protestant Reformation. The next stage would be the convulsions, the 'shakings', which would announce the fall of Antichrist and the beginning of the final scenario, the 'Last Things'.

Such was the general scheme of 'prophetic history' which was adopted, with local variations, throughout the Protestant world. In Elizabethan England, where it was made popular by John Foxe's *Acts and Monuments*, it acquired a peculiarly English interpretation. England, it was there argued, was the nation which, above all others, had preserved Christianity in its pure form. Even during the worst period of the raging of Antichrist, it was an Englishman, John Wyclif, who had shown the way to later reformers, and in the reign of Mary the martyred English bishops, Cranmer, Latimer and Ridley, had died in defence of a national, as well as a Protestant tradition. Similarly English kings, from King John onwards, had shown the way to the Tudor monarchs who, like Constantine and Theodosius, had reasserted the authority of the Christian Prince. Thus the Protestant English episcopate and the

---

* Hobbes' famous remark that 'the Papacy is not other than the ghost of the deceased Roman Empire, sitting crowned upon the grave thereof' is not a mere metaphor: it was an essential element in prophetic history. The same point is made by Milton in his *Treatise of Civil Power in Ecclesiastical Causes*, where he states that Roman Catholicism is not a religion at all (and therefore can make no claim for toleration) but 'a Roman principality rather, endeavouring to keep up her old universal dominion under a new name and mere shadow of a Catholic religion'.

imperial English monarchy were the historic forces destined to lead the great crusade which would bring Antichrist down.

This interpretation was all very well in the later years of Queen Elizabeth when England was the champion of Protestantism against Rome and Spain, but it was less easy to sustain when the Stuart kings made peace with Spain, sought Spanish dynastic marriages, and contracted out of the promising convulsions of the Thirty Years War. By the 1630s it seemed that England had missed its chance: that Gustavus Adolphus was the true heir of Queen Elizabeth. And what was one to make of those new English bishops who seemed to have no appreciation of the divine plan of history, who disowned the Waldensian and Albigensian tradition and even hedged their bets on the identity of Antichrist? Conservative men did not like these innovations but they did not despair: they hoped that time would bring a change of direction. Others became more radical. Disliking the new bishops, they turned against episcopacy itself, and revised history accordingly. Bishops, they now decided, even Protestant martyr bishops, were not defenders of Reformation but secret opponents of it: enemy agents left to operate behind the battle-lines of the holy war, 'limbs of Antichrist', still writhing tentacles of that giant octopus, whose grip would be loosened only if they were surgically cut off.

This new radicalism entailed a significant revision of doctrine. Hitherto the millennium had been placed in the past; beginning with the birth of Christ or the accession of Constantine, it had lasted till AD 1000 or 1300, and even so it had been disturbed by the birth and growth of Antichrist. But now it was switched to the future. After all, it could be said, if the Antichristian Roman Church were merely an extension of the pagan Roman Empire, the fulfilment of the prophecies which referred to the fall of that Empire must be postponed accordingly. Since the Papacy was now due to fall at any moment, that opened the exciting prospect of an immediate millennium such as had been expected by the radical Christians of the centuries before Constantine. The old medieval millennium was thus quietly devalued. Though not eliminated (for too much Protestant scholarship had been invested in it) it became a second-class millennium, not the real thing.

The new doctrine of the millennium was elaborated, early in the reign of James I, by a country clergyman in Bedfordshire, Thomas Brightman, who also emphasized the particular function of England. Indeed he supposed that St John the Divine, on Patmos, had had his eye fixed especially on such distant events as the rule of Thomas Cromwell and the Elizabethan recusancy laws, and that his account of the outpouring of the fourth vial was a prophetic reference to the forthcoming publication of Brightman's own book, which appeared posthumously, and abroad, in 1609. More important advocates of an imminent, as distinct from a past, millennium were two men of encyclopaedic learning, J.H. Alsted and Joseph Mede. Alsted was a professor at Herborn in Nassau; Mede, who may be the 'old Damoetas' of *Lycidas*, was the oracle of Milton's own college in Cambridge. Theologian, mathematician, natural scientist, astronomer, botanist, he reduced millenarian prophecy to a science, discovering the historical significance of every angel, every beast, every vial, every trump.

Though he never descended to such particulars, Milton always accepted the general scheme of prophetic history. In 1629, at the age of twenty-one, in his first great religious poem, 'On the Morning of Christ's Nativity', he described the binding of Satan, cast into the pit: how, at the birth of Christ,

> Th'old Dragon under ground,
> In straiter limits bound,
>   Not half so far casts his usurped sway,
> And, wrath to see his Kingdom fail
> Swinges the scaly Horrour of his folded tail.

That was the orthodoxy of the time, the orthodoxy of John Foxe, for whom he would always express his respect. Later, he would become more radical and would be critical of some of Foxe's heroes: of the Protestant martyr bishops, because they were bishops, and of Christian Princes, because Princes. The Christian Emperors, Constantine and Theodosius, he would find, had established popery, not the Gospel, and the Tudor monarchs had preserved prelacy instead of completing the Reformation. But he would retain the general framework of 'prophetic history': the raging of Antichrist, which began in full force in the time of Pope Sylvester II in AD 1000; his persecution of the true witnesses of the Gospel, the medieval heretics; the convulsions which were to precede his fall; and the grand finale of the Last Things. He would even contrive to fit the history of divorce, when that came to preoccupy his mind, into this great scheme. The complete ban on divorce, he would then discover, had followed 'the first loosening of Antichrist', and was, 'as it were, the substance of his eldest born' – just as Henry VIII's successful insistence on his own divorce was the first chink in Antichrist's armour.[11] The case of Mrs Milton was to be the second.

Like Brightman and Mede, Milton was also an English nationalist. He believed that the English were 'the elect people of God' and had a special role to play throughout history. Even in pagan antiquity, he declared, 'our ancient Druids' had made 'this island . . . the cathedral of philosophy to France', and since then, 'Britain's God' had always revealed himself first to 'his Englishmen'. So, although, like all puritan theorists, he respected 'our first reformers', the Albigensians and Waldensians of the Middle Ages[12] (and nothing would so move him, in the 1650s, as the massacre of the Waldensians in Piedmont, which would inspire his most famous sonnet), he gave his highest praise to 'the divine and admirable spirit of Wyclif', 'that Englishman honor'd of God to be the first preacher of general reformation to all Europe'. Wyclif, to him, was the torch-bearer at whose 'short blaze' 'all succeeding reformers more effectually lighted their tapers', and whose example showed 'the precedence which God gave to this island to be the first restorer of buried truth'.[13] Willibrord and Winfrid, Alcuin and Wyclif, were to Milton evidence that God had always 'had this island under the special indulgent eye of his Providence'; after Wyclif, the Reformation, and now the impending 'reformation of Reformation itself', were English achievements; and the fall of Antichrist and the second coming of Christ had been planned to come while 'this Britannick Empire' was at its 'glorious and enviable heighth'.[14]

Such was the fundamentalist, Christian scheme with which Milton combined his classical humanist philosophy. At first sight it seems, at least to us, an incompatible combination, for the two traditions seem inherently irreconcilable. After all, they were irreconcilable in history: one had driven out the other; and although many men, since the Renaissance, have tried, or claimed, to combine them, they have generally done so with the aid of some self-deception: they have worn either their Christian fundamentalism or their classical humanism lightly. This was apparent even among Milton's contemporaries. Those of them who sincerely believed in the theological system, like Cromwell, Vane or Harrison, were not devotees of the classical tradition, while those who believed in that tradition – the so-called 'classical Republicans' like Henry Marten and Henry Neville – were far from puritan, and had little patience with eschatology. But Milton genuinely believed in both traditions; he was learned in the literature of both; he thought deeply about them; and his life and poetry and politics were inspired by a heroic attempt to fuse them together.

How could they be so fused? The fusion occurs, I suggest, below the level of the language in which it is expressed, or even of conscious thought. For active millenarianism does not rise out of the texts by which it is justified. Its roots are psychological and social. It is the expression of a conviction that great events are in the making, requiring heroic effort, and that the present generation is called upon to meet that challenge, make that effort. In the early seventeenth century the Protestants of Europe recognized the challenge. It was the challenge of the Counter-Reformation, made vivid by the triumphs of the House of Austria in the Thirty Years War. They also felt capable of the effort required to meet it; for they were conscious of a new strength and a new spirit. That spirit expressed itself in several forms: in Paracelsian cosmology, in biblical fundamentalism, in the new enlightenment of Bacon.

Yes, even Bacon. The influence of Bacon, which grew immensely in the fifteen years after his death, was not merely philosophical: it was, or became, religious. Bacon was not himself a millenarian. He had little use for theology, which he saw as a wasteful diversion of intellectual effort, an obstruction to human progress; and he wished to keep religion separate from science. But there was a mystical spirit behind his vision of the future enlightenment and happiness of man, and at times he would find analogies and metaphors in Scriptural prophecy, just as he would also find them in pagan myths. He would even appeal to the book of Daniel: had not that obscure prophet said that 'many shall run to and fro and knowledge shall be increased'? And were not the recent journeys of discovery and exploration in every part of the globe precisely such a running to and fro, and therefore the condition and presage of such an enlightenment? Protestant enthusiasts seized upon these analogies and combined Baconian with their own millenarian views: they fitted the convulsions of Germany into the apocalyptic scheme, looked forward to the conversion of the Jews, and expected 'the renewal of all knowledge' as a stage in that divine process. Alsted and Mede were both enthusiasts of this kind. Writing during the catastrophic years of the Thirty Years War, they saw those catastrophes as the 'shakings' which were to precede and accompany the fall of Antichrist, the prelude to the new enlightenment.

In the 1630s, in the years of Milton's private studies, the fusion in his thought of millenarian with classical ideas is not yet visible. Perhaps this is because we do not possess his *Index Theologicus*, the record of his religious reading. What we see, in his poetry and his Commonplace Book, is the classical tradition – humanist, and aristocratic; a systematic study of history, ancient and medieval; and a resolution to dedicate himself to literature. Then suddenly, in 1637, there is a change. For the first time, we hear a discordant note. The Virgilian lyricism of *Lycidas* is crudely interrupted by a sudden, savage, irrelevant attack on the clergy of the time.

> Blind mouths! That scarce themselves know how to hold
> A Sheep-hook . . . etc. etc.

How are we to account for that sudden outburst? Nothing in Milton's previous history has prepared us for it. To be sure, he was brought up in a pious Protestant household, his father a convert from Catholicism; and of course Laudianism was now being enforced. Still, the savagery is surprising in one who had written a tributary poem to the Founding Father of Laudianism, Lancelot Andrewes, and who never objected to it on any grounds of doctrine. Even now he did not object to episcopacy as such. The blistering attack, limited to hireling clergy, is put into the mouth of a bishop: of St Peter himself, who appears as a bishop – Bishop of Rome too – with a mitre on his head. Clearly we are still a long way from the passionate anti-episcopal pamphlets of 1641. But perhaps we should not look too far forward, or seek too many reasons for Milton's outburst. His passionate themes are almost always found, on examination, to be generalizations from personal resentments – resentments which they splendidly transcend and absorb. So we may legitimately look for such an explanation here. I suspect that it is to be found in a traumatic but mysterious episode in his university career, several years before.

We know that Milton had a violent difference with his tutor at Christ's College, William Chappell; that he then suffered an indignity which he declared to be intolerable; that, according to Aubrey, who was informed by Milton's brother, his tutor whipped him; that he was rusticated for a term; and that, on his return, he was transferred to another tutor. Several years later, when Milton's defence of regicide had made him notorious, Bishop Bramhall wrote that he knew some very discreditable facts about his Cambridge career which he would not, even now, publish, since 'I desire not to wound the nation through his sides'; and he added that he had written to Milton 'long since about it roundly', but 'it seems he desires not to touch upon that subject'. Whatever it was that Bramhall knew, it probably came from Chappell. They were both bishops in Ireland, and both had been imprisoned together in Dublin in 1641. Clearly the episode was serious, and it may well have been on this account that he was not awarded a fellowship and so turned against the present establishment of the English

Church.* If so, the occasion of *Lycidas* – the death of Edward King, who had been with Milton at Christ's and (unlike him) had been made a Fellow – might well have touched that sore. It was a sore which was to erupt, a few years later, in a fearful rash.

But not now. For six months later Milton is on his way to Italy, and all dislike of popery or prelacy are, as far as we can see, totally forgotten.

3   A Spenserian epic

Why did Milton go to Italy in 1638? Clearly the visit had nothing to do with his supposed 'puritan' convictions. Nor was it merely for the sake of travel, of general experience. A visit to Italy was not yet an essential part of the English Grand Tour: indeed, good Protestants were advised against it: 'suffer not thy sons to pass the Alps' Lord Burghley had advised his son; Gallican France was safer. But Milton, who was deeply prejudiced against all things French, passed quickly through France, and never recalled his passage or named a single Frenchman that he met. His journey was essentially an Italian journey: it reflected his overpowering love of classical antiquity and the Renaissance revival of it. It was also a kind of liberation. Like so many Northerners, on their first visit to that delightful country, he would find his outlook transformed. In the country of Virgil and Tasso, those nasty puritanical frustrations which had intruded into *Lycidas* would dissolve, and in a Catholic country, dominated by papal and Spanish power, he would relish 'the old and elegant humanity of Greece and Rome'.

Milton's liberation is evident in the contacts which he made on that journey. His introductions were arranged for him by the ecumenical Anglican Sir Henry Wotton, the Provost of Eton, who had been charmed by the scholarly conversation of this young country neighbour. As a former ambassador, Wotton recommended Milton to his diplomatic colleague Lord Scudamore in Paris. Through the good offices of Scudamore, he was able to meet the famous Grotius, now serving as a Swedish ambassador in France. These are grand and

* Milton afterwards claimed that he had left Cambridge with the love and approbation of all the Fellows, and Parker, in his biography, accepts this, quoting as confirmation the statements of Aubrey, Phillips and Cyriack Skinner, none of whom can have known. In his earlier book, *Milton's Contemporary Reputation* (Columbus, Ohio, 1940), Parker was more meticulous. He there noted that at Cambridge Milton had almost no companions in study and made no friendships which survived graduation; that he had little good to say of the University; and that he was not invited to contribute to university collections of poetry.

flattering contacts for a young man who, hitherto, had led a retired life of study financed by an indulgent father; but they are not very puritan contacts. Scudamore was the most Laudian of laymen, the close personal friend of the Archbishop, to whom he owed his appointment. Grotius was an 'Arminian' exile from Holland, whom Puritans regarded as a crypto-papist. In Italy, Milton moved in a Catholic world – not only among Italian laymen but among *émigré* English Catholics and Catholic priests. In Rome, he was entertained to dinner, together with a party of English Catholics, by the English Jesuits,[15] availed himself of the help of the Catholic convert Lucas Holste, the Pope's German Librarian, accepted the invitation, and was charmed by the hospitality and courtesy of the Pope's nephew, Cardinal Barberini, the papal 'Protector of England', to whom he sent messages of almost unctuous thanks. Ten years later, he would make a savage attack on the memory of Charles I for having, in the same years, written with ordinary civility to the same Pope.

Milton's visit to Italy was a memorable experience. He had learned Italian in England, had read Italian history, and knew and loved Italian literature. He was charmed by the culture and urbanity of the Italian men of letters who received him and listened to him as he spoke of literature and his own literary ambitions. He would write to them afterwards, lamenting that he was stuck in England and not back in Italy with them: he would not then refer to the struggle for English liberty raging around him. To one of them, to whom he sent one of his Latin poems, he would apologize for 'some rather sharp words' in it about 'the Roman pope'. Such language, he would explain, was a necessary concession to vulgar English conventions . . . His prose writings, by this time, were crammed with furious denunciations of the Roman Antichrist, the Whore of Babylon, gorged with the blood of saints, etc. etc. But these, being in English, he did not send to his Italian friends. It is difficult to understand how Milton could have pretended to consistency in these matters. But the great advantage of egotism is that one need not be consistent: one only has to be one's self.

How little we know about Milton's Italian journey! Did he really meet Galileo, or did he merely drop that famous name in his retrospective self-dramatization? Did he really become intimate with those distinguished Italians to whom he would afterwards write and dedicate Latin poems, but who did not reply? Almost all that we know about him comes from himself, and some of it is suspect. It seems clear that he was courted as a possible convert. Aristocratic or cultivated Protestants were much wooed in Rome in those days. He claimed to have behaved with caution, but never to have disguised his religious views, for which there is some support,[16] and therefore to have been in danger of his life, for which there is none. But one thing is certain. He presented himself to the Italians, as to himself, insistently, compulsively, perhaps oppressively, as a poet: and not only as a poet but as a great poet, in *posse* if not yet in *esse*. That was to be the purpose of his life. Moreover, the poetry that was already filling his imagination, and would soon (he said) break forth, was to be epic poetry, a national epic.

Two of the men who, in Italy, exchanged complimentary verses with Milton refer to him already as an epic poet. One of them was a Roman poet, Giovanni Salzilli; the other called himself Selvaggi, but may have been an English Benedictine monk called David Codner.[17] Selvaggi declared that Milton was the equal of the two greatest of European epic poets, Homer and Virgil. Salzilli went further and declared him not merely equal but superior to Homer, Virgil and Tasso. Such judgments, at such a time, are grotesque, for Milton had not yet written a single line of epic poetry. Salzilli at least can have read nothing by him except a few experiments in Latin and Italian verse. We must assume that these egregious flatterers had allowed themselves to be bowled over by Milton's sales-talk about his proposed national epic; or perhaps they were ironical, gently ridiculing that sales-talk.[18] But six years later, Milton, who deplored the 'flattery and fustian' of Italian poets, was happy to publish these tributes to himself in a volume of all the poetry that he had so far written – which still did not include a single epic line.

Early in 1639, Milton began his homeward journey. Afterwards he would claim that he had abridged his travels, renouncing a visit to Sicily and Greece, in order to play his part in the civil war, of which he had received news; for how, he asked himself, could he enjoy the luxury of a foreign holiday when his fellow citizens were fighting for liberty? But this, once again, must be dismissed as retrospective romance; for first, no such struggle had broken out, or was yet in sight,* and secondly, he did not hurry at all, but travelled in a leisurely manner, stopping for two months in Rome, two in Florence, and dallying for an agreeable month in Venice. As for Greece, it is unlikely anyway that he

---

* Parker writes (*PMB*, p. 174) that 'we know for certain that at Naples he heard . . . of the imminence of civil war in England'. We know nothing for certain, except that Milton's statement is wrong; for he writes as if a state of civil war already existed: 'tristis ex Anglia belli civilis nuntius revocavit'. In fact the most that he can conceivably have heard at Naples was that the Assembly of the Scotch Kirk at Glasgow was being rather troublesome.

ever planned to visit that Turkish pashalik in which there were no men of letters, no academies, no hospitable ambassadors, and no encouragement for travellers. Finally, on his arrival in England, he made no attempt to take any part in any struggle for liberty or anything else: in his own words, he returned blissfully to his interrupted studies ('ad intermissa studia beatulus me recepi') and set up as a private tutor in London.

If we pause to consider Milton on the eve of the outbreak of the Puritan Revolution, we must conclude that he had, at that time, no political interests or ambitions. He had shown reluctance to take orders in the Church – a reluctance which he would afterwards dramatize into an exclusion from it; and in 1637 he had spoiled a good poem by a bad-tempered outburst against the unspecified clergy. But he had said nothing about politics. He had indeed republican opinions, which he would express, privately, in his Commonplace Book, but he did not publish them: they were classical ideals, quite unacceptable in England in 1639; he would only express them ten years later, when the republic was already a fact. The studies to which he now so happily returned – a systematic course of historical reading from Antiquity to the present – were not designed for immediate purposes: they were 'general intellectual preparation for later work'.[19] His personal ambitions were entirely poetical, and were concentrated on the idea, which dominated him at the time, of a great national epic.

Of that great epic – the greatest English poem, perhaps, that was never written – we know much, for Milton had talked much about it, in Italy as in England. He had described it in Rome, to Salzilli and Selvaggi; he had described it in Naples, to his host the Marchese Manso. On his return to England he began work on it. He wrote an epistle to Manso in Latin verse reporting his progress; and he dwelt upon it again in his Latin elegy on his old schoolfellow and bosom friend, Charles Diodati, who had died while Milton was in Italy. It was to be a poem on King Arthur: Arthur as the heir of mythical British kings; Arthur as a hero who descended to the Nether World to make war on the King of Darkness; Arthur as the pattern of chivalry, who, with his Knights of the Round Table, fought to defend Britain against the Saxon invaders and whose repeated victories culminated in the famous battle of Mount Badon.

Why Arthur? The reason is not far to seek. To the Elizabethans, under a Welsh dynasty, Arthur was not only a national hero; he was also the founder of British imperialism, the ruler of a vast maritime empire, including part of America. More important still, he was a sound Protestant; for British Christianity, in his time, had not yet been corrupted by the popery imported from Rome by St Augustine of Canterbury: it was the pure evangelical Christianity brought straight from Palestine by Joseph of Arimathea, if not by Christ himself. Finally, Arthur linked Milton with the poet whom he always venerated and regarded as 'his original', Edmund Spenser. Spenser, 'our admir'd Spenser', 'our sage and serious poet Spenser' was to him one of the 'great bards' who

> In sage and solemn tunes have sung
> Of Tourneys and of Trophies hung;
> Of Forests and inchantments drear,
> Where more is meant than meets the ear.

Spenser, in fact, was not only a great poet but also, by means of allegory, a great teacher, 'a better teacher', as Milton would afterwards write, 'than Scotus or Aquinas'; and Milton's epic was to be, like *The Faerie Queene*, an allegorical poem, his Arthur, like Sir Guyon or the Red Cross Knight, 'the pattern of a Christian hero'.

His mind thus filled with his Arthurian epic, it is unlikely that Milton thought much, in Italy, of puritan eschatology. To him Italy, 'the lodge of humanity and of all polite learning', was the natural home of the classical, not the millenarian tradition. But his Italian experience also emphasized an important general truth. He had read widely and thought deeply about both literature and history, and he believed that the two were inseparable. He also believed – it was a common belief at the time – that history was a cyclical process: that nations, by an organic rhythm, rose only to decline. It therefore followed that in any nation, science and the arts reached their perfection together with political and religious freedom; after which all, in the natural course of history, were destined to decay: for the virtue, which was at their heart, was subject to corruption. This is what had happened in ancient Greece and Rome, and it had happened too in Renaissance Italy which, with classical literature, had revived the classical virtues. But Renaissance Italy, as he had observed, had now passed its peak. Although individuals still retained some trace of its former virtue, and the relics of it were visible in the Italian cities, its living force had departed with freedom and independence, and the language itself, deprived of that invigorating force, had necessarily become degenerate. In other words, only in a period of national greatness, which in turn depends on classical 'virtue', can great poetry be written. As Milton wrote to a

Florentine friend in 1638, 'Where language is not cultivated, what does it mean but that the souls of men are slothful and gaping and prepared for any servility? Conversely, never have we heard of an empire or state that does not flourish so long as it cultivates its language and is proud of it.' Ten years later he would say the same: 'by a certain law of fate, great acts and eloquence have commonly gone hand in hand, equalling and honouring each other in the same ages'.[20]

But if 'virtue', political and literary, had abandoned Italy, whither had it fled? Whither indeed, Milton would reply, but to Protestant Europe and, above all, to England: that is, of course, to the 'real' England, what England could be, if only it would resume its historic role, abandoned since the reign of Elizabeth. For Milton, with so many of his English contemporaries, looked back to the England of Queen Elizabeth: that robust, expansive, imperialist, nationalist England which had believed in its destiny as the leader of Protestant Europe and the pace-maker of the new enlightenment, and was so different from the peaceful, correct, disciplined, clerical England of Charles I.

Not that Elizabethan England was perfect in itself, for Milton was not, like older men, nostalgic for a past which he had known, and the old Queen had her conservative side. But at least England, in her time, had been moving in the right direction. If only it had continued on that course, then, thought Milton, great literature would again be possible in it; the captive Muse would be set free, his own tongue untied, and he could continue where Spenser had ceased. Moreover, since Christ was about to return, this great literary revival would coincide with the beginning of the millennium, of which also he would be the poet. England would thus be at the head of the nations, and of literature, just at the moment when the wheel of historical change was about to stop. Therefore, unlike Greece, Rome, Italy, it would not decline; its 'virtue' would not be corrupted: the Elect Nation would remain top dog of Christendom through the coming millennium.

4   Jubilee and resurrection

In looking back to the Elizabethan age Milton was not alone. All the critics of Charles I and Laud looked back to that golden age, which each man romanticized in his own way. To the politicians it was the age of political consensus, of harmony between Crown and Parliament. In November 1640, when Charles I was obliged to summon Parliament on their terms, they believed that they could restore that consensus. They had the initiative, and they were determined never to lose it. They had prepared the ground, devised the strategy, launched the campaign. Now they drove out the old ministers of State and destroyed the instruments of their rule. By the summer of 1641, by the judicial murder of Strafford and by making Parliament legally permanent, they had secured themselves, as they thought, against counter-revolution. Thus secured, they set out to complete the reformation of the Church. A synod of clergy was to be summoned for that purpose. Ultimately the King would recognize the true balance of power; 'a good correspondency with his Majesty' would be established; and politics would return to their old course, as in the days of 'Queen Elizabeth of glorious memory'.

Such was the aim of the politicians. They recognized that there would be difficulties to come, but they reckoned that, with normal political skill, such difficulties could be resolved. They did not expect revolution. But other men – unpolitical men, puritan enthusiasts, millenarians – thought differently. They believed that a historic moment had arrived: the last obstruction had been removed, the ancient prophecies were now about to be fulfilled, Antichrist to fall, the millennium of enlightenment to begin.

The excitement, the exhilaration and expectancy of those months is audible to us still. We can hear it in sermons and pamphlets, in utopian blueprints, parliamentary speeches and private letters. Men knew, instinctively, that this was not a mere change of course. It was a revolution, or the beginning of a revolution, of vast, even cosmic proportions, and it aroused the same boundless expectations as the revolution in Bohemia twenty-two years before. Then too the millenarian enthusiasts had expected a quick and complete victory and a sudden acceleration of history: the return of Elias, the fulfilment of the remaining prophecies, the new enlightenment, the renewal of all things. In fact all that followed was a seemingly endless war. But the enthusiasts did not despair: the fall of Antichrist, after all, was due to be attended by such convulsions. Now the revolution in England would surely give the decisive push. Such a push was clearly due, because, according to Dr Mede, it was time for the fifth vial to be poured out. The fourth had already been poured out when the Protestant hero, Gustavus Adolphus of Sweden, had entered the war and turned its course; the fifth was to coincide with the sack of Rome, the destruction of the Beast in his lair; then would come the conversion of the Jews, the overthrow of Ottoman power, the seventh trump and the second coming of Christ.

Faced with such splendid prospects, men who had emigrated, or contemplated emigration, from Laudian England, changed their minds: 'the change', as one of them put it, 'made all men to stay in England, in expectation of a new world'.[21] Others, in the same expectation, came to England. How sad that the two great prophets of the new age, Alsted and Mede, were no longer there to rejoice in it! Both had died in 1638, Mede in his Cambridge college, Alsted in Transylvania, whither he had fled from conquered Herborn. But both of them had left disciples who shared their enthusiasm. Alsted's most famous disciple was the Czech philosopher Comenius, whom the conquest of Bohemia had driven to take refuge in Poland. In the summer of 1641 he came to England and was received as the guru of the new age. Among Mede's many disciples in England was Milton, who would afterwards persuade himself that he too had come back to England expressly to take part in the struggle: the struggle in which the Elect Nation was to lead the world, through Baconian enlightenment, to the new millennium and the Kingdom of God.

Of course, in order to qualify for this *rôle*, England had first to be inwardly transformed. It must become a true Christian nation – that is, it must re-create the pure Protestant Christianity which it had received in apostolic times, and which now, after long centuries of anti-Christian oppression, was reasserting itself. That reassertion was not yet complete. Even after the overthrow of Laudian tyranny there was much to do. Here the classical, humanist tradition came into play. Instead of the Laudian bishops, or any bishops, a new élite of virtuous Christians must step forward and gradually, by education and leadership, fit the nation for its glorious destiny. Obviously no man was better qualified, in his own eyes, to preach this message than Milton. So he tore himself reluctantly (as he says) from 'the quiet and still air of delightful studies', suspended his work on the Arthurian epic, and threw all his energies, all his immense literary power, into propaganda for the revolutionary cause. For 'when God commands to take the trumpet and blow a dolorous or a jarring blast, it lies not in man's will what he shall say or what he shall conceal'.[22]

It was not, in any normal sense of the word, political propaganda. Milton had no sobering contact with politicians, no interest in their limited ambitions. His mind soared above such day-to-day matters. For him the long-awaited moment of fusion had come. How comforting to see the divine timetable so punctually observed! At precisely the right moment, when the great pageant was about to begin, England had stepped forward, true at last to itself. Supreme in religion, virtue and the promise of great literature, it would take its rightful place at the head of the queue to welcome the grand Visitor from Heaven. And this time there would be no corruption, no decline. With the Elect Nation in the right place at the right time, and its predestined poet at the height of his powers, the cyclical process would stop. History would be frozen: Milton could confidently call upon God to freeze it now, to 'stay us in this felicity'.[23]

To one so 'God-intoxicated' (as Carlyle would say) the Long Parliament was not, could not be, a mere political assembly. It was a glorious band of heroes, a sodality of Arthurian knights under whose leadership the world's great age was to begin anew. They were appointed by God to reform 'a great and populous nation' from corruption and blind superstition. In his imagination, Milton saw them 'sitting as gods among daily petitions and public thanks flowing in upon them', achieving more, in a few months, than 'the utmost performance of many ages', leading their country 'to such a deliverance as shall never be forgotten in any revolution of time'.[24] Through them civic humanism and millenarian Protestantism would be united, literature would flourish with freedom, and Milton would 'take up his harp' and 'amidst the hymns and hallelujahs of saints' offer 'at high strains, in new and lofty measures', to celebrate the divine mercies and marvellous judgments of God 'in this land throughout all ages': mercies and judgments 'whereby this great and warlike nation (instructed and inured to the fervent and continued practice of truth and righteousness, and casting far from it the rags of its old vices) may press on hard' – not to a mere political or social reformation, or even utopia, but to that day when Christ, 'the eternal and shortly expected King', shall 'open the clouds to judge the several kingdoms of the world' and establish his own 'universal and mild monarchy'.

Thus to Milton, even before civil war had broken out, the issue between King and Parliament was not a political debate, to be settled by a political compromise. It was the first act in a drama of the Last Judgment. There were goodies and baddies; and when the battle was over and Christ came down to judge the nations, there would be no doubt which was which. He would award the prize to 'religious and just commonwealths'. What that prize would be is not stated, but there is no lack of clarity about the fate of their defeated enemies. 'After a shameful end in this life (which God grant them), they shall be thrown eternally into the darkest and deepest gulf of Hell', where they shall for all eternity be spitefully trampled upon 'by all the other Damned, that in the anguish of their torture shall have no other ease than to exercise a raving and bestial tyranny over them as their slaves and negros'. In this economical way the Damned would be used to persecute the more Damned, and the saints would not need to soil their hands with the business. The more Damned, the essential agents of Antichrist, were now firmly identified as the whole order of bishops.

Such was the mood in which Milton, having put aside his great Spenserian poem, threw himself into the political controversy of 1641–2. It is not the mood of a politician – or indeed of anyone else. No other man combined with such intensity the two ill-assorted ideals of millennial Puritanism and classical liberty, or had fused them together so explosively, or was so blinded by his own explosion. He alone, wielding his vast erudition with a messianic spirit and in incomparable language, placed the present moment against the whole range of human history, and by forcing that history into a vast, predetermined scheme, gave to the politics of the moment an intoxicating ideological power. At least it intoxicated himself; for there is no reason to suppose that his eloquence, in the pamphletary babel of the time, reached the ears of any of the Arthurian knights of the shire and godlike city burgesses whose aim, at that time, was to work out a durable settlement with a difficult but legitimate and irreplaceable King.

For exactly a year – from May 1641 to May 1642 – Milton thundered against the bishops. He published five pamphlets in all. As literature, what wonderful works they are! Lyrical exaltation and blind passion glow through that magniloquent prose. How can anyone read them unmoved by the most opposite emotions? At times, when he looks forward to the new golden age, we feel ourselves transported, with him, to empyrean heights. Always we are dazzled by the sheer power of the writing: the incomparable richness of vocabulary, the exuberant metaphors, the buoyant spirits, the freshness and flexibility of style, the sudden colloquialism, the flashes of black wit – 'such a grim laughter' (and indeed it is sometimes very grim) 'as may appear in an austere visage'. But if we stay to look behind those winged words, at their meaning and intent, we can only be disgusted by the gross injustice, the hideous caricatures, the venomous, hysterical spite which they convey. For to Milton episcopacy was not, as it was to the politicians – even the most radical of them – a negotiable thing: it was an abstraction, a type of absolute evil. The politicians would have settled, in the end, for a 'moderate episcopacy'. They respected 'moderate divines' like the learned Archbishop Ussher, Bishops Davenant and Morton and other survivors of the pre-Laudian era. Milton would have none of this. 'Moderate divines indeed!' he exclaimed, 'neither hot nor cold!' and he attacked them all, throughout their whole history: 'to our souls a sad and doleful succession of illiterate and blind guides, to our purses and goods a wasteful band of robbers, a perpetual havoc and rapine, to our state a continual hydra of mischief and molestation, the forge of discord and rebellion'. Even 'those prelate-martyrs they glory of', Cranmer, Latimer and Ridley, were not exempt from his vitriolic tirades, and he urged that their very names, lest episcopacy be incidentally idolized in them, be 'utterly abolished'.[25] To him no virtue could redeem episcopacy. It was a horrible carnivorous monster 'filling her dark and infamous den with the bones of the saints',[26] and he denounced that 'tyrannical crew and incorporation of imposters', their plebeian origins, indecent wealth, ignorance, pride and gluttony, their idolatrous ritual, even their 'deformed and fantastic dresses' – 'palls and mitres, gold and gewgaws fetched from Aaron's old wardrobe or the Flamen's vestry'[27] – the smell of their socks and 'the loud stench of their breath', with the same hysterical hatred with which Hitler denounced his diabolical stereotype, the Jews.

So episcopacy was to be swept away. And what was to replace it? Milton, at this stage, does not stop to think. The essential thing is to abolish it. Now is the time; we have the means; why should we tarry? Faint or corrupted souls argue that monarchy will sink with episcopacy, or that the destruction of episcopacy will open the way to mob-rule: that 'if Adrian's wall be broke, a flood of sects will rush in'. Not at all, replies Milton: the royal dignity is not chained to 'the painted battlements and gaudy rottenness of prelatry'; by removing this dead weight, this battening parasite, we shall save 'the floating carcase of a crazy and diseased monarchy' and restore it to health. As for the sects, what are these so-called sects and their opinions? 'Give us the inventory!' In fact, protests Milton, they are 'no rabble, Sir Priest, but a unanimous multitude of good Christians', who, once episcopacy has gone, will shed their particular differences, joining and strengthening a reformed, national Protestant Church.[28] And then, when that is established and the stage-machinery has been set in motion, the great pageant of history will move forward. Christ, who went up from Galilee, will come down to England; the reception committee of Lords and Commons will be awaiting him; and the great poet will be in attendance to sing the triumphal introit: having staked his claim by this 'plain ungarnisht' prospectus, he will, as he says (addressing himself directly to Christ), 'take up a harp and sing Thee an elaborate song to generations'. For the world is not in decline, 'as fond and faithless men imagine'; though by a zigzag course, it has long been moving forwards to that great event; 'and all creatures sigh to be renew'd'.[29]

We may note that, at this time, Milton not only has no fear of the sects, he is also unafraid of 'the people'. 'The people', he insists, are not 'a mutinous rabble' but responsible, disciplined, rational persons. He will trust 'the capacity of a plain artisan', 'a carpenter, smith or weaver'.[30] Equally he trusts the Presbyterians, for are not they too determined enemies of episcopacy? Indeed, at the height of the euphoria, in July 1641, he had aligned himself with the group of Presbyterian clergy who wrote under the collective acronym of 'Smectymnuus'. One of these was his old tutor, Thomas Young, who perhaps brought him in. The most important and interesting of them was Stephen Marshall, parson of Finchingfield in Essex. Marshall was a famous preacher, the bellowing 'Geneva bull' of the royalist pamphleteers; for he could make many a church shake, and its congregation shiver, with his threats of damnation. He was also an astute politician, the trusted agent of the parliamentary leaders, who would call on him to preach on all important occasions. He would serve them in other ways too, securing signatures for monster petitions and whipping up absentee members to vote in parliamentary divisions. Marshall took note of Milton's support and even, in some of his grand parliamentary sermons, borrowed some of his phrases.* He was one of the very few men who read and approved of Milton the pamphleteer. For Marshall too, like many English Presbyterians, was a millenarian. Millenarianism was the intellectual cement which united the anti-episcopal party – or perhaps, by now, the vapour which concealed its opening cracks.

---

* In the peroration of his tract *Of Reformation* (May 1641), Milton dwells on the struggles of 'these fourscore years' of which this year, 1640–1, is the climax, and offers 'amidst the hymns and hallelujahs of saints . . . at high strains, in new and lofty measures to sing and celebrate Thy divine mercies and judgments in this land'. Marshall, in his thanksgiving sermon, *A Peace Offering to God*, on 6 September 1641, makes exactly the same point about this year being the climax of fourscore years, rejoicing that 'after our Lamentations we shall together sing canticles and hallelujahs unto our God'. In the same sermon, Marshall's promise of a 'jubilee and resurrection of both Church and State' echoes Milton's phrase in *Animadversions* (July 1641), 'the very jubilee and resurrection of the state'. The passage from *Meroz Curs'd* quoted in the next paragraph is similarly echoed in the words of *Of Reformation*. Parker, in his *Milton's Contemporary Reputation*, does not notice these parallels; nor does J.T. Shawcross in his monumental *Milton: a Bibliography for the Years 1624–1700* (*Medieval and Renaissance Texts and Studies* XXX, Binghamton, NY, 1984). Haller, *Liberty and Reformation in the Puritan Revolution* (New York 1955), pp. 58–9, notes, only to dismiss, the coincidence of *Meroz Curs'd* and *The Reason*; but the other evidence which I have cited suggests that it is more than a mere coincidence.

A few months later, when the King had left London and was mustering support for a return in force, Marshall preached a famous sermon to Parliament which would be published under the title *Meroz Curs'd*. In it he called down the curse of God on those who, like the men of Meroz, were negligent in making war on the enemies of Israel, and he appealed, in very Miltonic language, for a singer who would set forth 'in elegant and lofty verse' the great mercies of God to his nation. At precisely the same time Milton interrupted the argument of his pamphlet, *The Reason of Church Government*, written in support of Marshall and his allies, to advertise, at great length, his own qualifications for such a task. He presented himself as one of those rare persons who were inspired 'to cherish in a great people the seeds of vertu and public civility, . . . to celebrate in glorious and lofty hymns . . . the deeds and triumphs of just and pious nations, . . . to deplore the general relapse of kingdoms and states from justice and God's true worship'. It looks as if he were answering Marshall's advertisement, or at least that the two men were in collusion.*

Once civil war had broken out, Milton withdrew from the fray. Soon he would be preoccupied with his own matrimonial problems and the controversy caused by his tracts in favour of divorce. But he remained firm in his millenarian convictions. Millenarianism indeed gained strength in those years. It was stimulated by immigrants from abroad – hot-gospellers like John Cotton, the evangelist of Boston, Lincs., and Boston, Mass., returning from the challenge of New England, 'Baconian' enthusiasts like Samuel Hartlib, the promoter of all good causes, who had arrived in 1629, fleeing from the European war. In those years the works of Brightman, Alsted and Mede, all written in Latin, were published and popularized in English, and the regular parliamentary preachers repeated their message, protesting against any political settlement, any compromise.[31] The war, to them, was a holy war. What was the point of political compromise when Christ was on his way?

This was shown in 1643 at the time of Waller's Plot, when the 'moderate' royalist party at Oxford attempted to achieve such a settlement by secret treaty with the peace party in London. The attempt failed, and the war party celebrated its triumph with a service of thanksgiving. The sermon, almost inevitably, was preached by Marshall, who on all such occasions would 'lift up his nose like a porpoise and make St Margaret's Church ring of their deliverance'.

* Twelve years later, in *Defensio Secunda* (*CPW* IV, p. 627), Milton protested that he had never sought public employment; but perhaps he protested too much. He had accepted patronage in the 1630s; why should he not seek it in the 1640s?

Marshall declared that the book of Revelation, 'the darkest and most mystical book in all the Scriptures', was now perfectly intelligible. All the trumps had been blown, the vials were being poured out in regular order; the slaughter (if Scripture was correctly interpreted) was to last only three-and-a-half years; 'and then presently come in the glorious times which Christ hath promised'.[32]

Next month, the long-promised synod of clergy – the Westminster Assembly, as it was called – was set up. Approved clergy, nominated by members of Parliament, each for his constituency, met in Henry VII's chapel at Westminster, to determine the form of a national Church fit to receive the returning Christ. The prolocutor of the Assembly, Dr Twisse, was a man after Milton's own mind: a learned scholar, who had edited Mede's *Key to the Revelation* and had discovered the millenarian relevance of Bacon's work.[33] Another prominent member of the Assembly, Herbert Palmer, a stiff Presbyterian, was also a millenarian. This millenarianism of English Presbyterians thoroughly alarmed the Scottish representatives who sat with the Assembly: it had no basis in a society which lacked dynamism and a Church that was authoritarian, clerical and defensive.[34]

About the same time, Milton became a friend of Samuel Hartlib. It was Hartlib who had fetched Comenius to England in 1641; and now he invited Milton, as a fellow millenarian and fellow Baconian, to set out his ideas on the reform of education. In general terms, they agreed. 'The end of learning', Milton believed, 'is to repair the ruins of our first parents by regaining to know God aright'. So far, so good. But when they came down to particulars, there was a great difference. Hartlib was a democrat. He believed, like Comenius, in universal education, education made practical and learning made simple for simple, practical, unlearned men. Milton had no such egalitarian ideas. He believed in a highly educated, classically educated humanist élite, maintained, as he himself had been, in 'ease and leisure . . . out of the sweat of other men',[35] and in the tract which he sent to Hartlib he said so, very clearly. He would have no truck, he said, with 'what many *Januas* and *Didacticas*, more than I shall ever read, have projected'. *Janua* and *Didactica* were the titles of Comenius' educational treatises. Instead, he set out a plan of 'complete and generous education', to create, out of 'our noble and gentle youth', a public-spirited ruling class. It was an exacting course, to last from the age of twelve to twenty-one. Boys were to be sent to special local academies and there taught Latin, Greek, Hebrew, Aramaic, Italian (but not French); they were to study literature, history, oratory, mathematics, natural science, the art of war, politics, jurisprudence, music and much else; they were to be toughened by gymnastic exercises and prepared for leadership by military training. Then they were to go on a grand tour. Avoiding, like Milton himself, any contact with 'the Monsieurs of Paris', which would merely transform them 'into mimics, apes and kickshaws', they were to converse only with 'the best and most eminent persons in Europe'. Then they would return, fit to be heard with honour and attention when they spoke 'in Parliament or council'. It is hardly surprising that Hartlib's closest friend, John Dury, on receiving the tract, dismissed it as 'brief and general' and irrelevant to their purposes.

Milton's last pamphlet of the civil wars, *Areopagitica*, was published in November 1644. It was a protest against the censorship demanded by the Presbyterians of the Westminster Assembly, and particularly by Herbert Palmer, who, in a sermon to Parliament, had denounced Milton's treatise on Divorce 'as a wicked book . . . deserving to be burnt'. In it Milton declared once again that the convulsions of the civil war would lead to complete reformation and enlightenment; for 'when God shakes a kingdom with strong and healthful commotions to a general reforming', he raises up 'men of rare abilities and more than common industry', to revise accepted doctrine and to take 'some new enlightened steps in the discovery of truth'.[36] It was an uncompromising demand for complete freedom of publication, inspired by humanist and Baconian ideals, still fused with millennial expectations.

Seven months later, after the decisive battle of Naseby, the last great battle of the civil war, the two Houses and the Lord Mayor and Common Council of the City of London listened to another thanksgiving sermon by Stephen Marshall. Once again, Marshall placed 'these huge shakings of the nations' in the context of prophetic history, and he urged Parliament to commission 'a sacred record' of 'these wonderful works of God . . . for generations to come'. Hitherto the standard record had been John Foxe's *Acts and Monuments*. That work, said Marshall, was itself a continuation of the Bible, which was 'nothing but a chronicle, a book of Acts and Monuments of the Lord's wonderful works' in protecting his Church and destroying its enemies. Now it was time to continue Foxe. Some worthy faithful person should have authority and power 'as Mr Foxe had in Queen Elizabeth's days', to provide posterity with 'a faithful story of these last three or four years'.[37] For we may note that the battle of Naseby was fought three-and-a-half years after the King, by withdrawing from London to York, had effectively begun the civil war; and three-and-a-half years was the period which Marshall, out of Scripture, had assigned to the last convulsions of Antichrist.

Once again we ask, was Marshall thinking of Milton as the writer of his 'sacred record'?[38] Possibly, possibly not. All that we can say is that, if so, there was no immediate response. Later that year, Milton staked out his claim as a poet by publishing his early poems. This was the volume in which he so complacently printed the Latin verses of Salzilli and 'Selvaggi' ranking him with, or above, the greatest of epic poets. He also included, among his juvenile exercises, a Latin poem in praise of Lancelot Andrewes, the patron and model of the Laudian bishops, and a laudatory epitaph on a Roman Catholic countess; and one poem which, as he wrote, 'being nothing satisfied with what was begun', he had left unfinished, 'supposing' (as Dr Johnson would drily observe) 'his readers less nice than himself'. The volume, in short, was a hotchpotch of all the verse that he had so far written, good or bad, in Latin, Italian and English, uncritically thrust on the public, with an extravagant puff not for his present but for his future poetry.* Since Milton was in general chary of publishing his poems – till then he had himself published none, and would publish no more till *Paradise Lost* in 1667† – this rush into print is surprising. Perhaps it was his prospectus. If so, it had no effect. The volume fell still-born from the press. Early next year the Parliament appointed another, and vastly inferior, poet, Tom May, to be its official historian. May never finished his history: he died 'of a merry symposiack' in 1650. His credentials were few; but at least he had not blotted his copybook by writing against parliamentary censorship and in favour of divorce.

5   Withdrawal and return

In the summer of 1646 the civil war ended with the surrender of Oxford and the flight of the King to the Scots at Newark. The next two years were a period of intense political struggle – the most controversial

---

* The praise of Milton as a (future) epic poet, is repeated in the Virgilian epigraph,
baccare frontem
cingite, ne vati noceat mala lingua futuro.
In his pamphlets, Milton never refers to his present poetry, only to his future epic.
† Of those poems which had been published before 1645, the sonnet on Shakespeare and *Lycidas* had been tributary verses published in other collections; *Comus* had been published by Lawes (Milton apparently being reluctant); *Epitaphium Damonis* was privately printed and circulated in few copies, none of which survives.

period, perhaps, of the entire revolution. There was no thought, as yet, of deposing the King, far less of ending the monarchy. The question was, on what terms was the royal authority to be readmitted, what institutional changes were to be made, in Church, State and society, before it was readmitted, and how were those changes to be made secure? The answers to these questions were complicated by the shifts and struggles of unstable parties caught between the fear of royalist reaction and the threat of sectarian revolution. The threat of revolution was articulated by the radical democratic Levellers. Faced by it, one party, the more cautious and conservative, wished to make a quick settlement with the King and rely on their own political skill to control him, and on an established, lay-controlled Calvinist Church to control the sects. Another, trusting the King less, or the sects more, was prepared to keep up the pressure on the former and settle for toleration of the latter. But each party was prepared to bargain with the King if it could be sure of power. Each also had its reserve of force. The conservatives, as 'Presbyterians', relied on the 'mercenary' army of the Scots; their rivals, the 'Independents', relied on the victorious English army, which however had been infiltrated by the agents of the Levellers and the sects. In the course of the struggle the Presbyterians, who controlled the Parliament, sought, and failed, to disband the English army; the Independents then used that army to coerce the Parliament. Thus the parties were polarized and the royalists gleefully exploited their dissension.

All through this period of political turmoil, Milton lay low. According to his nephew, he 'lived a private and quiet life, still prosecuting his studies and curious search into knowledge'. The great pamphletary controversies provoked by the Levellers passed him by, nor did he ever, then or thereafter, mention them. He wrote little and published nothing. But inwardly it is clear that he suffered a profound change. The euphoria, the fusion of ideals which had inspired him in 1641–2, and which had sustained him, though perhaps with diminishing force, until 1645, was now dissolved. In 1641–2 he had believed that the victory of Parliament, and the abolition of episcopacy, would open the way to the new enlightenment, the regeneration of the national Church, the millennium. Now the victory had been won, the bishops had gone, but what was the result? Mobilized at Westminster, the Presbyterian clergy had shown themselves just as intolerant, just as greedy as the bishops had been: 'new Presbyter', as he then wrote, was 'but old Priest writ large'. The Parliament, which had once seemed to him an assembly of gods, had become a self-perpetuating oligarchy of profiteers. Enlightenment was blocked by censorship. There was no sign of the millennium.

Milton's disillusion, growing throughout those two years of frustration, was at its blackest, it seems, in the early months of 1648. Driven by the fear of anarchy, the Presbyterian leaders of Parliament were then seeking to negotiate a new treaty with the King, whom they had rescued from military custody. Meanwhile, royalist risings threatened to overtake even those negotiations and force an unconditional return to the old regime. After the euphoria of 1641 and 1645, this was a dreadful decline. How, Milton asked, could it have happened? What had become of the 'virtue', the civic spirit, the pure love of freedom which had animated the godlike senators of 1640–1? In those days he had noted in his Commonplace Book that Brutus and Cassius had 'felt themselves of spirit to free a nation but considered not that the nation was not fit to be free'.[39] No doubt he had believed that the England of Charles I, unlike Caesar's Rome, was fit and ready for freedom. Now he had come to doubt this. In his dejection, he went back to the old subject which he had once wished to turn into a national epic. He looked, with a more critical eye, at the golden age of Britain before the Norman conquest and that type of the Christian hero, King Arthur. He began his prose work, *The History of Britain*.

The History of Britain is of interest to us not in its own right but as a barometer of Milton's mind. It was not completed till later, nor published – and then incompletely – till later still. Dr Johnson was mystified by it. Neither as history nor as literature could he find any value in it. Why, he asked, should Milton have repeated 'the whole fable of Geoffrey of Monmouth . . . which he seems not to believe, and which is universally rejected?' The style of the book, he added, is harsh, although he admitted that it had 'something of rough vigour, which perhaps may often strike, though it cannot please'. However, Johnson presumed that the work was written, as it was published, after the Restoration. Therefore he placed it against the wrong background. In its proper context, it is less mysterious.

Milton had begun his studies of early British history before 1640, at the time when he was contemplating his Arthurian epic. He had then read systematically the chronicles of the dark ages and the documents published by the great antiquaries, Camden and Ussher. Those were the days when he had believed, with them, in the pure Christianity of the ancient Britons which the present age was to restore. But now, in the disillusion of a lost victory, that vision had dissolved. Closer study had anyway cast doubt on the veracity of those ancient chroniclers;

the great antiquaries too were dismissed as too fond of bishops, monks and 'old writings'; and what had once seemed a romantic era of Spenserian chivalry had become a dreary and meaningless prelude to centuries of monkish superstition, only fit to be recorded in wry, dry prose.

To Milton all history was one continuum, and the present was foreshadowed in the past. So, when he reconsidered the age of Arthur, he saw it as a prefiguration of his own time: a prefiguration, an analogy, a warning example. Britain in the sixth century, he now suggested, was in a general decline. Its people, 'given to vicious ease', had been so softened and corrupted by long servility that even a heroic figure like King Arthur, if indeed he existed, could bring no real revival; for although he gained a famous victory at Mount Badon, and thereby won a 'long calm of peace', that peace was not properly used and thus 'so fair a victory came to nothing'. The next generation, we are told, 'unacquainted with past evils, and only sensible of their present ease and quiet', forgot truth and justice, 'scarce the least footstep or impression of goodness remaining through all ranks and degrees in the land, except some so very few as to be hardly visible in a general corruption'; so the British kings degenerated into tyranny, and their eminent clergy were the props and profiteers of that tyranny . . .

The account is taken from the old British writer Gildas, but when we read about the ancient British clergy – how they were 'pastors in name but indeed wolves intent upon all occasions not to feed the flock but to pamper and well line themselves'; how they were 'bunglers at the Scripture, nay forbidding and silencing them that know, but in worldly matters practis'd and cunning shifters', insisting on 'niceties and trivial points to keep in awe the superstitious multitude' – we recognize the language. It is the language of *Lycidas*. We have moved forward to modern times. The unexploited victory is the victory over the Spanish Armada; the corrupting peace is the peace of King James; the tyrannical kings and their sycophantic clergy need no introduction; and the few just men hardly visible in the general corruption are that dwindling band of parliamentary heroes whose praise Milton had once so ecstatically sung but of whose virtue and constancy he was now far more sceptical.

But the parallel did not stop here. In a passage which, long afterwards, when he published his work, was quietly removed from it, Milton went on to pose a topical question. Why, he asked, did the old Britons, once they were free of Roman rule, not achieve a perfect commonwealth? Why did that great opportunity 'pass through them as a cordial medicine through a dying man, without the least effect of sense or natural vigour?' For answer, he switched back to the present. The cause, then as now, he insisted, was a moral failure. Then he digressed to the present, to the failure of the Long Parliament, in which private interest had replaced its old public spirit, its *virtù*. The members of Parliament in 1648 were still largely the same men whose heroic virtue he had so lyrically hailed in 1641. But this virtue had now been rotted by the infusion of a base bourgeois spirit: 'some who had been called from shops and warehouses, without other merit, to sit in supreme councils and committees, as their breeding was, fell to huckster the commonwealth', battening on new impositions, taxes, excises, 'not to reckon the offices, gifts and preferments bestow'd and shared among themselves'. The Westminster Assembly, which had met with such high hopes, had proved no better: the Presbyterian clergy, whom Milton had once joined in the crusade against the bishops, had merely sought to replace the old prelates in all their vices, teaching 'compulsion without convincement' and seizing into their hands fat livings, headships of colleges, rich city lectureships, 'setting sail to all winds that might blow gain into their covetous bosoms'.

Altogether, Milton concludes, it was not lack of strength or courage but the civil vices of 'ruler, priest and people' which, now as then, had brought the nation, 'after many labours, much bloodshed and vast expense, to ridiculous frustration'. All of which showed that liberty was not to be granted to every man that claimed it; for 'liberty hath a sharp and double edge, fit only to be handled by just and virtuous men', perhaps not by Englishmen at all (so much now for the Elect Nation), but by men of 'solid and elaborate breeding' in whom civil virtues have been implanted by 'foreign writings and examples of best ages': 'men more than vulgar, bred up, as few of them were, in the knowledge of ancient and illustrious deeds' – in other words, an élite educated, as Milton had been, on the best classical models. It was for lack of such an 'elaborate breeding' that the modern English élite, like the ancient British élite, had failed.

Milton's *History of Britain* was begun in a mood of hopeless pessimism, and this digression is the most hopeless part of it: so hopeless indeed that Mr Woolrych has recently sought to re-date it, seeing it as an 'afterthought' from the last days of the doomed republic: 'a despondent retrospective judgment on all that had been attempted from 1640 to 1660'. For how, he asks, can we reconcile this mood of

gloom with the 'vigorous optimism' of Milton's previous prose tracts?*
But to this we may answer that the latest of those previous tracts had
been written over three years ago, and how much had happened in
those intervening years! Historians must always look at history
forwards, as contemporaries saw it, as well as backwards, knowing
what followed. Who could have guessed, early in 1648, that Charles I,
by a desperate last gamble, would throw away all that he had gained
from the divisions of his enemies? To a rational man, who expected
others to act rationally, it might well have seemed, by then, that the
revolution had failed, that the civil war had been fought and won in
vain, that England was not, after all, the elect nation, nor those
'shakings' the last convulsions of Antichrist. In such circumstances the
exaltation of the earlier years may well have been followed by
depression: a trough as deep as the previous wave had been high. There
are other signs, too, of Milton's despondency. In the same months in
which he was writing the *History of Britain*, he wrote a verse translation
of a group of nine Psalms. They were Psalms 80 to 88, in which the
Psalmist laments that Israel, the land which God had chosen, has now,
for its backsliding, been laid waste; that it is surrounded by enemies;
that God, in his wrath, has turned his face away from it: 'Turn us again,
O Lord of Hosts . . . Wilt thou be angry with us for ever?'

Then, suddenly, in the summer of 1648, the Lord of Hosts, as it
seemed, relented. By calling in the Scots to renew the civil war even
while negotiating with the 'Presbyterian' Parliament, Charles I lost all
credibility, and, after their defeat, all hope. Fortified and justified by
the victory of Preston, pressed by the radical 'agitators' in his army,
Cromwell decided to cut through the restraining bonds of law and
throw the sword into the scales. The majority of the Parliament was

---

* Austin Woolrych, 'The Date of the Digression in Milton's *History of Britain*', in
Richard Ollard and Pamela Tudor-Craig (ed.), *For Veronica Wedgwood These: Studies in
17th century History* (1986). Mr Woolrych's chief argument is the depth of Milton's
despondency, which argues an irreversible defeat, and the similarity of his language
with that of his last pamphlets before the Restoration, which was indeed such a defeat.
But the later date seems to me liable to greater objections. If Milton had been writing in
1660, his passionate attack on the Westminster Assembly (effectively extinct since
1648) was an irrelevancy; and if he had been pronouncing judgment on 'all that had
happened from 1640 to 1660', why did he mention nothing that had happened since
1648? Similarity of language – an argument also used by Parker to re-date *Samson
Agonistes* – does not seem to me significant (in either case): Milton's language seems to
me remarkably stable throughout the period, and can equally be used to confirm the
earlier date: compare, for instance, the passage in the Digression on the Public Faith
and the avarice of parliament-men and clergy (*CPW* V, pp. 444–7) with the last lines
of the sonnet to Fairfax, written in the summer of 1648.

expelled, the King brought to trial and execution. Thereafter the obedient Rump of Parliament abolished the monarchy and the House of Lords and assumed complete power as a self-constituted oligarchy. It was precisely what Milton had advocated: an oligarchy of the Elect.

To Milton, the seizure of power by the army, the execution of the King and the setting up of the Republic were a tonic which dispelled his former gloom. The total rejection of legality, the resort to force, the dependence of the Republic on military power, and the political implications of this illegality, did not disturb him. He therefore recovered his spirit and decided, once again, as in 1641, to throw himself into the fray. Then it had been to attack the bishops as the obstructors of the divinely ordained historical process; now it was to attack their successors, the Presbyterian clergy, for their foolish objections to the execution of the King. So he wrote a treatise, 'to quiet the people', as he put it, or, as his sympathetic modern biographer puts it, to vindicate the act of regicide 'with wise and calming words'.[40]

'Wise and calming' are perhaps not the adjectives we would naturally use about Milton's treatise, *The Tenure of Kings and Magistrates*, his first essay in politics, or indeed about any of the works which, after that, he wrote as the official scribe of the revolutionary regime. In all of them, his immediate enemy is not the King, now safely dead, but his 'Presbyterian' defenders: the politicians who had drawn back from regicide and now refused to recognize the Commonwealth; the clergy who gave religious sanction to their refusal; and their foreign colleagues, the Calvinists of Europe. To Milton the Presbyterian clergy were the true successors of the bishops: successors to their vices of tyranny and greed, 'greased thick and deep with pluralities', 'gorging themselves like harpies on those simonious places and preferments of their ousted predecessors', 'a pack of hungry church-wolves . . . following the hot scent of double livings and pluralities, advowsons, donatives, inductions and augmentations'. His old ally Stephen Marshall was not spared: he too, by now, was a rich pluralist, lecturer at St Margaret's, Westminster, as well as parson of a fat living in Essex, with liberal grants from Parliament, a rich wife, and daughters who 'followed the height of fashion, with changeable taffetas and naked necks'.*

---

* Milton repeatedly sneered at the Presbyterian sermons on the text 'Curse ye Meroz', 'the very motto of their pulpits': a reference to Marshall's famous sermon on this text. The phrase about Marshall's daughters comes from the (unsympathetic) anonymous biography of Marshall, *The Godly Man's Legacy to the Saints upon Earth* (1680).

In one respect, indeed, the Presbyterians were even worse than the bishops. The bishops at least had been consistent in their support of Antichrist. The Presbyterians were half-hearted and half-witted men who, through corrupt interest, had betrayed their own revolution. Cowards and hypocrites, 'puling priests', 'apostate scarecrows', 'mercenary noise-makers', they had shrunk from the logical and necessary consequences of their own proclaimed doctrines. Had they not already resisted the King, preached war, celebrated victory? They had killed the King politically and militarily: why should they shrink from completing their own work by killing him physically? Of course it was not humanity or principle: it was for their own interest that, having reduced him to political impotence, they sought to keep 'the mere useless bulk of his person'. Any tears that they shed were crocodile tears: their 'only grief is the head was not struck off to the best advantage of them that held it by the hair'.[41] For in opposing regicide they were betraying their own philosophy. To prove the point Milton crammed down their throats the revolutionary arguments of earlier and bolder Scotch and French Calvinists: of Knox and Buchanan against Mary Queen of Scots and the Huguenot writers against the last Valois kings; and if these did not suffice (as indeed they did not), there were always the sound Old Testament examples of Ehud, Samuel, Jehu etc., who, though lacking such philosophical justification, had a direct warrant from God to disembowel the king of Edom, throw the queen of Israel to the dogs, and hew the king of the Amalekites in pieces before the Lord.

Milton's second spate of prose writings, from 1649 to 1654, labours the same theme. There is no original thought in them: the political ideas are entirely derivative, often lifted textually from his brief; and the controversial temper gets worse. For of course he was contradicted, and nothing so enrages the egotist as the assertion of dissent. Milton had shown this in the controversy over episcopacy. He showed it even more in the controversy over divorce when he had to stoop (as he complained) to the 'underwork of scowring and unrubbishing the low and sordid ignorance' of 'a presumptuous lozel', a mere serving-man, an idiot, a pork. Cannot a man walk peaceably in the world, he then asked, without being infested 'sometimes at his face with dorrs and horseflies, sometimes beneath, with bauling whippets and shin-barkers?' Now, after the execution of the King, he found himself thus doubly beset. The horsefly at his face was the eminent Calvinist scholar Salmasius, whose pen had been hired by Charles II. The whippets snapping at his shins were those naïve persons who had been carried away by the best-selling, tear-jerking presentation of the royal martyr in his solitude and sufferings, *Eikon Basiliké*.

Against these encircling enemies, Milton launched out more violently than ever. He poured scorn on the turncoat Presbyterians. He attacked 'the blockish vulgar' seduced by royalist propaganda. Exasperated by the obstinacy of the former and the gullibility of the latter, he forgot his proclaimed intention of sparing the person of the dead King. Who, he asked, was this King whom the Presbyterians had refused to kill and whom the people insisted on mourning? To the old charges of tyranny and treachery he added new charges of personal vice and crime: of lust and debauchery, which he invented;[42] of parricide, of having poisoned his father James I, which he repeated *ad nauseam*,[43] slavishly following his brief, *The Remonstrance of the Army*. He mocked the King in his adversity, as he ridiculed the present poverty of his heir. For good measure, he declared that the whole family was illegitimate, for was not James I really the son of Mary Stuart's favourite musician David Riccio? He even mocked the King's literary tastes. The poet who had once written of sweetest Shakespeare, Fancy's child, now sneered at Charles I's 'closet companion of these his solitudes, William Shakespeare'. As the ultimate insult, he poured scorn on his dignified bearing on the scaffold. That last royal act, which so moved all the spectators, and which Milton's colleague Andrew Marvell so eloquently commemorated, was to him a mere pageant, a comedy, 'a ridiculous exit': evidence not of dignity but of shamelessness, a brazen front concealing the hardened heart of a common criminal.[44] Alone of educated men, Milton personally insulted the dead victim of his party: his magniloquence, alas, was never matched by magnanimity.

As for Salmasius, whose learning Milton had once professed to venerate,[45] he, of course, could expect no quarter. He was overwhelmed with vulgar abuse. He was a foreigner, a grammarian, a pedant, a hired pedagogue, a monster, a madman, a liar, a pimp, a parasite, a henpecked eunuch, a Circean beast, a weevil, a bug, a dunghill cock, a filthy pig; and before long Milton was able to add that he was also dead, and to boast that it was his powerful rhetoric that had killed him. When all was over, he insisted that in spite of his blindness, he was not depressed. Why should he be? He had lost his sight, but in a worthy cause which had made him world-famous, writing against Salmasius

> In liberty's defence, my noble task,
> Of which all Europe talks from side to side.

To be the talk of Europe! This was certainly more than his slender volume of poetry had achieved. Six years later, when the Republic which he had defended was crumbling in ruin, he would still be trumpeting his victory 'against a famous and thought invincible adversary' and boasting of his Latin tirade as 'a written monument likely to outlive detraction'.

6   True liberty

Liberty, liberty, liberty . . . what did Milton mean by it? He certainly did not mean democracy. In 1642 he had been prepared to trust the judgment of a plain artisan, a carpenter, smith or weaver. That was when he assumed that such men would be guided by reason, his reason: that their freedom was his freedom. Not now. In the traumatic years 1646–8, he had revised his views. Public opinion had been against him on the subject of divorce, so what was the public? 'Owls and cuckoos, asses, apes and dogs'. Then came the glorious *coup d'état*: Pride's Purge and the act of regicide. But had 'the people' recognized their liberators? No. The success of *Eikon Basiliké*, its easy capture of 'the worthless approbation of an inconstant, irrational and image-doting rabble', proved that it had not. 'What a miserable credulous deluded thing that creature is which is called the vulgar!' Milton exclaimed. 'The blind superstition of the mob', 'the rage and torrent' of their 'boisterous folly' showed that they were 'by nature slaves and arrant beasts', 'not fit for that liberty which they cried out and bellowed for'.[46] Never, after that, could Milton concede freedom to 'the blockish vulgar'.

Nor to other groups. Not to Presbyterians after 1648: they were not to have freedom of the pulpit.[47] Not to Roman Catholics ever, for they were not Christians. Not to the Scots, who were rightly conquered for being Presbyterian, nor to 'the villainous and savage scum of Ireland': an 'accursed race', who, for 'their endless treasons and revolts' deserved only to be governed 'by edicts and garrisons'.[48] Not to women: as Dr Johnson wrote, he 'thought woman made only for obedience and man only for rebellion'. Nor did he believe in liberty guaranteed by institutions. Like so many of those who supported the Cromwellian revolution, he had little interest in political forms and no veneration for the ancient constitution so cried up by the men of 1640 and the later whigs. Virtuous men, not 'gibberish laws', were the only guarantors of true liberty. ' 'Tis not the common law nor the civil, but piety and justness that are our foundresses', he had written in 1641; 'they stoop not, neither change colour, for aristocracy, democracy or monarchy'.[49]

Nor do they stoop for mere numbers. He had no respect for majority decisions if the majority was against him, 'there being in number but little virtue'.[50] The eviction of the majority of the Long Parliament by Pride's Purge did not offend him: 'no question', he wrote, 'but it is as good and necessary to expel rotten members out of the House as to banish delinquents' – i.e. royalists – 'out of the land; and the reason holds as well in forty as in five'.* Thus the sound minority always had the right to eliminate the rotten majority and Milton had no objection when Cromwell, by the same logic, evicted the once sound minority, the Rump.

The liberty which Milton demanded was for an élite, an aristocracy of virtuous Protestants formed by a liberal education. Only such men were worthy of freedom, and it was their function to create a free commonwealth, to rule it and, by education, to raise up worthy successors who would perpetuate it. How such men achieved power, what institutions they used to perpetuate it, was a matter of indifference. 'Justice and Victory' are the only warrants, 'next under immediate Revelation'. The essential thing is that the virtuous should rule. Ultimately, liberty might be expanded by education; but it must be humanist education which can never reach common men: 'it is not agreeable to the nature of things that such persons should ever be free: however much they may brawl about liberty, they are slaves'.

And what, we naturally ask, is the purpose of this virtuous freedom? In 1641–2 it had been clear. Then Milton had believed that history was coming to a grand climax. In a unique historical conjuncture, a heroic generation was about to lead England to its rightful front seat for the great spectacle of the 'soon expected' second coming of Christ. Freedom was the necessary qualification for this privileged role. After 1648 some enthusiasts still held this view, though without its humanist content. With the execution of the King, they believed, prophetic history had been put back on course. John Owen, preaching to the House of Commons in 1649, would welcome 'the shakings of Heaven and Earth and all the powers of the world': God, he said, was overthrowing princes in order to establish his kingdom in England before 'the consummation of all'.[51] In the intoxication of victory Cromwell would use similar language: 'how shall we behave ourselves after such mercies?' he would exclaim after 'the crowning mercy' at Worcester in 1651: 'what is the Lord a-doing? What prophecies are now

---

* *CPW* IV, p. 328. The numbers, forty as opposed to five, are presumably a riposte to the statement of John Geree, who, in *Might Overcoming Right* (18 Jan. 1649), had pointed out that the King had imprisoned only five members of Parliament whereas Cromwell had imprisoned forty and 'secluded' more than a hundred.

fulfilling? Who is a God like ours?'[52] The Fifth Monarchists used the same language and believed that they could help God along by direct action. They spoke of a totalitarian dictatorship of the saints, 'terrible to carnal men'. Such language caused many old millenarians – men like the supple Stephen Marshall, or Thomas Goodwin, now comfortably established as President of Magdalen College, Oxford – to revise their views.[53] They did not wish to be in that *galère*.

Nor did Milton. Never, after 1645, did he suggest that the second coming of Christ, in which he still believed, was due now, or that political events in England were directly related to it. The complex of ideas which had dominated him in 1641–2 had been evacuated from his mind, and from now on his purpose was different. He still believed intensely in liberty, the liberty with which only good men could be entrusted, the liberty which had been gained by the revolution and must now be secured. But that liberty was no longer to be granted to the Church, any Church. There was to be no national Church, or indeed Church, or clergy, of any kind. The function of the State was to suppress Catholicism, atheism, blasphemy (under 'that prudent and well-deliberated Act' of 1650), and idolatry (which included the circulation of *Eikon Basilikê*), but at the same time to protect the freedom of all its Protestant subjects to believe what they wished, so long as they could find warrant for it in the Bible. For Milton himself had, by now, become a heretic.

With Milton's multiple heresies, which made him in the end 'a unique combination of semi-Arian, Arminian, Anabaptist, anti-sabbatarian, mortalist, semi-Quaker, "divorcer" and "polygamist" ',[54] we are not here concerned. It is enough to say that, having begun as an orthodox predestinarian Calvinist, by the later 1640s he knew that his own ideas were regarded as intolerable by any established Church. Therefore the only hope for heretics like himself was complete toleration, and the only sure way to complete toleration was the complete separation of Church and State and, within the Church, the complete abolition of the clergy. This therefore now became his prime object, and his politics consisted of giving propagandist support to whatever government would carry out such a policy. Such a government could, theoretically, be a monarchy; but monarchs were unpredictable and traditional monarchies, resting on established Churches, were obviously out of the question. So was any form of democracy, as we interpret the word. Liberty is for a small minority only, for an aristocracy of virtue. Since virtue, in the Machiavellian sense, was civic courage, the courage to make war against their natural sovereign and not 'shiver at the majesty and grandeur of some noble deed' – i.e. of regicide – that aristocracy defined itself. It was the Rump.

From the Rump, Milton hoped for two things: the abolition of a State Church, maintained by tithes, and a statute of toleration.[55] In the summer of 1652, in his sonnets to Cromwell and Vane, he pressed this policy on them. Vane, he believed, shared his views; so, probably, did Bradshaw, the President of the Council of State. But Cromwell was more cautious, and nothing was done. Then, in April 1653, Cromwell expelled the Rump. Its leaders, naturally, were outraged. They now saw Cromwell as a perfidious and ambitious hypocrite, usurper and tyrant. Bradshaw protested that no power under heaven could dissolve the Parliament. But Cromwell was inexorable. He had finished with them. He particularly turned on Vane, declaring him 'a juggler', without 'common honesty': 'Oh Sir Henry Vane, Sir Henry Vane, the Lord deliver me from Sir Henry Vane!'

In these circumstances it is surprising that Milton uttered no squeak of protest, kept his place as Latin Secretary, and appears to have welcomed the change. He became Cromwell's man. In December 1653 he even supported Cromwell when he effectively dismissed the 'Parliament of Saints' which had actually voted to abolish tithes – just what Milton wanted. It seems that he proposed to celebrate in prose the glorious reign of Cromwell: at least I do not know how else to account for the private collection of Cromwellian State papers which he was allowed to make at that time, and which remained unused in his hands.* It would not have been the first time that he saw himself as the historian, or the poet, of the revolution.

How are we to account for this sudden change? Perhaps, like Machiavelli, he now believed that, in a corrupted world, a free commonwealth must give way, temporarily at least, to a necessary Prince. If the Rump would not disestablish the Church, a military dictator might do so. So, in his first publication under the new Protectorate, he declared that 'there is nothing in human society more pleasing to God, or more agreeable to reason, nothing in the state more just, nothing more expedient, than the rule of the man most fit to rule'.

---

* The so-called 'Milton State Papers', a volume of documents covering the period 1653–8, and particularly rich for the period after the expulsion of the Rump in April 1653, unquestionably belonged to Milton. Masson suggested that Milton was planning a life of Cromwell. Parker (*PMB*, p. 959) thinks that he merely 'recognised the historical value of the documents and was intent on preserving them'; but the question is not why he preserved them but how they came into his hands. They were not documents that concerned him as Latin Secretary. I suspect that they were originally supplied to him for a purpose.

He was not against kings, he insisted: there were kings and kings. Queen Christina of Sweden, for instance, was a splendid monarch: she had expressed her admiration of his book against Salmasius . . . But at the same time he gave Cromwell his instructions, naming the advisers who were most likely to support the policy of disestablishment. He even included Bradshaw among them; but he was tactful enough to omit the name of his hero Vane.[56]

Fond hope! The Protector had not kicked the old republicans out in order to adopt them as his counsellors, and he had no intention of disestablishing the Church. However tolerant himself, he was a prisoner of social forces, and of reason of State. So, as time passed and he struggled to reconcile the country to his rule, he became more like a traditional monarch, with a personal court, an established Church, and a new House of Lords. As for the splendid Queen Christina, within a year that giddy blue-stocking would become a papist, abdicate her throne, and gad off to Rome. So Milton was disillusioned again. He continued to serve Cromwell, but he wrote no more public manifestos for him. He returned to his private studies, wrote a few private sonnets, and worked on his great theological *Summa*, the work which he regarded as his greatest treasure, his legacy to posterity: the formulation of his increasingly private and heretical religion.

He also resumed work on that old barometer of his political mood, *The History of Britain*.* His first new chapter recorded the reign of the Saxon King Egbert. Under Egbert, he wrote, there had been great hopes, 'the sum of things in this island, or the best part thereof', being reduced, as never before, 'under the power of one man, and him one of the worthiest'. We think at once of Cromwell, the unifier of three kingdoms, 'the man most fit to rule'. But these great hopes, Milton goes on, had soon failed, for 'when God hath decreed servitude on a sinful nation, fitted by their own vices for no condition but servile, all estates of government are alike unable to avoid it'. In other words, corruption invades even the élite. It was his regular refrain, virtuous freedom seeking and failing to break through corrupted slavery: the refrain which he would repeat, after 1660, in *Paradise Lost*, when he wrote that the Israelites would return

> back to Egypt, choosing rather
> Inglorious life with servitude,

---

* It is not certain when Milton resumed work on *The History of Britain*. It was certainly after 1652; probably after 1655 when he was free from the controversy with Salmasius and More. See C.H. Firth, *Essays Historical and Literary* (Oxford 1938), p. 64.

and in *Samson Agonistes*:

> For what more oft, in nations grown corrupt
> And by their vices brought to servitude
> Than to love bondage more than liberty,
> Bondage with ease than strenuous liberty.

7 A model of government

From this period of quiet study Milton was once again plucked out and thrust back into public controversy by the new political convulsions which followed the death of Oliver Cromwell in September 1658. At first the Protector's son Richard, by the sufferance of the army, sought to prolong his system of government; then, in the spring of 1659, the army's sufferance gave out: Richard was driven to abdicate and the grandees of the army, 'under the working of God's holy spirit' as Milton put it, brought back the Rump. So, after an 'interruption' of six years, Milton's old friends Bradshaw and Vane, with the rest of those stiff republicans and regicides whom Cromwell had locked out or locked up, returned to Westminster. In these promising circumstances Milton heard again the dolorous or jarring blast calling him to admonish the nation. Perhaps Richard, being weak, or the Rump, being virtuous, would accept the advice which Oliver had spurned. So, once again, he set out his programme: complete disestablishment of the Church, complete toleration for Protestants, no tithes for the clergy, no endowments for churches; and he appealed, once again, to 'the incorruptest counsel' of 'those Waldensians whom deservedly I cite so often' that 'to endow churches is an evil thing'.[57]

Alas, Richard was too weak and the Rump not virtuous enough; and nothing had been done (except positively to strengthen the established Church) when the army grandees struck again. On 13 October 1659 Major-General Lambert, seeing himself as the true heir of Oliver, once again forcibly dissolved the Rump. Milton was outraged by the coup. This time he saw no sign of the working of God's holy spirit. To him, the Rump, in its exile, had recovered its old virtue: it was 'the old famous Parliament which they had without just authority dissolved';[58] its members were 'the best patrons of civil and religious liberty that ever these islands brought forth', 'the authors, assertors and now recoverers of our liberty';[59] and their expulsion was 'illegal, scandalous, I fear me barbarous' – indeed, it was 'scarcely to be exampled among any barbarians, that a paid army should, for no other cause, thus subdue the supreme power that set them up'.[60] 'The supreme power that set them up' was, of course, a group of politicians which had previously been set up – and then (with Milton's full approval) knocked down again – by them.

Two months later the army found itself without credit and allowed the Rump to return. Unfortunately, by this time the Rump was without credit too. It sought to recruit its strength without diluting its republican virtue; but before it could do so, General Monck arrived from Scotland and commanded it, instead, to readmit the members whom Cromwell, in December 1648, had forcibly 'secluded' in order to bring the King to trial and execution. The Rump once again yielded to power; the 'secluded members' returned; and from that moment the Republic was doomed. Less than five months later a jubilant nation heard Charles II publicly proclaimed King.

It was in those five months of virtual anarchy that Milton at last turned his mind from religion to politics. Politics, to him, had always been subordinate to religion, but now, with the whole political system in danger, what point was there in arguing about the details of religious reform? If the monarchy were restored, the future would be with the Presbyterians or the bishops. Therefore it was essential now, at whatever price, to save the Republic. The question was, how could that be done? Hitherto the emphasis had been on virtuous men. 'Forms of government' had been regarded as secondary. But now the virtuous men had failed, or, like Cromwell, been corrupted. So perhaps it was time to think of sound institutions. Institutions, hitherto, was what the Rump had lacked. It was simply the accidental residue of the old House of Commons at war, continuing to govern with improvised machinery. In retrospect that now seemed unfortunate: it had enabled 'impatient or disaffected people' or 'ambitious leaders in the Army' to 'interrupt' its government. As Milton put it, 'when monarchy was dissolved, the form of a Commonwealth should have forthwith been framed . . . this care of timely settling a new government too much neglected, hath been our mischief'.[61]

So, belatedly, Milton himself devised a new constitution to secure the Republic. His model was simple. He would pickle the Rump, making it a permanent legislature, immune, as far as possible, to change and decay. It was to be kept in power by the army, which was also to be pickled and made permanent in its present form, and it was to govern through an executive, or Council of State, chosen by it and by the army, and also permanent. All members of the Parliament, the Council of State and the army command were to hold office for life, 'nothing moved unless by death or just accusation'. There were to be no elections. Natural wastage was to be remedied by nomination. The Council of State was to approve and organize local councils of approved gentry who would nominate suitable replacements. All members of government, Parliament, army command, local councils were to abjure monarchy or the rule of any Single Person, and swear to maintain full liberty of conscience. These were the two 'fundamentals' of the constitution.

Not much of a Parliament, we may say. No: Milton did not intend it to be. In fact he proposed that the very name of Parliament be dropped. It should be replaced by that of Grand Council or Supreme Council. The reason that he gave was that Parliament had 'outlived its honour by so many dissolutions'. This can hardly have been his real reason: a historic institution cannot be fatally devalued by one exceptional experience. We must assume that his real purpose was different: with the name, he would shed the historic character of an English Parliament, its precedents, its customs, its hard-won liberties. Circumscribed by new tests, made permanent and protected against change, his irremovable Grand Council would be a different institution altogether. As 'both foundation and main pillar of the whole state', it would be far safer than 'successive and transitory parliaments'.[62] It would preserve the Republic 'for ever'.

Milton's constitution also provided for local government. That was to be entrusted to the nobility and chief gentry – provided that they abjured monarchy and swore to uphold liberty of conscience. These nobility and gentry were to build 'houses or palaces befitting their quality' in their local towns and govern, legislate and judge 'without appeal' in all civil affairs. In this way every county was to be 'a little commonwealth' – a little commonwealth governed by a little Rump.[63] Thanks to this participation of the approved local gentry Milton thought that his ideal model of government could not be called an oligarchy: it would have 'the resemblance and effects of a perfect democracy'.[64] This view was not shared by others. To the republican Henry Neville, the Rump was anyway 'an oligarchy, detested by all men that love a commonwealth';[65] and to perpetuate it in its discredit by reducing still further the possibilities of change would render it more detestable than ever. The Protectorate, which Milton now described as 'a short but scandalous night of interruption',[66] had been more tolerable to Englishmen only because it had shown some signs of shifting from a military to a civilian base and becoming a traditional monarchy with traditional Parliaments. But Milton sought to go back to the system from which Cromwell, sensibly, had sought to escape. Most Englishmen would have agreed with the contemporary critic who wrote that the system set forth in Milton's *Ready and Easy Way to establish a Free Commonwealth* was 'the most ready and easy way to establish downright slavery upon the nation that can possibly be contrived'.[67]

Such was the model of government by which Milton thought that the Restoration could be forestalled and the English Republic made permanent. In the rapidly changing political situation, it was revised in detail, but its essential character was constant: reliable republicans were 'to sit perpetual' at every level of government. It was a counsel of despair, and totally unrealistic. And yet Milton believed that this fossilized and reactionary oligarchy could be continued 'even to the coming of our true and rightful and only to be expected King . . . our only Saviour, the Messiah, the Christ . . . the universal Lord of all mankind'.[68] For Milton still believed in the coming millennium, though he had ceased to speculate on the timetable or to suppose that it was about to begin in England in a blaze of Baconian enlightenment, with a grand chorus of four hundred knights of the shire and godly burgesses, and himself, in his garland and singing robes, playing the solo part in the centre of the stage.

Two months after the publication of the last version of Milton's *Ready and Easy Way*, the monarchy was formally restored. Milton went into hiding and, somehow, survived. When his safety was assured, he returned to the original purpose of his life: his long-deferred epic poem. It was not now a national epic, an Arthuriad: that ideal had long ago been dissipated, its chivalric content puffed away as idle fancy,

> fabled knights
> In battle feigned,

its historical base, or the residue of it, rendered down into the *caput mortuum* of his harsh dry *History of Britain*. From history he had turned to the Bible, from Spenserian romance to a *Summa Theologiae*. Perhaps, after all, Spenser was not a better teacher than Aquinas. So, he completed his great heretical compilation, *De Doctrina Christiana*. But that great *Summa* was not merely self-contained. Like his study of history, his study of theology was to provide the basis for his intended allegorical poem. The fabled knights and battles feigned would be transported from history to pre-history, from Avalon and Camelot to Heaven and Hell, in *Paradise Lost*.

8 The end of ideology

If we look at Milton's 'political' career as a whole, we can see that it falls into three stages. First, there is the year 1641–2, the stream of pamphlets against the Laudian bishops, of which the savage digression in *Lycidas* is a premonitory symptom. Then, in 1649–54, there are the attacks on the Presbyterian and popular opponents of regicide. Finally, in 1659–60, there are the desperate attempts to fend off a royalist restoration by establishing a permanent oligarchy. At each of these three stages, as throughout his life, Milton moved on a high plane of generality from which he seldom descended. His battles were like the battles of his angels, fought in the empyrean void, with coruscating arms, to the accompaniment of thunder and lightning. His enemies too (at least until Salmasius appeared) are abstractions, not named persons: changing stereotypes of evil. Nevertheless, behind the abstractions and the metaphors, we can detect some consistency. Let us try to summarize it.

Milton saw the contest of his time not as a political struggle but as a crusade, and himself as having a commission to direct it. His pamphlets are not proposals but commands. In 1641, in the euphoric period of the Long Parliament, he pushed himself into the company of the Smectymnuans. Presumably he wished to be taken up by them. Perhaps he was taken up: at least he was taken seriously by their political activist Stephen Marshall; and in 1645, in the second phase of euphoria, after Naseby, when Marshall pressed Parliament to appoint an official rhapsodist, it may be that his eye was on Milton. I have suggested that the publication of his poems at that time – poems to which he never referred in any of his writings and which he presented only as the earnest of a future epic – may have been as a prospectus for such employment. Then came the years of depression, 1646–8. But in 1649 all was suddenly changed, and his re-entry into the fray, with his *Tenure of Kings and Magistrates*, may have been a new bid for influence. If so, it was successful. The pamphlet caught the eye of authority and for the next decade he was the official propagandist of the Republic. In 1653 he may have been designated, or have designated himself, as Cromwell's historian. Afterwards he lost faith in Cromwell, but kept silent till his death. Then, in the last crisis of the Republic, he put himself forward again, pressing his advice alternately on Monck and 'the people' – that is, on 'the godly party', the only 'people' he recognized. In all this, he clearly saw himself less as a practical politician than as a prophet: like the old Hebrew prophets who were also poets inspired by God to denounce and direct a chosen but wayward race.

In so far as he concerned himself with politics, Milton was a republican. This is evident from his Commonplace Book even before the civil war made republicanism a practical option. Republicanism was part of his classical humanist inheritance. However, it was not, for him, as for some of the members of the Rump, a divinely ordained polity. No form of government, for him, was absolute: like Cromwell, he regarded forms of government as 'dung and dross compared with Christ'. In 1641–2 he thought, or hoped, or pretended, that episcopacy could be detached from monarchy, which could then, as under Queen Elizabeth (for all his reservations about her), co-operate in preparing the way for the millennium. In 1649, when the Republic had been established, he became more intransigent. He then hoped that other nations would follow the English example: even if their monarchies were 'not illegal or intolerable', they were still 'as a lordly scourge . . . to be abrogated'.[69] However, when Oliver Cromwell took power, Milton forgot his opinion that only 'a race of idiots' would allow its welfare to depend on one man:[70] and when Queen Christina was said to have approved of his work, she too was excepted from the general censure. On Cromwell's death, Milton's republicanism reasserted itself, but even then it was not absolute: at one desperate moment he was prepared to accept Monck as Lord Protector, if only he would keep out Charles II, from whom nothing was to be expected but revenge.

If a republic, however desirable, was not the ultimate aim of Milton's propaganda, what was? Some men, through revolution, sought social change. The Levellers, the Anabaptists, the Diggers, the Fifth Monarchy men, preached a social as well as a religious gospel. So, in a less radical way, did the Cromwellians: Henry Ireton, Hugh Peter, some of the Rumpers, of the Major-Generals. Milton did not. The only positive function which he allowed to government was education, and in that – in 1660 as in 1644 – he was resolutely humanist and élitist: as always, his own experience was to be the norm for other men. Social grievances, as such, meant little to him. If he opposed tithes, that was not because they were an economic burden to the peasantry but because they were the maintenance of an established Church. He had no sympathy with the social demands of Levellers or Fifth Monarchy men. His positive aims were purely religious; and because he believed, at first, that history was on his side, and that there was a constant supply of virtuous men ready to help it forward, his politics consisted merely in removing the impediments in their way.

Alas, history was not on his side, and he over-estimated the stock of human virtue. So he was doomed to see the mirage of victory dissolve and his supposed allies, one after another, 'corrupted'. By the 1650s he was on the defensive, envisaging not a reception committee for the Messiah but new institutional devices to preserve the virtue of a dwindling élite. By 1660 it had dwindled almost to nothing, and he was isolated in his illusions. What then was he to do? His ideology had disintegrated. The aristocracy of virtue had receded into the past, the millennium into the future. Baconian enlightenment – at least as he had envisaged it – was a forgotten dream. He was totally blind. What could he do except retreat still further into his ego and bring out at last the riches buried in it? So, thanks to the clemency of the restored house of Stuart, we have those two great poems, *Paradise Lost* and *Samson*, in which that marvellous wealth and power of language, purged at last of its brutal application, finds its ideal subject: himself.

That the Satan of *Paradise Lost* is Milton's hero has often been stated, and of course denied. What cannot be denied is that the spirit and the sentiments which he ascribes to the ruined archangel are precisely those which he had expressed in his own person in his prose pamphlets. This indeed is perfectly logical. For Milton did not repudiate kingship *per se*: he only repudiated it on earth, among men; and he repudiated it there, explicitly, because our only King is in Heaven. To that heavenly King he willingly ascribed all the attributes, and the deference, which his proud spirit refused to Charles I. So, in *Paradise Lost* there is no nonsense about an aristocracy of virtue: God has subjected the old angelic aristocracy to an absolute monarchy with all modern trappings: a hereditary Crown Prince, a dazzling court, a hierarchy of courtiers. He now rules by decree, is addressed under 'imperial titles' and expects 'adoration': angels bow, kneel, prostrate themselves before him. He is approached through clouds of odoriferous incense. He disposes of an immense angelic bureaucracy and a formidable standing army, equipped with secret weapons, atomic and chemical. His vengeance is terrible: one word of disobedience and the offender is cast 'into utter darkness . . . without redemption, without end'. Naturally Satan, a proud rebel, defeated but unbroken, uses against this vindictive, sanctimonious tyrant the same forceful language which Milton has used against His earthly equivalent. Blake wrote that Milton 'was of the Devil's party without knowing it': without knowing it because, while consciously seeking to discredit the Devil, he unconsciously, even necessarily, creates him in his own image. Even if we find means to evade this paradox, the conclusion remains. As Saurat wrote, 'the hero of *Paradise Lost* is Milton himself . . . What need has Milton of a hero in his poem? He is his own hero'.[71]

Even more so in *Samson*. Here there is no ambiguity. For Samson is Milton: Samson the Nazarite dedicated at birth to God, Milton the child prodigy dedicated by his father to religion. Both had accepted the dedication. Both stood alone, confident in their strength and virtue, self-constituted leaders of their tribe against the enemies of its God. Both are betrayed by those they trusted and find themselves isolated among those triumphant enemies. Both are blind, but even in their blindness are unbroken in faith and spirit, dreaming of resistance and revenge. How Milton savoured the idea of revenge! It runs through his work, a constant theme: revenge on the bishops for being bishops ('Let your severe and impartial doom imitate the divine vengeance'); vengeance on the Piedmontese persecutors of the Waldensians ('Avenge O Lord, thy slaughtered Saints . . .'); vengeance on the wicked at the return of Christ. *Paradise Lost* begins with the terrible vengeance wreaked by the King of Heaven on his defeated rebels, and their 'study of revenge, immortal hate' in return. *Samson* is a drama of revenge, pure and simple, and it ends happily with its achievement ('O dearly bought revenge, yet glorious!'). And then also, in *Samson*, we recognize another now regular theme of Milton: his hatred, grown almost paranoid since *Eikon Basiliké*, of the common people. He could not, under the restored monarchy and its censorship, express his hatred of royalists, and the Presbyterians, outmanoeuvred and defeated, deserved pity rather than attack. But the common people, the 'miscellaneous rabble', 'irrational and brute', were not to be spared:

> Nor do I name of men the common rout,
> That wandering loose about
> Grow up and perish as the summer fly,
> Heads without names no more remember'd,
> But such as Thou hast solemnly elected,
> With gifts and graces eminently adorn'd,
> To some great work, Thy glory.

In those words, Milton looked back on his own past. Had he not himself been solemnly elected, his gifts and graces dedicated to some great work for the glory of God? Originally, that work was to have been

the allegorical Spenserian epic which he had begun before 1640. That
had soon foundered: its historical base had proved unsound, and the
excitement of revolution had demanded other subjects. Then, in the
barrenness of victory, his whole sustaining ideology had crumbled.
Re-examining the Bible with exact humanist scholarship guided by
'the spirit', that is, his own private judgment, the only final criterion,[72]
he found that the old panoramic interpretation of history which Foxe
and his successors had deduced from it was no longer valid. The
Papacy might still be Antichrist but the Reformation itself was no
longer a decisive breakthrough. At best, like Wyclif's preaching, it was
a short blaze, soon quenched: when the angel Michael set out to Adam
the course of human history, he did not mention it. And if the
Reformation was devalued, what was left? The continuous Protestant
thread had been taken out of history, leaving it a disordered tale of
dismal oppression by established Churches and secular tyrannies:

> So shall the world go on
> To good malignant, to bad men benign,
> Under her own weight groaning, till the day
> Appear of respiration to the just,
> And vengeance to the wicked, at return
> Of Him so lately promised . . .[73]

But when that shall be, we do not know.

After this drastic revision of his own thought, it was clear that Milton
could not give to the Puritan Revolution any historical significance.
Those 'shakings' which he had once wished to celebrate in an elaborate
song for generations as the priming of the millennium, now became just
another of those melancholy episodes in which nations, grown corrupt,
have lost first their inward, then their outward liberty,* so that noble
regicides, like Brutus and Cassius, or romantic re-creators of lost
grandeur, like Cola di Rienzi, are doomed to fail.[74] So, when his friend
Henry Oldenburg suggested to him that he write the history of the
revolution, he declined. Those commotions, he wrote gloomily, 'merit
oblivion rather than publication'. However, the elaborate song could

---

* Yet sometimes nations will decline so low
  From virtue, which is reason, that no wrong,
  But justice, and some fatal curse annext,
  Deprives them of their outward liberty,
  Their inward lost.

Paradise Lost **XII**, lines 97–101.

still be sung. It would still be a great allegory of the human condition. It would not be a Spenserian romance based on a historical reconstruction of the golden age of Britain in the context of prophetic history. It would rest on the firmer foundation of the Bible, now re-interpreted. In it the glittering fragments of his once coherent ideology could still be used to embellish, and sometimes to conceal, his secret heresies.

Abbreviations

The following abbreviations are used in the footnotes and source notes.

ABL   John Aubrey, *Brief Lives*. (Where pages are cited, the edition used is A. Clark, 2 vols, Oxford 1898.)

AO   Anthony Wood, *Athenae Oxonienses*, ed. P. Bliss (5 vols, Oxford 1813–20).

BHG   *Briefwisseling van Hugo Grotius*, ed. P. C. Moelhuysen & B. L. Meulenbroek (The Hague 1928–61).

BL   British Library.

Bodl.   Bodleian Library.

CA   Peter Heylyn, *Cyprianus Anglicus or the history of the life and death of . . . William Laud* (1668).

CHR   Edward, Earl of Clarendon, *The History of the Rebellion and Civil Wars in England*, ed. W. D. Macray (6 vols, Oxford 1888).

CJC   *The Correspondence of John Cosin D.D.*, ed. G. Ornsby (Surtees Society), vols LII (1868), LV (1870).

Clar. SP   *State Papers collected by Edward Earl of Clarendon* (3 vols, Oxford 1773–86).

CPW   *Complete Prose Works of John Milton* (8 vols, New Haven 1953–80).

CSPD   *Calendar of State Papers, Domestic*.

HMC   Historical Manuscripts Commission Reports.

PMB   W. R. Parker, *Milton, a Biography* (Oxford 1968).

P.RO   Public Record Office.

SP   State Papers.

UWW   *The Whole Works of . . . James Ussher with a life of the author*, ed. C. R. Elrington & J. M. Todd (17 vols, Dublin 1847–64).

WWL   *The Works . . . of William Laud*, ed. W. Scott & J. Bliss (7 vols, Oxford 1847–60).

Sources

Introduction

1 'The Paracelsian Movement', in *Renaissance Essays* (1985).
2 On this subject see my essay 'Three Foreigners' in *Religion, the Reformation and Social Change* (1967).

1 *Nicholas Hill, the English Atomist*

1 *ABL*, 'Nicholas Hill'.
2 Grant McColley, 'Nicholas Hill and the *Philosophia Epicurea*', in *Annals of Science* IV (1939), 392.
3 Ben Jonson, *Epigrams*, no. 133.
4 See David McPherson, 'Ben Jonson's Library and Marginalia', in *Studies in Philology* LXXI (5 Dec. 1974), 51–2.
5 Ben Jonson, *Works*, ed. P. and E. Simpson and C. H. Herford (1925–52) I, p. 145.
6 E.g. in Sir John Mennes' *Musarum Deliciae* (1655).
7 *ABL*, 'Nicholas Hill'.
8 John Donne, 'Catalogus Librorum Aulicorum Incomparabilium et non Vendibilium', included in *Poems* (1650); reprinted as *The Courtier's Library*, ed. Evelyn M. Simpson (1930). Mrs Simpson dates the work between 1603 and 1611.
9 *De Chymicorum cum Aristotelicis et Galenicis consensu ac dissensu* (Wittenberg 1619).
10 Kurd Lasswitz, *Geschichte des Atomistik* (Hamburg and Leipzig 1890) I, p. 441.
11 Ibid. I, pp. 473, 479. Basson's work is his *Philosophia Naturalis adversus Aristotelem*.
12 Mersenne, *Quaestiones celeberrimae in Genesim* (Paris 1623), cols 1837–8; cf. *L'impiété des déistes* (Paris 1624), pp. 211–40, *Vérité des sciences* (1625), pp. 78–83. The subtitle of the second of these works ('ensemble, la réfutation des dialogues de Jourdain Brun') shows the main enemy.
13 Burton, *Anatomy* (Everyman ed.) II, pp. 54–5.
14 W. H. Stevenson and H. E. Salter, *The Early History of St John's College* (1939), p. 367.
15 In interpreting the process of Wood's enquiries, I am grateful to Mr Mordechai Feingold. Cf. his book *The Mathematician's Apprenticeship* (Cambridge 1984), p. 84.
16 Henshaw's evidence is in Bodl. MS Wood fos. 175v–176; see also *ABL*, 'Nicholas Hill' and 'Edward de Vere, Earl of Oxford'.
17 *Iractatus de globis et eorum usu* (1594).

284

18 Pierre Lefranc, *Sir Walter Ralegh Ecrivain* (Paris 1968), Jean Jacquot, 'Harriot, Hill, Warner and the New Philosophy', in John W. Shirley (ed.), *Thomas Harriot, Renaissance Scientist* (Oxford 1974).
19 MS Wood F. 42. fos. 174–5.
20 MS Tanner 306, fos. 110, 112.
21 Brotherton Collection MS Lt. 52.
22 *Notes and Queries* (1880), p. 152 (21 Feb.). The entry is signed 'Fama' – i.e. Fa(lconer) Ma(dan).
23 *Philosophia Epicurea*, propositions 142, 147, 148, 151, 446, 453.
24 The history of the Basset family has now been vividly illustrated by Muriel St Clair Byrne's splendid edition of *The Lisle Letters* (Chicago 1981); on which see my essay in *Renaissance Essays* (1985).
25 Tristram Risdon, *Survey of Devon* (ed. 1811), p. 336.
26 Joseph Hunter (ed.), *The Life of More by Cresacre More* (1828), p.lxii.
27 The evidence for the identification of 'Ro. Ba.' as Robert Basset is given in A. W. Reed's Appendix I to *The Lyfe of Syr Thomas More . . . by Ro. Ba.* (EETS 1950), pp. 301–10.
28 PRO SP 12/274/20. Printed in H. Foley, *Records of the English Province of the Society of Jesus* (1877–84) IV, pp. 646f.
29 *CSPD* 1591–4, pp. 209, 246; 1598–1601, p. 181.
30 PRO SP 14/6/1 (examination of Rich. Bellew and Nathaniel Austin, servants to Sir Robert Basset); HMC *Marquess of Salisbury* XV. 288.
31 *Liber Ruber Ven. Collegii Anglorum de Urbe* (Catholic Record Society 1940), p. 133.
32 Sir William Becher to Camden 18/28 January 1609, in *Gulielmi Camdeni . . . Epistolae*, ed. T. Smith (1699), p. 125.
33 Basset's wanderings and return can be followed in *CSPD* 1603–10, pp. 64, 301; 1611–19, pp. 5, 64, 70, 71, 71; HMC *Marquess of Salisbury* XV. 288. XVI, 3, 438; XVII. 203; XVIII. 37, 61, 120, 135–6, 213, 252, 461; XX. 203; XXI. 129; PRO SP 14/65/95; SP Venice 99 bundle 2 fo. 250; HMC de Lisle & Dudley IV. 276, 280, 297.
34 For Sweet's arrest in 1621 see *CSPD* 1619–23, pp. 311, 320; HMC, City of Exeter 109–11; George Oliver, *Collections towards illustrating the Biography of English Catholics* (Exeter 1838), pp. 201, 291, and *Collections illustrating . . . History* (Exeter 1857), pp. 6–8; H. Foley, op. cit. IV, pp. 648, 653.
35 Foley, op. cit. IV, p. 653.
36 Ibid. IV, pp. 648, 653. Foley refers to Oliver's *Collectanea*. But elsewhere (VII, p. 858) Foley implicitly denies Oliver's identification of Southcote Hill, 'the *socius* of Sweet', with John Wood by suggesting that 'Captain Hill, once a pirate at sea, afterwards a lay brother with the Jesuits', was 'probably the person actively engaged in his native country in 1621 with Fr. John Sweet'.
37 Foley, op. cit. VI, p. 679.
38 J. L. Vivian, *The Visitations of the County of Devon* (Exeter 1895), pp. 486–7. Cf. W. Pole, quoted in Prince, *Worthies of Devon* (ed. 1810).
39 See Frances Yates, *Giordano Bruno* (1964), pp. 207–8.
40 Fludd states that he and Paddy had pursued their Hermetic studies since they had lived together in St John's College. See his dedicatory letter to Paddy in his *Medicina Catholica* (Frankfurt 1629).
41 For Gwinn and Bruno see Frances Yates, *John Florio* (Cambridge 1934), pp. 55, 92–3, 97, 204.
42 For Northumberland and Bruno see Yates, *Giordano Bruno*, p. 297; Henry Percy Earl of Northumberland, *Advice to his Son*, ed. G. B. Harrison (1930), p. 70. Northumberland owned and annotated Bruno's *degli Eroici Furori*: see G. R. Batho, 'The Library of the Wizard Earl: Henry Percy ninth Earl of Northumberland', *The Library* 15, 5th series (1960), 246–61.

43 Alexandre Koyré, *From the Closed World to the Infinite Universe* (Johns Hopkins Press 1957), pp. 42–3.
44 Paolo Rossi, 'Nobility of Man and Plurality of Worlds', in Allen G. Debus (ed), *Science, Medicine and Society in the Renaissance: essays to honor Walter Pagel* (1972) pp. 131–62.
45 *Philosophia Epicurea*, prop. 481.
46 Jean Jacquot, 'Harriot, Hill, Warner and the New Philosophy', in Shirley (ed.), op. cit, pp. 113–14.
47 Thomas Wilson, 'The State of England, anno Dom. 1600', in *Camden Miscellany* vol. XVI (1936), p. 2.
48 H. B. Wilson, *The History of Merchant Taylors' School* (1814), pp. 623–4.

2   *Laudianism and Political Power*

1 Robert Ashton, *The English Civil War: Conservatism and Revolution* (1978), p. 110.
2 Nicholas Tyacke, 'Puritanism, Arminianism and Counter-revolution', in Conrad Russell (ed.), *The Origins of the English Civil War* (1973).
3 Kevin Sharpe, 'Archbishop Laud', *History Today* (August 1983); Peter White, 'The Rise of Arminianism', *Past and Present* 101 (November 1983).
4 On Corro, see Paul J. Hauben, *Three Spanish Heretics and the Reformation: Antonio del Corro, Cassiodoro da Reina, Cypriano de Valera* (Geneva 1967). On the purge of the Erasmists in Seville see Marcel Bataillon, *Erasme et l'Espagne* (Paris 1937), pp. 749–50.
5 H. C. Porter, *Reformation and Reaction in Tudor Cambridge* (Cambridge 1958), pp. 376ff.
6 Overall's notes on this controversy are in Cambridge University Library, MS Gg i.29. 16–56.
7 *The Diary of Baron Waldstein*, tr. and ed. G. W. Groos (1981), pp. 93ff.
8 See Stephen A. Bondos-Green, 'The End of an Era: Cambridge Puritanism and the Christ's College Election of 1609', in *Historical Journal* XXV (1982).
9 *CHR* I, p. 118; *CA*, pp. 63–4.
10 *BHG* I, no. 248; 'Naudeana et Grotiana', Nat. Lib. Palat., quoted by R. Pintard, *Le Libertinage érudit dans la première moitié du XVIIe siècle* (Paris 1943), p. 324; Grotius, *Parallelon Rerumpublicarum liber tertius* (Haarlem 1802), ch. XXIV, pp. 34–5, quoted in Hans Bots et Pierre Leroy, 'Hugo Grotius et la réunion des Chrétiens', *Dix-Septième Siècle* (1983), 451ff.
11 'simillimum Casaubono Erasmum', *BHG* I, no. 334.
12 *BHG* I, no. 271.
13 Cosin's notes of the conversation are printed in [J. Gutch], *Collectanea Curiosa* (1781) II, p. 20. They were acquired by Thomas Smith for his Latin life of Cosin, printed in *Vitae Quorundam Eruditissimorum et Illustrium Virorum* (1707), and are in the Smith MSS in the Bodleian Library. Cosin's letter to Grotius is in *BHG* I, no. 660 – he wrote two years after the event, having waited till Grotius was out of prison.
14 Montagu to Cosin, in *CJC* I, p. 64; *CA*. For a scholarly and convincing study and interpretation of de Dominis, see Noel Malcolm, *De Dominis (1560–1624): Venetian, Anglican, Ecumenist and Relapsed Heretic* (Strickland and Scott Academic Publications 1984).
15 Hales' letters to Carleton from the Synod are published in vol. III of *The Works of the Ever-Memorable Mr. John Hales of Eaton* (Glasgow 1765).
16 Tyacke, loc. cit.
17 Neile's career is examined in Andrew Foster, 'A biography of Archbishop Richard Neile' (D. Phil. thesis, Oxford 1978).

18 'Praesul Wintoniensis [i.e. Neile] egregie te miratur et amat' (Dorislaus to Grotius, 19 June 1630, in *BHG* IV, no. 1518).
19 Franciscus Junius to Grotius, August 1622, in *BHG* II, no. 783.
20 *CA*, p. 82.
21 Printed in *CJC* I.
22 William Leo, *A Sermon preached . . . the Funeral of . . . Daniel Featley* (1645).
23 Cambridge University Library, MS Add. 22(c) fo.7.
24 *CJC* I, p. 154.
25 BL Add. MS 29587, fo. 41.
26 *CJC* II, p. 383.
27 *BHG* III, no. 1342, cf. 1382.
28 W. Notestein (ed.), *Commons Debates 1629* (Minneapolis 1921), p. 13. S. R. Gardiner, *Documents of the Puritan Revolution*, (3rd ed., 1906) pp. 77–82.
29 J. H. Overton, article on Cosin in *DNB*.
30 The Huguenot was the famous scholar David Blondel. See *BHG* IX, p. 490.
31 *CJC* I, p. 95.
32 *WWL* VII, p. 275.
33 David Lloyd, *The Statesmen and Favourites of England* (2nd ed. 1670).
34 *CA*, p. 74; cf. *CJC* I, p. 214.
35 See John G. Hoffman, 'John Cosin's Cure of Souls: Parish Priest at Brancepeth and Elswick, Co. Durham', *Durham University Journal* (1978).
36 T. Fuller, *The History of the Worthies of England* (1662), s.v. 'London'. The reference is to Howson's *Certain sermons made in Oxford, A.D. 1616* (1622).
37 Macaulay, 'Francis Atterbury', in *Complete Works* (Albany edition 1898) X, p. 391.
38 John. G. Hoffman, 'The Arminian and the Iconoclast', in *The Historical Magazine of the Protestant Episcopal Church* XLVIII (1979), 301.
39 *CJC* I, pp. 161–99.
40 *CJC* I, p. 203.
41 *CJC* I, pp. 204–10.
42 *CJC* I, p. 207.
43 Roger Howell, Jr, *Newcastle-upon-Tyne and the Puritan Revolution* (Oxford 1967), pp. 83–6.
44 *CJC* I, pp. 212–27.
45 *CJC* I, pp. 66, 217–19, II, pp. 299–300.
46 *CA*, p. 227.
47 *AO* III, p. 306.
48 William Prynne, *Canterburies Doome* (1646).
49 [Gutch], op. cit. II, pp. 68–9.
50 *CJC* I, p. 44.
51 On royal mandates generally see Mark H. Curtis, *Oxford and Cambridge in Transition* (Oxford 1959), pp. 26–7.
52 On the election of Beale see Thomas Baker, *History of St John's College, Cambridge*, ed. J. E. B. Mayor (Cambridge 1869), I, pp. 213–15.
53 For the election of Ralph Brownrigg at St Catharine's see MS Baker XXVII. 46–8, printed in J. E. B. Mayor (ed.), *Autobiography of Matthew Robinson* (Cambridge 1856), pp. 131–46.
54 Ward's letters to Ussher, in the Bodleian Library, Tanner MSS, are printed in Richard Parr, *The Life of James Ussher* (1686). For his correspondence with his pupils see Curtis, op. cit., pp. 208–11.
55 *Articles exhibited in the Parliament against William Beale D.D.* (1641); J. O. Halliwell (ed.), *The Autobiography . . . of Sir Simonds d'Ewes* (1845) II, p. 111; C. H. Cooper *Annals of Cambridge* (Cambridge 1842–53) III, p. 268; *UWW* XVI, p. 9; *The Diary of John Rous* (Camden Society 1856), p. 79; Hilton Kelliher, 'The Latin Poems added

to *Steps to the Temple* in 1648', in Robert M. Cooper (ed.), *Essays on Richard Crashaw (Salzburg Studies on English Literature: Elizabethan and Renaissance Studies*, no. 83), Salzburg 1979, pp. 14–34.

56 Hilton Kelliher, *ant. cit.*

57 *Monita pro sacello* in BL MS Harl. 7019, fo. 71.

58 'Superpellicea . . . non angusta, non arcta, sed late in orbem patentia et usque ad talos deducta'. Ibid.

59 The secret correspondence of Beale with Laud is preserved in the Cambridge University Guard Book. I owe my knowledge of this source to the work of J. D. Twigg, 'The University of Cambridge and the English Revolution' (Cambridge Ph.D. thesis 1983).

60 Cambridge University Library, MS Baker VI, 152–5. Internal evidence clearly shows that the document is by Cosin.

61 Beale was attacked for this in the Short Parliament (H. Heywood and T. Wright, *Cambridge University Transactions during the Puritan Controversies* II (1854), p. 433) and again in 1641 (*Articles exhibited . . . William Beale D.D.*, art. 8).

62 On Cosin's activities in Cambridge, see John G. Hoffman, 'The Puritan Revolution and the Beauty of Holiness at Cambridge', *Proceedings of the Cambridge Antiquarian Society* XXII (1982–3).

63 *CSPD* 1640, pp. 518–19.

64 Cooper, op. cit. III, pp. 47–52, 198. For Cosin's post-Restoration plan for a university library see *CJC* II, p. 383.

65 BL MS Harl. 7019.

66 *The Journal of William Dowsing of Stratford* . . ., ed. R. Loder (Woodbridge 1786). Reprinted several times; e.g. in Cooper, op. cit. III, pp. 364–7.

67 'The Consecration of the Chapel of Exeter College, Oxford', Trinity College Dublin, MS 533/3. I owe this reference to Professor Michael Reeve. See also J. A. Wickham Legge, *English Orders for Consecrating Churches in the 17th Century* (Henry Bradshaw Society vol. 41, 1911).

68 W. Twisse, preface to Mede, *Apostasy of the Latter Times* (1641).

69 S. R. Gardiner, *History of England from the Accession of James I to the Outbreak of the Civil War* (1900) V, p. 352. On Montagu's moderation cf. Peter White, 'The Rise of Arminianism Reconsidered', *Past and Present* 101 (Nov. 1983), 50.

70 *WWL* VI, p. 57.

71 HMC *House of Lords MSS* XI (*Addenda 1514–1714*), p. 436.

72 *Autobiography of D'Ewes* I, pp. 82, 114, 120; cf. pp. 101, 201, 265, 388–9, II, p. 65.

73 Geoffrey Soden, *Godfrey Goodman* (1953), pp. 152–3.

74 *WWL* VII, p. 582.

75 John Selden, *Table Talk*, s.v. 'Popery'.

76 For Prynne, and his part in the campaign against Laud, see William M. Lamont, *Marginal Prynne* (1963).

77 W. Prynne, *Rome's Masterpeece* (1643).

78 *WWL* III, p. 219.

79 On Normington, who afterwards went to Rome and became a Benedictine monk, see Edward Chaney, *The Grand Tour and the Great Rebellion* (Geneva 1985), pp. 236–40.

80 Cooper, op. cit. III, pp. 258, 287–8; BL MS Harl. 7019, fos. 56–60.

81 Lucy Hutchinson, *Memoirs of Colonel Hutchinson* (Everyman edition), pp. 40–1.

82 *WWL* IV, p. 223.

83 Baker, ed. cit. I, pp. 220–1.

84 See his ironical pamphlet, *A long-imprisoned malignant his humble submission to the Covenant and Directory* (1647); also *Dr Martin, late Dean of Ely his opinion . . .* (1662).

85 See Hilton Kelliher, 'Crashaw at Cambridge and Rome', *Notes and Queries* (Jan. 1972).

86 *BHG* II, nos. 653, 858, 869.
87 *BHG* III, no. 1152, and cf. Appendix 12 (p. 465).
88 Bots and Leroy, art. cit., p. 466.
89 Franciscus a Sancta Clara, *Deus Natura Gratia* (Lyon 1634).
90 The attempts to prevent the condemnation of Sancta Clara's book are described in letters of Fr. Wilford (*alias* Reade, *alias* Selby) to Leander Jones (see below) among Windebank's papers in Bodl. MS Clar. 6, fos. 20, 54, 75.
91 For Leander Jones see Gerard Sitwell OSB, 'Leander Jones's Mission to England 1634–5', *Recusant History* no. 5 (1959–60), 132ff.
92 [Lord Saye and Sele], *Vindiciae Veritatis* (1654), p. 33. That this anonymous work is by Lord Saye was suggested as a possibility by Valerie Pearl in her article 'The Royal Independents in the English Civil War' (*Transactions of the Royal Historical Society* 1968). It has been demonstrated by John Adamson in his Ph.D. thesis (Cambridge 1987) on 'The Peerage in Politics 1645–9'.
93 Milton, *Of Reformation* (1641), in *CPW* I, p. 583.

3 *James Ussher, Archbishop of Armagh*

1 Nicholas Bernard, *The Life and Death of . . . Dr James Ussher* (1656).
2 Richard Parr, *The Life . . . James Ussher* (1686).
3 Parr's difficulties with the censorship are shown by his correspondence with Archbishop Sancroft, quoted by Elrington (see next note). Examination of his book shows that it is a miserably botched affair, printed in distinct collations, some folio, some quarto, in irregular order.
4 Elrington's Life of Ussher forms vol. I of his edition of *The Whole Works of . . . James Ussher* (Dublin 1847–64), here cited as *UWW*.
5 *UWW* I, p. 302.
6 R. Buick Knox, *James Ussher Archbishop of Armagh* (Cardiff 1967).
7 *UWW* I, p. 193.
8 R. Baxter, *Reliquiae Baxterianae* (1696), p. 206.
9 Gilbert Burnet, *The Life of . . . Bishop Bedell* (1685), p. 86.
10 *WWL* VII, p. 275.
11 Hugh Kearney, *Scholars and Gentlemen, Universities and Society in Pre-Industrial Britain* (1970), p. 67.
12 *AO* I, p. 669.
13 See Katherine R. Firth, *The Apocalyptic Tradition in Reformation England* (Oxford 1979), p. 76 etc.
14 See William Haller, *Foxe's Book of Martyrs and the Elect Nation* (1963). Foxe did not, in fact, single out England as an 'elect nation' (see Firth, op. cit., pp. 106–9), but he did insist on the function of the secular monarch as the legitimate patron of true religion against papal usurpation; and this, of course, served nationalist propaganda in England. Cf. Frances A. Yates, *Astraea* (1975), pp. 38–51.
15 Kearney, op. cit., p. 68, shows that Ussher took copious notes on Ramus for himself and for his pupils. A list of his books in Trinity College, Dublin, MSS D-1-3 and D-1-5, includes ten works by Ramus.
16 Trinity College, Dublin, MS 550.
17 *UWW* XV, p. 184.
18 *UWW* XV, p. 63.
19 *UWW* XV, p. 90.
20 *The Diary of John Evelyn*, ed. E. S. de Beer (Oxford 1955), III, p. 156.
21 *UWW* XV, p. 67, cf. p. 149.

22 Richard Stanyhurst, *Brevis Praemunitio pro futura concertatione cum Jacobo Usserio* . . . (Douai 1615).
23 The discourse was first published in the form of an 'epistle' annexed to *A Friendly Advertisement to the pretended Catholickes of Ireland* (1623) by Sir Christopher Sibthorp, an Irish judge and a friend of Ussher. It was printed separately, in a slightly extended form, in 1631 (see p.146).
24 *UWW* XV, pp. 191, 266.
25 *UWW* XV, pp. 205–7, 211, 214–18, 262–7, 327–9.
26 Heylyn's criticism of Ussher, implicit in his biography of Laud, *Cyprianus Anglicus* (1668), is explicit in his *Respondet Petrus*.
27 *UWW* I, p. 153. Cf. Knox, op. cit., p. 45.
28 *WWL* VI, p. 332, VII, pp. 212, 287, 387; *The Earl of Strafford's Letters and Dispatches* (1739) (hereafter cited as *Strafford Papers*) I, p. 344; *UWW* I, pp. 172–6; *HMC Hastings* IV, p. 66.
29 *Strafford Papers* II, p. 249.
30 *UWW* XV, p. 573.
31 Knox, op. cit., p. 51.
32 *CA*, pp. 207, 216, 278.
33 *UWW* XV, pp. 433, 445, I, p. 156; *Strafford Papers* I, p. 299.
34 *Strafford Papers* II, p. 120.
35 Gilbert Burnet, *Life of Bishop Bedell* (1685), p. 86.
36 *UWW* I, p. 118.
37 *UWW* I, pp. 191–8.
38 *Historiae de Controversiis quas Pelagius eiusque reliquiae moverunt libri* VII (Leiden 1618). It was written in reply to the work of the strict Calvinist Jan de Laet, *Commentarii de Pelagianis et Semi-Pelagianis* (Harderwijk 1617).
39 *UWW* XV, pp. 477–8.
40 *BHG* V, p. 22, Grotius to Jean de Cordes 12 Feb. 1632; *UWW* XV, pp. 501, 555, 559.
41 For Laud's comments on it, see his letter to Vossius of 3 July 1632 (*WWL* VI, p. 299).
42 *Veterum Epistolarum Hibernicarum Sylloge* (Dublin 1632).
43 Gibbon, *Decline and Fall of the Roman Empire*, ed. J. B. Bury (1909), IV, p. 62.
44 *UWW* XV, p. 561. The letter from Prideaux to Ussher which Elrington (following Parr) dates 17 August 1628, and which refers to the work as already published, is misdated. Internal evidence shows that it was written in 1639–40.
45 Giraldus Cambrensis' 'Expugnatio Hibernica', the only contemporary account, was published by Camden in his *Anglica, Hibernica, Normannica, Cambrica, a veteribus scripta* (Frankfurt 1602).
46 Sir George Wentworth to Bishop Bramhall 11 June 1640, *Rawdon Papers*, ed. Rev. Edward Berwick (1819), pp. 78–9 (quoted without mention of source by Elrington, *UWW* I, p. 207).
47 Ibid. The text as given in *Rawdon Papers* (and cited by Elrington) reads 'Mr Pryn is very much with his Lordship'. 'Pryn' must be a misreading of 'Pym' (Prynne was anyway still a prisoner in Jersey at the time); but I have not been able to check the MS, which seems to have escaped from the Rawdon MSS calendared in HMC *Hastings* IV.
48 'Reverendissimus Primas adhuc Oxoniae haeret, inter libros istos manuscriptos, ut audio, tantum non sepultus'. John Morris to Jan de Laet, 7 October 1640, printed in J. A. F. Bekkers (ed.), *Correspondence of John Morris with Johannes de Laet 1634–1649* (Assen 1970), p. 43.
49 As Ussher wrote, with reference to communion with foreign Protestant Churches which had dispensed with episcopacy, 'I have ever declared my opinion that Episcopus et Presbyter gradu tantum differunt, non ordine'. *UWW* I, p. 258.

50 Milton, *Of Prelatical Episcopacy*, in *CPW* I, pp. 623–52.
51 *Reliquiae Baxterianae* (1696), p. 62.
52 'Ipse toto hoc tempore belli Oxoniae haeret, unde hic male audit'. John Morris to Jan de Laet, 10 January 1644–5, in Bekkers (ed.), op. cit., p. 97.
53 The evidence of Ussher's doubt about Predestination is given in a letter of Hammond, enclosing the written testimony of Brian Walton, Peter Gunning and Herbert Thorndike. These documents were printed in *Nineteen Letters of the Rev. Henry Hammond*, ed. P. Peck (1739), and reprinted by Elrington (*UWW* I, pp. 290–4).
54 S. R. Gardiner, *The Great Civil War* I (1886), pp. 392–4.
55 *UWW* I, pp. 236, 248.
56 *UWW* XVI, p. 203.
57 Ibid.
58 Williams' letter to Hérault is in Trinity College, Dublin (MS D-3-24, fo. 48). It is dated 19 April 1644 *stylo novo* – i.e. precisely at the time when the rival Irish delegations were in Oxford.
59 *CHR* I, p. 470.
60 Bernard, op. cit., p. 100.
61 Ibid., p. 190; cf. Evelyn, *Diary*, ed. cit. III, p. 157.
62 See William M. Lamont, *Marginal Prynne* (1963), pp. 138–9; *Richard Baxter and the Millennium* (1979), pp. 94, 110, 122, n.86. Here, as earlier (see above p. 104) Prynne played the part later played by Titus Oates.
63 For Milton see *PMB*, p. 1091.
64 Bernard, op. cit., p. 28.
65 Anthony Grafton, 'Scaliger's Chronology', *Journal of the Warburg and Courtauld Institute* 48 (1985), 121.
66 Nabonassar had at first been identified as Shalmaneser, King of Assyria (2 Esdras 13:40); but Scaliger correctly separated them (Grafton, art. cit., 122–3).
67 'De regibus Israelis, quis sanus promiserit se aliquid dicere quod certum esse jurare possit?' Scaliger to Calvisius 21 May 1607, cited from MS by Grafton, art. cit., 101n.
68 James Barr, 'Why the World Was Created in 4004 BC: Archbishop Ussher and Biblical Chronology', *Bulletin of the John Rylands University* (John Rylands Library vol. 87 no. 2, 1985).
69 See especially his letter to the Huguenot Hebraist Louis Cappel, published in *UWW* VII, pp. 589–609.
70 On this see Elrington in *UWW* I, pp. 269–70; Parr, op. cit, pp. 52, 95.
71 The moment of Creation, says Ussher, 'incidit in noctis illius initium quae XXIII diem Octobris praecessit' – i.e. at about 6.00 in the afternoon.
72 *UWW* VIII, p. 21.
73 Hales, op. cit. I, p. 230.
74 'non obstante solis vel statione in diebus Josuae vel retrocessione in diebus Ezechiae'. *UWW* VIII, p. 7.
75 For Scaliger's withering remarks on Lydiat see Jacob Bernays, *Joseph Justus Scaliger* (Berlin 1855), pp. 179–81.
76 Cf. Grafton, art. cit., 134.
77 H. Prideaux, *The Old and New Testament connected* ... (1714–18) I, p. xxv.
78 P. Giannone, *Il Triregno*, ed. A. Parenti (Bari 1940), I, pp. 5, 60, etc.
79 On Newton's chronology see Frank E. Manuel, *Isaac Newton, Historian* (Cambridge 1963).
80 'Historia dogmatica ... de Scripturis et sacris vernaculis'. *UWW* XII, p. 279.
81 *UWW* I, pp. 304, 321–2.
82 For Ussher's manuscripts, see William O'Sullivan, 'Ussher as a Collector of

Manuscripts', in *Hermathena* LXXXVII (May 1956), 34–58; for their acquisition by Trinity College see T. C. Barnard, 'The Purchase of Archbishop Ussher's Library in 1657', in *Long Room, Bulletin of the Friends of the Library*, Trinity College, Dublin, No. 4 (autumn and winter 1971).

4   *The Great Tew Circle*

1 *ABL*, 'Lucius Cary'. The account is paraphrased in *AO* II, p. 567.
2 See *The Life of Edward Earl of Clarendon* (Oxford 1759) I, pp. 37–45. The character of Falkland in *CHR* is in vol. III, pp. 178–90.
3 *CHR* III, p. 180.
4 See *The Lady Falkland her Life* (London 1861). This work was written by one of Lady Falkland's daughters and published from a MS of the English Benedictine nuns of Cambrai, now in the archives of Lille.
5 Thomas Triplet, in preface to Falkland, *A Discourse of Infallibility* (1651).
6 Clarendon, *Life* I, pp. 33–4.
7 Cited from the MS of *The Lady Falkland her Life* (see above, note 4) by Sister Veronica Delany, *The Poems of Patrick Cary* (Oxford 1978), pp. xvii, xx.
8 For the circumstances of Chillingworth's conversion and reconversion see Robert R. Orr, *Reason and Authority, the Thought of William Chillingworth* (Oxford 1967); for his relations with Lady Falkland see *The Lady Falkland her Life*.
9 'A Session of the Poets', in *The Works of Sir John Suckling*, ed. T. Clayton (Oxford 1971), I, p. 75.
10 *The Genuine Remains of Thomas Barlow* (1693), p. 324. Barlow was a Calvinist who, by astute compliance, contrived to prosper through every political change. He also exercised himself to keep the University 'from being poisoned with Pelagianism, Socinianism, popery, etc.' (*AO* III, p. 1058).
11 Falkland, *Discourse . . .*, preface.
12 Clarendon, *Life*, p. 51.
13 Barlow, *Genuine Remains*, pp. 324–9.
14 Clarendon, *Life* I, p. 31.
15 [reference lost]
16 Clarendon, *Life* I, p. 29.
17 *Clar. SP* II, p. 386.
18 Sir Charles Firth, *Essays Historical and Literary* (Oxford 1938), p. 118.
19 *Clar. SP* II, p. 358.
20 [Edward Earl of Clarendon], *Animadversions upon a book intituled Fanaticism fanatically imputed to the Catholic Church* (1673).
21 T.S. (i.e. Thomas Smith, of Christ's College, Cambridge), preface to Jean Daillé, *A Treatise concerning the right use of the Fathers* (1651).
22 *AO* II, p. 571.
23 See H. J. McLachlan, *Socinianism in 17th Century England* (Oxford 1951), pp. 121–5. The phrases quoted are from the All Souls Library Minute book recording the transaction.
24 [H. Hammond], *A View of Some Exceptions . . . by a Romanist, to the Lord Viscount Falkland's Discourse . . .* (Oxford 1646). These exceptions are not those of Holland but of another anonymous Roman Catholic writer.
25 David Mathew, *The Age of Charles I* (1951), pp. 222–31.
26 G. G. Perry quoted by J. W. Packer, *The Transformation of Anglicanism 1643–1660, with special reference to Henry Hammond* (Manchester 1969), p. 89.
27 C. V. Wedgwood, *The King's War, 1641–1647* (1958), p. 27.
28 Clarendon, *Life* I, pp. 91–3.

29 George Thomason, the bookseller who collected the pamphlets as they were published, ascribed one (E.242.16) to 'Falkland, Chillingworth and the rest of the university', and two (E.244.39) to Chillingworth.
30 See Clarendon's own account of their collusion in *CHR* III, pp. 38–53.
31 Clarendon, *Life* I, p. 49.
32 *ABL*, ed. Clark, I, p. 370.
33 *Clar. SP* II, pp. 166–68.
34 Bodl. MS Clar. 39, fos. 92–4, printed in *Clar. SP* I, pp. 535–7.
35 Ibid., fo. 160, printed in *Clar. SP* I, pp. 538–9.
36 *Theologian and Ecclesiastic* VII, 285–6, XII, 375. For Patrick Cary in general see Sister Delany, op. cit.; Pamela Willetts, 'Patrick Cary and his Italian Poems' and 'Patrick Cary, a sequel', in *British Library Journal* II.2 (1976), IV.2 (1978); Edward Chaney *The Grand Tour and the Great Rebellion* (Geneva 1985), pp. 282–3.
37 Lady Theresa Lewis, *Lives of the Friends and Contemporaries of Lord Chancellor Clarendon illustrative of Portraits in his Gallery* (1852) I.
38 *ABL*, ed. Clark, I, p. 365.
39 On Payne, who had scientific interests and was, with Hobbes, one of the scientific friends of Sir Charles Cavendish, see M. Feingold, *The Mathematician's Apprenticeship* (Oxford 1984), pp. 74–5.
40 BL MS Harl. 6942, no. 128.
41 *AO* III, p. 1014.
42 [Clarendon], *Animadversions*, p. 187.
43 *Clar. SP* I, p. 322.
44 C. Butler, *Historical Memoirs Respecting English, Irish and Scottish Catholics* (1819–21) IV, pp. 423–4.
45 Cressy, *Fanaticism fanatically imputed to the Catholic Church* (n.p. 1672), pp. 164–5.
46 [Clarendon], *Animadversions*, pp. 186–7.
47 Clarendon, *A Brief View and Survey of . . . Leviathan* (Oxford 1676), p. 320.
48 Edward Knott, *A Direction to be observed by N. N. . . .* (1636). Knott repeated the charge in *Infidelity Unmasked, or the Confutation of Mr Chillingworth's Religion of Protestants* (Ghent 1652).
49 Quoted by [H. Hammond], *A View of Some Exceptions*, p. 21.
50 Sir John Suckling, 'A Summons to Town', in *Works*, ed. Clayton, I, pp. 70–1.
51 *ABL*, 'John Hales'.
52 See his *Account of Religion by Reason* (1637) in *Works*, ed. Clayton, I, pp. 168–80.
53 McLachlan, op. cit., pp. 133–4.
54 Ibid., pp. 121–2.
55 Ibid., pp. 67–9.
56 [Clarendon], *Animadversions*, pp. 187–93.
57 Falkland's reply in Falkland's *A Discourse of Infallibility* (1660), p. 241.
58 Ibid., pp. 187–8. Cf., for other citations of Erasmus, pp. 16, 111, 123, 217.
59 See Orr, op. cit., p. 122.
60 *CHR* II, p. 321.
61 *Discourse* (1660), p. 138.
62 Orr, op. cit., pp. 122–3.
63 Cressy, *Exomologesis* (Paris 1647), p. 93.
64 McLachlan, op. cit., p. 8.
65 Ibid., pp. 55–60.
66 Chillingworth, *The Religion of Protestants*, ch. iv §. 16, note.
67 Castellio's *Conseil à la France désolée* (1562) was translated into Dutch at du Plessis Mornay's instigation in 1578.
68 Falkland, *Discourse*, p. 265; Chillingworth, *Religion of Protestants*, ch. I § 41; *Nineteen Letters of . . . Henry Hammond*, ed. P. Peck (1739), Letter VI (cit. Packer, op. cit., p. 188).

69 Cressy, *Exomologesis*, p. 59.
70 Izaak Walton, *Lives*, 'Life of Hooker'.
71 *CHR* II, p. 152.
72 See my essay *Edward Hyde, Earl of Clarendon* (Oxford 1975), pp. 13, 21.
73 *BHG*, V, p. 15.
74 Ibid., I, p. 428.
75 PRO SP Dom. 16/214/38.
76 An English translation of Grotius' *De Veritate Religionis Christianae* was published in 1632 (see above p. 218); his *Defensio Fidei catholicae de satisfactione Christi* was printed in Oxford in 1636; his poems were printed in London in 1639. Two editions of *De Veritate* were printed in Oxford in 1639 (one with the imprint of Leiden). *Christ's Passion*, George Sandys' translation of *Christus Patiens*, printed in London in 1639, was reprinted in 1640. The arguments of Grotius are often used in Chillingworth's *Religion of Protestants*.
77 [Clarendon], *An Essay on an Active and Contemplative Life* (Glasgow 1765), p. 43.
78 'Εξοσκύλορ illud Thucydidis, ὅπερ ἐδέξατό τις σχῆμα τῆς πόλεως, τοῦτο δίκαιον ξυνδιασώζειν (*BHG* I, p. 195). The letter is to de Thou.
79 *BHG* I, p. 800 (Grotius to Lingelsheim).
80 *BHG* IV, p. 392.
81 Roland H. Bainton, *Erasmus of Christendom* (1970), p. 225.
82 McLachlan, op. cit., p. 9n.
83 Hooker, *The Laws of Ecclesiastical Polity*, III.i. 8–11; V.lxviii.5.
84 *BHG* II, pp. 214, 216, 221, 232, 233.
85 Erasmus, *The Praise of Folly*, cit. Richard H. Popkin, *The History of Scepticism from Erasmus to Descartes* (Assen 1964), p. 5.
86 P. S. Allen (ed.), *Erasmi Roterodamensis Opus Epistolarum* III, p. 365.
87 See, for instance, *BHG* I, pp. 179, 372.
88 Grotius, *De Veritate . . .*, preface.
89 Reply to White in *Discourse* (1660), p. 265.
90 *Religion of Protestants*, ch. I § 41.
91 'me quoque hortante et adiuvante'. Grotius to Lancelot Andrewes, 19 November 1619, *BHG* II, p. 595.
92 For Sandys and his book see especially Gaetano Cozzi, 'Sir Edwin Sandys e la Relazione dello Stato della Religione', *Rivista Storica Italiana* (1967).
93 *H. Grotii Epistolae quotquot reperiri potuerunt* (Amsterdam 1687), p. 865.
94 *CHR* III, p. 39.
95 Clarendon, *Life* I, p. 53.
96 John Fell, *The Life of . . . Dr Hammond* (1661), p. 16.
97 *Religion of Protestants*, ch. II § 1.
98 Clarendon, *Life* I, p. 58.
99 *CHR* VI, p. 124.
100 Clarendon, *Life* II, pp. 12–14.
101 Clarendon, *Animadversions*, p. 136.
102 Falkland, *Discourse* (1660).
103 The phrase is that of Cressy, *Exomologesis*, pp. 13–14.
104 'I did never love too curious a search into that which might put a man into a wheel and circle him so long between proving Scripture by Tradition and Tradition by Scripture, till the Divell finde a meanes to dispute him into Infidelity and make him believe neither'. *A Relation of the Conference between W. Lawd and Mr Fisher the Jesuite* (1639), p. 59.
105 BL MS Harl. 6942, no. 4.
106 John Worthington, 'Life of Joseph Mede', in *The Works of Joseph Mede B.D.* (1664).
107 *ABL*, ed. Clark, II, p. 176.

108 The work is entitled *La Vérité des sciences contre les Sceptiques ou Pyrrhoniens* (1625). On this see Robert Lenoble, *Mersenne ou la naissance du mécanisme* (Paris 1943).

109 Birch, 'Life of Robert Boyle', in *Works of the Hon. Robert Boyle* (1744) I, pp. 12–13. Chatsworth, Duke of Devonshire's MSS, Boyle to Earl of Cork 16 November 1640; cf. *Lismore Papers*, ed. A. B. Grosart (1886–8), V, p. 72.

110 Sir T. Browne, *Religio Medici*, ed. J.-J. Denonain (Cambridge 1955), pp. 27–80.

111 For Descartes and Pyrrhonism see especially R. Popkin, op. cit., ch. X, 'Descartes: sceptique malgré lui'.

112 Clarendon, *Animadversions*, p. 76.

113 Cressy, *Exomologesis*, p. 99.

114 'Et si daretur Deum non esse' (*De Jure Belli ac Pacis*, Praelim).

115 Orr, op. cit., p. 23.

116 MS Lille, quoted by Delany, op. cit., p. xviii.

117 'Studia certe, optimum omnis maestitiae levamen, quam sint aspera atque incondita, ademto doctorum virorum commercio, nemo est qui nesciat', Grotius to Lancelot Andrewes, 19 November 1619, *BHG* II, p. 595.

118 Clarendon, *Life* I, p. 43.

119 Chillingworth, *The Religion of Protestants*, ch. VI § 56.

120 Ibid., ch. II § 1, 30.

121 Ibid., Preface § 35, 40; Additional Discourse I.

122 Falkland's defence of Arminianism is recorded in Sir Ralph Verney's Notes of Proceedings in the Long Parliament in J. Bruce (ed.), *Verney Papers* (Camden Society 1845), p. 121. His attack on the Laudian bishops is in *A Speech made to the House of Commons concerning episcopacy* (Feb. 1641). The quotation from Clarendon is from *CHR* III, p. 186.

123 For Chillingworth's silence on Laud see Orr, op. cit., pp. 146–7.

124 See *A Draught of a speech concerning episcopacy by the Lord Viscount Falkland* (Oxford 1644). This draft, found among Falkland's papers after his death, had evidently been written for the Root and Branch Debate at the end of May 1641.

125 Edward Earl of Clarendon, *Religion and Policy, and the Countenance and Assistance each should give to the other* . . . (Oxford 1811).

126 Hales, *Works* I, pp. 170–1.

127 Evelyn to Pepys, 20 Jan. 1703, in J. R. Tanner (ed.), *Private Correspondence . . . of Samuel Pepys 1679–1703* (1926), II, p. 301.

128 Clarendon, *An Essay on an Active and Contemplative Life*, printed in *Essays Divine and Moral, a Collection of Tracts of the Rt. Hon. Edward Earl of Clarendon* (1727).

129 Bodl. MS Clar. 126, 'Cursory and Occasional Considerations', nos. 33, 59. The praise of Bacon is in nos. 27–32.

130 *Clar. SP* II, pp. 288, 355–6; Bodl. MS Clar. 12.

131 *Clar. SP* II, pp. 348–50.

132 Clarendon, *Life* I, p. 47.

133 *CHR* I, p. 57.

134 See Chillingworth's letter to 'dear Harry' printed in his *Collected Works* (Oxford 1838), p. xx. 'Harry' is most probably Henry Coventry – cf. C. J. Stranks, *The Life and Writings of Jeremy Taylor* (1952), p. 447; the 'Mr Coventry' mentioned by Chillingworth is probably Francis.

135 The letters from Hammond to Sheldon, and some other related letters and papers, are in BL MS Harl. 6942. They were used, and many of them quoted, by N. Pocock in a series of articles entitled 'Illustrations of the State of the Church during the Great Rebellion' in *The Theologian and Ecclesiastic* vols VI–XV (1849–53). Unfortunately Hammond dated his letters by day and month only. Pocock supplied the year for those letters that he quoted; but the evidence often does not permit certainty.

136 *A View of Some Exceptions to the Practical Catechism* (1647).
137 *Theologian* XII, 376, XIII, 323, XV, 182.
138 Bodl. MS Clar. 29.
139 BL MS Harl. 6932, no. 105.
140 Ibid.
141 C. Barksdale, *Nympha Libethris or the Cotswold Muse* (1651).
142 C. Barksdale, *The Disputation at Winchcombe Nov. 9 1653* (Oxford n.d.).
143 *PMB*, p. 395.
144 Baxter, *The Grotian Religion* . . . (1658), p. 89.
145 *Letters and Papers of Robert Baillie* (Edinburgh 1842) III, pp. 400–1, 406.
146 P. Barwick, *Vita Johannis Barwick* (1721), pp. 164–6.
147 Ibid., p. 189. On Lushington see above, pp. 184, 202.
148 *Letters and Papers of Robert Baillie* III, p. 444.
149 *CHR* VI, p. 164.
150 For Dryden's scepticism before his well-timed descent into Catholicism, see his preface to *Religio Laici*. Gibbon's tribute to Chillingworth is in his autobiography, *Memoirs of my Life and Writings*.

5   *Milton in Politics*

1   Christopher Hill, *Milton and the English Revolution* (1977), pp. 156, 199.
2   Ibid., p. 226.
3   Ibid., p. 5.
4   Ibid., pp. 69, 71, 97–8.
5   See A. B. Worden (ed.), Edmund Ludlow, *A Voyce from the Watchtower, Part V, 1660–2*, R. Hist. Soc., Camden Fourth Series vol. 21 (1978).
6   Milton's overriding egotism was well brought out by Denis Saurat in his important work *Milton Man and Thinker* (1944).
7   *PMB*, p. 965; Saurat, p. 181. In fact Saurat is far more emphatic than Johnson on Milton's egotism.
8   Saurat, op. cit., p. 48.
9   John Phillips, in Helen Darbishire (ed.), *Early Lives of Milton* (Oxford 1932), p. 19.
10 The 'shakings' were supplied by the minor prophetic Haggai (2: 6–7): 'And I will shake the heavens, and the earth, and the sea, and the dry land; and I will shake all nations'.
11 *CPW* II, p. 706.
12 Parker (*PMB*, p. 883), noting that Milton read Pierre Gilles' *Histoire ecclésiastique des églises réformées*, which was first published in 1644, remarks that this 'may mark the beginning of Milton's interest in the Waldensians'. But such a suggestion is quite superfluous. The Waldensians and Albigensians had been familiar figures in Protestant genealogy for many years. Cf. above pp. 128, 134, 143 etc.
13 *CPW* I, p. 526, II, pp. 232, 553, 704, 707.
14 *CPW* I, pp. 614, 704, 861, II, pp. 231, 553.
15 On Milton's companions on this occasion see Edward Chaney, *The Grand Tour and the Great Rebellion* (Geneva 1985), pp. 244–5.
16 In a letter from Nicolas Heinsius to Vossius, cited in J. Milton French, *Life Records of John Milton* (1949–58) III, pp. 316–17.
17 Chaney, op. cit., pp. 245–6.
18 In 1642, in his *Reason of Church Government* (*CPW* I, p. 813), Milton says that he has considered attempting epic poetry after the model of 'the two poems of Homer, and those other two of Virgil and Tasso'; so we may suppose that he had used similar language in Italy.

19 J. H. Hanford, 'The Chronology of Milton's Private Studies', *PMLA* XXXVI (1921).
20 *CPW* I, p. 330, V, p. 40.
21 John Winthrop, cited in D. Masson, *The Life of John Milton* (1859–94) II, p. 585.
22 *CPW* I, p. 803.
23 *CPW* I, p. 614.
24 *CPW* I, p. 922, II, pp. 226–7, 538–9.
25 *CPW* I, pp. 535, 603.
26 *CPW* I, p. 857.
27 *CPW* I, p. 521, cf. pp. 611–12.
28 *CPW* I, pp. 786–8.
29 *CPW* I, pp. 706–7.
30 *CPW* I, pp. 933–4.
31 On the millenarianism of the Fast Preachers see John F. Wilson, *Pulpit in Parliament* (Princeton 1969), especially chapter VII.
32 S. Marshall, *The Song of Moses and the Song of the Lamb* (15 June 1643).
33 Twisse there quotes Daniel 12:4, 'Many shall run to and fro, and knowledge shall be increased', and comments that he has found 'in a certain manuscript' an interpretation of this verse relating it to the recent 'opening of the world by navigation and commerce'. The 'manuscript' must have been a copy of Bacon's works – either *Novum Organum* (ch. XCIII) or one of the other passages in which he makes similar remarks (*Works*, ed. Spedding, III, pp. 220, 584, 612).
34 For Scottish horror at the millenarianism of the English 'Presbyterian' leaders see *Letters and Papers of Robert Baillie* (Edinburgh 1842) II, p. 313.
35 *CPW* I, p. 804.
36 *CPW* II, p. 566.
37 S. Marshall, *A Sacred Record to be made of God's mercies to Zion* (19 June 1645).
38 The suggestion is made by Michael Fixler, *Milton and the Kingdoms of God* (1964), p. 104.
39 *CPW* I, p. 420.
40 *PMB*, p. 347.
41 *CPW* IV, p. 346.
42 *CPW* IV, pp. 373, 408, 520.
43 *CPW* III, pp. 352, 438, IV, pp. 372, 451.
44 *CPW* IV, pp. 309, 361, 371, 508.
45 *CPW* I, p. 781.
46 *CPW* III, pp. 339, 601.
47 *CPW* VII, p. 424.
48 *CPW* III, p. 303.
49 *CPW* I, p. 605.
50 *CPW* VII, p. 415.
51 John Owen, *Righteous Zeal encouraged by divine protection* (31 Jan. 1649); οὐρανῶν οὐρανία, *The Shaking and Translating of Heaven and Earth* (19 April 1649).
52 W. C. Abbott, *The Writings and Speeches of Oliver Cromwell* II (Cambridge, Mass., 1939), p. 483.
53 On the retreat from millenarianism by prominent independent preachers see John F. Wilson, op. cit., pp. 225–9.
54 *PMB*, p. 496.
55 Don M. Wolfe, *Milton in the Puritan Revolution* (2nd ed. 1963), p. 88.
56 *CPW* IV, pp. 637–9, 671–82. Cf. Wolfe, op. cit., pp. 96–100.
57 *CPW* VII, p. 307.
58 *CPW* VII, p. 324.
59 *CPW* VII, pp. 274–5.

60 *CPW* VII, p. 327.
61 *CPW* VII, p. 430.
62 *CPW* VII, p. 434.
63 *CPW* VII, pp. 383–4.
64 *CPW* VII, pp. 331–2.
65 *Burton's Diary*, ed. J. T. Rutt (1828), III, p. 134.
66 *CPW* VII, p. 274. That this phrase refers to the whole Protectorate of Oliver Cromwell is convincingly argued by Austin Woolrych, 'Milton and Cromwell', in *Achievements of the Left Hand*, ed. M. Lieb and J. T. Shawcross (Univ. of Massachusetts Press 1974), pp. 185–218; and cf. his comments in *CPW* VII, pp. 85–7.
67 *The Censure of the Rota*, cited in Parker, *Milton's Contemporary Reputation*.
68 *CPW* VII, p. 374.
69 *CPW* III, p. 237.
70 *CPW* III, p. 542.
71 Saurat, op. cit., p. 184.
72 *De Doctrina Christiana* in *CPW* VI, pp. 582–91.
73 *Paradise Lost* XII, lines 537–42. Cf. Saurat, op. cit., p. 164.
74 *CPW* IV, pp. 683–4.

Index

Abbot, George, Archbishop of Canterbury: a morose sour man, 29–30, 41, 50; his refrigerating breath, 54, and cold shoulder, 54, 56; his unfortunate hunting accident, 64; a disastrous reign, 69; eclipse and death, 64, 77, 149

Abraham, his dates revised, 160–1

Acontius, Jacobus, 95, 189–90, 192, 194

Adami, Tobias, 5

Adams, Sylvester, Fellow of Peterhouse, 107

Aglionby, George, 166, 178

Ahaz, his recording sundial, 160

Albigensian heretics, early witnesses to the truth, xi, 128, 135, 143, 148, 238–9, 241. cf Waldensians

Alcuin, English instructor of foreigners, 241

Allen, William, Cardinal, 23

Alsted, J. H., millenarian encyclopaedist, 240, 242, 251, 256

Alvey, Yeldard, Arminian vicar of Newcastle upon Tyne, 73

Andrewes, Lancelot, Bishop of Winchester: intellectual leader of Arminians, 46–8, 227; 'our Gamaliel', 65; misses archbishopric, 49–50; relations with Grotius, 54–5, 97; anti-papist, 68,

95; praised by Milton, 243; mentioned, 56, 57, 59–61, 70, 81, 92, 97, 143, 152, 219, 243, 259

Anne of Austria, Queen Regent of France, 154

Ansley, a malcontent Somerset man, 22

Antichrist, who is he? 45, 128; the Pope? 128; James I and Ussher think so, 50, 132, 135; Bidle too, 224; Stanyhurst does not, 135; Arminians hedge their bets, 96; his birth, heyday and impending fall, 127, 135–6, 237, 240–1

Antiochus IV Epiphanes, King of Syria, 158

Arianism, 188, 198

Aristotle, attacked by philosophers of Nature, 5–6; and by Nicholas Hill, 2n, 31–2, 37; and by Ramists, 125; and by Ussher, 143; defended by Laud, 143

Arminianism, in England, 41, 44–7, 51; in Cambridge, 56–7; captures court, 60–2; battle for power, 62–8; attacked as appeasement of popery, 68, 193; but anti-papist, 68; its doctrines, 94–7, 194–8; politicized, 80, 98; does it lead to popery? 105–9; Arminianism and Laudianism, 97, 114, 208, 227; Ussher urges Charles I